W0006763

NEO-TRADITIONALISM IN ISLAM IN THE WEST

Orthodoxy, Spirituality and Politics

Walaa Quisay

EDINBURGH
University Press

Edinburgh University Press is one of the leading university presses in the UK. We publish academic books and journals in our selected subject areas across the humanities and social sciences, combining cutting-edge scholarship with high editorial and production values to produce academic works of lasting importance. For more information visit our website: edinburghuniversitypress.com

Cover: Baraa Quisay and Esteshhad Quisay

Edinburgh University Press Ltd
The Tun—Holyrood Road
12(2f) Jackson's Entry
Edinburgh EH8 8PJ

Typeset in 11/14pt EB Garamond by
Cheshire Typesetting Ltd, Cuddington, Cheshire

A CIP record for this book is available from the British Library

ISBN 978 1 3995 0277 1 (hardback)
ISBN 978 1 3995 0279 5 (webready PDF)
ISBN 978 1 3995 0280 1 (epub)

CONTENTS

ACKNOWLEDGMENTS

بِسْمِ اللَّهِ الرَّحْمَـٰنِ الرَّحِيمِ

I first embarked on the journey that culminated in this book in 2015. Initially, I was hoping to solve a puzzle: how do the politics of space impact subject formation in neo-traditionalist Muslim spiritual retreats? Not long after, I found myself swimming in deeper waters and navigating much larger conundrums. The question I found myself asking was: is this embodiment of tradition unamenable to the imperatives of modern power?

I owe much of my intellectual growth, and this book, to the sharp insights, kindness, support, and generosity of my family, mentors, friends, and editors. I would like first to thank Dr. Mohammad Talib. He has been much more than a supervisor and mentor to me. It is very rare to find true intellectual genius, immense spiritual humility, and kindness in one person, but he was just that. The lessons I acquired from him I will need a lifetime to actualize, but I am nonetheless very lucky to have been given the opportunity to learn them. I would also like to express my deep appreciation to Professor Walter Armbrust and the Faculty of Oriental Studies at the University of Oxford for their continued support throughout my D.Phil. This project has benefited immensely from the thoughtful critiques of my examination committee, in particular Professor Emad Shahin and Dr. Moin Nizami. Their sharp insights have helped shape my scholarship in a profound way.

I would also like to express my utmost gratitude to my mentors and friends – without whom this book would not have been possible. I am especially grateful to Shaykh Hasan al-Shafi'i, Joshua Ralston, Tom Woerner-Powell, John R Hall, Yahya Birt, Mohammad Fadel, Ovamir Anjum, Adam Sabra, Juliane Hammer, Omid Safi, Kecia Ali, Andrew Fiala, At-Tijani Abdul Qadir Hamid, Abdelwahab El Affendi, Hizer Ali, Usama al-Azami, David Warren, Shuruq Naguib, Natana J. DeLong-Bas, and Emad Hamdeh. I am enormously grateful for their mentorship and their invaluable support and feedback. Their insights have strengthened and indeed often changed my course of analysis and have revealed important nuances to me.

I have benefited from the intellectual engagement, profound scholarship, and friendship of Danish Qasim, Abdallah Hendawy, Razan Idris, Basit Iqbal, Miray Philips, Zaid Adhami, Michael Mumisa, Joseph Kaminski, Luisa Barbosa, Dzenita Karic, Eyad Abuali, Fatima Rajina, Andrew March, Yassir Morsi, Muneeza Rizvi, Mira AlHussein, Mutaz Al Khatib, Sahar Ghumkhor, Asim Qureshi, Khadijah El Shayyal, Farah El Sherif, Rahma Esther Bavelaar, Michael Mumisa, David Coolidge, Ermin Sinanovic, Besnik Sinani, Feryal Salem, Saadia Yacoob, Abdullah Alaoudh, Taghrid Al Sabeh, Mohammed Bushra, Muhammad Amasha, Micah Hughes, and Sami Al Arian.

I would also like to express my deep appreciation for Edinburgh University Press, and especially to Louise Hutton, Emma Rees, and Isobel Birks for reading and re-reading my drafts, and to Michael Ayton, the copy editor. I would like to show my appreciation to the anonymous reviewers for helping me develop this book and for strengthening my arguments. Completing this book would have been impossible without the insights of Thomas Parker. Furthermore, I would like to express my gratitude to the institutions and funding bodies that have supported my research. I am grateful to the University of Manchester and Edinburgh University for their immense support. I am also thankful to the Arts and Humanities Research Council (AHRC) and the Leverhulme Trust for supporting my research.

I am immensely grateful to my friends who supported me and shared indispensable insights throughout the project, including: Sara Mohamed, Sousan Ibrahim, Firdevs Bulut, Aysenur Gosken, Mohamed Soltan, Majd Dahoud, Fatima Said, Halem Henish, Habiba Shebita, Nusayba, Hodan, Ebadur Rahman, Imad Ahmed, Nesrien Hamid, Abdelrahman Ayyash, Mona Arafat, Hossamuddin Rami, Muhammad El-Labban, and Gamal Diab. A special thanks to Zainab Shah, Omar Henish, Deema Ayyash, Olivia Hendawy, Aban Alaoudh, and Hassan and Maryam Abdelali.

I would like to show my appreciation to Sarah Drews Lucas. Thank you

viii | NEO-TRADITIONALISM IN ISLAM IN THE WEST

for being a teacher and friend. Thank you for filling my world with music and books. Thank you for being the person I can talk Bob Dylan, Leonard Cohen, and Joni Mitchell with. I would also like to show my appreciation to my extended family, particularly the people of Dirshay and Ad Dilinjāt – my success is your success.

Above all, my greatest thanks goes to my parents—Hamed Quisay and Eman Atuian. Thank you for all the profound lessons you have taught me. Thank you for exemplifying the unyielding commitment to truth, justice, beauty, and faith. I am proud to be your daughter. I also would like to thank my partner-in-crime, study buddy, and sous-chef Amr ElAfifi. Thank you for being there in the good times and the bad. I love you. I would also like to thank my four sisters: Gehad, Esteshhad, Eman, and Baraa, for being especially supportive of me. And a massive thanks to Baraa for painting this incredible book cover and to Esteshhad for the editing. I am especially grateful to my father and mother-in-law—Ahmed and Selwaan—for indulging me in long (and I am sure tedious) discussions around this book.

Finally, this book is for all those condemned to the margins. God's mercy knows no centre and no margin. This is for my friends, uncles, mentors, and those who might never get a chance to read this book. This is for my friend Suhaib Saad. Thank you for being the shining light that never dims. Thank you for introducing me to a world full of books, ideas and faith. This is for ʿammū Tawfik Ghanem. Thank you for teaching me that true genius can only be through mercy, love, and integrity. Thank you for teaching us what it means to be free. This is for Habiba Abd Elaziz, Alaa al-Siddiq and her Baba—Shaykh Mohammad al-Siddiq. This is for Shaykh Salman Alaoudh and for all the prisoners, exiles, and martyrs.

FOREWORD

In the Name of Allah, the Most Gracious, the Most Merciful.

I am truly honored and delighted to be writing the foreword for this invaluable work on Islamic Sufism. For decades now, Islamic Sufism has garnered attention from generations of Western scholars of Islam. Classical works and translations have been produced on Omar Khayyam, Rabia Basri, and Imam al-Ghazali—as well as the poets of Persia and their Arab counterparts and *Shaykhs* of Sufi orders. The seeds they have planted have grown to bear fruit in the East and West alike. Here we are, generations later, still studying the layered dimensions of Islamic esotericism.

Indeed, the interest in Islamic Sufism has increased remarkably in tandem with the proliferation of international religious associations by Al Azhar and its many global initiatives. It is also important to note the tremendous role women have played in amplifying scholarship on Islam. The first presentation I recall attending in a Western institution on Islam was by the late German scholar Annemarie Schimmel at the School of Oriental and African Studies in the 1970s.

I see Dr. Walaa Quisay as a continuation of a tradition seeking to give justice to the lived experience of Islam, as well as to honour its tradition. This book is unique for its contribution to Sufi revival in the West and Sufism writ large. It explores how the texts, scholars, and students travel, change, and mould their subjectivities across political and religious circles.

Dr. Quisay's exploration of this new iteration of Sufism deserves much attention. It is only natural that, in the age of modernity and postmodernity, religious groups form around the promises of harmony and for religious seekers to feel existentially anxious. The book's oscillation between intellectual critiques and engagements of prominent *Shaykhs*—Hamza Yusuf, Abdal Hakim Murad, and Umar Faruq Abd-Allah—and the religious lives of their followers speaks volumes for how seriously we should take these relationships and how rigorously we should study this phenomenon.

Beyond Sufism per se, we are pushed to think of tradition, its maintenance, recreation, and abandonment within our conceptions of both religious and political authority. Sufism's transition from local practice to transnational movement(s) means that its image can often be franchised in lieu of its essence and its image in lieu of its reality.

To this promising scholar, I say: these tents may have become houses, and houses grand edifices—but their dwellers have not changed. For this is human nature, and by the Divine breath, the human heart is nourished from an unending source—belonging neither to an East nor a West. I dedicate to this promising scholar these lines of poetry:

نَقِّل فُؤادَكَ حَيثُ شِئتَ مِن الهَوى *** ما الحُبُّ إلّا للحَبيبِ الأوّلِ

كَمْ مَنزِلٍ في الأرضِ يَألفُهُ الفَتى *** وحَنينُـــهُ أبـــداً لأوّلِ مَنـــزِلِ

Move your heart to every desire,
Love belongs to your first love alone.
No matter how many places a man lives in on earth
he always longs for his first home.

We thank you for introducing those in the East to their brethren in the West in a world that unites in praising the Lord of the Worlds. I gift you these lines of poetry as well:

لا تَقُل دارها بشرقيّ نجدٍ *** كلّ دارٍ لِلعامِريّة دارُ

وَلها منزلٌ عَلى كلّ ماءٍ*** وَعَلى كلّ دمنةٍ آثارُ

Say not that her abode is in East Najd,
Every abode is an abode for 'Amriyya,
Her [deserted] encampment is near every water pool,
And every dunghill bears impressions [of her presence].
May Allah grant you success.[1]

Professor Hasan al-Shafi'i
Member of The Council of Senior Scholars of Al Azhar
Faculty of Dar al-Ulum, Cairo University
Dean of The Academy of the Arabic Language

INTRODUCTION

On December 28, 2021, Hamza Yusuf and Jordan Peterson recorded a long-awaited interview in which they talked about Islam, theodicy, postmodernity, and religious co-existence. It had been seven months since Peterson had first announced his intention to interview Yusuf. Yusuf, now about 61 years old, spoke with as much passion and conviction as he had done as a young religious leader (shaykh) in the early 1990s. Except now, Yusuf is not decrying Western imperialism and capitalism. Instead, he is addressing with the utmost conviction the symbiosis of conservative Western values with core Islamic principles. He fervently notes that the preservation of private property is, as the conservative Cold War philosopher Richard Weaver called it, the "last metaphysical right." Yusuf echoes much of the anxieties Weaver had expressed in the late 1940s. It is the same fear that Peterson is now heeding—an impending decline of Western civilization. The decline of religion, vocation, social and gender distinctions—and, most importantly, the decline of the sacred in modernity—is a marker for civilizational collapse.[1] For Yusuf, the Muslim civilizational crisis and the Western civilizational crisis are prompted by the same postmodern condition.

Peterson—a professor of psychology at the University of Toronto—became renowned as a culture war polemicist after a video appeared of him refusing to use gender-neutral pronouns at a university protest.[2] Peterson combines a Jungian approach to myth and mysticism, self-help, a shared albeit confused critique of Marxism, feminism, and postmodernism, and a call for the return to traditional society. This traditional society, exemplified by a sense of order and stability, has fallen into disarray or chaos.[3] Yusuf has long shared this critique of the disorder heralded by modernity. For Peterson, the "order" and "culture" in traditional societies were characteristically masculine; chaos—exemplified by the postmodern condition—is distinctly feminine.[4] Dubbed "custodian of the patriarchy," Peterson decries the attack on masculinity and the purported attempts to feminize men by the Left.[5] This distinct critique of feminism attracted young men across cultures—including many of Yusuf's avid fans.

The two men—Hamza Yusuf and Jordan Peterson—appeared side by side on a split screen. Peterson announced, "The reason our culture is riven apart by political trouble at the moment is that issues that should be discussed at the level of the sacred have started to be discussed at the level of the political." He went on to add:

> So there is a pervasive accusation against ... Western culture, in particular, coming from the more radical side of the left, claiming that [it] ... is a tyrannical patriarchy and an oppressive colonial enterprise ... It looks to me like, without that container, the guilt we have about the arbitrariness of life and the arbitrariness of our privileges can start to be overwhelming, and then it can also become weaponized. This is certainly happening at the present to a dangerous degree.

Many young Muslims who gravitated toward Hamza Yusuf's approach to traditional Islam found Peterson's critiques of postmodernity equally compelling. He had garnered the support of many young Muslim men anxious about an impending crisis of masculinity caused by hypergamy and feminism as well as the decline of the sacred, hierarchy, and gendered archetypes purportedly found in traditional societies.[6] It is no coincidence that Hamza Yusuf's interview with Jordan Peterson would prove so significant. It inaugurated Muslims in a shared narrative of Western civilizational decline and its accompanying anxieties. As such, Muslims shared in the political imperatives of its resolution.

Yusuf retorted:

> [That is what happens] if you don't have a religious worldview that gives meaning to those situations. For instance, one of the most important aspects of the Qur'an is that it really gives answers to these inequities in the world ...
>
> The Qur'an says that one of the hallmarks of a believer is gratefulness and gratitude ... There are many verses in the Qur'an that talk about "We

have raised some of you over others in privilege as a test to show who will be the best in action?" What are you going to do with those privileges? How are you going to respond to those tribulations? So, if you have a worldview that actually incorporates all of the problems in the world and gives them meaning, then it enables people to look at them in a very different way. Whereas if you remove that, you're stuck with just Marxist resentment and envy.

For others, this forged relationship between Yusuf and Peterson illustrates a more troubling phenomenon. Yahya Birt—a scholar of contemporary Islam—characterized Yusuf and other religious leaders as acting as "conduits who provide legitimacy towards some figures attached to white nativism."[7] Birt went on to add:

What makes me uneasy, more so in the case with Hamza Yusuf, is that his engagements with populist recruiters for the radical right like Peterson … But more so as I would say working directly with the Trump presidency on the Committee of Unalienable Rights, which essentially wanted to take the culture wars into US constitutional law.[8]

Hamza Yusuf, a white Californian shaykh and public pedagogue, first converted to Islam in the late 1970s. Since then, he has risen to high prominence in the Muslim community as a religious leader. In 2008 he founded the Zaytuna Institute, which would later become Zaytuna College—the first accredited Muslim liberal arts college in the United States. Yusuf's prominence has led him to take on leadership roles such as serving as a religious advisor to President George Bush after 9/11, acting as a member in Mike Pompeo's Committee of Unalienable Rights, and becoming vice-president of the UAE-based Global Center for Guidance and Renewal and the Forum for Promoting Peace in Muslim Societies.

Upon his conversion, Yusuf traveled across North and West Africa to study Islam in *traditional* centres of Islamic knowledge. In the 1990s, he returned to the United States, where he began transmitting the knowledge he had attained. He was among a growing trend of convert religious leaders—who were mainly white (although there were significant Black religious leaders, including Zaid Shakir and Ibrahim Osi-Efa) and almost exclusively male. His distaste for and sustained critique of modernity exemplified the worldview of many Anglo-American converts to Islam at the time. Abdal Hakim Murad (a white British convert to Islam) and Umar Faruq Abd-Allah (a white American convert to Islam) worked closely with Hamza Yusuf and established religious learning institutions and communities and amassed large followings. Yusuf, Murad, and Abd-Allah became leading figures and authorities propagating a revival of traditional Islam in the West.

Together they formed a significant orientation within Anglo-American Islam (I call neo-traditionalism) that emphasizes the primacy of a notion of "tradition" and sees a moral and political imperative in its resurrection. With the emergence of a new wave of right-wing populism in the United States and Europe, neo-traditionalist religious leaders (shaykhs) have intervened to reframe the larger historical, religious, and political narratives Muslims place themselves in. The sense of alienation Muslims feel, they contend, is part of a larger story of the dislocation of human societies from the sacred in post-modernity. It is the story of the decline both of Western civilization and traditional Muslim societies. This shared past was distinguished by a sense of harmony and beauty. God was in charge of history. Humans acknowledged the omnipresence of the sacred and manifested it in their aesthetics. This traditional world had a metaphysical arrangement whereby the spiritual, political, and social were all in equilibrium. The political disjuncture and chaos—manifest with the rise of the Left and Islamist politics—are emblematic of a loss in equilibrium.

To their community of followers and students—known as "seekers of sacred knowledge"—Yusuf, Murad, and Abd-Allah represented a connection to an authentic religious tradition marginalized by modernist voices. The shaykhs guide seekers through a paradigmatic critique of modernity that stresses the importance of reconnecting with the tradition. Modernity, as such, dislocated Muslims from a normative religious belief and practice—on the one hand—and from a metaphysically sound worldview on the other. Islamic (Sunni) orthodoxy was traditionally established through a religious adherence to one of the four *fiqhī madhhabs*—Ḥanafī, Mālikī, Shāfiʿī, and Ḥanbalī. Muslims believed in one of the two normative schools of *ʿaqīda*—the Ashʿarī and Māturīdī schools. Furthermore, Muslims were traditionally Sufi and the majority followed Sufi *ṭuruq*.[9] These methods were developed and transmitted through an unbroken chain of transmission from student to teacher all the way back to the time of the Prophet.[10] These methodologies, therefore, represent the prophetic *sunna* and are corroborated by authoritative scholars throughout history.[11] The shaykhs thereby focus on affirming spirituality, self-purification, and religious orthodoxy, and advocating for the notion of a traditional metaphysical worldview and recognition of and deference to spiritual (and political) authorities.

In an imperative to revive the tradition, each year, seekers of sacred knowledge embark upon a spiritual retreat called Rihla—organized by the shaykhs. In these retreats, seekers leave behind their modern lives to reconnect with tradition. Rihla is typically located in places with spiritual significance in the East, much like the pockets of tradition where the shaykhs had once studied. The impulse toward spiritual travel to the peripheries of the East, where tradition had been preserved, was enshrined in the seekers' imagination. In these spaces, the shaykhs provide traditional orientations to the sacred world in Islam, and a rejection of the modern world around them. That is, the retreat provides both "ways of seeing" and "what is to be seen" as part of Islam within modernity. The central thrust of the sites of the transaction of sacred knowledge is to "school" the seekers in different narratives of the spiritual decline under the modern condition. As spatially disconnected from modernity, in these retreats, the seekers can comprehend the critique of modernity as outsiders to it, untarnished by its concerns or assumptions. This becomes a place where tradition is imagined and performed, and where meanings are constructed. The traditional values and social critiques are presented by the shaykhs as metaphysical principles. They contend that these values are disembodied in modernity, which has done away with the metaphysical lens by which traditional people saw the world.

In this book, I examine the ways in which leading neo-traditionalist shaykhs—Hamza Yusuf, Abdal Hakim Murad, and Umar Faruq Abd-Allah—and the seekers of sacred knowledge navigate modernity, tradition, and politics. These seemingly abstract concepts are articulated for the moral, religious, social, and political guidance of the seekers. Given the variety of these shaykhs' political affiliations, this book engages with themes of political quietism and stability, political and religious subjectivities, race, and gender, and the political role neo-traditionalists play in global politics, as well as the convergence with the religious Right. In the book, I argue two main points. First, the notion of tradition is not entirely theological or stable; rather, it represents an antidote to the felt loss of modernity. The active "unlearning" of modernity in the space of the retreat is consequently a project of refashioning the political and religious subjectivities of the seekers. Second, the political re-orientation of the seekers' subjectivities is complicated by the shaykhs' political commitments and discourses—mainly as the seekers reflect on it outside the space of the retreat. The seekers I interviewed in neo-traditionalist spaces relate their beliefs in terms of a spiritual journey or as a story of becoming. The meanings they assign to objects and experiences in the neo-traditionalist retreat are also framed in reference to their personal story and how it fits within the larger story of the "tradition." The shaykhs, acting as transmitters and narrators of the tradition, stand between its construction and its performance.

I provide different contextual backdrops so as to locate how meanings are formed, understood, practiced or rejected. For the seekers, this relates to navigating their own subjectivities, their relationship with the outside world, and their understanding of faith. The seekers' religious and political subjectivities are subsumed in the larger story of Islam in the United States and the United Kingdom. Neo-traditionalism, thus, challenged different, inherited notions of religious orthodoxy and problematized the political identities of Muslims in the United States and the United Kingdom. For the seekers, notions of religious orthodoxy and political identity could no longer just be inherited but instead needed to be found. That said, I cannot claim that this newfound trend caused an epistemic rupture; rather, it introduced articulations of orthodoxy and ideal subject formations that the seekers had to contend with.

While Muslim communities in the United States and the United Kingdom do share certain commonalities, there are significant differences. This is particularly true for the historical as well as the socio-economic standing of the communities. Most significantly, the history of Islam in the UK—and consequently the inherited political legacy of Muslims in Britain—is the history of Empire. After the Second World War, there was a mass migration of people from British territories, as there was a need for unskilled labor to remedy the war shortages.[12] This coincided with the subsequent dissolution of the British Empire, the partition of India, and the formation of new nation-states in the Indian subcontinent.[13] In 1962, the government passed the Commonwealth Immigration Act, which facilitated a mass migration of unskilled labor along with the workers' families.[14]

The new British Muslims were overwhelmingly South Asian, and most followed religious trends that were already dominant in the Indian subcontinent. As Humayun Ansari explains, "Segregation [between different Muslim groups followed chain migration], and previously ethnically mixed Muslim communities increasingly fragmented according to village-kinship, tribal, ethnic and sectarian affiliation."[15] The Muslim community did not develop a homogeneous communal identity based on religion, but rather developed into several smaller communities. The tapestry that would form British South Asian Islam was dominated by the Barelvis and Deobandis.[16] The denominational divide between the Barelvis and Deobandis seemed to be the primary marker of difference in the development of Islam in Britain, and would later be revealed in the educational institutions (*madāris*) they built.[17] The Tablighi Jamaat was also a major force and kept close links with the Deobandis.[18] There was also a minority Jamaat-i Islami and Ahli-i Hadith presence.[19]

Meanwhile, the history of Islam in the United States is rooted first and foremost in Black history and culture. As Sylvia Chan-Malik has shown, "Islam's ideological and material presence as a minority religion in the United States is ineluctably linked to histories of blackness and Black people and culture."[20] While many enslaved Black Muslims were forced to convert to Christianity, many Black Muslims—both enslaved and free—practiced Islam well into the nineteenth and even into the early twentieth century.[21] In the 1920s, Indian Ahmadiyya missionaries proselytized to the Black community, who they found more receptive to Islam. In that period, other Black-led Muslim movements emerged—most notably the Moorish Science Temple established in Chicago by Timothy Drew.[22] For many, Islam represented a return to an imagined ancestral religion different from the Christian faith that was forced on their grandparents. Islam was a theology and a political statement of resistance and identity.[23] Later, in 1930, Wallace D. Farad (aka Farad Muhammad) established the Nation of Islam (NOI). Edward Curtis notes: "One of his chief lieutenants, Georgia migrant Elijah Poole (later known as Elijah Muhammad), saw in Wallace D. Farad what Ahmadi followers saw in Ghulam Ahmad. Poole believed that Farad was the Christian Messiah and the Islamic Mahdi. But Poole went even further. He also declared that Farad was God in the flesh, and he, Elijah Poole of Georgia, was the Messenger of God."[24] Elijah Muhammad also preached completed economic and political self-determination for Black people, as opposed to "integration." After Malcolm X joined the NOI, he swiftly became a prominent figure in the movement, inspiring many others to join. However, Malcolm split with the Nation in 1964 and converted to Sunni Islam; many others would follow him.

After Elijah Muhammad died in 1975, his son Wallace Muhammad succeeded him as the leader of the Nation of Islam. Soon after assuming the leadership of the Nation, Wallace Mohammed adopted the name Warith Deen Mohammad and restructured the movement significantly. He moved it toward Sunni Islam, renamed it the World Community of Al-Islam in the West (WCIW), and in 1976 liquidated its businesses.[25] As a result, there was a significant factional schism. A group led by Minister Louis Farrakhan, unhappy with this shift, revived the Nation of Islam and the teaching of Elijah Muhammad. Still, W. D. Muhammad's community quickly became the largest Muslim organization for Black Muslims and pushed many significantly toward Sunni Islam.[26]

While, up until the mid-1960s, the majority of Muslims in the United States were Black, the religious and ethnic structures of the Muslim community changed when the Hart–Celler Immigration Act of 1965 abolished the immigration quota imposed on certain regions such as Asia and South America.[27] It heralded mass migration of Muslims from the Middle East and South Asia who were from professional, urban, and predominantly Sunni backgrounds.[28] Most of these new immigrants were more affluent and more educated than the average American and, indeed, than their British Muslim counterparts. As a result, these Muslims tried to preserve a religious identity as well as harmonize their civic belonging with a hegemonic racial American culture.[29]

In the 1980s, the identity formation of Muslims in the US and the UK was enriched with the arrival of new immigrants from around the Muslim world. The excesses of economically liberal and secular dictatorships in the Muslim world prompted migration from these countries. The plight of the *ummah* had become a less abstract and more visible issue, hotly debated in mosques and university campuses. Lines between political and economic migration were often blurred, as economic liberalism and political repression went hand in hand.[30] Many of the new immigrants found a voice in exile and became advocates working in conjunction with representative institutions to further their causes. Beyond formal activism, which was effective, but with which perhaps only a minority were directly active, the interactions between the Muslim community forged a sense of brotherhood and solidarity. The political ongoings in the Muslim world had become a lived reality, rather than something the Muslim community identified with only on principle.

By the late 1980s, Islamic *da'wa* movements had emerged and, notably, became interested in developing notions of orthodoxy. These worked to re-orient Muslims' religious belief and practice as well as converting non-Muslims to the faith. Some were financially linked to foreign governments (especially Gulf countries) and others were independent initiatives. Saudi Arabia had gained some religious legitimacy from Muslims across the globe. Many Muslims around the globe looked to Saudi scholars such as Muḥammad

Naṣir-ud-Dīn al-Albānī, Bin Bāz, and Ibn al 'Uthaymīn for guidance on the correct beliefs and practices un-tampered with by innovations.[31] These Salafi scholars sustained a sense of skepticism toward religious methodologies developed after al-Salaf aṣ-Ṣālih (the pious predecessors: the first three generations of Muslims)—except for that developed by a handful of figures such as Ibn Taymiyyah and Ibn al-Qayyim.

The Salafi *da'wa* provided a doctrinal framework for the establishment of a faith community whereby the faithful are joint as brothers in their practice and their beliefs.[32] This was especially popular among the already disenfranchized segments of society. Salafism provided a theological doctrine that was unmediated by the liberal sensibilities of the West. The Salafi *da'wa* also had an appeal which other religious groups did not have.[33] Salafism fostered a sense of community that claimed to transcend racial or cultural parameters, which was liberating and empowering on one level. On another level, there was an increasing sense of cultural loss and erasure. This period simultaneously saw a significant theological rift within Salafi circles, leading to what is commonly known as the "Salafi burnout."[34] This caused a great vacuum and disillusionment for many in the Muslim communities in the United States and the United Kingdom. Many, as a result, looked toward neo-traditionalism in the aftermath of the "Salafi burnout."

Methodology

When I first set out to conduct this research, I experienced challenges I had not previously anticipated. The increased state surveillance of the Muslim community renders the exercise of ethnographic research fraught—particularly if the research is conducted by an outsider.[35] Even for insiders, like myself, navigating the field is not without its challenges. Like other scholars, I found that my personal spiritual journey was at the center.[36]

Judith Okely argues that when fieldwork is assumed to be the simple collection and relation of data, the knowledge it produces has in-built positivist assumptions. It claims a level of objectivity or scientific method.[37] If the anthropologist's attempt to capture a truth outside their personal subjectivity is not a tenable project, it still could be argued that neither is shining the spotlight on one's subjectivity. This dichotomy, however, fails to see that what is at stake is more than just authorship and subjectivity; it is the accurate representation of the field itself. I found that in the debate on the scientific value of intersubjectivity in research, I had two options. One was to edit and erase the intra-subjective relationships that were so central to my fieldwork and interviews, and the other was not to do that, but instead to risk the unscientific burden of talking as a believer with a spiritual journey and a concern for truth and significance. It was indeed the latter position that made much of the fieldwork notes possible.

For the seekers I interviewed, the spiritual and the political were deeply linked. In many ways, I was an insider. I too was a seeker. My position as a researcher did not change that, at least with the younger seekers. They too were interested in Islam and the shaykhs from an academic perspective. To them, I was enacting a more formalized version of what they were doing in Rihla, albeit in a secular university. For that reason, the ages of my interviewees ranged from 18 to 34. Older seekers were less inclined to see me in the same way. They were more reserved and unsure about my project. This may have been partly due to my age; I started the fieldwork when I was 23 and ended it when I was 29. It could have been due to the scope of my research—including its political and seemingly polemical concerns. After all, I was working in a secular university. I was not affiliated to any Sufi *ṭarīqa*, nor did I have a shaykh or spiritual guide. To the younger seekers, I was like them. I was navigating modernity, tradition, and politics. I was trying to understand the feeling of the retreat and process the information transmitted to us by the shaykhs. Like many of the seekers, I had a spiritual journey. At first, I tried to keep a somewhat ambiguous tone so as not to lead the discussion or centre it around my own narrative. I later found that, especially with female interviewees, only a degree of reciprocity could make the discussion intelligible:

> "How did you decide to do this?"
> "Do you know that feeling, Walaa—that feeling of being lost?"
> "What about you, would you ever consider having a shaykh?
> I don't think I can do it again."
> "How was Rihla for you, first time around?"

As these questions popped up during my interviews, I knew I could simply apologize and say that they were outside the scope of the research; alternatively, I could explain. Three years prior to starting this research as a part of my doctoral program, in 2012 I was an undergraduate student at the School of Oriental and African Studies. I had moved to the United Kingdom for university after spending my childhood between Egypt, the Gulf, and the UK. At university, I encountered a diversity of intra-Islamic beliefs that were not as evident in Muslim majority countries. Some were concerned with "correcting" religious beliefs and practices, others had political concerns about the conditions of Muslims in the West and around the world, and still others were concerned with spirituality. On the recommendation of a university friend who was also a *murīd* of Shaykh Nuh Ha Mim Keller, I applied to Rihla in 2012. I had no prior knowledge of Shaykh Hamza Yusuf, Shaykh Abdal Hakim Murad or Dr. Umar Faruq Abd-Allah, except for having passingly seen their program, *Rihla*, on the Arabic channel MBC.

The year 2012 was important for me and other Arab seekers. The people of Tunisia, Egypt, Libya, Syria, and Yemen were going through not just a radical political change but also a transformation in possibilities and human potential. This coincided with the twilight of the euphoria of revolutionary change and the consequent deep existential disappointment at violence and massacres. The message in Rihla was unique. First and foremost, take care of your heart; know your place in the cosmos and learn humbly from religious authorities that know better. This was far removed from the revolutionary instinct to topple all authorities. Each seeker has a spiritual journey and is in need of a spiritual guide to take them through this journey. The experience set out my personal journey of discovery. My journey, as well as that of other seekers, was never completely internal. The lived social and political realities of the seekers outside the space of the retreat presented at times a harmonious and at other times a tenuous relationship with neo-traditionalist social and political critiques.

In 2016, Donald Trump was elected President of the United States. It was a divisive win, especially for Muslims living in America. Prior to his election, there was already increased political tensions in the West and around the world. The promise of change and political autonomy was seemingly squashed in the Arab world, only to be replaced by violence. The political vacuum in the Middle East gave rise to what is known as the "Islamic State in Iraq and Syria" or "ISIS." As the War on Terror first waged by George Bush took even more complex turns, Muslim communities in the West were put under more pressure. This sparked different reactions from different segments of the Muslim community. One reaction was to try to forge alliances with other minority groups on the Left. This did not just include ethnic minorities, but also sexual minorities from the LGBTQ community. This seeming move to the Left became one of the biggest political triggers of the neo-traditionalist trend, as they see Muslims losing their system of beliefs for the sake of maintaining an activist disposition.

Aside from Islamophobia, the other issue plaguing the Muslim community was that of anti-Black racism. On the one hand, more and more young Black Muslims have been addressing anti-Blackness in the Muslim community. On the other hand, police shootings, state-sanctioned racism, and the seeming indifference of the (non-Black) Muslim community to the plight of Black people and Black Muslims in particular has disillusioned many in the younger generation of older immigrant (Arab and Subcontinent) imams. While this has caused increased political engagement for some seekers, it inspired a sense of escape for others. The promise of a post-racial Islam based on orthodoxy rather than on seemingly left-leaning politics made the neo-traditionalist trend more attractive than "activist Islam."

Between 2015 and 2021, I interviewed forty of the retreat participants—twenty-four females and sixteen males. They were from various different religious and ethnic backgrounds, and all of them felt that embarking upon the retreat was a part of their spiritual journey. Some attended the Rihla retreat with Hamza Yusuf, Abdal Hakim Murad, and Umar Faruq Abd-Allah; others attended the Alqueria de Rosales retreat with Umar Faruq Abd-Allah or its sister "Spring Lodge Retreat" in Nottingham. The retreat in Nottingham was organized by Ibrahim Osi-Efa and brought the shaykhs of the "East" from whom neo-traditionalists derive their authority—namely Habib Ali Jifri, Abdurrahman ould Murabit al-Hajj, and Habib Kadhim as-Saqqaf.

The interviews took an in-depth look at the seekers' family backgrounds and religious journeys, their encounters with the shaykhs, their experiences of and reflections on the retreats they attended, and, finally, their assessment of the political and social messages disseminated by the shaykhs. The longest interview lasted a total of eight hours spanning three days, and the shortest lasted around forty-five minutes. All the interviews were recorded and transcribed. The interviewees were given pseudonyms to ensure their anonymity. I had several informal conversations and exchanges with prominent members of the neo-traditionalist community, including interviewing Habib Ali Jifri.

Some seekers gave me access to their lecture notes as well as the schedule and reading materials they were given in the retreat. Additionally, I attended two retreats. The first, in April 2015, was the short neo-traditionalist Spring Lodge Retreat in Nottingham, where I conducted "participant observation."[38] In 2017, I also attended the Rihla retreat in Malacca, Malaysia, where I was much more limited regarding my research method. I was allowed to record the lectures that were already in the public domain through the livestream, and was also allowed to describe the setting and the scheduling of the retreat—all of which were also in public domain.[39]

Chapter Outline

The book consists of three parts, which showcase respectively: (1) trajectories of disenchantment; (2) the project of re-enchantment; and (3) the overall implications of this project for its seekers and for the wider Muslim community.

Part One: Stories of Disenchantment

In Chapter 1, I locate the historical emergence of neo-traditionalism, its intellectual, theological, and institutional formation, and its claims to authority. First, I examine the historical factors that contributed to the rise of neo-traditionalism in the United States and the United Kingdom. This newly emergent trend was first represented by a handful of shaykhs—most of whom were converts to Islam. Of these shaykhs, this book focuses primarily— although not exclusively—on Hamza Yusuf, Abdal Hakim Murad, and Umar Faruq Abd-Allah as pioneering figures. These shaykhs had returned from so-called "traditional centers" of religious learning in the Muslim world with the intent of reproducing the traditional pedagogical styles in the West. I furthermore outline how the notion of "tradition" is employed by neo-traditionalist shaykhs and, in turn, what I mean by "neo-traditionalism." Starting from Ḥadīth Jibrīl, the neo-traditionalists identify the three components of the faith—Islām, Imān, Iḥsān—as the basis for the methodological arrangement of orthodoxy and orthopraxy.

In Chapter 2, I explore the different narratives of modernity that provide a basis for the shaykhs' anti-modernist polemic. They provide a hybrid theological-sociological narrative and critique of the advent of modernity. Modernity, they explain, is not simply a temporal designation, but rather a system of values and beliefs that had developed over time which impacts how people perceive their social reality and their relationship with God. They provide a critique of modernity in the secular Western as well as the Muslim-specific context—which is reflected in their religious polemics against modern Muslim trends. They employ two narratives of modernity to explain modern decline in the Muslim and the non-Muslim context: disenchantment, and the decline of metaphysics. The chapter then explores the importance Sufism and later neo-traditionalism garnered after 9/11 and the subsequent War on Terror. The fostering of so-called "moderate" alternatives to political

Islam prompted the US and the UK governments to seek alliances with neo-traditionalist shaykhs.

In Chapter 3, I show how the religious retreats—organized by the neo-traditionalist shaykhs—become a spatial representation of the tradition. The retreats are typically held in secluded locations, often in the so-called "East." Many of the seekers embarking on the retreat are motivated to forge a spiritual connection and find self-actualization in the sacredness of this re-enchanted space. They are also there to escape the alienation of secular modernity—as experienced by a religious minority. Secular spaces can sometimes be unwelcoming to religious beliefs, especially when they are seen as irrational. Additionally, the burden of visibility as a Muslim, some seekers note, means that Islamophobia and racism can sometimes be inescapable. Many have noted feeling politically burdened with the concerns and prevailing violence facing Muslims. On the other hand, the dominance of leftist discourses as well as identity politics had seemingly transformed Islam as another "alternative" identity from the host of "others" to the status quo. There is often a great deal of vulnerability in these spaces, as many seekers try to make sense of personal difficulties through spiritual connection. In this chapter, I also examine how the shaykhs' whiteness functions within this space as a "blank slate." It is deemed to be authoritative outside the burdens and contingencies of the so-called "cultural" Islam of immigrant communities, the purported theologies of protest of Black Muslim communities, and gender bias. This "blank slate" Islam evades the problems of subjectivity, as it instructs seekers to transcend it. Furthermore, I show how the male domination of the space engenders tradition as masculine and modernity as feminine.

Part Two: Places of Re-enchantment

In Chapter 4, I explore the transformative significance of the space of the retreat. There, the notions of authority and the conditions for plausibility change. By this, I mean how the space functions in rendering certain discourses plausible and viable—and others implausible. The space maintains its figurative position as one outside of modernity in its seclusion from even the societies in which it is found. Shaykhs frame their sophisticated critiques of modernity as a form of devotional spiritual practice. The seekers learn about modernity so that they may "unlearn it." In this re-enchanted space, the disenchantment of modernity is therefore critiqued as an existential other. The retreat becomes a space where neither the particularities of modern subjectivities nor the political pressures of the outside world are allowed. The conditions of plausibility change due to the symbolic authority of the space of the retreat, which allows for a kind of metaphysical intervention unpoliced by modernist or political dispositions. I explore how the political and social interventions made in the retreat are framed as providing a metaphysical perspective on the profane world outside. Another central component this chapter explores is how authority and order are constructed and affirmed in the space and outside. The top-down enforcement of rules reaffirms the discrepancy of power between the seekers and the authority of the retreat conveners. In this space, discipline and religious accountability are important in fostering a sense of hierarchy and obedience. This is affirmed especially by the symbolic authority of the *shaykhs* as spiritual leaders and saints. Seekers disseminate and derive meaning from the stories of *karāmāt* (saintly miracles) they have heard. This sanctification of authority is of the utmost importance, as finding a *shaykh* or a spiritual guide is a big theme in the retreat. The shaykhs' contentions, whether regarding race, gender or politics, thereby become metaphysical interventions that exist outside subjective claims or even religious interpretation.

In Chapters 5 and 6, I examine how the shaykhs' anti-modernist polemics and appeal to tradition inform their political positions. I show how the narrative of the decline of metaphysics in modernity relates to politics. Before modernity, they contend, Muslims recognized the metaphysical arrangement of the world—which promoted a sense of harmony. This meant that the traditional world had a metaphysical arrangement whereby the spiritual, the social, and the political were in equilibrium. This was reflected in everything from architecture to clothing, and it reflected the way in which people see society and government, gender identities and gender roles, and how traditional people saw tribulations. Furthermore, they understood the metaphysical value and purpose of calamity. The notion of political stability and harmony entails cosmic stability.

In Chapter 5, I examine how Hamza Yusuf uses the notion of a "metaphysical lens" to critique different forms of political dissent, activism, and revolutions as cosmic destabilizers. Yusuf explains that in modernity people have been so consumed with their discourse of grievances that they cannot see tribulation through a metaphysical lens that might account for their misdeeds that warranted these tribulations. The modern hyper-critique of power structures allows for a sense of perpetual victimhood which bars people from introspection and responsibility. Yusuf contends that this was the result of the internalization of a Marxist epistemic framework and critical theory, especially in activist circles. I show how Yusuf uses this to critique dissent in Muslim-majority and Muslim-minority contexts as well as presenting his discourse on the Black Lives Matter movement. In Chapter 6, I examine the way Abdal Hakim Murad and Umar Faruq Abd-Allah address the question of race and gender. I show how the shaykhs use the "decline of metaphysics" narrative—which borrows from different Christian narratives on modernity and the "civilizational crisis" facing the West—to construct specific notions of an "American" or "English" Islam. Metaphysics, they contend, is at the heart of the modern confusion over gender roles and identity. The imbalance created by the modern world has caused dissolution of the family structure and a disorientation in terms of gender identities.

Part Three: Locating Neo-traditionalism in Modernity

In Chapter 7, following on from the metaphysical principles that are presented as the traditional basis for navigating politics, I explore Hamza Yusuf's role in global and domestic politics. In the United States and the United Kingdom, neo-traditionalists among other Sufi groups were used as a tool for achieving soft power. It was not only Western governments that were interested in cultivating neo-traditionalism as a moderate alternative to political Islam. After the Arab Spring, Arab governments, particularly that of the UAE, worked closely with Hamza Yusuf and his shaykh, Abdullah bin Bayyah, to develop an alternative religious discourse by establishing the "Forum for Promoting Peace in Muslim Societies." Bin Bayyah and Yusuf urged young Muslims to privilege the path of peace over justice and not to be consumed with the discourse of victimhood. This relationship with the UAE sparked controversy due to the country's role in the region—such as the destructive war on Yemen and the UAE's support for counterrevolutionary autocrats.

In Chapter 8, I show how seekers understand and accept, reject, or negotiate the political positions of the shaykhs and how this shapes their perspective on neo-traditionalism. In the space of the retreat, where the foremost authority of the tradition is upheld by the coherence of the space, modernity seemingly does not intrude. However, as seekers leave the enchanted space of the retreat, they must navigate the modern world with its political baggage. Furthermore, the burdens of the seekers' subjectivities and their different relationship with locales of power make the shaykhs' metaphysical interventions in politics more difficult for some to accept. The post-racial, anti-political introspective claims of the retreat become problematic when the pressure of Islamophobia or other political contexts encroach. I show how the seekers make sense of the discourse on political activism as well as on the alliance of conservative believers. Finally, I explore the implications the debate on spiritual abuse has had in neo-traditionalist spaces. The seekers navigate these in one of three ways. For some seekers, the discrepancies reach a point beyond reconciliation. They too go through a "burnout," while others—despite being a small percentage of seekers—accept the political positions of the shaykhs uncritically. For the majority, however, the claims of tradition become privatized. Seekers can sometimes accept the validity of the traditional political claims while simultaneously retaining their independent political dispositions.

STORIES OF DISENCHANTMENT

1

LOCATING THE (NEO)TRADITIONAL

Printed on the cover of the Rihla retreat course pack are the words "Islam, Iman, Ihsan: the three foundations of the faith."[1] Each year hundreds of hopeful seekers of sacred knowledge, hailing from different parts of the world, and significantly, from North America, the United Kingdom, and Australia, embark on this spiritual journey. Through the retreat, they wish to reconnect with an Islamic tradition that is unmediated by the modernist aberrations that have for so long hampered faith. Outside the profane West, seekers reside in the seclusion of cities believed to possess some form of spiritual significance. There they study the traditional sciences under the tutelage of the renowned shaykhs—namely Hamza Yusuf, Abdal Hakim Murad, and Umar Faruq Abd-Allah, among others. Through their study of Islām, Imān, and Iḥsān at Rihla, the seekers become rooted in the authentic Islamic tradition they believe to be increasingly inconspicuous in the modern world.

The basis of this tradition is derived from a ḥadīth found in Imām al-Nawawī's compilation of the forty ḥadīths. It was narrated on the authority of ʿUmar ibn al-Khaṭṭāb that a man appeared before the Prophet Muḥammad and his companions. His garments were pristine white, and his hair was the darkest black. There were no signs of travel on him. The companions of the Prophet did not recognize him. He sat next to the Prophet and asked, "Muḥammad, what is Islām?" The Prophet responded, "To testify that there is no deity worthy of worship than Allah and that Muḥammad is his messenger, to perform the ritual prayers, pay alms, fast Ramadan, and perform the ḥajj if able." The stranger responded, "You speak the truth." The stranger then asked, "Muḥammad, what is Imān?" The Prophet responded, "It is to believe in Allah, His angels, His books, the Last Day, and fate, both good and bad." The stranger responded, "You speak the truth." The stranger then asked, "Muḥammad, what is Iḥsān?" The Prophet responded, "It is to worship Allah as though you see Him, for though you cannot see Him, yet He sees you." The stranger responded, "You speak the truth." After the stranger departed, 'Umar asked the Prophet if he knew the stranger. The Prophet responded, "This is Jibrīl; he came to teach you your religion."[2]

Seekers learn that the authentic tradition begins with Ḥadīth Jibrīl. The courses in Rihla reflect that. They are taught that the three sacred sciences of *fiqh*, *'aqīda*, and *taṣawwuf* were developed by divinely guided scholars so that believers may ascertain true Islām, Imān, and Iḥsān. Adhering to a correct practice of *fiqh*, or "sacred law," is central to the practice of Islām. According to the tradition, seekers are advised that it is incumbent to follow a single *madhhab* from the four agreed-upon *madhhabs* in the Sunni tradition—Ḥanafī, Mālikī, Shāfi'ī, Ḥanbalī, although, in Rihla, seekers may only choose to study one of three *madhhabs*—Ḥanafī, Mālikī, or Shāfi'ī. Brenden Newlon notes that although the shaykhs in the retreat affirm the orthodoxy of the Ḥanbalī madhhab, they have their doubts as to whether there exists an intelligible study of this madhhab uncorrupted by modernist Salafi impositions.[3] Secondly, the correct tenets of faith, or Imān, stipulate following two credal schools of Ahl al-Sunna (*'aqīda*)—the Ash'arī and the Māturīdī schools of theology. Finally, the shaykhs emphasize that the practice of Iḥsān (spiritual excellence) also developed as a distinct science in the tradition of *taṣawwuf* (Sufism).[4] These religious sciences were preserved in unbroken chains of transmission throughout history. These sacred sciences, however, were marginalized in the onslaught of modernity.

This chapter explores the emergence of neo-traditionalism through its renowned public pedagogues (shaykhs) and their students (seekers of sacred knowledge). The shaykhs who spearheaded this movement since the mid-1990s have subsequently amassed a following of dedicated believers—many of whom had been disillusioned with their religious environments. The shaykhs founded prominent programs and institutions for religious learning dedicated to transmitting traditional knowledge. The notion of "tradition" becomes a defining feature in their theological and intellectual orientations. It is both layered in its definition and authoritative in its claims. It refers to theologies, temporalities, personifications, and a spatial representation of good belief and practice obscured by a profane, heterodox, and ultimately modernist other. This chapter shows that tradition is not a fixed entity for neo-traditionalist shaykhs. Instead, it reflects the antidote to the felt loss of modernity and the loss of the spiritual.

The Revival of a Lost Tradition

In the late 1980s, a group of young seekers of sacred knowledge returned home to the United States and the United Kingdom after years of studying the Islamic sciences in "traditional" centers of learning in Syria, Egypt, Yemen, Morocco, and Mauritania. At the time, they comprised, mainly but not exclusively, young converts, whose dedication to the rigorous study of faith had led them to long and sometimes arduous spiritual journeys. These seasoned seekers—now shaykhs and teachers—were troubled by the seeming religious vacuum and the lack of adequate study of the traditional sciences in the West. They found that the growing salience of Salafism and Islamism had resulted in a crisis of knowledge. To their new following, these young shaykhs were distinctly Western but had an awe-inspiring mastery of the Arabic language. They could move freely from complex notions of Western philosophy to medieval Islamic texts to the legacies of saints and mystics, constructing meaningful linkages.

Three white converts stood out as leading advocates for tradition (neo-traditionalists)—Hamza Yusuf, Abdal Hakim Murad, and Umar Faruq Abd-Allah. They gave lectures and *khutbas* (religious sermons) and set up educational programs such as the Rihla program and institutions such as Zaytuna College and Cambridge Muslim College. To their community of followers and students, they provided both a philosophical and a theological diagnosis of the spiritual malaise of modernity. In turn, they represented a connection to an authentic religious tradition that was in decline due to modernity and seemed to be woefully missing from their communities. At that time, the Salafi *da'wa* was experiencing severe challenges to its credibility in the United States and the United Kingdom. Salafism's dramatic rise and relative decline after the mid-1990s left a vacuum. These new shaykhs preached a resolutely dissenting form of "orthodoxy," temporal references, and moral geographies to the UK- and US-based Salafis.

The Salafi Burnout

The Salafi *da'wa* first emerged in the United States and the United Kingdom in the 1980s.[5] In the subsequent decade, the influence of the Salafi *da'wa* expanded beyond those who identified with the Salafi appellation. Salafi lectures and *khutbas* were easily accessible on cassette tapes and the internet. *Da'wa* materials—pamphlets and booklets—were readily found in mosques and university prayer spaces. Salafis advocated a form of religious orthodoxy based on the Qur'an, the Sunna of the Prophet, and the example of al-Salaf aṣ-Ṣālih (the pious predecessors: the first three generations of Muslims)—as opposed to the purported innovations of the latter communities.[6] Unlike the neo-traditionalists, Salafi shaykhs were critical of the Ashʿarī and the Māturīdī creeds due to their incorporation of philosophical reasoning, which the *salaf* did not do. Instead, they advocated for Ibn Taymiyyah's approach to creed, or Muḥammad ibn ʿAbd al-Wahhāb's Kitāb at-Tawḥīd. In the matter of *fiqh*, Salafis were closer to the Ḥanbalī *madhhab*, although they "claim that an ijtihad based on probative proof text (dalil) that contradicts an established school's opinion is to be accepted as superior."[7] This is in stark contrast to the neo-traditionalist approach, which stresses the importance of *taqlīd*—the "recognition of the importance of the madhhab tradition as both a legal identity and as setting the broad parameters within which a jurist might operate."[8] As for *taṣawwuf*, Salafis rejected it categorically because it enshrines blameworthy innovations (*bidʿa*) that were not in the Qur'an or Sunna, or practiced by the pious predecessors of Islam.

In its heyday, Salafism was a growing phenomenon among both converts and second-generation Muslims in the United States and the United Kingdom. The appeal of Salafism lies partly in its claims to an Islamic authenticity outside contingent cultural practices. Sadek Hamid notes that many converts and second-generation Muslims "found in the Salafi perspective a 'de-culturalized' Islam, an approach to a religious commitment that seemed to be intellectually rigorous, evidence-based and free of perceived corruptions of folkloric religion."[9] This approach to intellectual rigor and an appeal to an authentic truth flourished on university campuses and in other academic settings. The personal religious conviction became a primary identity marker marginalizing ethnicity (at least in discourse). Being a Salafi, one identified foremost with Islam and principally with its foundational texts and the example of the *salaf*. As Hamid put it, "joining the Salafi *da'wa* meant acquiring membership of a multi-ethnic supranational identity."[10]

This empowered Muslim converts who had long been marginalized in South Asian and Arab mosques and communities. In the UK, West African and Afro-Caribbean Muslims—many of whom were converts—spearheaded the Salafi movement and created a uniquely Black British Salafi culture and community. In 1975, they founded the Brixton Mosque, often called "the revert mosque" or "the Jamaican mosque." [11] Initially, the mosque was not Salafi in its orientation, but in 1993, a new Salafi leadership was elected.[12] Since then, the Brixton Mosque has become one of the most prominent Salafi hubs and convert-run mosques. Likewise, the Salafi *da'wa* became prominent among many Black Muslims in the United States. Many in the Black community lived on both the economic and political margins. Salafism provided a theological doctrine that was unmediated by liberal sensibilities. Further cementing the Salafi *da'wa*, the University of Madina offered full scholarships to study in Saudi Arabia. Salafi shaykhs, such as Bilal Philips, Abdullah Hakim Quick, Ali al-Tamimi, Dawud Adib, Abu Muslima, and Abu Usama, became essential figures in the *da'wa*.[13]

However, the seeming salience of Salafism at the time was fraught with contestation and factionalism. By 1995, Salafi organizations in the US and the UK, mirroring the conflicts between global Salafi factions, faced significant theological schisms. This originated in Saudi Arabia after the First Gulf War, when a young generation of Salafi scholars—arguably influenced by the political literature of the Muslim Brotherhood—questioned the permissibility of a Muslim political alliance with the United States, which would entail their military presence in Muslim lands. This movement—known also as the Ṣaḥwā Movement—was headed by Salmān al-'Awdah and Safar al-Ḥawālī.[14] They were countered by another set of young scholars—notably influenced by Rabī' al-Madkhalī. The proponents of the Madkhalī approach were decidedly apolitical and vehemently opposed to the ideas of the Muslim Brotherhood.[15] They contended that *khurūj 'an al ḥākim*—which they translated as any opposition to a leader—was impermissible even if the leader was tyrannical.[16] Salafi institutions such as the US-based Qur'an and Sunna Society or the UK-based Jamiyat Ihya Minhaj as-Sunna fragmented due to the rift between supporters of the Madkhalī approach and those who advocated a more politically vocal approach. This partly led to what came to be known as the "Salafi burnout."

"Salafi burnout" is "a term that describes a dramatic loss of faith and a steep decline of religious practice" due to a decreasing commitment to Salafism.[17] Abdal Hakim Murad first coined the term as a polemical intervention and a cautionary tale. Murad explains that the Salafi burnout shows a trajectory that starts with "An initial enthusiasm, gained usually in one's early twenties, loses steam some seven to ten years later. Prison and torture—the frequent lot of the Islamic radical—may serve to prolong commitment, but ultimately, a majority of these neo-Muslims relapse, seemingly no better or worse for their experience in the cult-like universe of the Salafi mindset."[18] Murad's depiction of Salafis as "neo-Muslims" or "Islamic radicals" reveals several things about the fraught relationship between neo-traditionalists and Salafis. From the outset, it shows the extent of their contending views of orthodoxy and indicates that Salafism comes to represent an enduring "religious other." It also indicates the overt securitization of religious polemics. Nevertheless, the Salafi burnout did come to represent a sociological phenomenon in the United States and the United Kingdom. It did not necessarily follow the trajectory outlined by Murad. On an institutional level, the vitriol between competing Salafi factions made them more insular. Ultimately, it led to the decline in these institutions and, consequently, the commitment of those who belonged to them. On a personal level, many adherents of the Salafi *da'wa*, for various reasons, found that belonging to the community or believing in its ideals was no longer sustainable.[19]

The Rise of Neo-traditionalism

As the Salafi *da'wa* was experiencing severe challenges to its credibility by the mid-1990s, the neo-traditionalists, who at the time comprised only a handful of young shaykhs, rapidly gained popularity. These young shaykhs espoused a tempered affinity to Sufism as intrinsic to traditional Islam. They believed in the legitimacy of the *madhhabs* and delved deeper into the philosophy of Divinity outlined in the Ash'arī creed. Their character and religious makeup differed from all other actors in the Islamic scene. For many Muslims increasingly disillusioned by Salafism, this opposing discourse of orthodoxy resonated as spiritually expansive and intellectually rooted. Their discourse appealed to born Muslims and converts alike. Ironically, much like Salafism, the neo-traditionalist appeal to religious authenticity and its seeming "post-racial" identity attracted many who felt cultural contingencies impeded this religious authenticity.

Hamza Yusuf, a charismatic white Imam from California, was at the forefront of the movement. In the mid-1990s, Yusuf captured his Euro-American Muslim audiences with his mastery of the Arabic language. He married an understanding of traditional Islam with a counterculture critique of American imperialism, capitalism, secularism, and modernization. Yusuf's religious speeches were passionate, sometimes bordering on revolutionary messianism.[20] Cassette tapes of his lectures were in high demand. Yusuf was joined by Abdal Hakim Murad—an English convert. Murad did not gain the mass appeal that Yusuf had. He was tempered in his demeanor and measured in his words. Still, Murad became one of the most influential advocates for neo-traditionalism. His public scholarship inspired many Muslims frustrated by the prevailing anti-intellectualism in Muslim spaces. Umar Faruq Abd-Allah joined them a few years later. He, too, was a prominent white convert born in Nebraska. A decade older than Yusuf and a little over a decade older than Murad, Abd-Allah had been an academic for many years. He was not, however, just known for his academic astuteness. Abd-Allah was respected for his exemplary spiritual piety, which led many to seek his spiritual guidance. Their communities of seekers have changed and matured in many ways since the 1990s. They, too, have undergone considerable intellectual and political shifts. They are no longer the underdogs challenging Salafi domination of religious spaces, and their influence far exceeded their expanding community of seekers. Yusuf, Murad, and Abd-Allah gained international notoriety for their religious scholarship and advocacy, regularly making it to the 500 Most Influential Muslims list.[21]

Hamza Yusuf was born Mark Hanson in Walla Walla, Washington State, in 1958, but grew up in Marian County in Northern California.[22] He is referred to as Shaykh Hamza Yusuf; he sometimes goes by "Hamza Yusuf Hanson" in policy spaces.[23] Yusuf has Scottish, Greek, Irish, and Northern European heritage.[24] He was born into an affluent family. His maternal grandfather founded *Screenland Magazine*, an influential entertainment magazine. He later sold it, joined the oil business in Bakersfield, California, and helped found Callon Petroleum Company. This made his family exceedingly wealthy. Later, upon rediscovering his Greek Orthodox faith, Yusuf's grandfather dedicated himself to a life of piety to become the Greek Orthodox Church leader in Ignacio.[25] As a result, Yusuf was baptized into the Greek Orthodox Church. His grandfather even encouraged him to attend Greek Orthodox summer school in Greece at twelve. Yusuf's father—David Joseph Hanson—met his mother—Elizabeth Anne George Hanson—in 1956. He had been a Second World War veteran and an academic. David Hanson earned a liberal arts degree from Columbia University and a Master's degree in philosophy. Initially, Yusuf's parents lived in Walla Walla, where his father taught English literature at Whitman College.

They later moved to the San Francisco Bay Area, where David Hanson joined his father-in-law's oil business and continued to work in the oil industry until his final days.[26]

On the other hand, Yusuf's mother was very involved in the 1960s and 1970s counterculture scene. Yusuf recalls that she spent her life fighting injustice; she marched behind Martin Luther King and Cesar Chavez.[27] She was a committed civil rights activist and an environmentalist.[28] Even well into her eighties, she was protesting the Iraq War.[29] Yusuf's mother was baptized into the Orthodox Church but was raised Catholic. Like many in the counterculture movement of the 1960s and 1970s, however, Elizabeth Hanson moved on from her Catholic upbringing. For most of Yusuf's life, she was a member of a Buddhist Songhai and practiced Tibetan Buddhism.[30] Her uncle, George Fields, had owned a metaphysical bookstore in the 1930s. There, he sold New Age treatises on Buddhism, Sufism, and Gurdjieff's Fourth Way.[31] Yusuf recalls her teaching him and his siblings a more ecumenical form of spirituality in which all religions had some truth, and that religious affiliation was essentially random.[32] He added that she believed that "religion is largely arbitrary ... that people generally follow religions of the families that they are born into, and there's something very arbitrary about that. If I were born in Sri Lanka, I would be a Buddhist or a Hindu. So that really struck me." He went on to add: "Heidegger calls it thrownness. You are kind of a historical product, and most people don't ever challenge their thrownness, the fact that they're just thrown into an environment that determines how they view the world, what they think, and how they worship."[33] As a result, she tried to instill a deep respect for all religions. When Yusuf was twelve, she took him to a mosque.[34]

By the age of sixteen, Yusuf had developed a keen interest in mysticism. Sufi groups at the time flourished in the San Francisco Bay Area, where he lived, and the counterculture scene flourished there too. "Sufi dancers and singers, utilizing chants from a variety of religious traditions (including some of the Arabic Names of God or asmā' al-ḥusnā), performed at Grateful Dead concerts and were featured in the psychedelic–spiritual scene that characterized so much of the Bay Area youth culture during that era."[35] In 1976, Yusuf went to a small spiritual bookstore in Ojai, California. There he came across a metaphysical treatise written by Abu Bakr Siraj ad-Din called *The Book of Certainty: The Sufi Doctrine of Faith, Vision, and Gnosis*. He did not know it then, but Siraj ad-Din was the renowned English convert Martin Lings. The book contained esoteric commentaries on the Qur'an. He recalls finding the language inaccessible, yet it provided something he felt he was missing—a sense of certainty. Yusuf set the book aside and bought a copy of the Qur'an.[36] Yusuf noted a year later: "When I was 17, I was in a very serious car accident that led to a really deep reflection on transition—the possibility I could have died in that accident. I felt ... I hadn't really done anything with my life spiritually."[37] Yusuf was introduced to Islam soon after.

Yusuf met a couple from Mecca living in Santa Barbara; they had been devotees of an eccentric and exceedingly charismatic Scottish shaykh, known to his followers as Abd al-Qadir as-Sufi.[38] Abd al-Qadir, born Ian Dallas, had been a successful writer, actor, and playwright. Dallas had traveled to North Africa in 1967, where he converted to Islam. A year later, in Morocco, he met his spiritual guide—Shaykh Muhammad ibn Habib. Shaykh Muhammad ibn Habib then appointed Abd al-Qadir as the Muqaddam (representative) of his *ṭarīqa* (Sufi order), the Ḥabibyyah Ḍarqawiyyah—a branch of the Shādhilī Sufi order.[39] He then announced that he had the authorization (*idhn*) from Shaykh Muhammad al-Fayturi Hamudah to join the branches of the Ḥabibyyah and the Aliwyya orders in the Ḍarqawiyyah order.

Due to the upsurge of New Age spirituality in the 1960s and 1970s, Dallas's devotees at the time consisted primarily of white converts who were a part of the hippie movement.[40] Dallas was also a part of the 1960s hippie counterculture movement—which brought together radical politics, esotericism, art, and a peace-and-love ethos. He befriended Eric Clapton, George Harrison, Bob Dylan, Kenneth Tynan, and Ronald Laing. Like many of his contemporaries, Dallas set out on a spiritual journey to ascertain spiritual truths. He first set up a *zawiya* (Sufi lodge) in a West London apartment building in Bristol Gardens.[41] Many of his devotees moved into the building, signaling the first experiment with communal living. In 1975, as-Sufi moved his devotees to a secluded area near Norwich—a city one hundred miles northeast of London. He intended to set up a pure "Muslim village in England."[42] As with most communes set up in the 1960 and 1970s, this experiment eventually failed. This resulted from logistical reasons—such as lack of adequate finances and essential services to sustain the community—and the fallout from as-Sufi's increasingly authoritarian hold.

Hamza Yusuf—then still Mark Hanson—met with as-Sufi's devotees several times before converting to Islam. At eighteen, in 1977, Yusuf dropped out of junior college and left the United States to join as-Sufi's community in Norwich. Soon after, Yusuf gained a reputation as an astute student and became well-respected in the order.[43] In the late 1970s, Yusuf was already in contact with and under the tutelage of the Emirati scholar Abdullah Ali Mahmood, who convinced him to pursue his Islamic education in the UAE. There he studied for four years. During his time in the Emirates, Yusuf studied *tajwīd* (Qur'anic recitation), *fiqh*, *'aqīda*, poetry, rhetoric, logic, and other classical Islamic disciplines.[44] In addition to his formal studies in the Islamic Institute of Al Ayn, Yusuf also studied privately with scholars including Abdullah ould Siddiq. Abdullah ould Siddiq, the then *muftī* of Abu Dhabi and a native of Mauritania, introduced him to West African scholars, including Shaykh Abdullah bin Bayyah—who later became Yusuf's shaykh.[45]

Yusuf's teachers convinced him to move to North Africa to continue his religious education. In 1984, Yusuf decided to do so. He also decided to terminate his relationship with Abd al-Qadir as-Sufi and his movement—now dubbed the Murabitun World Movement. Nevertheless, between 1984 and 1988, Yusuf lived in Algeria, Morocco, and Mauritania—visiting Spain intermittently. During his time in Mauritania, he met a man who would become his shaykh—Murabit al-Hajj Muhammad ould Fahfu. The image of Murabit al-Hajj would later play an essential role in how neo-traditionalists construct, imagine, and perceive the notion of tradition. In 1988, Yusuf returned to the United States to study as a nurse with the intention of returning to Mauritania. Although Mauritania would always remain a point of reference, Yusuf settled in the United States, and there, his *da'wa* journey began.[46]

Umar Faruq Abd-Allah (Wymann-Landgraf) shares some similarities with Yusuf regarding the trajectory of his conversion and upbringing.[47] Abd-Allah was born in 1948 in Columbus, Nebraska. He has Swiss, German, English, and French Huguenot heritage.[48] Abd-Allah was raised in a pious Protestant household in both the Presbyterian and Lutheran traditions. Like Yusuf, he came from an astute academic background. His parents—Donald Eugene Weinman and Grace Marian Weinman—were academics. His father was a professor of Organic Chemistry, and his mother had a Master's degree from the University of Georgia.[49] In 1964, his family relocated to Columbia, Missouri, where his parents took up positions at the University of Missouri. Like Yusuf, Abd-Allah was involved in a traumatic accident when he was a teenager. Although this did not lead him to convert, he was spiritually changed by it.[50] Following in his parents' footsteps, Abd-Allah enrolled in the University of Missouri with a dual degree in History and English Literature. In 1969, he was awarded the Woodrow Wilson Fellowship to pursue a PhD at Cornell University in English Literature.

At Cornell, Abd-Allah read *The Autobiography of Malcolm X*, which inspired his conversion to Islam in 1970. Two years later, he changed his degree and transferred to the University of Chicago. There he studied Arabic and Islamic Studies under the supervision of renowned modernist Islamic scholar Fazlur Rahman. In 1978, Abd-Allah received his doctorate with honors for his dissertation on Mālikī *fiqh*.[51] From 1977 to 1982 he taught at the University of Windsor (Ontario), Temple University, and the University of Michigan.[52] In 1982, he left for Spain, where he taught Arabic in Abdul Qadir as-Sufi's Murabitun community.[53] The Murabitun community had already been undergoing a great upheaval. The commune experiment as-Sufi, founded in Norwich, failed soon after. According to the accounts of nostalgic adherents, the community did not have the means to be self-sufficient, resulting in food shortages.[54]

Ziauddin Sardar presents a grimmer narrative. He first met Abd al-Qadir as-Sufi in 1972 and was the only non-white regular at their *zawiya*. Sardar recalls:

> The disciples were ordered to purify themselves with the water of the Unseen. Their hearts had to be cleansed of the ailments which veiled them from the presence of the Knower of the Unseen. The purification involved the Sheikh—Abdul Qadir—who was "purified of fault," pouring the water of secret sciences that flowed from the presence of the Unseen into the heart of the devotees. Those who refused to be cleansed in such a way lacked the inner sight to recognize the qualities of the Sheikh. Abdul Qadir was now the absolute master of the Bristol Garden community. He chose husbands for his female devotees, ordered male disciples to divorce their wives, and generally regulated all aspects of the lives of all his followers.[55]

According to Ian Abdal Latīf Whiteman, an early *murīd* in the community, in addition to as-Sufi's charismatic authoritarianism, his aversion to the nuclear family and his commitment to radical politics shaped the trajectory and eventual downfall of the community. In his memoir, Whiteman laments: "Whether his dream was for a kind of experimental Sufi *kibbutzim* (socialist communes in Israel) or a Maoist re-engineered society and cultural revolution, we shall never know, but I was very unhappy that he tried to come between some of the followers and their parents, then between the followers and their children and finally between the husbands and the wives."[56] Whiteman related embittered recollections of the charismatic power as-Sufi yielded. As-Sufi had ordered his devotees to divorce their wives—with which most, including Whiteman, complied. He stressed that this was "proof that we had all temporarily lost our minds."[57]

Sardar notes that after moving his community from the Bristol Garden community in London to Norwich and Granada, Spain, as-Sufi named his group the Murabitun. He set out to "create a 'new species' of 'Islamic man who was a fitting follower of the Messenger.'"[58] When Abd-Allah first went to Spain to join the community, he left behind a successful academic career. However, it became increasingly apparent to him that the insular nature of the group was a problem. Abd-Allah's intellectual astuteness became a challenge to Abd al-Qadir as-Sufi's monopoly on power. The breaking point for Abd-Allah was when he challenged as-Sufi for stating that there were no Muslims—in the Muslim world—who truly understood Islam. Whiteman explain, "He [Umar Faruq Abd-Allah] too had to flee the city in the end as the politics got ever more vicious. He tried to stand up to what had become an oppressive regime amongst the community but was driven out in a very unjust and ignoble fashion."[59] When Abd-Allah left Spain for Morocco, as-Sufi sent Hamza Yusuf after him to persuade him to return. However, it was only a matter of time before Yusuf left as well. Abd-Allah never refers to Ian Dallas by name, but often mentions that he was tricked by a false shaykh who betrayed the community's trust.[60] Abd-Allah then relates that although it took him time to trust again, he eventually found a true shaykh who became his shaykh.

In 1994, Abd-Allah was appointed Lecturer in the Faculty of Islamic studies at King Abdul Aziz University in Jeddah, Saudi Arabia.[61] In 2000 he returned to the United States, where he founded the Nawawi Foundation in Chicago—which is now defunct. Since then, he has collaborated and worked with neo-traditionalist networks on many educational projects. Abd-Allah's current shaykh is Shaykh Muḥammad Ḥaydara al-Jīlānī of the Qādirī *tarīqa* in the Gambia. He is also a Sufi shaykh in this *tarīqa* and takes *bayʿah* (allegiance from initiates in the Sufi order). Aside from teaching annually at Rihla, Abd-Allah also organizes his own spiritual retreat called "The Zawiyah." This takes place in Alquería de Rosales in Spain, and has recently taken place in Egypt.

The religious trajectory of Abdal Hakim Murad differs slightly from those of both Hamza Yusuf and Umar Faruq Abd-Allah. Born Timothy John Winter in 1960. Murad came from a middle-class and highly educated background. His family consisted of Norfolk congregational ministers. He was from a "mainstream Anglican" background, yet he considered himself a non-conformist Anglican as he was not convinced about the Trinity. His father, John Winter, was a renowned modernist architect.[62] From a young age, Murad seemed alienated from modern life and skeptical about the core principles of his religion.[63]

In an article about his conversion, Murad recalls a story that instigated his spiritual musings:

> In my teens, I was sent off by my parents to a cottage in Corsica on an exchange with a very vigorous French Jewish family with four daughters. They turned out to be enthusiastic nudists. I remember being on the beach and seeing, conjured up before my adolescent eyes, every fifteen-year-old boy's most fervent fantasy. There was a moment when I saw peach juice running off the chin of one of these bathing beauties, and I had a moment of realization: the world is not just the consequence of material forces. Beauty is not something that can be explained away just as an aspect of brain function. That was the first time I became remotely interested in anything beyond the material world. It was an unpromising beginning, you might say.[64]

Murad studied at the elite Westminster School before studying at the University of Cambridge.[65] When he was at Cambridge, he decided to join the Unitarian Church. In the meantime, he was learning Arabic intending to move to the Gulf amid the oil boom. Murad was not looking to convert, he explains, yet Islam "ticked all the boxes that my inherited Christianity left vacant." He says, "this was a shocking realization because, by temperament, I really didn't want to take any major step or do anything exotic. I saw myself as very English."[66]

Unlike Yusuf or Abd-Allah's fascination with the esotericism of the counterculture, Murad's aversion to it is what led him to Islam. Haifaa Jawad explains:

> Being a teenager in the 1970s, when there was no limit or boundary to what a young man or woman could do, must have had a crucial impact on his view of life and its meaning. This set him on the road to looking for a new direction and another worldview with a deeper meaning of life and spirituality. And this direction he found when he decided to embrace Islam, a religion that, like no other, asks of its followers' strict conformity to its tenets.[67]

Upon converting to Islam, Murad briefly joined the Tablighi Jamaat.[68] He then went on to spend six years in the Middle East, three of which he spent in Egypt studying in al-Azhar and the remainder of which he spent between Saudi Arabia and Yemen studying informally with shaykhs (notably some Baʿalawī shaykhs like Ḥabīb Aḥmad Mashhūr al-Ḥaddād).[69] In 1989, Abdal Hakim Murad returned to the United Kingdom.

By the mid-1990s, Yusuf and Murad had become increasingly active—as part of a budding transnational Euro-American network concerned with the propagation of the tradition. To this end, Murad published articles for *Q-News*—a British Muslim publication founded in the early 1990s by Fuad Nahdi. Like Murad, Nahdi had been a student of the Baʿalawī shaykh Ḥabīb Aḥmad Mashhūr al-Ḥaddād.[70] In these articles, Murad often provided critical interjections to his advocacy of the tradition by juxtaposing it with the inauthenticity of Islamism and Salafism. Murad would argue that Islamists' and Salafis' theological and political blunders are premised on their modernist dispositions. Murad's interventions resonated with many. Masʿud Khan was among them. Khan was a young British Pakistani computer scientist at the time. He had come from a Barelvi background. Growing increasingly worried about the impact of Salafism on the Muslim community and simultaneously disillusioned with Barelvi mosques, Khan found Murad's interventions necessary. He began to transcribe Murad's lectures alongside those of Nuh Ha Mim Keller—another white convert who was advocating for traditional Islam—and shared them online.[71] The internet was still a new medium to which primarily young educated professionals had access; this was the key demographic they mostly influenced.

Yusuf's lectures were also becoming increasingly popular among Muslims from immigrant backgrounds. By 1993, Yusuf was already addressing the North American Muslim community at ISNA (Islamic Society of North America). By 1995, Yusuf was invited at the behest of Ibrahim Osi-Efa—a Nigerian British Muslim shaykh—to speak at the Islamic Forum of Europe.[72] Osi-Efa and Masʿud Khan thought it was necessary to create sustainable religious programs that introduce the community to traditional sciences. Along with Hamza Yusuf, they first set up "Deen Intensive," "Light Study Programs," and the "Rihla Programs," which were small study circles and retreats.[73] These programs aimed to deepen seekers' knowledge of traditional Islamic sciences. The "Light Study" program would typically last for a day, while "Deen Intensives" would often be for a weekend or three days. The Rihla retreat, however, was much longer. It would last from three weeks to a month. The Rihla retreat—or Rihla for short—was founded in 1996. The first

Rihla was held in Nottingham in the United Kingdom. It was later followed by Rihlas in Morocco, Spain, Saudi Arabia, Turkey, and Malaysia.[74] In 1996, Yusuf simultaneously founded the Zaytuna Institute in California alongside the Iraqi philanthropist Hesham Alalusi.[75]

As the network of shaykhs, committed to an understanding of tradition and their institutions, grew transnationally, so did the need to explicitly define their beliefs, identities, and goals. In 1999, a meeting took place at the Islamic Foundation in Markfield, Leicestershire, in England, between several neo-traditionalist figures. The meeting aimed to decide the organizational structure and future of the group. Among those present were Hamza Yusuf, Abdal Hakim Murad, Umar Faruq Abd-Allah, Ibrahim Osi-Efa, and Nuh Keller.[76] Nuh Keller was adamant that all adherents ought to follow a Sufi *ṭarīqa*. Hamza Yusuf contended that it was a personal choice.[77] The meeting concluded by agreeing on some overarching thematic principles. There would be no "movement" per se; instead, they would be a loose affiliation of shaykhs and students who agreed on some overarching theological tenets. These include, first and foremost, an affirmation of the importance of traditional Islam. This means a religious adherence to one of the four *fiqhī* madhhabs—Ḥanafī, Mālikī, Shāfiʿī, and Ḥanbalī, following one of the two normative schools of *ʿaqīda*—the Ashʿarī and Māturīdī schools—and affirming the importance of *taṣawwuf*. Although Yusuf did not actively advocate *ṭarīqa* allegiance—as Marcia Hermansen contends—he contributed to a culture in which more people became receptive to *ṭarīqa* affiliation.[78]

Since then, the loose affiliation of shaykhs has developed a multi-generational and transnational epistemic community. The members shared notions about the validity of particular forms of knowledge or "specified truths."[79] This community extended from the United States and Canada to the United Kingdom and Australia—despite the strong US and UK centrism. The early pioneers of its formation were Hamza Yusuf (Hanson), Nuh Ha Mim Keller, Zaid Shakir, and later Umar Faruq Abd-Allah in the United States, and Abdal Hakim Murad (aka Timothy Winter) and Ibrahim Osi Efa in the United Kingdom. The generation of neo-traditionalists that succeeded them includes Usama Canon, Yahya Rhodus, Omar Qureshi, Faraz Khan, Asad Tarsin, Walead Mosaad, Feraidoon Mojadedi, Mustafa Davis, and Abdullah bin Hamid Ali in the United States.[80] In the United Kingdom, the second generation of neo-traditionalists included Aftab Malik, Faiz Qureshy, and Haroon Hanif. Faraz Rabbani and Afroz Ali played an essential role in teaching and building institutions in Canada and Australia. They derive their authority from so-called "traditional" luminaries of the East—such as Abdullah bin Bayyah, Muhammad al-Yaqoubi, Habib Ali Jifri, Murābiṭ al-ḥāj ould Faḥfū, and Ḥabīb Aḥmad Mashhūr al-Ḥaddād, among others. The more senior religious figures in the West are often designated "shaykhs" or "Imams." By contrast, the younger ones are often called *ustadh or sīdī*—establishing an informal scholarly hierarchy.[81] They act as theologians advocating for a tradition long abandoned in modernity, and as spiritual philosophers and sociologists of the modern world.

As evidenced, the authoritative voices that constitute neo-traditionalism are almost exclusively male. Likewise, the pedagogues from whom they derive their authority too are male. While this is by no means unique to neo-traditionalists, it does have significant implications for the formation of "tradition" as a category. As Sajida Jalalzi notes, "religious authority is traditionally coded as masculine, while masculinity is also configured as essentially authoritative."[82] Consequently, it indicates that "tradition"—or traditional authority—lies primarily with male figures. On the outliers of the neo-traditionalist community, however, a small number of female *ustadhas* gained notoriety—such as Ustadha Saraa Sabbagh, Ustadha Shazia Ahmad, and Ustadha Muslema Purmul, as well as *shaykhas* from a proto-Syrian Sufi sisterhood called Al-Qubaysiat—most notably Tamara Gray and Shehnaz Kerim. Unlike their male counterparts, however, they are poised to speak to female-specific audiences on female-specific issues. Furthermore, except for Tamara Gray, they are referred to by the generic title "Ustadha" (religious teacher) rather than "Shaykha" (religious leader). Hence, the construction of female religious voice allows only for limited access and transmission of the tradition since the female voice is specific while the male voice is universal.

Neo-traditionalism

The neo-traditionalist shaykhs became custodians of the tradition in the West that has long been marginalized and obscured by modernity. They share a theological commitment to the "tradition:" that is, a commitment to the *fiqh*, *ʿaqida*, and *taṣawwuf* as traditional methods of ascertaining true Islām, Imān, and Iḥsān, "traditional" Islamic pedagogy, and an epistemological rejection of modernism and its purported Muslim aberrations. The methods of traditional Islam were preserved through unbroken chains of transmission. Kasper Mathiesen explains that it is central to the neo-traditionalist conception of "traditional" Islam that it had been passed down in a chain from teacher to student all the way back to the time of the Prophet. This makes it firmly rooted in the Sunna and corroborated by authoritative scholars throughout history.[83] This is as true for *taṣawwuf* (as the science of *Iḥsān*) as it is for *fiqh*. Hamza Yusuf, Abdal Hakim Murad, and Umar Faruq Abd-Allah elaborate on five dimensions of "tradition"—theological, temporal, civilizational, intellectual, and authoritative.

Yusuf defines traditional Islam as "the 'plumb line,' the trunk of the Islamic tree ... whose roots are firmly buried in the soil of Prophethood. Over time, tributaries sprout from the 'plumb line' and eventually die out, but the line continues because ... tradition [is] based on isnad—sound, authentic, reliable transmission of sacred knowledge."[84] For Murad, tradition "is a return to the civilizations' time-honored root-epistemology, the *uṣūl*, and the employment of the cumulative wisdom of the Muslim centuries in all its amplitude (*madhhabs, taṣawwuf, kalām*)."[85] Abd-Allah notes that, as Heidegger points out, modernity is "post-traditional." He contends that the notion of "tradition is fundamentally connected with the transmission, from living people to living people. In Islamic civilization, that sense of tradition through transmission applied to everything."[86] Modernity, the neo-traditionalists contend, has disrupted the continuity of the tradition by reformulating normative traditional methods and denying their original authority.

This notion of "tradition," however, is not universally recognized by all. It seems to make a distinct authoritative claim in the Western context that does not translate outside. In my interview with Habib Ali Jifri in 2015, I asked how he would define this religious and intellectual orientation. Interviewing in Arabic, I attempted to explain "tradition" and "traditionalism" while retaining all its authoritative claims. I offered two translations—*turāth* or *taqlīd*. Habib Ali seemed to take mild offense at both terms. For one, the term *turāth* directly translates as "heritage." The notion of *turāth* does not make a religious claim to orthodoxy; instead, it was the sum of the intellectual output of Muslim societies regardless of its religious validity or orthodoxy. Some scholars cite the books of *turāth*. However, that makes little claim regarding their religious standing. The project of *turāth* revival in the twentieth century is connected to a reformist Arabic intellectual impulse to revive and discuss the totality of the intellectual and theological output of the past. The notion of Islamic heritage or *turāth* includes aspects that may be conceived as heterodox or even heretical. Translating it as *al-Islām al-turāthī*, therefore, did not work.[87] I tried to translate it as *taqlīd*. *Taqlīd* is a crucial methodological block of the "tradition"; however, it does not encapsulate the whole meaning of "tradition."

I presented my dilemma to Habib Ali Jifri—who is often considered a "traditional" scholar by Western shaykhs. He interjected with his own term. He stated that he belonged to *al-madrasa al-'aṣīla*, which translates as the "authentic school." His use of the notion of "*'aṣālah*"—authenticity—is vital for two reasons. Firstly, it makes an exclusive claim to authenticity and orthodoxy. Secondly, the notion of *'aṣālah'* was developed partly from Arab reformist intellectuals' debate on modernity.[88] *'Aṣālah'* was used to counter a contemporist[89] view—or "*mu'āṣara.*" The "*'aṣālah'–'mu'āṣara*" debate shows how the perception of the "modern" shapes the way the tradition is understood. After all, it can only be from the vantage point of view of the now that the past could be conceived as "traditional" and have meanings assigned to it. Although Habib Ali insisted on using the term "*al-madrasa al-'aṣīlah*," the term was not used by Western neo-traditionalists and seemed to have disappeared even in Eastern circles.

The term "neo-traditionalism" came to be used as a self-definition in Abdullah bin Hamid's article "'Neo-Traditionalism' vs. 'Traditionalism.'"[90] Bin Hamid, a neo-traditionalist shaykh who sometimes teaches in Rihla and is a Zaytuna college faculty member, was inclined against using "traditional" as self-denomination. He explained that the "neo-" in "neo-traditionalism" indicated that although he is a proponent of restoring (or at least attempting to restore) what was lost of what he calls "sacred history," it cannot be fully restored.[91] He adds: "This orientation cannot rightly be called 'traditionalism' because truly authentic traditionalism can only be known and practiced by those who have not been influenced by modern thinking. And all of us living today, in one way or another, have been influenced by modern thinking. So, the past cannot completely ever be retrieved."[92] Here, Ali indicates that time is not a purely secular conception but a religious and moral category constantly decreasing in value. Normativity and religious orthodoxy exist within the confines of time, and as time passes, their ability depreciates.

However, the notion of neo-traditionalism does not have the same conceptual capital for some seekers. According to one seeker at the Spring Lodge retreat, positing a "neo-traditional"–"traditional" dichotomy is erroneous. He added: "This revival [of tradition in the West] is not abstracted from the [traditional] continuum; it is within it. We are not a generation who have found an encoded message that we are trying to decipher and then reconstruct a move-

ment from it." He then began to outline the neo-traditionalist historical narrative of the modern decline. "Due to various socio-political conditions, the
heirs of that tradition have been obscured. The proper Islamic tradition has
been marginalized. So that continuum hasn't ceased but has become inconspicuous. And now you have these satellites in rural areas in Mauritania; in
Hadramawt, and places like Syria, these traditions are preserved in communities that are on the fringes now where before they used to be in the center."

His contention demonstrates that the notion of tradition is multi-layered.
The tradition indicates a history of orthodox belief as it was normatively established in time and is being depreciated in modernity. Temporality, therefore,
entails a system of meaning and values. The passage of time is not to be taken
for granted but rather is a depreciation of the value of truth. Additionally,
the tradition can be located geographically. The past and its authority exist in
places and people. To revive the tradition, the authority of these traditional
locations needs once again to be re-centered.

The conceptualizations of neo-traditionalism have been, for the most,
more descriptive than analytic. These often stress a theological claim of the
centrality of *taqlīd* in *fiqh*, *'aqīda*, and *taṣawwuf*, a form of nostalgia with a
somber reference to a lost past and a critique of modernity. Sadek Hamid and
Kasper Mathiesen opt for the term "traditional," emphasizing the theological
location of the tradition. As an objective category in time, it could therefore
depreciate or be regained to a degree in this attempt to revive the tradition.
That is to say, one can be of a sufficiently "traditional" orientation in modern
times and therefore be more religiously orthodox than those who espouse other
modernist interpretations of Islam. There are some significant limitations to a
purely descriptive approach. For example, Abbas Berzger, Brenden Newlon,
and AbdelWahab El-Affendi describe traditional orientation as nostalgia or
historical romanticism.[93] Other Islamic trends, including so-called modernist
approaches, also maintain a reference to the past that is highly nostalgic. The
"Golden Age of Islam" trope is not unique to neo-traditionalists. Nostalgia
implies that the reference to the past is a rhetorical tool rather than an authoritative claim.

The fundamental problem with this descriptive approach is that it assumes
that neo-traditionalists employ an objective theological category of tradition, which is only ornamented with a romantic appeal to the past. In fact,
what is "lost" is continually and constantly being reformulated, performed,
re-adapted, and negotiated to fit modern concerns and consumption while

retaining its discourse of authenticity and orthodoxy. For example, as their social critiques expand, the notion of tradition encapsulates a lost Western tradition undergoing a civilizational crisis in modernity.[94] Therefore, it is necessary to explore the different trajectories and forces that go into the negotiation and eventually construct the tradition and "traditional" principles. Therefore, the "neo-" in neo-traditionalism is not an attempt to suggest the existence of an alternative "tradition" (or even an attempt to deny the existence of this one), but rather shows how the discourse on tradition, modernity, and religious orthodoxy functions as an ongoing attempt at meaning-making outside modernist constructs.

Tradition Personified: In Space and Person

In the neo-traditionalist narratives, the notion of "tradition" appears objective rather than a constructed or imagined category. It indicates authentic and authoritative forms of belief, practice, and method. It is both temporally and geographically situated. One can historically situate where orthodoxy was established and show the meanings and the value system it produced. Additionally, as the secular passage of time in modernity decreases the value of tradition, it moves away from the geographic centers to the peripheries. The peripheral pockets where tradition has been purportedly preserved are presented as places untouched by modernity and uncorrupted by modern politics. They are both protected and sanctified by the scholars and saints within them. As neo-traditionalist shaykh, Yahya Rhodus relates:

> Sometimes you have to go to a special place in the Muslim world like Fes or Tarim or many of the other beautiful pockets that still exist of traditional societies, and you go, and you visit the righteous; you visit their graves and understand that the *awliyā'* ... are the way and the means through which Allah distributes his generosity here in the earth.[95]

The Western impulse to position the East as an archival—albeit mute—authority is replicated in both the shaykhs' discourses and the seekers' imaginaries. This is evident in how Hamza Yusuf cites Mauritania as an enchanted reservoir of tradition and his claim to authority. In a BBC interview, Yusuf describes his journey to Mauritania:

> One day a man comes from Mauritania named Shaykh Abdurrahman ...
> Looking at this man for me was looking at someone coming out of the

seventh or eighth century. I asked, who is this man? They told me that this is the son of one of the greatest scholars of the Sahara, whose name is al-Mura-bit al-Hajj ... Here is this American kid from Marion County in Northern California in the middle of the Saharan desert, and here is this shaykh, and this is the divested man. He has given up the world. He is in a state of complete submission.[96]

Zareena Grewal explains that Yusuf's depiction of his shaykh, Murabit al-Hajj, evokes the trope of the "noble savage." The people of Mauritania are described "in terms of cultural essences, as only quasi-human, half living in an unearthly realm."[97] In Yusuf's discourse, and consequentially in the seeker's imagination, Mauritania represents an "enchanted" pre-modern. Grewal adds, "He refers to the [Mauritanians] as prem, residual traces of ancient, vanishing, and utopic cultures that have miraculously survived into the dystopic modern world."[98] Mauritania's enchantment meant that in the desert and villages, their lived reality was, in effect, vulnerable to the intervention of the *otherworldly*. Yusuf adds:

> The desert people of Mauritania are halfway into the unseen world; their dreams are so extraordinary. I mean, we know this about Aboriginal peoples; they are connected to the dream world 'ālam al-khayāl, the imaginal world. I am seeing this in these people. You think of water, and suddenly someone is handing you a bowl of water.[99]

Grewal points out that Yusuf's Mauritania origin-story single-handedly changed the religious imagination of young Muslims, creating a fantastical image of Mauritania.[100] This image presents Mauritania not only as a geographic location of the past but also as an enchanted land. In the desert, the world remains porous to the intervention of the *otherworldly*, which means that the boundaries between the heavens and earth are blurred in Mauritania. The religious purity and piety of the land untouched by modernity and sanctified by the presence of saints indicates that, unlike the modern West, Mauritania has not been disenchanted.[101] Grewal points out that although the Mauritania fantasy looms in the Western Muslim imagination, very few know the country's history or politics. They only know the myth.[102]

Traditional places that represent the traditional ideal must represent the past but still stand outside time, unscathed and not sullied by profane politics or even the mundane day-to-day. On this basis, although the retreats are often located in Muslim countries, they are highly secluded from the wider society. The sacred pockets or fringes are not just contrasted with the "profane West", they tell the story of the demise of the Muslim centers themselves. The sacred utopias are, in fact, a vindication of the Muslim postcolonial dystopias.[103] Yusuf explains: "Mauritanians—really West Africans—still have an incredible pride and culture, of language and religion whereas most of the Arabs have had their pride taken away from them because they are a defeated people. They co-opted the conqueror's culture."[104]

When Yusuf traveled to Mauritania thirty years later, his tone on its traditional exceptionalism shifted. No longer was he the young seeker of sacred knowledge living among Bedouins in the Mauritanian desert; he was now being honored in the country's capital of Nouakchott for his contributions.[105] On a podium overlooking the audience of Mauritanian men and women, he remorsefully recites these verses:

> As for the tents, they seem like theirs (in the past).
> But the women of the encampment are unlike theirs.
> I swear by the one whose home Quraysh makes pilgrimage to,
> seeking to kiss the blessed corner in its valley
> My eyes have never seen the tents of a tribe.
> But that I remember my beloved in its precincts.[106]

Yusuf expresses disappointment at the country's relative modernization efforts and the changes he has witnessed in the Mauritanian people who have become modern. "Mauritania has changed a lot," he remarked, lamenting a loss. He related the Mauritania he knew and had traveled to as a young man in the 1980s, seeking spiritual guidance from its traditional scholars. He met his spiritual guide in the middle of the desert. Yusuf explains to this Mauritanian audience that Islam used to be preserved in the most traditional forms in their country. The seekers of spiritual knowledge, he explained to them, once lived in tents and drank from wells. For him, being in Mauritania was as though he had traveled in time to a different century. In the Mauritanian desert, there was no electricity and no television. He recalled that he would hear the recitation of the Qur'an from every house.[107] He would observe as seekers gathered stones and recited their ancestors' most refined poetry. Unfortunately, he exclaimed, Mauritania is not what it used to be. Young Mauritanians are now watching American films. Modernity—as he put it—has brought technology to the country and caused moral decline, opening them to the potential for civil strife. Mauritania should not follow the path of its Arab counterparts, who had experienced the so-called Arab Spring, in attempting revolutionary change.[108] Such radical unsettling can only lead to chaos and a loss of its pre-served beauty.

The Mauritanian past that Yusuf evokes relates to his narrative of modernity. Tuwamarat was one of the many pockets in the Muslim world that escaped modernity's ravages and even time itself. There, Islam was not a political ideology void of spirituality as it had been in other postcolonial Muslim centers and the West.[109] He felt that this idealized depiction of Mauritania, perhaps incomprehensible to the ordinary Mauritanian, was increasingly threatened by the advent of technology. In contradistinction to the Mauritania Yusuf knew, Muslims in modernity have been alienated from their tradition. This tradition entailed both a commitment to religious normativity and a metaphysical way of conceiving reality—as understood by Muslims in the past and in traditional pockets in the Muslim world.

For shaykhs and seekers, Mauritania is not the only spatial location of the tradition, and Murabit al-Hajj is not the only personification of it. These moral geographies, where the tradition is purportedly preserved, exist in the mosques of Morocco, villages in Syria, Yemen, and marginal centers in Egypt. It is personified by saintly scholars of the East—such as the Yemeni Baʿalawīs (most prominently Ḥabīb Aḥmad Mashhūr al-Ḥaddād, Habib Ali Jifri, Ḥabīb ʿUmar, and Ḥabīb Kādhim as-Saqqāf), or the Syrian Shadhillīs shaykhs (such as Muhammad al-Yaqoubi), or the Mauritanian shaykhs (such as Murābiṭ al-ḥāj ould Faḥfū or Abdullah bin Bayyah).

The Western shaykhs—Hamza Yusuf, Abdal Hakim Murad, and Umar Faruq Abd-Allah—stand between two symbolic geographies and intervene in two different stories. For one, their religious personas were shaped through their connection with the East. They attained the traditional knowledge through the *suḥba* or the spiritual companionship of the traditional scholars of the East. They are no longer seen as spiritual voyeurs in the East but as a part of it, touched by the charisma of saints and sacred geographies. They absorb not just exoteric knowledge but also the *ḥāl* (esoteric station) of the great scholars they study under.[110] A whole array of meanings and symbols are constructed on this basis. The second geography the shaykhs stand by is that of the West—to which they are indigenous. They talk from the altar of the West as authentic insiders—seemingly unmediated by identity politics. As an essential meaning, the tradition is transmitted from Eastern scholars to Western seekers and from sacred Eastern geography to a Western one through the mediation of these shaykhs. The transmission of tradition crosses spatial and temporal boundaries mediated by them. Their authority and charisma are derived from this precise positioning.

Tradition functions as an authoritative and objective category of truth and a critique of the modern condition. At the outset, as I have elucidated, it is theologically rooted through an interpretation of Ḥadīth Jibrīl whereby the three components of the faith—Islām, Imān, Iḥsān—are the basis for the methodological arrangement of orthodoxy and orthopraxy through a committed adherence to *fiqh*, *ʿaqīda, and taṣawwuf*. In this chapter, I have shown the role Hamza Yusuf, Abdal Hakim Murad, and Umar Faruq Abd-Allah played in propagating the tradition among Muslim communities in the West. On the precipice of the Salafi burnout, these shaykhs have built institutions of religious learning and have developed communities rooted in their understanding of religious normativity and a powerful critique of modernity. This tradition, they contended, is preserved by saintly scholars in marginal pockets of the Muslim East that are unscathed by modernity. Neo-traditionalism, as I have argued, assigns moral categories to different temporal epochs and geographies. On the other hand, tradition—in the shaykhs' discourse—has functioned as a sustained critique of the decline of the sacred in modernity. Modernity, as I will examine in the next chapter, becomes a locus for both the shaykhs' critiques and the seekers' anxieties.

2

MODERN TIMES

In his distinctive all-white *thawb* and turban with a long white veil draped across, Umar Faruq Abd-Allah—or Dr. Umar, as the seekers often refer to him—sat in an Ottoman-style lecture hall. He presented his concluding lecture in a series of lectures titled "Modernism and Post-Modernism in the Light of the Prophetic Belief."[1] These lectures were designed to explain to the seekers the allusive notion of "modernity." Abd-Allah clarifies that modernity is not simply a temporal designation but a set of desacralized principles with distinct genealogies. These principles have clear implications for Muslims' beliefs, practices, and worldviews. He begins by identifying the critical process by which the world came to be modern.

A German social scientist named Max Weber—Umar Faruq Abd-Allah announced—declared that the world we inhabit had become disenchanted. This process is called *Entzauberung*. Abd-Allah proceeded. It means the removal or the emptying of magic from the world. Before this age of modernity, he tells the seekers, human beings lived in a world that was "enchanted." As human beings, we acknowledged and accepted the intervention of angels and *jinn*, sorcerers, and white magic in our material world. The world around us, he announced, has become depopulated of these unseen realities. This is "a type of genocide in my belief," Abd-Allah passionately declared. Once, human beings had "porous selves" that were vulnerable to the intervention of the *otherworldly*. Now, the self is "buffered" from such interventions. Man, he affirmed, had become a "disciplined free agent that is living in a disenchanted, secular world."[2] This critical process of disenchantment occurred after the

Protestant Reformation in the West and with the rise of the Wahhabi movement in the Muslim world. Disenchantment, he concluded, has resulted in the development of modern mechanistic, materialistic, secular, and rationalistic worldviews. Even religious believers are now modern.

Abd-Allah relates a distinct narrative of what has gone wrong for believers. Like Hamza Yusuf and Abdal Hakim Murad, he asserts that the paradigmatic shift from tradition to modernity impacted all aspects of life. For the shaykhs, the major challenges believers and even civilizations face are caused by the advent of modernity. The problem of progress is at its heart a theological, metaphysical, social, and political matter. For the seekers of sacred knowledge, the consequences of modernity hinges upon their devotional practices and views of orthodoxy and orthopraxy. The seekers experience disenchantment as distinctly Muslim subjects coming of age amid the War on Terror. Facing a crisis in religious authority, they search for certainty and authenticity in belief and belonging. The neo-traditionalist shaykhs become central contenders in the quest for religious authority in the West. They outline the legitimacy of their approach through a critique of modernity that links secularization to religious and political extremism. In turn, seekers integrate their personal narratives of religious becoming into the broader neo-traditionalist narratives of counter-modernity.

Narratives of Modernity

Abdal Hakim Murad explains that traditional Islam "can claim to represent a more intellectually and morally coherent response to the present emergency of Muslim integration than either secular scientism or Islamism."[3] The twin modernist aberrations of secular scientism and Islamism reflect the antagonists in the wider intertwined neo-traditionalist narratives on modernity. These relate to the story of Western decline and that of the Muslim decline. These two narratives frequently overlap. The Western story does not merely pertain to the crisis of meaning in Western modernity. It also reflects what the pre-modern West looked like when it still had a semblance of meaning and social order. The story of modern decline in the Muslim world is also not just a story of modern decadence. It is one of the willful losses of the sacred past due to theological failures and political blunders. Modernity, as such, is not a "coming-of-age" narrative. Rather, it reflects an accumulated failure of the promise of progress which transformed the traditional theocentric perspective on the world into the modern anthropocentric view.[4]

The neo-traditionalist shaykhs refer to two overarching trajectories of modernity in their critiques—disenchantment, and the decline of metaphysics. These are not separate or distinctive narratives; together, they formulate and explain the ills of modernity. These ills have culminated in a theological and civilizational crisis. The modern denial of metaphysical essences has brought about a form of radical relativism. This, in turn, formed a crisis of meaning in the world. This is reflected in everything from modern art to political extremism to gender identity and the atomization of truth. The second metanarrative the shaykhs integrate into their discourse is the Weberian notion of disenchantment. They present its genealogy from the Protestant Reformation, in effect showing the impact of the process of rationalization that led to secularization and the disenchanting of the world.

In parallel with the formulated critiques of Western modernity, the shaykhs present a narrative of the development of modernity in the Muslim world. In many ways, this narrative replicates their earlier narratives in its trajectories and conclusions. They argue that Protestant-like variations—namely the Salafi and the Wahabbi movements—developed and forged a break with the tradition in the Muslim world. This consequently caused the disenchanting of the Muslim world. In this narrative, the result was the development of Islamist movements[5] that have resulted in epistemological and political havoc. The shaykhs contend that these movements have taken on a neo-Marxist framework, further voiding Islam of its true essence. In doing so, they argue that the modern Muslim rejection of metaphysics led to the development of Islamist movements.

The Decline of Metaphysics

The decline of religious learning in modernity, the shaykhs note, has inevitably led to the decline of metaphysics. "We live in the most anti-metaphysical age; a society without metaphysics will surely die," Umar Faruq Abd-Allah announced in his lecture during Rihla.[6] The result we see, he explains, is the rise of Islamic extremism.[7] For the neo-traditionalist shaykhs, the central narrative of the decline of metaphysics provided a backdrop to their intellectual, theological, political, and social critiques of the modern world. It also provides a strong link between notions of tradition and notions of metaphysics. Hamza Yusuf explained to his students in a lecture at Zaytuna college that the study of "metaphysics" in the past might have been reserved for the elite. However, the implicit knowledge of metaphysical truths was held by even the laity (al-ʿawām). This knowledge had been passed down through their *ṭarīqa* affiliations and in Friday khuṭbah.[8] Yusuf elaborates that metaphysics is the "science of abstraction." It is "the attempt to grasp the nature of things in their immaterial and universal essences ... Metaphysics aims to understand first principles, including causation itself, its nature, scope, and limits."[9] Abd-Allah contends that seeing the world through a metaphysical lens meant that everyone in the past understood what the "first principles" were. People understood the meanings underlying their subjectivities and purpose on this earth. He went on to add that modern people do not understand what the "first principle" even means. "In this anti-metaphysical world we live in, our expectations are low. We look at modernist Muslims; their theology is superficial because their metaphysical expectations are low."[10] This has turned intelligent people away from religion and led to the development of religious extremism.

Hamza Yusuf traces modernity's anti-metaphysical standpoint to the development of nominalism. In metaphysics, nominalists deny the existence of universals.[11] Yusuf explains that the triumph of the nominalists over the essentialist approach of the realists decoupled the link that philosophy and theology had with one another. The domains of philosophy and theology, now de-coupled, paved the way for the empirical sciences to reign supreme.[12] Abdurrahman Mihirig contends that Yusuf is presenting a quasi-Thomist Catholic reading of the development of modernity. He adds that nominalism was in fact the influence the normative Ashʿarī position of the likes of William of Ockham. Mihirig explains: "It was the Ash'ari school, in its attack on Aristotelian physics and metaphysics, that paved the way for nominalism and empirical science. They were moderate nominalists whose work was readily taken up by opponents of Thomas Aquinas and Aristotle."[13] Indeed, in his article Yusuf does not shy away from asserting the merit of the Catholic narrative. Yusuf states: "Currently in the West, it is the Catholic Church alone that maintains a rigorous ethical approach that is rooted in metaphysical principles."[14] In fact, the Catholic narrative pervades even the Muslim narrative of modernity.

Muslims with a sound belief in the past viewed the world through a "metaphysical lens."[15] They had implicit knowledge of their position within the wider cosmos, as manifested in *tasawuuf* and *ʿaqīda*.[16] In the tradition, Muslims recognized that the cosmos was organized, layered, and meaningful; they had an understanding of recognized spiritual and political authorities. The notion of authority and hierarchy is crucial, in that they provide a sense of stability—be it the epistemic stability of "orthodoxy" or political stability.[17] Abd-Allah explains that the pre-modern metaphysical arrangement of the West—which is not very different from the Muslim worldview—was "based on a view of a cosmic hierarchy. That led to a particular type of laws for the people and a social hierarchy (which we may not agree with) that embodied these laws and spoke to that reality."[18] Abdal Hakim Murad shared Abd-Allah's contention wherein he argued that the social order in the West was predicated on a metaphysical arrangement. The collapse of that order and the decline of metaphysics has thus brought on a crisis of meaning.[19]

With the decline of the theocentric worldview, the metaphysical de-linking of the natural world and transcendence entailed a devaluation of the institutions of pre-modernity. Abdal Hakim Murad explains that the structures that governed, restrained, and restricted society—in Western Christendom—have disappeared with the departure of ontology, metaphysics, and ethics.[20] For example, he goes on to clarify that "fundamental things like family, like class, nation, language, neighborhood, things that gave people meaning are now all up for grabs."[21] So with the decline of these coordinates and hierarchies in modernity, the very definition of culture changes. In the past, culture gave people in society an indication of which class they belonged to. For example, people who frequented opera houses and theatres knew what class they belonged to. In modern times, people no longer belong to classes because the meanings they entailed were essentially voided.[22] These coordinates were predicated and informed by some form of metaphysics or a metaphysical understanding; this is no longer present.

Disenchantment

The second critical process of modern decline is disenchantment. The shaykhs often use Charles Taylor's interjection in the Weberian disenchantment narrative to describe the modern secular condition. As Omar Qureshi—one of the instructors at Rihla—explained in his lecture on the ethical treatise of the Mālikī scholar Muḥammad ibn 'Abd al-Raḥman al-ījī, the main feature of this "secular age" is the loss of transcendence. [23] Qureshi contended that Charles Taylor's magnum opus *A Secular Age* provides a necessary context for transforming our ethical worldviews from pre-modernity to modernity. He explains that modern man lives in what Taylor calls the immanent frame. The immanent frame does not allow for interpretation or mediation between the natural world and gods, spirits, or magic. With the loss of the anchoring of the cosmos toward transcendence, modern man atomized his existence and lost meaning. Qureshi was not alone in outlining the narrative of disenchantment as a pretext for the modern decline. Abdal Hakim Murad, using Taylorian vocabulary, explains the condition as the "felt flatness of modernity."[24] Umar Faruq Abd-Allah further elaborates that, according to Taylor, modernity's "Supernova" had collapsed over the past few decades. "This is his way of describing a breakdown in the philosophical underpinnings of modernity that others before him called dissolution."[25]

The defining feature of the pre-modern, enchanted world that disenchantment eliminated was that the world and human beings were vulnerable (porous) to the intervention of the *otherworldly*—saints, god, demons, or just magic.[26] According to Weber, rationalization and disenchantment are the inevitable coming-age story of modern society.[27] A rationalistic mechanistic worldview replaces the old metaphysical one. "Man's emancipation from traditional religious metaphysics—that once connected him to the totality of his own being through sacred space, sacred text, sacred figures, rituals, and religious institutions—leaves him disconnected and existentially adrift."[28] The enclosed systems of meaning rooted in religious interpretations of reality had become atomized. Disenchantment had simultaneously transformed man into a rational subject and disoriented him from transcendental meaning. This disorientation has left him with a sense of longing for lost innocence.

The process of disenchantment reached its pinnacle with the Protestant Reformation, and especially with Calvinist Protestantism.[29] Protestantism unintentionally paved the way for the rise of Western rationalism through its theological protests that affirmed the centrality of the *this-worldly* over the *otherworldly*.[30] Weber argues that Protestantism engendered its own demise in its rational quest for purpose. It inadvertently demonstrated the importance of secular forms of worldly legitimation. This led to the affirmation of the importance of scientific ontology in replacing metaphysics.[31] This was instrumental in the development of modernity.

The shaykhs work within the Weberian narrative while simultaneously subduing it. They argue that, first, there was the enchanted world that was vulnerable to the forces of magic. The cosmos was composed of layered, recognized hierarchies (such as the Church), meaningful and porous. It was oriented toward transcendence. Using Taylor, they contend that before our present state of disenchantment, man lived in a world of "spirits, demons, and moral forces."[32] Not only were these forces recognized as real, but their centrality to human existence was not doubted. The enchanted world was essentially inhabited by spirits, demons, angels, and saints; it was a world inhabited by God.[33] Hamza Yusuf explains: "The problem with modern society is that it is horizontal. The vertical alignment has been lost. Previous peoples, even pagans of the past, had a deep sense of vertical alignment."[34] The process of disenchantment, which worked to eliminate magic, resulted in a general breakdown of order and meaning in the cosmos through the vertical connection between heaven and earth. "Taylor encapsulates this imaginary shift as ... the move of spontaneously imagining our cosmic environment as an ordered, layered, hierarchical, shepherded *place* to spontaneously imagining our cosmic environment as an infinite, cavernous, anonymous *space*."[35]

The cosmic environment essentially becomes devalued, voided of "charged" meanings, and decentered from any notion of objective truth. Unlike the "porous self" of pre-modernity, the human agent becomes the "buffered self"—one "no longer vulnerable to the transcendent or the demonic."[36] Now, we live in a world haunted by the remnants of transcendence, haunted by what was once an enchanted cosmos. This new modern buffered self is in search of its identity now that it has lost its meaning and position in the cosmos. Umar Faruq Abd-Allah argues that modern identities are extremely powerful because they provide a sense of meaning in a meaningless world. Therefore, people hold on to them with fanaticism and sometimes violence.[37] Abdal Hakim Murad clarifies that this is what Charles Taylor dubs the "age of authenticity."[38] This authenticity refers to an understanding that people must uncover their way "of realizing their humanity" alone without referring to or confirming a model imposed by a previous generation or a religious or political order. Furthermore, Hamza Yusuf explains that with no essential nature of the self, the modern person is urged to liberate themselves "from the shackles of a socially constructed reality and recreate an 'authentic' human being in 'its' own absolute and immaculate conception of what it means to be a person."[39] The cult of individualism is insular.[40] It becomes trapped in a culture of unbridled materialism and accumulation by removing any reference to transcendence and all essential meanings. It constantly needs to actualize its meaning, but it cannot. This explains the perpetual crisis of identity that Muslims have in the West.

Muslim Narratives of Modernity

I greeted Junaid at the beginning of our interview. We had become good friends since I had first told him about my research project. He half-jokingly asked me, "What is wrong with your people [in Egypt], man?" Somewhat confused, I asked him, "What do you mean?" He responded, "Why are so many deviant ideas coming out of Egypt? First, you had 'Abduh and the Islamic modernists, and then you have Quṭb." This question was both interesting and somewhat bewildering. I come from an Egyptian background, but I never considered Muḥammad 'Abduh or Sayyid Quṭb "countrymen." Instead, I only saw them as relevant to the development of Islamic thought in recent history. I asked Junaid to elaborate on these Islamic modernists' purported "deviance." One of his favorite classes in Rihla, he explained, was on the genealogies of radicalization. Junaid added:

> I absolutely loved Aftab Malik's class on radicalization [in Rihla]. It was so eye-opening. I told you I am very passionate about the history, geopolitics, and sociology that creates such fanatical groups. I realized a lot of it was a result of postmodernity and postcolonialism's breaking from the tradition. Today, a lot of people actually feel like breaking up the tradition is a good thing. The *ustadh* explained that the tradition is there as a safeguard. It made me revere the tradition more and revere the shuyūkh of the past more because of the effort they did to preserve this *dīn* [religion]. I mean if it weren't for them, there would be ten times more groups like ISIS walking around.

In the retreat, the narratives of Muslim modernity highlight how Islamic modernism, which led to the development of Islamism and extremism, resulted from the tradition's rupture, which eventually produced radical groups.

The generalized narrative of modernity, often related by the shaykhs, expounds their narratives of intellectual, theological, and political decline. I call this the "Protestantization narrative." The neo-traditionalist shaykhs contend that there had been an Islamic Reformation instigated by Protestant-like Muslim movements—namely the *Salafiyya* and the Wahhabi movements. These movements deconstructed the "established," "traditional" modes of religious authorities and initiated Muslims into a form of Islamic modernity. The shaykhs draw some parallels between the Weberian narratives of disenchantment after the Protestant Reformation and the aftermath of the so-called "Islamic Reformation." In this narrative, the result was the development of Islamist movements that have led to epistemological and political havoc. Just as in the context of Western modernity, they contend that the underlying epistemic structures of Islamism are based on a Marxist epistemic framework.

The antagonists in these narratives of modernity are the scholars, activists, and thinkers who—in countering colonial modernity—adopted its language and imbibed its epistemic structures. The narrative of Muslim modernity, which the shaykhs provide, echoes their discontent with Western modernity. Like the Protestant Reformation, the Muslim Reformation was violent and metaphysically defunct. Abdal Hakim Murad contends, "The Islamic world is now in the throes of its own reformation, and our Calvins and Cromwells are proving no more tolerant and flexible than their European predecessors."[41] This narrative presents Muslim Protestants, Muslim Catholics, and an ongoing violent Islamic Reformation. In an interview with *Cairo Review*, Hamza Yusuf explained: "In Saudi Arabia two hundred years ago, a movement emerged which was a puritanical movement which was a radical departure, it was more of a protestant movement against a kind of Catholic Islam. It was more of a protest movement against a traditional Islam. People say Islam needs a reformation; this is what we're witnessing."[42]

Evoking the Weberian analysis, Yusuf presents his negative assessment of the Reformation and modernity. In another interview, he explains, "People ... say Islam needs a reformation, no, it doesn't! The Reformation was a bloody war between Catholics and Protestants, with the Protestants in effect saying get back to hadith, which is what's happening within Islam now. But Islam doesn't need a reformation. Islam needs a restoration."[43] Yusuf's transposition of the Catholic narrative onto the Muslim narrative provides insights into the neo-traditionalist self-framing as analogous to Catholicism and the "religious other"—as a form of Islamic Protestantism.

The Muslims' first encounter with Western modernity—during the French occupation of Egypt—had a lasting traumatic effect on them. Muslims were faced with their weakness relative to the military might of Napoleon's army. The impact of French and later British colonialism led Muslims to ponder the collapse of their civilizations. As such, the postcolonial religion is haunted by the ghost of Empire, unable to reconcile its past glories with its fallen present. This psychological trauma informs the political and religious agendas of that type of Islam, particularly its Islamist off-shoots. They inadvertently become obsessed with seizing political power and are impacted by secular ideologies borne of the colonial moment.[44] Hamza Yusuf explains the implications of this trauma:

> [Muslims] identified the crisis with a lack of know-how. Most Muslims believed that the reason that we were colonized was that the West got ahead of us. Hence, they directed all of their young people to study things like engineering and medicine because if we could just get the know-how and learn how they do these magical things, we'll restore our greatness again.[45]

Yusuf goes on to add that the Muslim response to colonialism was that of weakness and insecurity. Instead of trusting in their spiritual and scholarly authorities, they became concerned with achieving material success to counter the colonial powers' encroachment. Muslim seminaries, such as Al Azhar, had been instrumental in preserving the tradition then began to modernize. They introduced the study of natural sciences—as the study of theology and metaphysics consequently suffered. The quest for scientism and progress replaced the ethical concerns rooted in these fields.[46] Hamza Yusuf contends, "New narratives were put forth to explain the malaise of Muslim societies, placing the blame squarely on the abandonment of 'worldly' sciences and on the scholars who emphasized spirituality and 'otherworldliness.'"[47] The subsequent induction of Muslims into the logic of scientism has placed the metaphysical principles in which the Muslim world had been organized into question. Lay people with politicized agendas replaced traditional authorities and reformulated and dismantled the religious methodological structures.[48] The traditional scholars were pushed to the fringes while a new stratum of Muslim authority emerged—the "professional" Muslim or the Muslim "intellectual."

From that position of insecurity and assumed inferiority, the so-called *Nahḍa*, or Islamic renaissance movement, was born in the nineteenth century. The architects, who in this Protestantization narrative are "our Calvins and Cromwells," forged a break with the Islamic tradition. The story, as it develops, is therefore primarily predicated on colonial modernity as an epistemological point of reference. The *Nahḍa* had been proceeded by a quasi-Ḥanbalī movement in the Najd—founded by Muhammad ibn 'Abd al-Wahhab—in the eighteenth century. Together they form the early seeds of Muslim modernity. Akin to Protestantism, neo-traditionalists contend, so-called "Wahhabism" relied on a form of uncompromising literalism. It rejected the established orthodox authorities and their methods. Abdal Hakim Murad dubbed this a "Protestant error."[49] Like the Calvinist puritan rupture, the Wahhabi movement transformed how Muslims approached scripture, religious authorities, and their religious subjectivities. This subsequently led to the Wahabbi's attacks on Sufi practices and rituals, such as intercession, which disenchanted the Muslim worldview.[50]

The *Nahḍa*—according to Yusuf—"undermined the spiritual authority of the scholars of Islam, making them appear backward and foolish by promoting the idea that the scholars' religious cosmologies paled before the impressive pillars of modern science."[51] 'Abduh, who was no more than a stooge for the British Empire,[52] essentially secularized the study of Islam.[53] In doing so, he and his reformist counterparts innovated an epistemic shift in how Muslims understand Islam that was divorced from the tradition. 'Abduh's student, Rashīd Riḍā, married Wahhabism and the so-called "liberal Salafism" of the *Nahḍa*,[54] consequently inspiring the development of Islamist movements. Riḍā's thought comprised three elements—a reference to the *salaf al-ṣāliḥ* as a template for religious reform, a call for reconciling and accepting modern science, and a political agenda for change.[55] According to the neo-traditionalists, these had clear implications for religious methods of belief and practice. Under the guise of the reference to the *salaf*, Riḍā "advocated the abandonment of authoritative scholarship."[56] Essentially, what this meant was that he had rejected *taqlīd* as a viable jurisprudential method. Riḍā popularized much of the anti-*taqlīd* polemics. He utilized notions of rationality and anti-institutional and theological stances entrenched in post-Enlightenment modernist thought to make Islam compatible with modern science.[57] Riḍā and many of his contemporaries called for Muslim societies to take a more active role in their political destinies. As Yusuf put it, he believed "the Muslims were far too 'otherworldly'—that the Sufis had taken hold of their understanding to such a degree that they really forgot about the world itself."[58]

Hamza Yusuf and Abdal Hakim Murad trace Riḍā's influence to the development of one of the most influential Islamist movements—the Muslim Brotherhood.[59] Riḍā's political theology was predicated on the belief that the decline of the Muslim world was a direct result of the lack of commitment Muslims have to their faith. This, in turn, transformed Islam into an ideology. Umar Faruq Abd-Allah thus points out that the project of Islamism as an ideology, like Marxism, entails conducting a form of social engineering. It is predicated on a combative worldview as opposed to the traditional harmonious ordering of the world. Ideology sees the world through the prism of victors and vanquished; therefore, it is inherently militant and violent.[60] Indeed, for the shaykhs, Islamists have, de facto, internalized Marxist epistemic structures. As the shaykhs argue, the Marxist epistemologies that Islamists have internalized are based on a utopian view of justice on earth. This materialist and anti-metaphysical worldview leaves no space for heaven, hell, or God's action. In the zeal and confidence in human power to achieve material heaven on Earth, this framework requires a revolutionary unsettling of the world.

Hamza Yusuf cites Sayyid Quṭb and his Islamist interlocutors as an example. In their re-interpretation of classical Islamic texts, they framed Abū Dharr—one of the companions of the Prophet—as a Marxist figure fighting for the poor. In this paradigm, the only framework that exists is that of the oppressor and the oppressed.[61] This concocted dichotomy does not allow for a metaphysical view of existence or tribulation.[62] As upholders of this dichotomy, Islamists have justified the use of violence and rebellion against leaders and the state. In doing so, Islamists have transformed Islam into a predatory force[63]—making it, as Yusuf explains, "a refuge for angry youth who use it as a political platform to rage against the injustice of the West."[64] This anger is a manifestation of the metaphysical decline of Muslims in modernity. The Islamist movements have perpetuated a cycle of violence in the world. They have reduced Muslims' receptivity to inward and outward Islamic knowledge. This led to a big crisis of meaning that is ongoing for Muslim youth—which has left the religion as a form of Islamized Marxist totalitarianism. Umar Faruq Abd-Allah argues that the Islamists' angst to achieve uniformity and unity in the Muslim world is comparable with the Marxist bid for equality. The result is a form of Maoist or Stalinist Islamic totalitarianism.[65] Islamism, according to Abd-Allah, for that reason is inherently totalitarian.[66]

The Crisis of Authority and Moderate Islam

This sustained critique of modernity did not develop in a political vacuum. The seemingly perennial question the shaykhs were responding to, "Does Islam need its own Reformation?," first developed amid a colonial gaze. Orientalists pondered over the possibility of Islam, and, in turn, of Muslim subjects following in the footsteps of Christendom in its rationalization, modernization, and, ultimately secularization. Shortly after the 9/11 attacks, US President George Bush announced the beginning of the War on Terror, and this question gained a sense of renewed urgency. The propensity (or lack thereof) of Islamic doctrine and Muslim people to undergo a process of reformation that will inevitably lead to secularization became a central security concern. This became akin to asking how best to neutralize the innate violent tendencies of Islam for a people who will not secularize.[67] In addition, the question of who speaks for Muslims or what constitutes religious authority in Islam also attained a sense of urgency. Although Muslims have long been concerned with the question of religious authority, it gained a new securitized dimension after the War on Terror. In his speech announcing the War on Terror, George Bush addressed the Muslim world, stating, "Either you are with us, or you are with the terrorists."[68] This became a warning call to Muslim communities in the United States and all over the West, just as it was to Muslim communities and governments worldwide.

The dichotomy emerged between a good, acquiescent, and moderate Islam amenable to liberal and secular citizenship and a bad, fundamentalist Islam incompatible with Western values. The hard power strategies of internally waging the War on Terror altered Muslim life in the United States. In October 2001, Attorney General John Ashcroft arrested around 1,200 Muslim men with suspected ties to terrorism using the corrosive powers of Patriot Act counterterrorism legislation. They had no access to lawyers and were held without being charged with a crime.[69] The Muslim community felt increasingly targeted and surveilled. This included undercover police officers in mosques, Muslim student organizations, and other Muslim spaces. Many American Muslims were put on "the government's No-Fly List of suspected terrorists and subsequent refusal to remove their names unless these citizens agreed to spy on friends and families."[70]

The trope of the Muslim insurgent or ticking time bomb, as a result, led to heightened suspicion and the racial profiling of Muslims. The Muslim insurgent archetype that shaped much of the War on Terror discourse has a long history. Sylvia Chan-Malik explains that the roots of Islam as a religious-racial archetype that signifies insurgency—the notion that Muslims are actively engaged in activities that rebel against and undermine Western "freedoms and democracy"—predate the War on Terror.[71] The Black Muslim insurgent long served as an archetype fuelling white anxieties. Chan-Malik adds that this "laid out the ideological groundwork for how Islam and Muslims would exist within the nation's boundaries, as vehicles of harm to white Americans and U.S. liberal democracy."[72]

The soft power strategies of the War on Terror included supporting and empowering a "moderate" form of Islam to curtail the theological potency of a "fundamentalist" other. The subtext behind many of the debates around religious authority was geared toward resolving the question of fundamentalism. The state became an important interlocutor with a vested securitized interest in "who speaks for Muslims." From its vantage point, the state identified moderate Muslims as those who "can be worked with" as opposed to "those who cannot."[73] The marker of who an apt partner is was contingent on many variables such as suitability, amenability to liberal and secular citizenship, and legitimacy within the community. Saba Mahmood notes that as a result, the state functioned as a de-facto theologian authorizing practices and doctrine as legitimate only if they could be brought under the purview of civil law.[74] As such, it worked at reformulating religious subjectivities to "render them compliant with the liberal political rule."[75] Indeed, the War on Terror prompted many American Muslims—particularly those from immigrant backgrounds—to rethink their religious identity and sense of belonging. This seeming clash between a "Muslim" and "American" identity—which centered on narratives of integration and acculturation of immigrants—marginalized the experiences of Black Muslims, who had been the majority Muslim population until the 1970s.[76] Su'ad Abdul Khabeer argues that the political and religious subjectivities of Muslims from immigrant backgrounds represented a normative ideal within the Muslim community, in popular narratives on Islam in the US, and with state policymakers.[77] The Muslim becomes an inherently foreign other needing political assimilation and religious moderation.

As in the United States, the discourse of assimilation and moderation became a cornerstone of government policy in the United Kingdom. In 1997 when the New Labour government led by Prime Minister Tony Blair was elected, it worked at expanding its constituency. Blair tried to foster a good relationship with the Muslim community by building ties with the newly formed umbrella organization, the Muslim Council of Britain (MCB).[78] Consistent with the political aims of the Labour Party at the time, the MCB worked to promote a mode of "active citizenship." For Blair's government, religious organizations, like the MCB, were seen as "repositories of social capital" and a way for the party to expand its electorate.[79] As a result of this budding relationship, the government allocated funding for Islamic schools, passed religious anti-discrimination legislation, launched the first government-backed British Hajj delegation, and developed a recognition of the Equality Gap.[80] However, the MCB and the Labour government's relationship became strained after 9/11. In the immediate aftermath of the attacks, the MCB and the Labour government seemingly established a united front. The MCB categorically condemned all acts of terror, while the Labour government affirmed its support for the Muslim community.[81] In the meantime, as in the United States, the Blair government passed draconian counter-terrorism legislation positing that terror suspects could be detained indefinitely.[82] The government had hoped that its relationship with MCB would keep the Muslim community's support. The decision of the government to join the war efforts in Afghanistan was the straw that broke the camel's back. The MCB could not support the war efforts and damaged its relationship with the Labour government.

In 2005 after the 7/7 train bombings, the government changed its strategies and partners in the Muslim community. Instead of seeking out a larger constituency in the Muslim community, the New Labour government sought "moderate" allies in the War on Terror. This shift led to the founding of the Prevent strategy (also known as "Preventing Violent Extremism" or PVE) in 2007. The then-Secretary for Communities and Local Government, Ruth Kelly, announced the Prevent agenda to create a "British version of Islam."[83] By 2008–9, the Government relied heavily on Prevent strategy; around £140 million was set aside for Prevent-funded community projects. Stephen Jones notes:

> At a rhetorical level and in decisions about the allocation of public funding, the interpretation of Islam became more salient. Ministers such as Kelly began to quote Muslim intellectuals such as Tariq Ramadan, suggesting they offered a vision for a fully integrated British Islam. Islamic Studies was named by the Labour Government as a "strategically important subject" in 2007.[84]

As in the United States, the discourse of moderation created the categories of a "good" Muslim versus a "bad" Muslim. In turn, the role of the good Muslim leader or "good imam"—as Jonathan (Yahya) Birt notes—had been defined by the state as an amenability to "civic religion."[85]

Sufism emerged as the model of "good" and "moderate" Islam. The UK government initially sought out Quilliam—an anti-Islamist think tank founded by ex-Hizbut Tahrir members—and the Sufi Muslim Council (SMC) as partners in the War on Terror and examples of moderate Islam. The founder of SMC, Haras Rafiq, explained that the Council was founded "partly due to government leaders' request for 'moderate Muslims' to have their voices heard."[86] Hisham Kabbani, one of the leaders of the Naqshbandi Haqqani Sufi order, stood out as one of the most prominent political voices advocating for Sufism as a "moderate" alternative to fundamentalism (now an umbrella term used to depict Islamism and Salafism). In fact, "the SMC can be viewed as a British offshoot of Shaykh Hisham's and his aides' long-term project of advancing their mission of Sufism as a positive counter-force to the alleged threat from 'Wahhabis.'"[87]

Kabbani's political journey started in the US. The State Department began cultivating a relationship with Sufi groups, particularly Kabbani, in the late 1990s.[88] In 1998, he founded the Islamic Supreme Council of America. Kabbani fostered an image to The State Department of Sufism as "peaceful, apolitical, and moderate" in contradistinction to other Muslims who were possible extremists.[89] He enraged Muslims at the time by stating that "extremism has been spread to 80 percent of the Muslims in the U.S.," and that "there are more than 2,000 mosques in the U.S. ... and 80 percent of them are being run by extremist ideologies."[90] Soon after 9/11, Abdal Hakim Murad remarked that Kabbani was "brushed aside as a dangerous alarmist" and that Muslim organizations "are no doubt beginning to regret their treatment of him."[91]

Neo-traditionalism and the War on Terror

Although the orientalist gaze that rendered Sufism as a faux-spiritual practice against the muscular authenticity of the Salafi and Islamists' sharīʿa-centric worldview persisted, the authenticity discourse of neo-traditionalists had more capital. Unlike modernists and progressives, whose worldview was easily amenable to secularity, neo-traditionalists have legitimacy within the Muslim community.[92] That is not to say that neo-traditionalists were the only Muslim allies in the War on Terror. Policymakers courted secular Muslims, progressive Muslim intellectuals and scholars, "moderate" Islamists, and even *madkhalī* Salafis in the War on Terror. These relationships were not always sustainable and often fraught with contradictions. It is worth noting that although the state undoubtedly has the upper hand, these religious communities have theological, ideological, and political commitments that can temper their relationship with the state.

In the immediate aftermath of 9/11, George Bush sought out Hamza Yusuf from among a number of Muslim representatives and advisors. Before 9/11, Yusuf was staunchly critical of the West and US foreign policy. Even on the infrequent occasions he had advocated for quietism, it was posed as a rejection of Western materialism. There was a notable shift in his discourse. In the White House prayer meeting in September 2001, Hamza Yusuf stated, "Islam was hijacked on that plane."[93] Yusuf urged Muslims away from a "discourse of anger" and instead urged them to focus on introspection and be more self-critical.[94] He affirmed that there was a true Islam, a "good" Islam devoid of violence or terror.[95] In his meeting with George Bush, Yusuf gifted him a copy of the Qur'an and *Thunder in the Sky: Secrets of the Acquisition and Use of Power*—a book on the traditional Chinese philosophy of power.[96] As his advisor, Yusuf warned him against naming his military operation in Iraq and Afghanistan operation "Infinite Justice." He explained that this is one of the nighty-nine names of Allah and would offend Muslims. Instead, Bush renamed the campaign "Enduring Freedom."[97] Yusuf's rationale, which seems to be principally concerned with avoiding blasphemy, was quite similar to that of his shaykh, Abdullah bin Bayyah. In 1977, Bin Bayyah, the Minister of Justice in Mauritania, was sent to Libya on a mission, where he befriended Colonel Muammar Gaddafi. Bin Bayyah used the amicable relationship to dissuade Gaddafi from taking a "Qur'ānist" position of rejecting the Ḥadīth corpus.[98] Seemingly, affirming an orthodox position surpassed advocating for political reform. Similarly, Hamza Yusuf felt that the war's theological framing was an important point of conjecture.

At the time, Yusuf's neo-traditionalism was framed as a progressive and civil religion that did not counter modernity but rooted modernist positions in an authentic tradition. This was the impression Geneive Abdo—a policy expert—had when she interviewed Yusuf. Prefacing the interview, Abdo writes:

> As I approach the wooden front door, I wonder if I should put on my black headscarf. I give the matter much thought. In the Islamic world, it would be unthinkable to visit a sheikh at his home without the scarf, but there are divergent views in America. I want to show respect to Sheikh Hamza, but on the other hand, he knows that I am not a Muslim.[99]

Yusuf calmly notes that Abdo does not have to wear the *hijab*. They discuss Zaytuna, Islamism and extremism, and Islam in America. Abdo notes that Yusuf appeals to a younger generation of Muslims who "can no longer rely upon imams stuck in the mentality of the Old Country."[100] She adds, "While their parents never challenged an imam, who might tell them, for example, that setting off fireworks on the Fourth of July is forbidden in Islam, their children ask for religious proof in the Koran or the *hadiths*."[101] Abdo also noted that both Yusuf and his shaykh, Abdullah bin Bayyah, issued a *fatwa* allowing Muslim women in America to don a hat or not cover their head at all if they feared harassment on account of their *hijab*. She explained that this versatile approach distinguishes Yusuf's followers from the older population of immigrant Muslims.[102] This Islam was culturally unmarked and could easily be integrated into the American religion.

In the United Kingdom, constructing a British Islam, combating extremism, and neo-traditionalism also intersected. By 2006, *Q-News*—the magazine that Abdal Hakim Murad frequently wrote for—published its final issue. Fuad Nahdi, soon afterwards, founded the Radical Middle Way project (RMW). Inspired by Abdullah bin Bayyah's call for an "alliance of virtue," the RMW brought together the network of neo-traditionalist shaykhs of the West and their spiritual guides in the East for this set goal.[103] These included Hamza Yusuf, Abdal Hakim Murad, Umar Faruq Abd-Allah, Faraz Rabbani, Abdullah bin Bayyah, Ali Goma, Habib Umar bin Hafiz, and Habib Ali Jifri, among others. The raison d'être of the RMW was to promote a mainstream, moderate understanding of Islam after the 7/7 London bombings.[104] By that time, public funding for religious groups aimed at fostering social cohesion and preventing extremism was readily available. Jones noted that in "the second half of the 2000s RMW received considerable public support—for example, £350,000 in 2009 from the Department of Communities and Local Government."[105]

The RMW focused on engaging and educating young Muslims to present a convincing and positive religious discourse promoting mercy, public service, and civic participation as emblematic of Islamic values, and challenging illegitimate theological arguments favoring violence and terrorism against civilians.[106] Since its inception, the RMW was involved in the making a British Islam consistent with the goals of the New Labour government. Correspondingly, the government framed the integration of Muslim immigrant communities as a security concern. This was one of the main areas of concern for the RMW—and by extension, for neo-traditionalism, as I will later show. The RMW, however, experienced a severe crisis in its legitimacy, as Abdul-Rehman Malik—a journalist for *Q-News* and an employee of RMW—noted that there was "a big trade-off in terms of fighting for credibility and fighting for the money to operate."[107] There was also increasing criticism from the British public. *The Telegraph* published an article criticizing the government for its public spending and for mismanaging funds allocated for counterterrorism initiatives. It singled out the RMW for spending over £1.2 million and questioned the effectiveness of its approach.[108] Following the General Election in 2010, a Liberal–Conservative coalition replaced the New Labour government. This new government decided to cut the funding of RMW as it did not engage in counterterrorism in the way, or to the extent, that the government would have liked. As a result, the organization went through a rapid decline. Unlike the MCB, however, it continued to have a good relationship with the government.[109]

Neo-traditionalism, as I have shown, retains its potency as an interlocutor and ally in the War on Terror. It has also maintained extensive legitimacy within the Muslim community as an orthodox religious movement distinguishing itself from Islamism and Salafism. Through the neo-traditionalist paradigmatic critiques of modernity, in their religious retreats, I have traced the shaykhs' assessment of disenchantment and the decline of metaphysics in the modern world. These processes have instigated secularization and a rise in religious extremism. Through an intellectual trajectory I have called "Protestantization of Islam," I have argued that the shaykhs transpose a critique of Western modernity onto a Muslim narrative in which a Muslim reformation overtook a traditional and Catholic-like Islam. Modernity, they have explained, is not simply a temporal designation but a system of values and beliefs that has developed over time, impacting how people perceive their social reality and relationship with God. This has impeded the traditional theocentric worldview in both the post-Christian West and the Muslim world. In this chapter, I have contextualized the significance of their critiques in the wider Islamic discourses that emerged after the War on Terror. The governments of the United States and the United Kingdom were interested in cultivating a "moderate" religious alternative to political Islam. As such, I have shown, this prompted a keen interest in developing neo-traditionalism among other Muslim groups as an ally in the War on Terror. In the book's next section, I will outline the neo-traditionalist project of reviving the tradition as a project of re-enchantment after the prevailing conditions of disenchantment in modernity. Muslims, as I will examine, find refuge from their alienation in the modern world in spiritual retreats—whereby the burdens of their subjective "baggage" seemingly lift.

PLACES OF RE-ENCHANTMENT

3

TRAVELERS TO TRADITION

In the Black Sea province of Samsun, Shaykh Abdal Hakim Murad presented the first lecture of his annual Rihla series—"Contentions." These contentions are a set of poetic one-line aphorisms often read as enigmatic riddles that elucidate broader spiritual commentaries.[1] They are loosely modeled after the aphorisms of the thirteenth-century Mālikī Shādhilī jurist and *murshid* Ibn ʿAṭā Allāh al-Iskandarī's "Ḥikam al-ʿAṭāʾiyya." Murad cites a wide range of complex theological, political, sociological, and philosophical concepts and debates to elucidate the salient anxieties of modernity. In Rihla, he gives extensive commentaries on these aphorisms. Notwithstanding the commentaries' academic density and intellectual rigor, the true purpose of this lecture series and the aphorisms is devotional.

In this first lecture, Murad sat cross-legged on a small couch on stage— donning a green turban. He began by making a resolute statement:

> Ours is an age which is categorized by what Zygmunt Bauman calls liquid modernity ... there is something about modernity which is so mobile ... Everything which used to constitute people's fixed coordinates has been liquidized and put into the blender of what is modernity ... Every value we adopt is provisional and makeshift, and there are no absolutes.

He went on to add:

> Charles Taylor in his book *A Secular Age* ... has reflected on this. The paradigm shift represented by late modernity is more drastic and more

challenging than any previously experienced by human beings ever. Whereas earlier societies were driven by the assumption that behind the carapace of matter there lies a world that is more real and more luminous and more true, instead for us, there is only matter.

Murad tried to further illustrate to the seekers the consequences of liquid modernity for their immediate reality. "If you have just traveled here by air," he explained, "you will know that governments spend billions to create portals for their countries that tell you nothing about these countries. Modernity is so anxious about having a location and having a place that its symbolic structures have to look away from that and celebrate the nowhere-land of late modernity and postmodernity."[2]

Over a hundred seekers of sacred knowledge who have embarked on this spiritual journey to Samsun to study the traditional sciences under Murad and other Western shaykhs listen resolutely. They sit and try to comprehend the complex debates he conjures and the intellectual material he presents as they take notes. The absence of meaning or the tremendous void created by modernity speaks to a larger truth that led many seekers to the Rihla program. The radical interrogation of meaning, as Murad argues, liquidizes certainties and essences and nullifies meaning. It leaves the modern Muslim disenchanted and alienated from a cosmic reference that—according to Murad—was self-evident to traditional peoples.[3]

This chapter shows that the project of reviving the "tradition" is akin to a form of "re-enchantment" surrounded by the supposed condition of disenchantment. The retreat becomes an alternative space or, as Umar Faruq Abd-Allah calls it, an "island of culture."[4] These secluded islands of culture become traditionalized spaces carved out of modernity. They are meaningful spaces from the outset in that they are meaning-generating spaces. The seekers are escaping from their unique experience of disenchantment as religious minorities and racialized subjects. They integrate their quest for selfhood within the wider neo-traditionalist narratives on modernity. For them, this quest is seemingly more profound than the question of political identity. The neo-traditionalist retreats are part of a growing trend of "spiritual tourism," which comprises "the quest for personal meaning from and through travel."[5] The charisma of these re-enchanted spaces and the charisma of the shaykhs function as bridges transporting the seekers to the tradition.

Seekers in a Secular Age

The spiritual retreat phenomenon has a tenuous relationship with modernity. From the outset, "The popularity of retreats highlights the problems of modernity in many participants' minds—too fast-paced, with no time to relax and reflect. Religious and spiritual retreat therefore becomes spaces of anti-modernity, intended for those people who need a break from living modern lives."[6] Notwithstanding its embedded critiques of modernity, however, in many ways the retreat phenomenon is subsumed in the very modernist paradigms it attempts to counter. While it can be argued—as I will show—that the genealogy of the "spiritual retreat" can be traced to Madame Blavatsky's spiritual travels to the "East," I contend that spiritual retreats are an offshoot of the failed experiences of communes and communal living and the larger category of spiritual travel. Gauthier notes that the quest for spirituality—through spiritual retreats and spiritual tourism more broadly—is a result of the rise of consumer culture and consumer-based spirituality:[7] meaning that the escape from capitalist modernity in the space of the retreat is not only curated by the very capitalist modernity it seeks to escape but also follows in its very trajectories. This is evident in the rise of "wellness retreats" and even "corporate retreats." When seekers opt to go to neo-traditionalist retreats, they are already inoculated with secular values as regards what the retreat ought to entail and mean.

Embarking on the retreat—whether lengthy like Rihla or short like the Spring Lodge Retreat—disrupts mundane modern life.[8] For the seekers, I interviewed, it is not leaving behind just a busy work life where a degree of disenchantment is felt. It is also leaving behind their racialized identities, gender expectations in the liberal public sphere, dealing with Islamophobia, and all the perceived political burdens of their subjectivities. A retreat promises to essentially vacate these temporal concerns and to connect them to a tradition. This tradition can then inform the seeker of alternative paradigms for dealing with modern concerns. For a short period, the retreat provides seekers with the option of opting out of modernity. They are sought out when a seeker's quest for transcendence is borne out of the "perceived collapse of the established social world."[9] As the political realities seem grim, the notion of modern progress becomes open to interrogation. Uncertainty, therefore, leads people to question the narratives they find themselves in and to try to find new accounts.[10] The establishment of "traditional" and "enchanted" forms of temporary living in the retreat often highlights the tension that modern concerns will eventually catch up with the seekers once they leave the spatial confines of the retreat.

Seekers, however, do not embark on the retreat with the intent of temporarily unsettling their mundane secular lives. They go with the hope that their lives will be forever transformed by it.[11] Alex Norman posits that there are five overarching categories of experience that seekers often strive to achieve on their spiritual journeys. Most of the seekers I spoke to identified with four or more of these categories in their personal motivations. The first is *spiritual healing*; this "includes the search for spiritual, emotional, and psychological healing."[12] Many seekers have noted having had the desire to go to Rihla for a long time but were finally prompted to go after an event that had unsettled their life—such as a painful break-up of a relationship or a divorce. The second is *spiritual experimentation*; this is "where spiritual tourists experiment with different cultures and religious philosophies or immerse themselves in different religious traditions and practices."[13] This is the least common motivation for seekers in the retreat; however, Islamized forms of spiritual experimentation definitely exist. This includes seekers who experiment with different approaches to Sufism and go to different retreats and those who experiment with competing Islamic ideations.

Norman notes that the third motivation is the *spiritual quest*; by this, he means "travel to search for meaning and personal discovery."[14] The purpose of the Rihla retreat, as Zaid Shakir explains, is to inform, first and foremost, personal, individual change; the change ought to start from within.[15] Most of the seekers share this search for selfhood and higher meaning. The fourth motivation is *collective spirituality*.[16] In neo-traditionalist retreats, spiritual quests and collective spirituality are mutually constitutive. The articulation of self-fulfillment in the retreat is governed by the boundaries of the community of seekers.[17] Multiple selfhoods are constructed internally by each individual's spiritual journey, but also succumb to the limitations put upon it by the rituals and the orientations of meaning and the degree to which one ought to accept the spiritual authorities in the retreats. The last motivation is *spiritual retreat*; this is "where people seek socio-geographical escape, meaning that people seek experiences away from their home and home culture and use secular attractions for spiritual purposes."[18]

The socio-geographic escape that the retreat provides is deeply alluring for reasons beyond travel. Neo-traditionalist retreats share themes as well as motivations with New Age (NA) spiritual tourism. The retreats are less likely to take place in the West. Even when they take place in the West, they are more likely to "easternize" the space by inserting ornaments and symbols and adorning clothes that are not Western. This is precisely because these spiritual retreats are premised on a critique of the spiritual and, at times, materialist excesses of the disenchanted modern West. Alex Norman notes, "The deeply rooted critique of the West is evident at every turn."[19] The main difference between Muslims at a neo-traditionalist retreat and NA spiritual tourists is their religious commitment and their conception of Eastern spaces. These spaces are not just meaningful because they are "spiritual." They are meaningful because they are Islamic and connect the seekers to their personal traditions. Muslims come to the retreat not as strangers trying to uncover an Eastern tradition. They come as believers wanting to return and relearn their personal spiritual and exoteric traditions in a manner they had not before. They are essentially recovering what was lost, and in doing so, they are reconnecting to moral geographies that belong to them, but that they did not know existed.

Alien in belief

Jamillah was a freshman at university; her family migrated from Syria a few years back. As we spoke, she depicted her deep sense of alienation before Rihla. She explained, "Shaykh Hamza gave me this idea that religion can sometimes look like this mythical, mystical thing where you believe in angels. I always felt a lack of confidence talking about that because the secular world sees the world only in empirical terms." She added:

> When I went to university, we had loads of information coming to us. Things that would change your values and be really critical of what we believe. Like gender ideas, race ideas. Everything is a social construct. I didn't know how to refute it in a way that was academically acceptable or at the same level as their argument. I don't want to be against everything they are saying. At the same time, I want to stand my ground and see what my cultural, religious principles and beliefs are. I didn't have a strong background in that. So after my first year of university, I thought it would be a perfect time for me to go to Rihla. I knew if I were to argue or refute, I would have [to have] the vocabulary that the shuyūkh have and that I would know that this is a correct vocabulary.

Charles Taylor argues that the defining feature of the secular age is not necessarily the loss of belief, but rather the "conditions" and "contestability of belief."[20]

By this, he means that there is "a move from a society where belief in God is unchallenged and indeed unproblematic, to one in which it is understood to be an option among others, and frequently not the easiest to embrace."[21] Admittedly, I took this for granted when I first set out to conduct the interviews. In my mind, I wanted to address the question "how to be a Muslim?" Or, why is neo-traditionalism more appealing for seekers than other forms of Muslim expression? It quickly became increasingly evident that the question the seekers would rather address was "why to be (or remain) a Muslim at all?" This is not necessarily a question as to whether or not God exists. Rather, it asks if there is still a need for religion in a modern rationalist world. In doing so, the seekers needed first to address the contestability of belief.

Saffi Ullah was a decade or more older than Jamillah. He shared many of her concerns, but seemed more resolute in his answers as he reflected on the beginning of his spiritual journey many years previously. "In high school," he told me,

> I was introduced to the idea that if I wanted to, I could change religions. I had to ask myself, what is it about my faith that makes me so certain that it is the correct one? It was a shock that the only reason I was a Muslim was because I was taught to be one by my parents. I had to think about epistemology and notions of truth. You know, to think about "how I think about thinking." From then on, I began my journey. I considered changing faith to a different one, but I didn't find one that ticked the boxes.

The contestability of their religious belief did not always lead seekers to resolute conviction about one thing. Still, it sometimes opened them up to a plethora of beliefs, philosophies, and value systems. Interestingly, however, the religious claims to authenticity and orthodoxy also functioned as a commodity in the spiritual marketplace. Sophia Rose Arjana notes that the spiritual marketplace often casts "Eastern" mystical traditions and practices as commodities to be consumed.[22] Although Arjana was studying the "spiritual, not religious" phenomenon, some of these New Age adherents' experiences are shared by people who are religious. In this instance, there are some intersections between the New Age (NA) and New Religious Movements (NRM). Olsen and Timothy explain that NA and some NRM (true in the case of the neo-traditionalists) share a suspicion of modernity—which includes "meaningless jobs, the alienation, and subjugation of nature." They add: "This suspicion fuels the conviction that modern urban life is at best less authentic than life in the past and at worst is a toxic illusion." This leads seekers "to seek for this authenticity in Indigenous spiritualities and traditions that emphasize 'the oneness of humanity, nature and the cosmos.'"[23]

The seekers' entanglement with New Age movements follows two main trajectories. Some experience neo-traditionalism as one manifestation of the esotericism they have encountered on their path to spiritual enlightenment. Others experience neo-traditionalism as an authentic spiritual corrective to the "spiritual, not religious" phenomenon of New Age spirituality.

This was Nawal's experience. I spoke to Nawal a few weeks after Rihla. She related to me the beginning of her spiritual journey:

> All I knew about Mawlana Rumi were the quotes people posted on Facebook. I believed in the things he said although I did not know who he was. I used to read that book, the "Secret," and I was very interested in Buddhism. This was a couple of years before I decided to go to Rihla; I was very much into these philosophies. I felt like I was the master of myself. For a second, I was awakened! [I told myself] What am I doing? I don't believe in this. I believe in the teachings of the Prophet!

Nawal's realization of the religious authenticity of the spiritual teachings of Rumi is an important feature of neo-traditionalist reading of the tradition. Rumi becomes a hallmark of Islamic orthodoxy—as Ḥanafī *faqīh*—rather than a heterodox, non-denominational love poet as the New Age movement often paints him. For Amine, a Moroccan seeker, this very claim to authenticity is an important function in the spiritual marketplace and does not contradict it. The retreat provided a promise of a true Islamic orthodoxy preserved by the tradition. Amine contended that Salafi and reformist movements in Islam had de-emphasized and transformed Muslim subjectivity so that it no longer recognized hierarchy. This eventually led to the breaking of the chains of transmission and the devolution of orthodoxy. At the same time, he expressed a pluralistic approach to spirituality. He explained:

> For the past three years, I have been influenced by Hindu philosophy. It seeped its way into my religion and my Islam. I have been influenced by Mooji and Ramdas. I have had experiences that are non-Dualistic. I have come here (to Rihla) to bridge the gap between my experiential knowledge and the latter. That is why I am trying to attain knowledge rooted in Qur'ān, the Sunna, and the consensus of the scholars.

Amine's fascination with Eastern religions is shared by some, but not most seekers. Instead, the instinct to find "his Islam" and the articles of faith that speak to "his truth" and conviction prevails in many of the seekers' spiritual journeys. This, of course, makes the adherence to a "traditionalist" designation a more complex process, that makes a claim for religious orthodoxy but also follows many of the trajectories of New Age spirituality.

Alien in belonging

On June 14, 2017, a fire broke out in West London in the Borough of Kensington and Chelsea. It ravaged the 24-story residential building called the Grenfell Tower. Across the UK, people watched as the building collapsed in a blaze. Livestreams of the residents screaming were broadcasted as the public watched helplessly. Around seventy-two people died in the fire and many more suffered serious injuries.[24] This tragedy struck the British working class. It became emblematic of vicious social inequalities. John Preston writes, "There was an obviously racialized and classed position of those in the tower: asylum seekers, Muslims, BAME [Black, Asian and minority ethnic] and white working class, as well as middle class immigrants and British nationals."[25] It was not lost on the surviving residents of Grenfell nor on the wider community that "the inadequate and unsafe construction of the tower block, the siting of primarily economically disadvantaged BAME people in the tower, the cladding on the tower to make it more appealing to (predominantly) white and middle class neighbours in Chelsea" were the main contributing factors to the fire.

The wider Muslim community in Britain rallied around the survivors. A few minutes from the fire was a mosque—Al-Manaar Muslim Cultural Heritage Centre temporarily housed the survivors. It was Ramadan. The overwhelming sense of grief and anger united marginalized communities in solidarity.[26] That same year saw a surge in Islamophobic attacks in London— including an attack on worshippers in the Finsbury Park Mosque during Ramadan. Furthermore, terrorist attacks were carried out in London and Manchester. Sara, a British seeker of sacred knowledge with dual Pakistani and Moroccan heritage, went to Rihla that year. Having been overcome by grief and fatigue, she explained, "It really affected me. I feel negative emotions intensely, and that often manifests physically. I was so incredibly broken and upset that I cracked my tooth." Sara was also battling her simultaneous hyper-visibility and invisibility as a Muslim woman amid an intense sense of grief. She felt seen, exhausted, and not heard. She explained:

One of the reasons I decided to go to Rihla, was all the attacks that have been happening, especially in that period. There was the Grenfell tragedy.[27] This really, really shook me this time around. It got to a point where you just feel so exhausted by everything. You know something is wrong. And you know it is very clear. I was just so exhausted by it. And by the narrative constantly portrayed about what Muslims are, what Muslims believe, Islamism, or this sort of stuff. I needed a space where I could see what Islam was. So now you're surrounded by it all the time; I needed that rejuvenation.

The feeling of hyper-visibility and simultaneous invisibility resonated with Nermin. I became good friends with Nermin in Rihla and afterwards. She was of a Sudanese-Egyptian background. She had moved between Egypt and the Gulf as a child before permanently settling in Virginia. A few years previously, Nermin's parents had decided to retire and move back to Egypt, leaving her and her siblings in the United States. At the time of our interview, she was a graduate anthropology student at a university in New York; however, during her time as an undergraduate she studied at the University of Virginia.

We spoke only two months after her alma mater was put in the national limelight. On August 11– 12, 2017, a coalition consisting of white supremacists, neo-Nazis, Klansmen, and alt-right dubbed "The Unite the Right" marched in the town of Charlottesville, in which the University of Virginia was situated.[28] They were protesting the vote for removing the Confederate statue of Civil War general Robert E. Lee.[29] They were chanting phrases such as "blood and soil" and "You will not replace us." Facing sizeable counter-protesters, they started chanting "White lives matter." Virginia Governor Terry McAuliffe declared a state of emergency.[30] One of the white supremacist marchers drove his car into a group of counter-protesters, killing one and injuring thirty-five others.

Nermin recalled these events. Unlike most commentators, she was not shocked that this had happened in Charlottesville. She explained:

> When I was at the University of Virginia, I had the problem of not being able to speak up because I am a minority and because it was super white. You probably heard what happened in Charlottesville.[31] I know most of them [the white supremacist protesters] were not university students, but some of them were. A lot of the students were upper-class, Republican conservatives. So, it was unsafe for me to speak. In many [of] my classes, I would just stay

silent; I just felt unsafe to speak. I'm surrounded by all these people that can't even see me and don't even acknowledge that I exist.

She added:

Now, in grad school, I have another problem. You can't bring your own narrative to this secular blank slate. You can only bring in Islam as a critique but can't go beyond that. It is just an intensely secular space that limits the conversations you can have or what is considered viable scholarship. I wanted to go to Rihla before digging even deeper in grad school to find out what Islam says about the "self," about "human nature," about "God" and all these questions.

Nermin felt a more subtle form of racism in graduate school. Her identity as a Black Muslim woman was accepted and celebrated, but not on her terms. Rather, her identity was curated as another "alternative" identity among the host of "others" differing from the status quo. This, however, not only worked to reaffirm her marginalization in the public sphere and the centrality of the status quo, but also distanced her from the sense of her "authentic self" outside the dominant frameworks. She explained: "I was feeling kind of stuck in this circular cycle, you know? I thought maybe I was not in a space conducive to the kind of changes I wanted in my life. I thought Rihla would give me the courage to seek out other spaces and friendships that might help me cultivate the sense of 'self.'" Nermin's quest for selfhood is emblematic of the experience of many seekers of sacred knowledge. As a religious minority in the secular West, they have a unique experience with disenchantment. Positioned as racialized subjects in between the different nodes of Western modernity, the seekers navigate not only religious belief and practice, but also greater questions of meaning and selfhood.

Alien in becoming

In their quest for selfhood, most seekers note experimenting with different religious and secular ideations before encountering the neo-traditionalist shaykhs and coming to the retreat. This is what Anabel Inge termed "delayed conversion." By this, she means that "Involvement [in a religious group] occurs only after exploration of and experimentation with other groups has proven disappointing, prompting a reinvestigation of the original group, which subsequently emerges as more attractive."[32] The seekers had to contend with their family's religious backgrounds and the religious and secular discourses they encountered and adopted along the way. Many of the seekers were raised in secular or non-observant households, while others came from observant families of varying degrees of religiosity. Some were raised in non-Muslim families and were converts; others came from Salafi backgrounds. Some seekers were raised in Deobandi or Barelvi families, and others came from families that belonged to the Nation of Islam. Some did not belong to a particular denomination but had a mainstream American or British Sunni background, attending ISNA conferences and other umbrella Muslim initiatives; others came from Islamist families that were aligned to the Muslim Brotherhood or Jamaat-e-Islami. Some of the seekers were raised in the Warith Deen Muhammad community, while others had Sufi backgrounds. Finally, some seekers were raised in progressive or liberal households.

It is easy to assume clarity and stability in these religious categories. While some families provide a semblance of religious stability, many others are in flux. This could be for various reasons—social mobility, migration, an eclectic approach to religion, the religious evolution of one or more of the family members, a parent undergoing a spiritual crisis, and moving or breaking away from a religious community. The seekers are as ethnically diverse as they are religiously diverse. Some articulate their newfound belonging to neo-traditionalism as a direct affront to the "cultural" Islam they grew up with, or the salience of Salafism in their immediate religious environments. Some express being torn between competing accounts of truth—that of their religious upbringing and that of the shaykhs at Rihla. Others express alienation from the very neo-traditionalist discourses that had once attracted them.

Ahmed—more than most—exemplified the complexities of delayed conversion. He had come from an ethnically and religiously mixed background. His father was North African and Muslim; his mother was Irish Catholic. Ahmed's father was not religiously observant for most of his life but wanted to raise his children as Muslims, despite Ahmed's mother's wishes that they be raised Catholic. Ahmed's father put Ahmed and his eldest brother in a weekend Arabic school. Ahmed recalls looking up to his older brother—who had become increasingly more religious in adulthood. He started studying Islam and joined the Tablighi Jamaat. He encouraged Ahmed—a teenager then—to go to an Islamic school. As his brother's involvement in Tablighi Jamaat increased, so did his parents' fears. His brother grew out his beard and wore Shalwar Kameez. His parents were not happy about this sudden surge of religiosity. Still, Ahmed's brother taught him to pray. His brother mellowed after meeting Shaykh Babikr, a prominent Sudanese Sufi shaykh in London.

Ahmed then enrolled in an Islamic school. He explained that his Islamic school had initially leaned toward "traditional" Islam. His Islamic Studies teacher was a Barelvi Pir, and he also studied with a white convert, Dr. Matthew Tariq Wilkinson, a student of Abdal Hakim Murad. Dr. Wilkinson tried to instill in his students a strong British identity which, in Ahmed's words, "was critical but respectful" of the British Empire. Ahmed explained that there was an unfortunate Salafi infiltration and takeover of the school. This was when he started to change.

Ahmed explained:

> I was confused but started becoming impressed by their zeal. I started reading Salafi materials and websites. Then, I gave up playing the violin; I started rolling up my trousers. I liked the idea that there was this monolithic "true" Islam. We were so passionate about it, and that was the ammunition and armaments to challenge the elders. It made me, as a youth, feel incredibly knowledgeable about Islam and gave me authority. It was also very simplistic. The flawed logic of Wahhabism is incredibly attractive to uneducated youth. You could literally have an excuse not to study philosophy or understand the pluralistic nature of Islam by declaring it as *bid'a*. After becoming taken with Wahhabism, I started arguing horribly with my brother every day in front of my family. It negatively impacted my mum. We argue about everything from *fiqh* to wiḥdāt al-wujūd. And every time, I "won" because I had ammunition from extremist websites. And my brother just had himself and a job [that kept him from studying]. I had time to read that stuff. It just put my mum off Islam even more. Anyway, I felt guilty, so I started watching videos of Shaykh Nazim [of the Naqshabandi *ṭarīqa*].

Ahmed stressed that the anti-intellectual attitudes young people acquired from Salafism shielded them from true introspection. It amplified their propensity to polemics and an arrogant disposition, all the while justifying their mistreatment of others. He half-jokingly noted, "It just gives you an opportunity to be anti-social. And feel good that you couldn't talk to girls not because you have no game but because it was 'ḥarām.'" The notion of Salafi orthodoxy fell short. In turn, the neo-traditionalist shaykhs provided an argument for Islamic orthodoxy that was both intellectually supported and did not discard spirituality. Ahmed decided to go to a Sufi retreat.

Ahmed's spiritual journey did not stop there. After the retreat, he felt
spiritually elevated:

> After that, I was spiritually high, started having dreams. I was literally doing
> ṣalāwat [supplications for the Prophet] so much. And I had visions like I was
> walking in a circle. Someone said it might have been ṭawāf [circumambula-
> tion around the Kaaba]. And I had a vision where I thought I felt the pres-
> ence of the Prophet but behind an empty bookcase. I got back to the UK.
> Then I started having nightmares. Horrible nightmares. And then I started
> not sleeping. I started compulsively reading Salafi websites. That's when I
> became pretty much a hardcore Wahhabi. I cringe now when I think of it.

Ahmed later met other, more knowledgeable people in graduate school and
slowly moved away from Salafism toward the neo-traditionalist approach.

For many seekers growing up, Salafi orthodoxy was almost as axiomatic
as the Islamic orthodoxy. It also had some appeal. The prevailing pedagogical
attitudes promoted by Salafism emphasized individual learning. There was a
constant invocation by seekers of Salafism, its purported intellectual fallacies,
and its excesses. Even those who did not experience a so-called "Salafi phase"
conjured the hardline Salafi excesses as an omnipresent religious "other" which
they were reacting against and responding to.

As attractive as Salafism may have been, seekers argue, it causes an intellectual decline. Saffi Ullah recalls being exposed to Salafism at a young age,
"I would lie to you if I said I didn't find it extremely seductive because I do
consider myself an autodidact. I was a math and science guy. That's why I
found the Salafi doctrine so appealing. Why do you need a mediator when the
text is right in front of you? I now find the Salafi doctrine one of the greatest
mistakes."

Saffi Ullah's parents moved him and his siblings to Saudi Arabia at a young
age. Saffi Ullah's mother was from a conservative Deobandi background, and
his father was secular. At first, he found that Salafism was attractive in a way his
religious education was not. He explained, "I went to a madrasa with a 'back-
home' imam, and the quality of education was rudimentary." Like many, he
soon became disillusioned with the lack of intellectual and theological rigor
that Salafism at school presented. There is also another dynamic at play. Like
many second-generation socially mobile young Barelvis, many young Muslims
from Deobandi backgrounds found neo-traditionalism appealing. Unlike
Salafism, it stressed adherence to a madhhab and has a sustained reference

to Sufism. This was, in many ways, like the Islam they grew up with and recognized. Like Salafism, however, it had the appeal of an Islam purportedly outside cultural contingencies.

This was a part of the appeal of neo-traditionalism for Sabrina. I spoke to Sabrina days before she planned to make *bay'ah* to Umar Faruq Abd-Allah. In our conversation, Sabrina explained that the Islam she grew up with, or "her father's Islam," as she called it, was purely ritualistic and "cultural." She explained, "In the afternoon, we would have an hour and a half of Islamic school. We would learn stuff like *'aqīda, sīrah, and* memorization but it was not spiritually building. Because the majority were Muslim, Islam was very cultural." Sabrina had a renewed sense of faith when she moved to the United States for university. She was faced with the choice she had pondered on when she was a teenager: "why stay Muslim?" "why practice Islam?" She also met her husband in the United States—a white convert. Sabrina juxtaposed her father's Islam with that of her husband. Her father was a graduate of Al Azhar and had studied at seminaries in Egypt. He was also loosely affiliated with political Islam. She explained that because of their backgrounds, Malaysian Azhar graduates are emotionally broken, so their understanding of religion is filtered through culture and the emotional baggage they project onto religion. On the other hand, her husband does not experience conflict in his Islam. He came to Islam intellectually, so he provided her with the religious guidance she lacked growing up.

In many seekers' articulated stories of becoming, there has been an overt frustration with so-called "cultural Islam." Islam, embedded in the cultural practices of immigrant Muslims or Muslim communities outside the West, purportedly lacked religious authenticity. Culture reified as subjective baggage represents many of the seekers' frustration with their upbringing. In contradistinction, the Islam that neo-traditionalists provide, as many of the seekers have noted, is a religious one without the baggage. Nawal, an Arab seeker, for example, explained that the first time she had watched one of Hamza Yusuf's lectures on YouTube she had showed the clip to her parents. She said, "I got my parents to show them how real Muslims are. These are the real Muslims!" Zareena Grewal argues that for many second-generation Muslims, the notion of "culture" is often juxtaposed with a "pure Islam." They present Islam born of the Western context as outside the contingencies of culture. These second-generation Muslims, therefore, have a higher "moral ground" than the cultural Islam of their parents.[33] The seekers identify their hybrid identities in the abrogated "Western" category. Seekers from immigrant backgrounds use this to differentiate themselves and their purportedly "Eastern" parents or grandparents. The Islam of the predominantly white neo-traditionalist shaykhs provides an added dimension to the cultural-pure Islam juxtaposition.

Mahdi Tourage notes that the hyper-performativity of "muslimness" creates the "white shaykh" ideal. He contends that these white shaykhs would perform a form of religiosity that affirms the audience's beliefs.[34] There are, however, layers of analysis missing in Tourage's argument. Outside the performance of "muslimness," white neo-traditionalist shaykhs provide an account of immigrant Islam that we must consider when reflecting upon the seeker's "cultural" versus "pure" Islam typologies. In Yusuf's "pure" Islam typology, Mauritania stands out as an archetype space unimpacted by the profane modern or postcolonial baggage. The narrative of the "postcolonial religion" posits that the Muslim response to colonialism was that of weakness and insecurity. Instead of trusting in their spiritual and scholarly authorities, Muslims became concerned with achieving material success to counter the encroachment of the colonial powers. This led to the modernization, and even Protestantization, of Islam.[35]

Yahya Birt argues that neo-traditionalist white convert leaders have had a tendency to juxtapose the pristine classical Islam they had converted to with a cultural and contingent immigrant Islam. He goes on to explain:

> within neo-traditionalism, there is a hierarchy of non-white traditional Muslim cultures that it views as having been least adversely affected by Western modernity. There is a romance, if you like, of the authentic sage of the East who imparts timeless, undisturbed tradition, accessed by an accomplished translator who is only a simple mediator of it to the Anglophone West. The translator is positioned as someone who has no agency, no interpretive power or political agency, but is merely like a relay station changing Morse code into Latin characters. I think we should not be so naïve, as translation is always an interpretive and hence political act. [36]

There are multiple things at stake in Birt's characterization. First, the "traditional" spaces and the traditional "authentic sage of the East" archetypes represent a projected hierarchy rather than a real one. For example, the "Syrian" or "Mauritanian" are only significant if they reinforce the projected image. Once they have political or contingent "cultural" concerns they can no longer represent an ideal. Second, what Birt characterizes as the "political act of translation" is in fact a particular contingent "cultural" and subjective baggage of whiteness presented as universal and axiomatic. Third, the seekers are asked to accept contingent whiteness as objective while simultaneously disavowing their own subjectivities as modern or cultural baggage.

In this neo-traditionalist narrative, lay people with politicized agendas replaced traditional authorities and reformulated and dismantled the religious methodological structures of the tradition.[37] It contends that this pushed traditional scholars to the fringes while a new stratum of Muslim authority emerged—the "professional" Muslim or the Muslim "intellectual." Grewal points out that they typically had a revivalist or Islamist background. They were often critical of the 'ulamā' or "traditional" scholars in the East.[38] She points out that most had secular college degrees, usually doctors and engineers, rather than graduates of madrasas and seminaries.[39]

This narrative—often posited to elucidate the pitfalls of a cultural Islam that has been professionalized and secularized—is exaggerated. It stresses the difference between an older Islamic "immigrant" vanguard that is typically unlearned and has a secularized understanding of Islam and Western neo-traditionalists—who are more rooted and have studied under traditional scholars. Although many immigrant Muslim figures had "secular" university backgrounds, a great deal of literacy in Muslim majority countries, well into the mid-twentieth century, came from formal and informal religious education. Therefore, it is not strange for an engineer, a doctor, or even a self-described Muslim intellectual to have spent the better part of their life under the tutelage of "traditional" shaykhs. Likewise, many popular neo-traditionalist shaykhs in the West are a product of secular education as, indeed, are doctors and engineers. This narrative highlights the purported subjective formation that renders the immigrant professional Muslim envious of but acquiescent to Western modernity—due to their ignorance of the tradition—and the neo-traditionalist fundamentally connected with a rooted understanding and rejection of modernity. The real difference between the immigrant vanguard and the neo-traditionalists does not lie in their pedagogy, but in how they relate to "traditional" authorities. While the so-called "professional" Islam may profess skepticism with what neo-traditionalists call "traditional" 'ulamā' of the East, the neo-traditionalists see these latter as key to mending the broken chain of tradition.

Secondly, we cannot aptly analyze the construction of whiteness, as Tourage has, without showing how these shaykhs themselves see and talk (or ignore) their own whiteness. When accounting for his racial positionality, Hamza Yusuf argued that the color "white," to him, is merely a skin pigmentation, not a political ideology.[40] The role whiteness performs in a hegemonic environment renders it invisible or even post-racial. This Islam becomes a blank slate almost outside the confines of subjectivity. Since having become disillusioned by neo-traditionalism, one of the seekers noted, "they see themselves as inherently objective; while we are all subjects." This "objectivity" too extends to the maleness of the *shaykhs*. While male shaykhs tend to dominate most Muslim spaces in the West, in this particular context the male voice comes to represent that of the tradition. By contrast, the female voice is in need of being brought under the purvey of tradition. Women are subsumed within modernity and do not sit comfortably within the tradition, while men can—by retrieving their innate dispossession—step outside of modernity. Hence, the experiences and subjectivities of women are invariably gendered and modern while men can be rational and objective. For this reason, *ustadha*s typically teach women, while *ustadh*s and shaykhs teach both men and women.

The shaykhs' whiteness and maleness allow their subjectivities to be seemingly unburdened and untroubled by the political particularities that keep their counterparts constantly asking identity questions. At the same time, whiteness posits itself as a baseline and outside of culture; hence, its concerns are not perceived as "baggage," but rather as axiomatic. For example, Abdal Hakim Murad explains that true Islamic understanding exists beyond the baggage of subjectivities. The "*fiṭra*" of a Palestinian under bombardment would be unlike his own. Living a comfortable life in Cambridge means that your *fiṭra* is not damaged or altered by a sense of injustice.[41] For that reason, people burdened by unjust circumstances tend to understand scriptures in more extreme ways. This is perhaps the main argument neo-traditionalists have against so-called "identity politics," and echoes Sabrina's concerns about her father's religiosity. From this perspective, their understanding of Islam and politics is not burdened with subjectivity.

Michael Muhammad Knight explains:

> Immigrant Muslims are ... denied credibility as bearers of authentic Islam when their homeland practices are perceived as riddled with heretical innovations and "cultural" interference ... For transnational Muslims, this means abandoning homeland languages, dissolving their national backgrounds within an American Muslim "melting pot," and rejecting traditional

practices that have been marked as un-Islamic, thus arriving at "pure" and cultureless Islam.[42]

Seekers, however, encounter and often internalize racialized accounts of Islam. The promise of "whiteness" in this instance, or of the "post-racial" Islam, is the promise of achieving an Islam that could transcend social and political contingencies of immigrant or Black Islam that impinge on a pure, culture and race-free religious orthodoxy—as the neo-traditionalist shaykhs present it. As such, seekers can access an authentic Islamic tradition that their parents cannot. They have access to the authentic traditional ethos and a deepened knowledge of lands where tradition has been preserved—essentially a "good Eastern geography" as opposed to the "bad, heterodox, and postcolonial Eastern geographies" their parents come from.

This was a lingering dilemma for Hamida after Rihla. She was a young seeker in her twenties. Hamida's parents had migrated from West Africa after she was born. Her father had always been Muslim, but her mother converted to Islam after she got married. In America, someone gave them a copy of the *Final Call*—the official newspaper of the Nation of Islam. She added:

> I remember my parents telling us that they read the books and the newspaper and watched lectures of the Honorable Minister Louis Farrakhan, and they just fell in love with it. Although my parents were already Muslim, the Nation of Islam enlightened their path. For my parents, being in the Nation of Islam was not always easy—especially during that time.

Hamida's parents encouraged an ecumenical approach to religion. She studied at a Sunni Islamic school and was raised with Sunni and Shia Muslims. After Rihla, she looked back with mixed feelings, particularly at the discourses of the shaykhs on race and politics:

> In Rihla, it was very difficult listening to some of the teachers. Sometimes I felt like they were very insensitive to my reality. They're saying it is not the Prophetic way to go out in the streets and yell at police officers. You have to also understand that people are angry; people are upset; people feel injustice. But then they [the shaykhs] are like these people have no *adab*. I think if someone was murdered in our community then it is your responsibility to go out there and show the community your support if the community wants you to walk with them on the street and make them feel better. Why not stand by your community to make them feel better?

She went on to add that not seeing that Black issues are Muslim issues is

> [w]hy you have entities like the Nation of Islam. They can be dedicated to the Black issues that the American Muslim community does not want to focus on. In programs like Rihla, when the conversations they have neglect minorities in Islam, it makes you feel like you don't belong. In Rihla, there were no Black scholars teaching me and only one woman. Being a Black Muslim woman traveling across the entire world to come and study, I see different people teaching me, which is great, but then I don't see myself in those circles.

Knight notes that the neo-traditionalist narrative on building an "American Islam" has

> pathologized African American and transnational Muslim communities as lacking authenticity in one category or the other, and often both. These discourses widely represent African American Muslims as struggling to overcome "heterodox" traditions, lack of qualified religious scholarship, and an anti-Islamic fixation on race to earn recognition as "real" Muslims. At the same time, immigrant Muslims are imagined as gradually assimilating to become "real" Americans ... For African American Muslims, this means transcending the "holy protest" of "Black Religion," leaving behind the legacy of "proto-Islamic" movements such as the Nation of Islam and Moorish Science Temple, and somehow becoming simultaneously more American and more global.[43]

Danish Qasim—an advocate against spiritual abuse—elaborated on the racialized component of this claim to orthodoxy. He explains that some of the white neo-traditionalist shaykhs felt that the advent of white converts to positions of religious leadership was a result of divine retribution against the religious failures of immigrant Muslims. Qasim went on to add:

> I have heard many prominent neo-traditionalist shaykhs use Qur'anic ayah 5:44 which states {You who believe, if any of you go back on your faith, God will soon replace you with people He loves and who love Him, people who are humble towards the believers, hard on the disbelievers, and who strive in God's way without fearing anyone's reproach.} They would tell us that for that reason, Allah replaces born Muslims with converts ... I used to call this "Sufi Manifest Destiny." When statements such as "Islam in America will be

led by white converts" got out, the teachers would desperately try to make it seem like they were just rumours or spread by zealous students when in fact, they were the originators.

Qasim added:

> Only converts could determine who the real *awliyā'* of the East were. We were told we are blinded by culture while they are Muslims without any cultural baggage. They have a pure Islam. The only respected non-converts were cultural Syrians and Moroccans who maintained a culture of *nasheeds* and *taṣawwuf*, or descendants of saints they respected. They had to make up for not being converts through other spiritual variables. Interestingly, this does not always apply to white convert women—who were assumed to be influenced by feminism.

Here Qasim demonstrates two aspects of subjectification—first, that the revered non-white cultures could only be held in the same regard if they live up to the spiritual abstraction of their reality. Similarly, for white women, their inherent womanhood renders them closer to modernity, and in turn their subjectivities become incompatible with tradition and thus must be brought under its purview.

Eman had gone to Rihla in 2012. She had, since then, spent years trying to decipher and understand her experiences. She explained that almost everyone she had previously connected with in neo-traditionalist spaces had undergone some form of burnout and had left. Her struggles were very personal and reflected the tensions in her family. Eman's mother was a white convert from Texas, and her father was a Pakistani immigrant to the United States. She had a modest background that had oscillated between working- and middle-class, depending on the economic climate. She had first been inspired by her mother to go to the retreat:

> Because my mom was a convert, it was important for her to hear Islam being articulated in a way different from the types of imams or shaykhs you would normally find. We would listen to Hamza Yusuf for hours and hours on road trips. Still, there was this lingering suspicion that my dad had that he would sometimes talk about. He felt something intrinsically shifting in the Islamic tradition he knew. And it was really hard for him to pinpoint or articulate what that was.

Eman witnessed her mother go through a religious burnout as she grew older. She, too, became disillusioned with the Muslim spaces she was once a part of. This led Eman to question many things, including the function of race in the space. Her mother had introduced them to neo-traditionalist spaces. As Eman said, her mother later "dropped out of the lecture scene." She (the mother) has since joined New Age esoteric circles where it was "less about religion and more about psychedelics." Eman wondered about her mother's religious trajectory. Her conversations with her mother led her to believe that there was something intrinsically capitalist in her mother's religious trajectory—from the consumption of idealized Muslimness to finding alternative idealisms when this was no longer sustainable. All the while, so-called "cultural" Islam was perceived as inherently problematic. Eman wondered if her father's suspicion of neo-traditionalist spaces might *not* have stemmed from his not having proper access to orthodoxy or tradition. Maybe he understood it too well, and was uncomfortable with its grand claims. She concluded that perhaps the cultural contingencies she once problematized might, in fact, tell a more complex story of Islam.

Facing the East

For other seekers, however, there is a constant construction of meaning, to integrate every seeker's personal spiritual journey with the wider narratives of tradition and modern decline. They therefore set out to recover and reconstruct personal histories and geographies that presumably existed before a modernist and Wahhabi intrusion. The contention repeated across the board was that "our people in Somalia" had been Shāfiʿī and Sufi, or "our people in Libya" had been Mālikī and Sufi, or "our people in Egypt" had been Ḥanafī and Shāfiʿī and Sufi until the Salafis came. We no longer knew our culture, or the finer aspects of "devotional law" or *taṣawwuf*. This invariably allowed for cultural, spiritual, and, ultimately, political stagnation and poverty. These new national myths reaffirm the seekers' rootedness in a long history of tradition that, on the one hand, is aesthetically rich and pure. On the other, it blames political and economic blunders on religious change in society—rather than on colonialization or postcolonial authoritarian nation-states. This myth encapsulates the spirit of a nation in its harmonious past maintained through aesthetics and destroyed by their dissipation.

The East functions as an important starting point for the neo-traditionalist shaykhs. Abdal Hakim Murad elaborated on the East–West dichotomy in a

2010 *khuṭba* in the national mosque of Malaysia. He decries the modern West thus: "Where there was once truth and meaning, there is now confusion and relativism." [44] A true seeker is not content with this absence of meaning, he goes on to add. Serious people will still go to the "East" in search of meaning, for the East remains a place of *ishrāq*—a double-entendre indicating both sunrise and enlightenment. Modern people's hyper-focus on materialism results from their dire state of spiritual meaninglessness. He contends: "The fact that the East seems to be technically behind and structurally decrepit should not in the eyes of serious seekers be a discommendation. In fact, it is a good sign. If the East is lagging behind in the acquisition of ever more meaningless technique, then this is possibly a commendation." [45]

The East–West dichotomy in this neo-traditionalist narrative has multiple features. As modernity empties the West of its meaning and alienates it from a truth reference, this knowledge becomes preserved in pockets of the East untouched by modernity. From a Western modernist perspective, Murad explains, these areas' political and economic structural decrepitude may seem problematic; however, their material lack makes their spirituality possible. There is then the popular theme of spiritual travel or *riḥla*. Serious people (presumably Westerners lamenting the decline of meaning and tradition in their own societies) go to the East for enlightenment and meaning. As Grewal argues, the East for the neo-traditionalists represents moral geography and a depository or archive of meaning and tradition. [46] The charisma of tradition can move through geographies from the traditional and preserved East to the modern West. Therefore, the shaykhs become important because they carry both traditional knowledge and charisma.

The notion of setting out for the East to attain an enlightenment which had been eclipsed in the West itself has a somewhat complicated history with modernity. This trope was arguably first popularized with the journeys Madame Helena Blavatsky, the co-founder of the Theosophical Society, undertook to the East. [47] There it was said she studied under the great spiritual masters of the East and attained the sacred knowledge that was then disseminated in Western societies. The East represented an antidote to the modern, forever progressing, scientific, and rational West. Blavatsky and her European interlocutors' fascination with the East represented an escape by the West from itself, and a desire to objectify and consume an imagined East. Without distinctions between Eastern geographies, realities, or theologies, the so-called "metaphysical orient" becomes a focal point of orientation. [48] There was a sense that the immortal had become mortal in the West. The West had lost something of its essence, first with the Protestant Reformation and then with modernity. With its imagined cosmic significance, the East provides the prodigal sons and daughters of Western modernity with what they believe they have lost.[49] The East, therefore, functions solely as the West's vanishing spirit. It is a place of magic and mystery whose essences can be geographically transferred and consumed by the spiritual elite. That is not to say that the neo-traditionalists are somehow religiously or spiritually indebted to the Theosophical Society. Rather, the Western impulse to position the East as an archival—albeit mute—authority is Islamized and replicated in both the shaykhs' discourse and the seekers' imaginaries.

Nevertheless, the neo-traditionalist discourse around the retreats emphasizes both a historical authority and a geographic one, referring back to the "tradition." In the past, Muslims would travel to distant locations—or embark upon a riḥla—to study with scholars of Islam across the world. This indeed is how the chain of transmission or *isnād* was formed across geographic boundaries.[50] The retreats are not exactly a replication of that, but only an attempt to build upon and revive a traditional motif of travel for the sake of knowledge. The geographical dimension builds upon the imagined authority and charisma of the traditional "pockets" outside of modernity. Some retreats take place in consciously isolated regions with historic religious significance—like Malacca in Malaysia or Rosales in Spain. Others do not happen in such isolated areas, but the retreat is still made to be secluded from modern city life—like the retreat in Istanbul. Other retreats, in places with no history of Islamic presence or with minimal significance themselves, are imbued with religious symbolism and meaning, in an attempt to model them after the pockets in the Islamic East. This is true, especially, for retreats set in the West.

The Retreats

The travelers accessed the traditional essences preserved in these pockets through their intensive study under traditional scholars. These scholars were, in turn, an embodiment of tradition in character, essence, and understanding. By the authority of these "traditional" shaykhs in the East, Western neo-traditionalist shaykhs can make the tradition accessible in the modern West. The retreats—Rihla and others—become spatial or geographic bridges to the traditions. The seekers can be connected to tradition by virtue of studying under scholars who have studied under other scholars in a chain of transmission all the way back to the Prophet. The seeker studies the traditional religious methodology—in the form of the *fiqh*, *'aqīda*, *taṣawuuf* tripartite and in traditional spaces. All of this is enveloped in an air of sanctity.

There are three main types of neo-traditionalist retreats. There are retreats to the Eastern points of authority in Eastern institutions. These could be organized retreats such as "The Dowra" retreat in Tarim, Yemen, with the Ba'alawī Ṭariqa of Habib Ali Jifri, Habib Umar bin Hafiz, and Habib Kadhim As-Saqqaf.[51] There are semi-organized retreats, such as staying with the community of the American-born Sufi Shaykh Nuh Ha Mim Keller in Kharabsheh, Jordan, or otherwise permanently moving to this community.[52] Sometimes the retreats are wholly unorganized. Over the years, many have followed in Hamza Yusuf's footsteps to find the small village of Tuwamarat, where his shaykh, Murabit al-Hajj, resided. Some blogged about their experience of finding that little village in the middle of nowhere,[53] while others posted YouTube survival guides on how to navigate life without modern luxuries.

The second type of retreat is conducted by Western neo-traditionalist shaykhs outside their countries in places with some Islamic significance. This is the case with the Rihla retreat, for the most part—although this was not the case in the early years when financing was insufficient, and in 2018 where it was held in Zaytuna College. It is also true for Umar Faruq Abd-Allah's Zawiya retreat and Abdal Hakim Murad's Ghazali retreat. Both of these retreats are held in Alqueria de Rosales, an isolated agricultural plot in Andalusia. These retreats often last between three weeks and a month. The third type are the shorter retreats that do not happen abroad but are still usually in secluded locations—like the Spring Lodge retreat in Nottingham. These happen more frequently than the first two types and can last from two days to two weeks.

The first type of retreat, to places like Yemen, Mauritania, or Jordan, is the least commonly undertaken. Most people have neither the means nor the ability to travel. A few female seekers have noted that they attempted this journey but were restricted by the fact that they had no *maḥram*, or male chaperone. Still, many seekers harbor the dream that they can one day drop out of modern society and commit themselves to this sacred journey. One of these seekers is Anna. I met Anna at the Spring Lodge Retreat. She was born to an Algerian father and a Polish mother. After her parents divorced, she was raised as a Catholic. She relates the first time she felt a connection to Islam. Her paternal grandmother had come to visit her in Paris from Algeria. As she watched her pray, she realized that there was a big part of her identity she did not know.

She first found Islam, like many others, through the Salafi community. Quite quickly, she felt fundamental intellectual gaps in the community around her. She told me:

> I always wanted to go to Mauritania. I wanted to see Murabit al-Hajj. You know I am a Mālikī, and I love the desert. It was like a dream for me to meet him. When I read about him on the internet, I thought, oh my days! Subḥān Allāh, how can such a knowledgeable person be living in our time? I told myself I would get my sleeping bag and I would go and sleep in the tent. But because I am a sister, I couldn't do that.

Another female seeker at the Spring Lodge retreat was Meriem. She was a single mother with a special needs child whom she brought to the retreat with her. She recalls that her spiritual journey was especially difficult. She had married at a young age, and her husband had left her after their son was diagnosed. Later, she led what she described as a "party life." She had been brought to Islam by some female friends. Although she was born a Muslim, she describes herself as a "revert." Before going on the Spring Lodge retreat, Meriem had attended the Rihla retreat and the Zawiya retreat. She spoke to me in earnest about her desire to seek knowledge in the East:

> I would like to go to Yemen and Mauritania. I just want to tap into sacred traditional knowledge and tap into the teachings of people who have this ascetic life, this gnostic approach to life, the *zuhād*. I find so much peace in this kind of lifestyle. We have lived in the city for so long that we really become accustomed to things that are unacceptable to the simple human being.[54]

Meriem continued to relate many stories about traditional societies as told to her by Hamza Yusuf and other shaykhs. The subtle meanings in these places and the sound hearts of people are contrasted with the harshness and profanity of people in the modern West: "In Syria, a shaykh who was studying there told me, if someone were walking and eating, people would look at them and laugh and say, look, this is a person from the *jāhaliyya*. Imagine, there just walking and eating is considered bad *adab*."

For the seekers, the moral life and moral order in the traditional East are preserved in some way, making the character of the people wholly different from that of "modern" people. Traditional people are thus preserved outside the modern perversion of traditional values. Anna explains that this was how she felt when she went to study in Tarim after her attempts to go to Mauritania had failed:

> You are really shocked when you go there because people are so pure; they are so sincere. It is like something else. You know how we study with books, right? You don't need a book there; you look at how they behave and learn from that. Because they literally apply what they learn. I remember the sisters just looking at them and saying that they can learn so much about the *sunna* of the Prophet by just observing them.

The second type of retreat is perhaps the most popular form in the imaginary of the community of seekers, even if not everyone can afford to attend. Independent travel to the East may be a significant marker of religious authority. Still, it is neo-traditionalist retreats like Rihla or Zawiya or the Ghazali retreat that first give the seekers access to, and ferment, this kind of imaginary. Those who cannot attend physically get the opportunity to attend virtually via livestream, as Ashely, a white American convert who had attended Rihla, explained to me. Before coming to Rihla, she had followed the program on livestream very closely. It made her anxious to apply and attempt to get into the program. These retreats are organized by one or all of the neo-traditionalist shaykhs—Hamza Yusuf, Abdal Hakim Murad, and Umar Faruq Abd-Allah. They take a group of primarily Western students to places with some form of Islamic significance—often in the Muslim world and sometimes in Andalusia. These classes are conducted in English with a strictly regulated schedule of classes, breaks, and occasional recreational activities.

The spaces of the retreat and the figures of the shaykhs become endowed with a set of traditional meanings. Their symbolic significance is demarcated from the outset—even before the seekers embark upon the retreat. Unlike the liquidation and the devolution of meaningful spaces in modernity, the retreat asserts that the Muslim space has a meaning. In times of liquid modernity where there are no fixed coordinates or essential meaning, the retreat captures the essence of the tradition. For a few weeks, the seekers can live attuned to the traditional Muslim values and essence. This is done partly by relocating the retreat to the geographical points of traditional Islamic authority—be it Andalusia, Konya, Istanbul, Malacca, Fez, or the other similar locations in which the retreats were held. Murad outlines the meaning of space again during the Rihla retreat in Konya, chosen because it had been the birthplace of Rumi. He addresses the seekers thus:

We come here. Why not Grand Rapids? Why not Cambridge? Academic conferences nowadays can be wherever they like … Muslims believe that place is significant because everything in the world is composed of the concatenation of Allah's purposes. Nothing is kind of randomized. So what is significant about here? What air do we breathe?[55]

As Murad explains, from the perspective of the conveners of the retreat, these geographic locations possess the essence of the past—the tradition. Locating knowledge transmission in that space in turn brings religious knowledge together with the essential meaningfulness of the place. Unlike in Disneyland, as Murad continues to explain, where the hotel rooms may be cheaper, holding a retreat in Konya or Andalusia gives the seekers access to a system of significance lost in the modern world.

For the seekers, significance is not just found in the inherent geographical location of the space, but also in the idea of traveling to the traditional lands to acquire traditional knowledge—much like Hamza Yusuf's own Rihla to Mauritania. The seekers' access to the tradition is not automatic in their geographical relocation. The neo-traditionalist shaykhs become the bridges connecting the traditional East to the modern West. This is not because the East is inaccessible to the seekers. Many of these seekers come from these very "traditional" places. There are seekers of Moroccan, Malay or Turkish descent. The process of bridging East and West is, therefore, not a simple process of translation or making what is inaccessible accessible. Rather, it re-contextualizes the importance of the traditional spaces and the traditional scholars and saints who live in these spaces in relation to the religious experience of Western and westernized seekers.

Jamillah, a young Syrian seeker who attended a few retreats, including Rihla, described what the shaykhs meant in that space. She comes from a Sufi-inclined family. Her mother and father have their own shaykhs whom they follow, who still live in Syria despite the war. Jamillah studied at an American university and therefore identified more with Western culture than with an Eastern one. She pointed out the obvious discrepancy in finding Western shaykhs more accessible:

All these Western, American shuyūkh learned from traditional shuyūkh in the East. The source of knowledge is not just geographical; it was traditionally preserved. The shuyūkh came to the East and were then able to spread the tradition. So they have this traditional knowledge, and they also have the language to translate this traditional knowledge. This is huge because I don't think this existed before ... Shaykh Abdal Hakim Murad, Dr. Umar, and Shaykh Hamza Yusuf are so outspoken and accessible. You can just go to these retreats—as long as you pay—but the traditional shuyūkh in the East are hard to get to physically.

It is not always a question of the physical reality of getting to the Eastern shaykhs. The neo-traditionalist shaykhs mediate their ideas, intellectually contextualize them, and reaffirm their charisma for a Western Muslim audience to accept, as Amine noted:

> To study in Rihla with traditional and bonafide scholars like Shaykh Hamza Yusuf [is to study with scholars] who understand the West. So it is super easy to go study with any [Eastern] scholar but they don't understand the West. With Shaykh Hamza and many others over here in the Western liberal world they are still holding on to Islam in such a traditional way. They are going to be able to understand my experience to some degree more than some amazing Arab scholar who has only ever been to the West for like five days and hated it. Shaykh Hamza Yusuf is really educated in Western philosophies; Eastern scholars don't have that.

Amine stresses the role Western neo-traditionalist shaykhs play in bridging the traditional knowledge between East and West. In the space of the retreat, Abdul Haqq, a convert explained: "The retreats give us a platform with the scholars; to take that knowledge from them in a more intense environment. We have the opportunity to sit at their feet and learn the traditional way, which is the *baraka* (blessing)."

In the third kind of retreat, the role of the neo-traditionalist shaykhs remains the same, but the process of meaning-making takes on a more conscious and less inherent nature. They must carve a geographic space out of Western modernity. Often in secluded locations, these retreats conjure up the image of the traditional pockets of the East on the fringes, away from the modernized centers. When possible, these spaces are made to be secluded, too, from city centers and the hustle and bustle of modern daily life. These newly formed Western pockets are traditionalized in different ways. First and foremost, they are traditional by virtue of the presence of neo-traditionalist or Eastern scholars. These spaces are imbued with traditional Eastern symbolism. Both the retreat conveners and the seekers are involved in designating significance and attaching meaning to the space. These retreats are usually more convenient and less costly for the seekers. They last for a significantly shorter period, making them ideal for professionals and parents.

In the Spring Lodge retreat, I asked Mahmoud, a seeker, why they had chosen Nottingham as a location for the retreat. He explained that it was, in fact, only a prelude to a much longer and more intense retreat called the Trodden Path retreat set in Wales. Mahmoud continued:

> The aim of these retreats is to deal with the day-to-day life and spirituality in it. We forget that some of the saḥābah [companions of the Prophet] are said to have left Mecca and immigrated to the far fringes of the world. Some say that there were saḥābah (companions of the Prophet) buried in Wales! What a blessed place to have a retreat.

The retreat had marketed its connection to the tradition aptly; every lecture, dhikr, activity, food, and coffee was said to be significant and had some form of traditional meaning. The worldview, once objectified, becomes materialized or externalized. Nowhere did the conveners make any claim about the possibility of saḥābah or saints buried in these spaces. Mahmoud's comments highlight a central point about meaning-making. Seekers derive and construct meaningful links between the enchanted space of the retreat and the stories of traditional spaces, peoples, and times told to them by the shaykhs. It almost does not matter whether the saḥābah reached Wales or not. The mere fact that this story circulates among the community of seekers evokes the same imagery of the forgotten pockets where tradition was preserved. That little village in Wales does not become sacred because of the presence of the scholars alone. It becomes sacred because there may be hidden shrines of the saḥābah.

Despite the enticements of enchantment, seekers are sometimes prompted to depart from the constructed sacrality of the space and act as consumers of a service. The Spring Lodge retreat lasted two nights and three days and cost £275 per person, while Rihla typically lasts for four weeks and costs $3,300— not including the cost of the flights. The organizers of the Spring Lodge had major difficulties on the first day as people signed in. They were severely overbooked. Many who had traveled to the retreat did not have a room to sleep in and had to wait for hours as the organizers scrambled to find a solution. People were jubilant at first, citing that a true marker of a Muslim was patience and reliance on God. By midnight, many had still not been given a room to spend the night in and were camped out in the communal areas. One seeker, having finally lost her temper, alerted the organizer: "We have paid a lot of money for a service. I have worked hard for this money, but we are not getting our money's worth."

Masooda Bano contends that it is typically more affluent Muslims and social elites that attend the retreats, and therefore the appeal of neo-traditionalism lies among wealthier Muslims.[56] There is some truth in this. Many seekers come from upper-middle-class and upper-class backgrounds and can easily afford these fees. However, in my interviews, I found an equally compelling account of capitalist consumption and class difference in the retreats. Many of the seekers I spoke to had worked hard to raise the money for the fees by applying for scholarships, while others finally spent years raising the money to get to Rihla. Others noted that they simply spent all or most of the money they had at the time. Hall explains, "Among the alienated ... certain individuals entertain a utopian wish—of living in a new and meaningful world with others who share their dream. For them, neither previous class [n]or status identifications seem compelling; nor do individual deviance and perfunctory participation in ongoing institutions satisfy the urge toward a change of life."[57]

The communal living in the retreat allows—albeit for a short time—the radical unsettling of the seekers' modern subjectivities, including their class positioning. They all live in the same dormitories and eat the same food communally. In a way, they become equal believers without class. However, the seeming dissipation of class does not always happen on those terms. Eman recalled going to Rihla in Istanbul in 2012. At the time, the shaykhs were very close to the Turkish government. The seekers were hosted and given privileges by the Turkish government. They were invited to an extremely luxurious three-course dinner by wealthy business owners trying to court Hamza Yusuf. This intensified her alienation:

You know when it comes to my *dīn*, I take it very seriously. I prepared mentally, and I prepared spiritually for this trip. They always talk about this imān high in Rihla. It's like you're always seeking something or some form of escapism. When you're in these spaces, and you're not someone who is rich, you see it differently. I can't afford to escape my reality. I can't afford the clothes or catch constant flights to see my Rihla friends. It is not how it works. What really got me thinking hard about all of this was when I went to Rihla, and we were mixed up with Erdogan's family and sitting at, like, fancy dinners. I was so uncomfortable. I felt, like, where am I? Here I am sitting with these elites. And having this dinner that I don't even understand and felt thoroughly confused. It made me feel like a pawn or an accessory of some kind. It was not what I signed up for as a young knowledge seeker.

In Chapter 5, I provide greater context on the neo-traditionalists' fraught relationship with the Turkish government.

The impulse to set out for the East to seek meaning and vacate the political, social, and economic forces of modernity that impede the seekers as Muslim subjects in the West is, as Eman has noted, a fraught process. Political contingencies loom over the space of the retreat. Still, as I have shown, the seekers of sacred knowledge come to the retreats as travelers to tradition alienated from the modern world. Their experiences of disenchantment are two-fold. They have experienced disenchantment as believers in a secular age, as racialized subjects in the modern West, and as a generation of young people with identities and systems of belonging different from their parents'. In this, I have demonstrated that embarking upon the retreat fulfills the instinct to abandon modernity and its meaning-vacuum. This, as John R. Hall has called it, is a "collective deviance" against modernity and the seekers' modern subjectivities. These journeys are modeled after the neo-traditionalist shaykhs' personal journeys to the East; seekers harbor a dream of visiting the reservoirs of tradition unpolluted by modernity where true orthodoxy and traditional Islam are preserved. I have noted that the Western shaykhs act as mediators of space and tradition between the preserved East and a profane West. As white converts, they seemingly act as neutral-free bridges and objective translators of tradition. I have explained that the retreat thus possesses an implicit "promise of whiteness" in which the seekers, too, attempt to shed their modern racial, political, and social subjectivities. In the next chapter, I will show the cleavages manifest in the promise of whiteness as seekers' political and religious subjectivities are being refashioned.

4

FORMATION OF AUTHORITY AND CONDITIONS OF PLAUSIBILITY

"Some people would say it is a coincidence; I really don't believe it was," Sara proclaimed. Her voice was becoming increasingly emotional. Sara was back in London after having spent three weeks at the Rihla retreat in Malaysia. She continued to explain, "We were walking past the lobby area, and Dr. Umar was standing there. He was there with two other people, and they were in a fully-fledged conversation. I was walking past them and, in my heart, I remember thinking to myself, I really wish he would say *salām* to me even though I am really unworthy. I swear, Walaa, as soon as I said that in my head, he turned around, smiled at me, and nodded."

If the mere notion of spiritual travels and retreats instills in seekers such pervasive imaginaries, the reality of the experience and the physicality of the space becomes all that more meaningful. The retreat gives seekers access to a past, geographies, and charismatic scholarship that they feel they were barred from due to the ruptures of modernity. The shaykhs instruct seekers on the tradition and the traditional approach so they may navigate modernity as conscientious objectors to it. In turn, this provides tools for seekers with which to understand their social and political lives. In this chapter, I examine the way the retreat becomes a medium of re-enchantment after the supposed disenchantment of modernity. In doing so, I examine the way in which the plausibility structures—by which I mean the cognitive process by which something can be deemed plausible and potentially true while other things are filtered as implausible and potentially false—of modernity unravel in the space of the retreat. Furthermore, I show how religious authority is formed and transformed in the space of the retreat.

The chapter starts by introducing the space of the retreat, its charismatic and traditional value, and its sanctification. It then moves on to explore how authority is formed in the space of the retreat through the charismata of the shaykhs—as mediators of the tradition—and through the routinization of social time and control of the social space. The chapter then examines the changing plausibility structures in the retreat, the attempts to reform the religious and political subjectivities of seekers, and the attempt to construct the ideal Muslim and ideal citizen. Finally, the chapter demonstrates how the meaning-making process develops due to the changing plausibility structures. In particular, it explores how seekers make sense of the discourse around finding a spiritual guide or shaykh to help them traverse the spiritual path.

The Space of the Retreat

"There is no true engagement without detachment," Abdal Hakim Murad noted in one of his contentions.[1] In the space of the retreat, the seekers imbibe this contention as their approach to this transformative experience. Khaled explained this maxim to me by evoking another maxim he heard one of the shaykhs mention. "It is like being an empty cup." "Do you know the story of the sage and the cup?," he asked. "A sage once asked a seeker to pour tea into his cup. The seeker obliged and kept pouring. The tea spilled everywhere. The sage responded, you can only fill an empty cup." Khaled explained: "You must empty yourself so that the sage or shaykh fills you up." For seekers in the retreat, this motif becomes an orientation that elucidates Sufi notions of *tarbiyya*—cultivating virtues and good nurture. Umar Faruq Abd-Allah expounded this—in his lecture series on modernism and postmodernism—through the popular Sufi motif *takhliyya qabl al-taḥliyya*. This refers to emptying the self of the love of the world before one can spiritually beautify it.[2] Abd-Allah took this a step further: if one empties oneself of modernity and modernist dispositions, tradition becomes a reality one can realize. In turn, the seekers learn about modernity in the space of the retreat so that they may "unlearn" it.

The space maintains its figurative position as one outside of modernity in its seclusion from the societies in which it is found. The shaykhs constantly affirm the symbolic importance of being in Istanbul, Fez, Malacca, Andalusia, Konya, etc. The histories and essences of these places constantly intervene and provide a link to the tradition. The geographical location of the retreat is not random. Alqueria de Rosales implants the memory of what was once an Islamic Andalusia. The retreat in Istanbul reminds the seekers of an Ottoman past. This is not to lament the political losses Muslims have endured but rather to laud the timelessness and essences preserved in these spaces. It is no surprise that the material taught, whether *fiqh*, *'aqīda*, spiritual refinement, virtue, ethics or logic, etc., all refers to a historical moment of traditional authority.

They carry a form of essential authority that could be conjured or translated in the present—especially in the location of the retreat. The notion of timelessness could free the seeker from temporal concerns and the particularities of experience, thus opening them up to a religious discourse that is potentially utterly different. The retreat becomes an ideal space outside the contingencies of modernity. Modernity can therefore be critiqued as an existential other. In turn, the space of the retreat, too, opens seekers to the possibility of shedding their modern subjectivity as an existential other. The meaninglessness of their disenchanted life outside the retreat is trumped by the promise of enchantment in the retreat.

This promise of enchantment is particularly alluring after a personal crisis. In 2014, Hiba decided to go to Rihla after she had experienced heartbreak at the loss of a relationship she thought would end in marriage. After she found herself in Konya, she was immediately uplifted:

> The thought of being worthy enough to be here, in this space. I could have easily been anywhere else. I could have been mourning or crying at home in my bed, but Allah chose for me to be in a city where one of my favorite scholars is buried, and I'm surrounded by those He loves. I thought there must be something special about me. God must actually love me, right? Like there's no way he doesn't love me, and he's doing this for me.

The enchantment or "*imān* high"—as one of the seekers described it—is ingrained in the vocabulary the seekers use to describe their experience in the retreat. Seekers often describe the euphoria of both the "*imān* high" they experience and the validation that comes with finding themselves "worthy" of the space or of being in the presence of the shaykhs when they had previously believed themselves unworthy of it.

This space is saturated by meaning not just through its geographical significance but, from the outset, by the charisma of the shaykhs. As Farah, a Pakistani seeker in the retreat, declared:

The place [of Rihla] itself was sanctified. I think the Muzzafer hotel [the hotel in Malaysia where Rihla was held] was a blessed place. The presence of a walī [a saint] can change the spiritual dynamics of a place, like the presence of that walī sent by Shaykh ʿAbdul Qādir al Jīllānī many years ago. It is his blessing. The magnetic power in that place, I could easily have absorbed that when I was in the Rihla. When everyone has the same heart, the energy of the place is purified, and also the presence of the shuyūkh blesses the place.

The seekers were not alone in their sanctification of the space. In the retreat in Spain, one of the seekers noted that Umar Faruq Abd-Allah told the seekers, "Ibn Arabi is here." He explained that it was proof that the veils between the this-worldly and the otherworldly were being lifted in the retreat.

The seclusion of the retreats, however, prevents seekers from engaging with the living geographies where the retreats are held. They only experience idealized depictions of it. The seekers spend the overwhelming amount of their time in lecture halls and dormitories—only interacting with one another or with the shaykhs and retreat organizers. Independently, they can venture to a nearby supermarket, but not further. Any extended recreational activity outside the confines of the retreat's physical location is done communally. The shaykhs contextualize these recreational experiences according to what they mean for the overall project of re-enchantment. The seekers thus interact with and see the wider society in which the retreat takes place in these terms. For example, Meriem noted that when they all went to pray in a local mosque in Konya, there was an evident language barrier. This did not matter, for they spoke the same language—the language of love and *adab*. The Turkish "aunties" at the mosque become emblematic of this enchantment. Furthermore, unchallenged by mundane social problems or a political context, the retreat vacates these countries of any social, political, or historical particularity or baggage, leaving just its supposed essence and link to tradition.

Later, Meriem relayed to me a concern she shared with many seekers:

Coming back from *Rihla* is weird because it hits you; you are no longer on a spiritual high, and if you don't renew your intentions, you can really digress. It was a really surreal experience that brought you close to the creator and to the teachers and the people to sisters, really creating a bond ... When I came back, I was really struggling with my prayers, so my shaykh said often, people associate a spiritual high with the environment.

In the enchanted space of the retreat whereby theology, space, time, the authority of the shaykhs, and symbolism all came together to construct a meaningful experience, this system of meaning is vulnerable in the outside world.

In the Spring Lodge retreat, I interviewed two friends, Marwa and Najwa, who reflected on this very notion. They both came from Sufi families but were critical of the space of the retreat. Marwa was adamant about clarifying a point for me:

> The problem I keep having here is that people are asking me, "Are you spiritually elevated?" "Are you having a great spiritual time?" And, no, I am not! A part of the reason I am not having a great spiritual experience is that people are projecting this idea of spiritual experience on me. They say, well, those are our masters (the shaykhs), and they know better. Their idea of religion, God, and spirituality is somehow greater than ours. You need to have these sources and these chains so with a population untouched by modernity, but then this turns into a superstitious relationship.

Marwa and Najwa were bothered by the continuous process of meaning-making that the seekers engage in and try to project onto them. Like Hamida, they felt that this outpouring of symbolism reaffirming the narrative of the retreat renders criticism of the space and message difficult. From the outset, in advertising for the Spring Lodge retreat, the organizers made a point of saying that everything would be of traditional value—even the food would be "*sunna* food." In the communal eating space, they served eggs and porridge for breakfast. I asked a volunteer who was eating with us if this was, in fact, "*sunna* food." She responded: "Perhaps. The Prophet lived in the desert. He must have eaten grains." Later in the day, we were served a lamb biryani dish cooked with *Medjool* dates. This reimagining and reconstruction of what "*sunna* food" might entail raises an essential point about meaning-making. It is not about retrieving historical practices but about locating oneself in proximity to the tradition. Schemes of meaning invoked by the seekers are constructed collectively or independently and then shared with others. Hall notes that this space-specific meaning-making allows for identifying what is relevant and important and is collectively socialized and legitimated.[3] The seekers "cognize reality, focus attention, and interpret selected phenomena in ways that comprise alternative meaningful communal worlds."[4]

This could be seen in simple things, from dress to more significant matters such as how the seekers relate to the shaykhs.[5] For instance, in both retreats, men of all ethnicities were almost exclusively wearing the traditional Moroccan *djellaba*s and slippers, even though there were very few North Africans at either retreat. Among hundreds present, no one wore *Shalwar Kameez* even though seekers were largely South Asian. To them, they were adorned with the garments of the saints and scholars of North Africa—as they imagined them and as was described to them by the neo-traditionalist shaykhs. This was the Islamic attire of traditional people. Murad explains:

> If you look at drawings of how Muslims used to be a hundred years ago in Morocco or Cairo, it is very splendid and beautiful, but nobody dresses like that anymore. We might dress like Najdī Bedouins, perhaps, or I don't know, like a Pakistani peasant, but what we don't have is the splendor of the vestment of the Islamic world. Those are no longer understood.[6]

In Murad's discourse, the construction of the ideal Muslim is both racialized and classed. The performance of seekers, through their aesthetic representations in the retreat, reflects an aspiration to this ideal.

Formation of Authority: In Space and Time

The day begins twenty minutes before dawn prayers, both in Rihla and the Spring Lodge retreat. The seekers are strongly urged to wake up and go to the communal prayer area. Often led by a fellow seeker, they recite communal litanies (or *wird*) and a chapter of the Qurʾān—usually Sūrah Yasīn. According to one of the seekers, Rihla in 2017 was a "very Shādhillī" one, whereas the one she had attended in previous years was more "Baʿalawī." This was in reference to the choice of litanies recited as each ṭarīqa has its specific litanies, which initiates then recite. In the Spring Lodge retreat, for example, the seekers communally recited "Al Wird al Laṭīf" by Imam Ḥaddad—a litany from the Baʿalawī Ṭarīqa. This is the ṭarīqa of Habib Ali Jifri and Habib Kadhim As-Saqqaf, who were present. Afterwards, the seekers communally pray the *fajr* prayer. Except for the Friday prayer, every prayer is communally prayed in the same place.

Shortly after the communal *fajr* prayers and the recitation of litanies, seekers eat breakfast communally. The schedule in Rihla was as follows:

6:15 am:	Fajr prayers and *wird*
7:00–8:00 am	Breakfast
8:30–9:45 am	First class

10:00–11:15 am	Second class
11:30–12:30 pm	Third class
12:30–2:30 pm	Lunch and rest
2:45 pm	Dhuhr Prayer
3:00–4:15 pm	Fourth class
4:30–6:00 pm	Fifth class
6:15 pm	Asr
6:30–7:30 pm	Dinner
7:30 pm	Maghrib and *wird*
8:00–9:00 pm	Study Hall/sixth class
9:00–10:00 pm	Isha prayer and *wird* (and sleep)

The scheduling of classes was very rigid. Seekers in Rihla note that in their applications they are warned of this intensity from the outset. The classes start after breakfast and last until 10 p.m.[7] The seekers are advised to sleep as soon as the classes are over and not spend much time socializing with each other or their roommates since they have to wake up the next day before *fajr*. The dormitories house three in a room, or two for couples. There are two main breaks, one for lunch and the other for dinner. These breaks are often spent communally—either in the lunch hall or in other communal spaces. Some use this time to catch up on sleep. The sense of communality is heightened since very little time is reserved for individual introspection. The intensity of the scheduling impacts the reception of knowledge in different ways.

Temporality plays an essential role in the retreat. The routinization and organization of time and the enforcing of a schedule were important in constructing a traditional pedagogical space. That said, time was not the only aspect of the retreat that was regulated top-down. The retreat conveners put forth a dress code for both men and women, a code limiting engagement between the sexes, and a code for engaging with the shaykhs. Additionally, it was stated in the Rihla retreat pamphlets that the seekers could not venture out or leave for extended periods of time of their own volition unless they had the consent of the organizers and a reason to do so. The seekers were expected to attend every lecture. One noted that they needed to hide from the organizers when they decided to skip class to get some rest. The set-up of authority draws a clear boundary between the seekers at the retreat and the conveners. The hierarchy established from the outset reaffirms the top-down transmission of knowledge.

Indeed, discipline and religious accountability were very important in fostering a sense of hierarchy and obedience. Obedience was not differentiated by the age or position of the seeker; both old and young were expected to follow a set of rules. This had been explained to them at the very beginning in the orientation booklet:

> Attendance policy: Classes are NOT optional and are a required portion of the program. To be excused from this class, you must obtain prior permission from a designated organizer who will be made known to you.[8]

The booklet then went on to elaborate a system of accountability and punishment:

> *1st offence:* A meeting with a *Rihla* Team official. A verbal warning will be given.
> *2nd offence:* A meeting with the *Rihla* Team official. A written warning will be issued and the student will be put on probation.
> *3rd offence:* A meeting with the *Rihla* Team official. Immediate dismissal.[9]

Although most seekers did not seem to disagree with this in principle, the affirmation of spatial authority through a regulatory system had opened the doors to questions regarding agency. For example, as adults with careers, capable of making their own decisions in the outside world, why would they need to relinquish this capacity in that space? This question was especially amplified regarding the regulation of time, gender interactions, and dress (though to a lesser degree). Hamida noted that seekers were often strongly advised not to stay up past the lectures. In one instance, when they had, they were reprimanded by a Rihla Team official privately and then publicly. One seeker, called Amal, reflected on her experience in Rihla many years ago:

> The size of the group and the travel for the program precludes the kind of attention and energy that is needed to have a thoughtful exchange between scholars and students at a more equal level, and the traditional framework of the program makes Rihla more akin to programs in which students are meant to be vessels of their teacher's thoughts, not their own.

Eman and Shazia shared Amal's concern about how close control and regimentation of time and performance in Rihla fostered a sense of obedience. Eman recalled:

I was concerned about how much sleep we were getting, how we were shamed if we didn't wake up for *fajr* or do *tahjjud*. I couldn't talk to people at night after class because I was so tired. Now I think, why are you exhausting people? These are patterns of control in a way. You are really trying to put people in a place where they're more suggestible.

Eman explained that it took her years to decipher the experience. She added:

I remember them saying you shouldn't eat much; you shouldn't relax your back on the wall. It felt like micromanaging—from how you should behave in front of the shuyūkh to what you're allowed to wear to how much you can eat to literally the position you're sitting in. In the end, you feel like you have to be superhuman to even be at the feet of knowledge.

Shazia, in earnest, explained to me:

I don't think I went to a single *fajr* prayer there. I could barely get through the day. How am I supposed to go and sit for an hour? And yes, it's beautiful. It ended with *dhikr*. But how am I supposed to do that? I am barely functioning. I don't even think I realized that at the time until later when I looked back. I am like, wow, no wonder I ditched class; no wonder I was late. Some things would make you question, but if you question, you're being disrespectful. Can you imagine making a comment criticizing the space? I remember someone telling us not to sit in a certain way or not to wear jeans. I don't think I realized then that I was being treated like I was in the military.

Meriem experienced the rigid organization and routinization of time in the retreat, but she remembered it more fondly:

It was very tiresome, but we were running on spirituality caffeine. Even though we were tired, we were never late for classes, or we would be told off. We had bad coffee, but we loved it and needed it. We were up every day from 4 am to 11 pm. Subḥan Allāh, I didn't realize how hard it was to sit on the floor, but Shaykh Hamza said that historically sitting on the floor was the natural posture for the human body. Over the years, we have become so accustomed to chairs that we can no longer survive sitting on the floor even though this was the way traditional studying was done.

Social time, as Hall explains, comprises "subjectively transcendent ways of scheduling events and activities in relation to a group that person is in."[10] As individuals move between different social times, so do their interpreted experiences, imaginations, and conceptions of reality. This is not to say that these are always radically different. Sometimes they reaffirm one another. Some seekers, however, noted a slight discrepancy. Hamida remarked that, in retrospect, there were things, especially regarding race and politics, said in Rihla that had bothered her throughout. I asked whether she had spoken to the shaykhs or organizers about her concerns. She responded that these conversations only happened in her room with her roommates and the day after the retreat ended. The conformity established within the space of the retreat is affirmed by the fact that the shaykhs have the knowledge and the seekers do not. She explained:

> I talked to my roommates about it, but I didn't really talk to the shaykhs about it because I didn't know. I felt like I wasn't ready to talk to them because I was still in a place where I didn't feel eloquent and articulate enough. I do not have enough concrete evidence to support what I'm saying. So many of these conversations I could only have with my roommates in my room.

Truth claims and authority are reassessed and renegotiated in the private spaces in the rooms—outside the hierarchal knowledge transmission and authority in the retreat. The scarcity of time, however, limits the seekers' ability to do this. This reaffirms the dependence on the shaykhs to provide authentic knowledge, for as a seeker, what you know cannot be compared to what the shaykh knows. For Hamida and her roommates, the conditions for plausibility (i.e. schemas of knowledge thought to be plausible in space) were secured by space, time, and proximity to the shaykhs. When these conditions cease, they become a more open matter. Hamida explains:

> I felt like I didn't process everything. I just tried to take in what I could so I could reply in the end. By then, I was really exhausted. Like a lot of the mentors and shaykhs throw so much information. Many times you don't understand it, and you're not given enough time to process what you're learning. You don't know, and you can't ask questions. That makes you feel powerless and helpless. It is great sitting in lectures but then after if you're unable to analyze it and talk about what you're learning. You won't know what you don't agree with. These conversations are only happening in our rooms. I think it takes away from student involvement.

Among the seekers, there is an awareness of the impact and significance time has in forming the conditions of plausibility. Not everyone navigated the program immersion in the same way Hamida had. For Meriem, for example, to be immersed in unfamiliar knowledge reaffirmed by a set of narratives gave access to worlds that would not otherwise be intelligible. For her, the mythic time of the "tradition" and the temporal ordering in the retreat coincided. David Chidester states that mythic time is a kind of "temporal ordering of sacred stories" which creates a sense of continuity, not just through ritual observance but though a sense of accountability.[11] He notes that "the temporal subtext of myth, a forensic dimension runs like a unifying thread through religious stories about time."[12] Meriem confessed that she could only truly appreciate what time meant when she left Rihla.

Authority of the Shaykhs

In Rihla, the neo-traditionalist shaykhs, in particular Hamza Yusuf, Abdal Hakim Murad, and Umar Faruq Abd-Allah, are central to this mediation of spatial-temporal authority in the space of the retreat. In fact, for many of the seekers, studying under the shaykhs and "taking" knowledge from them is one of the main reasons they go to the (Rihla) retreat. The notion of "taking" knowledge or studying "under" is entirely different from studying with someone or studying knowledge. For it pertains to the position of the seeker in the chain of transmission. The shaykhs do not typically give *ijāza*[13] in the retreat; the students nonetheless imagine themselves in a chain connected to the tradition through the shaykhs. This is not a matter of pure meaning-making; in fact, it is one of the stated purposes of the retreat: that is, for students to learn in the traditional method from teacher to student.

In contradistinction, the Spring Lodge retreat placed a greater emphasis on Eastern shaykhs as a point of authority. Still mediated by their Western students, one could see the movement of knowledge in a chain being performed. Upon the stage and on chairs ornamented with Islamic geometric designs, the Eastern scholars Habib Ali Jifri, Habib Kadhim As-Saqqaf, and Shaykh Abdurrahman ould Murabit al-Hajj sat. Beside them on the far edges of the stage are the high-profile neo-traditionalist shaykhs who have studied under them. The crowd of seekers sits on the floor. The authoritative lecture is given in fifteen-minute intervals by an Eastern shaykh. It is then translated by a Western neo-traditionalist shaykh, who had previously studied under that Eastern shaykh. The final station is the floor where the seekers sit. The pervasive charisma of being physically located in the chain of transmission allows for the seekers to position themselves in the traditional chain of transmission.

The relationship they develop is not solely with the knowledge but also with the way the Eastern shaykhs speak or the light emanating from their faces. This rests on the shaykh's sheer physical presence.

In the Spring Lodge retreat, the shaykhs were all male; in Rihla, there was only one female *ustadha*. The gendering of religious and spiritual authority extends beyond the perception of the male voice as axiomatic or without subjectivity. It also reflects how female and male seekers position themselves in the tradition. As Zahra Ayubi notes, the systematic exclusion of Muslim women from classical training prevents their interpretative interventions from being seen as legitimate.[14] In traditional spaces, male seekers often frame their "collective deviance" from modernity differently from female seekers. Their spiritual journey is not an external search for meaning and significance. Rather, it becomes a search for an inner truth manifested in an authentic self. Modernity, as such, is feminized, and its discontents externalized. In these spaces, as Julianne Hammer notes, women are often perceived as having

> no choice but to challenge the traditional system of knowledge transmission and preservation, for there has historically been little space for them within such a system. And while women could historically acquire Islamic knowledge, their ability to build interpretive communities was hampered by their social and legal status in Muslim societies.[15]

As a result, the female voice becomes suspect and pushed to the margins of tradition and orthodoxy.

Thus, for male seekers, finding the external truth manifested in tradition becomes more a matter of reconciling it with an internal truth. Male seekers often position themselves as inheritors of the authority of the tradition rather than receivers of it, as in Salem's case. Using the "we" pronoun, Salem explained the importance of reviving traditional Islamic scholarship. The shaykhs, he explained, are the inheritors of the Prophet. Retreats become a place where the tradition is manifested and transmitted to him. He explained: "The retreats give us a platform with the scholars; to sit at their feet and take their *baraka*." This is then manifested in the uniquely masculine attributes of *futuwwa*. The notion of *futuwwa*—often evoked in neo-traditionalist circles—may be roughly translated as "spiritual chivalry." Salem explained that, in the retreats he attended, "The intention of the shaykhs is to revive the tradition and encourage us men and youth to master it so we can pass these traditions on."

The appeal to the Western neo-traditionalist shaykhs' authority is a salient, albeit complex feature of the retreat. For many seekers, the shaykhs' appeal is firmly rooted in their discourse of love. The centrality of love amplifies the beauty of Islam that is obfuscated in the modern world. Mysa explained, "I used to have a lot of difficulties understanding Shaykh Abdal Hakim Murad. This time, I tried to really listen. I was so shocked when I realized how great his emphasis on love is. I used to think he was the least spiritual. Now I think he might be the most." This, too, was Hiba's impression: "Shaykh Abdal Hakim Murad is very interesting. At first, he was like the most typical Englishman you've ever met in your whole life. Doesn't speak too much. But the minute he opens his mouth it's like Allah is speaking through him. I'm not saying that in a blasphemous way. I just mean he's divinely inspired." In contrast, Hiba continued to add that the connection she felt with Umar Faruq Abd-Allah was instantaneous. "I look at his face," she said, "and for some reason, I saw my father's face. I thought of my family. I thought of that boy that didn't like me; I thought I wasn't good enough. Then Dr. Umar looked and said Allah wanted you to be here this minute. For a minute, I thought, maybe I am good enough."

For the seekers I spoke to, Hamza Yusuf inspires fewer feelings of familiarity and intimacy and more awe and charisma. Most of the seekers were first introduced to neo-traditionalist spaces through Hamza Yusuf. His approach balances the intellectual, spiritual, and emotive, making him popular and accessible to a wider public. His appeal to an unapologetic, "undiluted" Islamic orthodoxy is why many seekers chose that space. Abdal Hakim Murad's approach is overall more stringently academic. Murad evokes and explores contemporary and medieval intellectual discourses in great depth. The depth and sophistication of his scholarly knowledge and discourse inspire awe. Umar Faruq Abd-Allah is considered by many to be a spiritual master and authority. On several occasions, Hamza Yusuf and even Habib Ali Jifri alluded to his *karamāt* (saintly miracles).[16] Students do not just consider his importance as a teacher of outer knowledge but also his importance as one with inward esoteric knowledge. Together, Hamza Yusuf, Abdal Hakim Murad, and Umar Faruq Abdallah bring the popular, the intellectual, and the esoteric.

Nevertheless, the cultivation of the shaykhs' authority is meticulously outlined from the beginning of the retreat, and throughout. In the handbook, clear directions are outlined regarding the etiquette with shaykhs. Seekers are also advised to follow a code of conduct throughout the Rihla program, including:

> Respect and show deference to the shuyukh (instructors) and program/site personnel.[17]

Each year, seekers are taught alongside their classes on *fiqh*, *'aqīda*, spiritual refinement, the etiquette of seeking knowledge, and finding a shaykh. This point was emphasized by Sarina, a seeker who had attended Rihla in 2017 and blogged about her experience. She noted:

> Knowing proper *adab* prepares our hearts so that it is ready to receive knowledge. The heart is like a window; light cannot shine through if it's dirty. We want our hearts to be in the best condition so that the Light of Allāh can pass through. One of our teachers, Ustadha Saraa Sabbagh, taught us the adab of seeking knowledge, which entails preparing ourselves for class, behaving in class, and treating our teachers. Ustadha Saraa wasn't the only teacher who put great emphasis on adab; all our teachers did, too.

Sarina then copied a passage from Deenstream—the online medium that posts video lectures from Rihla—of Feraidoon Mojadedi, from his class on Jalaluddin Rumi called *Key to the Mathnawi*, in which he said: "Your teachers are sometimes harsh with you because they know you can do better; bear this harshness with adab, or remain ignorant for the rest of your life." The stakes for obedience and deference become all that much higher, for it is through the teacher (or the shaykh) that you can reach the path of knowledge.

For some, the retreat is the first place in which they come across the concept of finding a personal spiritual guide or a shaykh. Every year, the Rihla program is held, and the seekers are taught a classical text in *taṣawuuf*. In 2017, this had been from Ibn 'Ashir's Murshid al-M'īn,[18] but they had previously studied a text by Aḥmad Zarruq.[19] In the margins of these sessions, the importance of finding a spiritual guide from which a seeker could gain guidance and consult on their spiritual journey is amplified. That said, the notion is not only introduced in *taṣawuuf* classes. It has a looming presence as the shaykhs cite the authority of their spiritual guides and lament the declining numbers of true guides in modernity. In modern times, the individual Muslim is left to their vices to delineate truth from the sources. Modernity rejects hierarchies as such—spiritual or pedagogical. The lack of spiritual guidance from true shaykhs has consolidated a sense of spiritual arrogance among young people. In spiritual cultivation class, seekers are taught that finding a spiritual guide is important if they are to navigate their spirituality correctly.

Nawal recalls the shock she had experienced when she had first gone to Rihla in 2014. It was the first time in her life that she had traveled alone without family. She explained she had not previously known of *ṭarīqas* or what it meant to be *murīd*, or have a shaykh; it was all new:

> I heard everyone should have a shaykh who can help them reach stages in the path of Allah, but I never knew how or what the shaykh does or how he can help. The Turkish ladies in Rihla would say, "I have my Shaykh; no, I have my Shaykh." I still did not know what the shaykh did. When I went into the *maqām* of Mawlāna Rumi, I said, "Oh Allah, please help me find my shaykh." So I was just there sitting. Shaykh Hamza came and sat next to me. After going out of Rumi's place, I was a different person. I knew things could not be like before, and that was it!"

"How did you feel about it?," I asked. She replied: "I didn't know what the shaykh does. I just knew he would facilitate the road for you, or he could give you protection. I didn't know that the shaykh may give you the *rabbānī* [godly] knowledge or *ʿilm ladunnī* [gnostic], and I was searching for a shaykh. At some point, you just want more. You have the prayers, but you want more than this knowledge."

Nawal went on to ask a shaykhs at Rihla about what the relationship between a *murīd* and his spiritual master entailed. One of the shaykhs at Rihla told her, "*ka'l nikāḥ*," as if it were a marital bond: "I said, how come? He said, 'It is like having a husband, he will know the details of your life.' I can't honestly make sense of that because if I were to have a shaykh like that, it would just be my husband. It doesn't make sense; you can't have contact with a male like that to make it halal."

She continued to tell me her story of trying to find a spiritual guide. "I was eager and curious, but curiosity killed the cat," she exclaimed. When she returned home, she was desperate to find a shaykh and could not think of anything else. That is when she became affiliated to a Baʿalawī center. She then retracted: "they could not have been real Baʿalawīs, but I joined because, in *Rihla*, they made us read the al-Wird al-Laṭīf."[20] There she studied *fiqh*, *ʿaqīda*, and *taṣawwuf*. In her heart, she stated, she felt that something was wrong:

You see all the ladies in the center falling in love with that shaykh. This shaykh would say if you get a job, tell me. If you got a proposal, you need to tell me. My parents said, of course, you will not do that. He is not your husband. So I had to flee. My personality was changing a lot. You can see what's happening. Afterward, I felt like I had lost knowledge, and I lost something. So I quit the search for the shaykh and the ṭarīqas. I started on my own. I went to the library and found the old books. So technically, do not rely on any person, even if he was the shaykh of the shaykhs. No one will do the work for you. It's your own path.

Her firm stance was intriguing. This was 2014, but she decided to go to Rihla again in 2017. I asked her if she had raised these concerns about the notion of spiritual authority with any of the shaykhs in Rihla. She said she had spoken with Umar Faruq Abd-Allah and Walead Mosaad, and briefly with Abdal Hakim Murad. Abd-Allah and Mosaad understood that the damage a "false shaykh" can have on someone's spirituality is immense and sometimes irreversible. The seeker needs to give themselves time to heal so they may trust again. Indeed, the shaykhs warned the seekers quite strongly about "false shaykhs." The existence of false shaykhs, however, does not diminish the importance of the institution.

Nawal described her meeting with Abd-Allah as follows:

Dr. Umar has the nūr [spiritual light] to know what the person in front of him wants to ask. He said it might be hard to get back to your state [her spiritual state before meeting the false shaykh], but it is not impossible. With the help of the shaykhs, they know the unseen so they can do something about it. I won't worry myself about it again. Allah will facilitate. If I need a shaykh, he will provide me with one.

Nawal paused a little and said, "But Shaykh Abdal Hakim Murad told me you need a shaykh." "In what context?" I asked. "He was talking about the self and [the] evil side of the soul. So I asked, how can I tame the evil? He said you need to have a shaykh. I said, well, what if I can't? He said Iḥyāʾ ʿulūm al dīn will be your shaykh." Indeed, the issue of spiritual authority and false shaykhs had a looming presence in the 2017 Rihla—as scandals have unfolded in the Muslim community around allegations of spiritual abuse. Mojadedi was asked after one of his lectures how one identifies a false shaykh and who can hopeful seekers trust. After some thought he replied, you could trust the shaykhs here.

Many seekers took this in their stride. The spiritual descriptions of the shaykhs and the occasional accounts of *karāmāt* (saintly miracles) serve a relational role. As much as it may be a description of what the seekers believe to be true about the shaykhs, it is also about what the space of the retreat means to them by being there. On account of the sanctification of the space by the shaykhs, it becomes quite unlike the "immanent frame" of the disenchanted modern world. The (re)enchanted space of the retreat is porous to the possibilities of transcendence. As the seekers are in the presence of these *karāmāt* (saintly miracles)—not necessarily witnessing them but receiving them, disseminating them, and legitimating them among themselves—they too become a part of this enchantment.

In one instance, Meriem noted that Hamza Yusuf had complimented her for grasping the class material so well. At first, she felt an intuitive sense of pride, which was then dwarfed by an overwhelming shame that her ego was taking over. She adds:

> Then a girl told me teachers could tell what's on your mind. I was like, oh my god! I was so frightened. Clearly, I never really knew that the teachers could tap into your thoughts, but [they had] that kind of spiritual inclination. Then it made perfect sense to relate how my experiences with my shaykh were. I was like, why didn't I know this? So what I used to do ... before every class with Shaykh Hamza is pray two *raka‘a nafl* [optional prayer] to cleanse my thought and for Allah to grant me honor in front of him and not move my heart with pride.

This particular account of Hamza Yusuf's *karāmāt* is important, for multiple reasons. For one, it is a fairly common account, but not because it is common knowledge. Indeed, many seekers were unaware of this story. Rather, it is told and retold by different seekers as a form of exclusive knowledge. The select who become aware of this are in the center of the enchanted space. They know how the *otherworldly* engages the *this-worldly*. Khaled related that this account of a saintly miracle known as *kashf* was fairly common in neo-traditionalist and Sufi spaces. He explains:

> They [some seekers and shaykhs] make it seem that everyone who has some sort of spiritual status can read your heart, you know? This could really play on the neurotic tendencies of people and make them feel more vulnerable and more likely to second guess themselves. Push people to be more of a

blank slate. It can also make people feel excited. On some deep level, people want to feel seen and acknowledged, but at the same time, it can be very ungrounding.

Khaled insisted, "I have never seen that from Hamza Yusuf. He doesn't promote it, but the culture around him is very broken." I asked him, "how so?" He explained, "There is an emphasis on the filthy, vile *nafs* and how we are inherently flawed. I remember somebody used to say *Kun ʿardan takun lillāhi ʿardan*—be earth, and you'll be more pleased to God. Just be dirt. It was a lot of breaking down the person and recreating his worldview within theirs."

The diffusion of miracle stories in these spaces does not just happen *across* seekers. It also moves from top to bottom. This is particularly so in the case of Umar Faruq Abd-Allah. I watched a famous video recommended by the seekers where Hamza Yusuf spoke of a *karāmāh* he had witnessed. In this intensely emotional video, Yusuf describes how Abd-Allah saved people in a car accident by lifting up the car.[21] During my interview with Habib Ali Jifri, he related the same story citing Abd-Allah's *aḥwāl*—or spiritual states. It is no surprise, then, that some seekers took *bayʿah* with Abd-Allah. With Abd-Allah especially, seekers relate an intense connection or a spiritual experience that supersedes any form of secular rationalization. One seeker related a story that Abd-Allah conveyed from his shaykhs, that in the primordial realm, when there were only souls, the souls of the youth were circumambulating around the soul of Hamza Yusuf, and that is why Yusuf has a secret with the youths.

Umar Faruq Abd-Allah, more than Yusuf or Murad,[22] has a spiritual presence. Most of the seekers described a sense of awe in his presence, which led a few to take him as their shaykh. This is not advertised in the retreat, so the relative secrecy of the ritual of pledging allegiance to him as a Sufi master gives the initiates a sense of a different level of spiritual connectedness. Meriem noted being taken over by his presence. She described it as follows: "When Shaykh Umar came, his presence totally boiled over us. I went up to him, completely dazzled by his radiance. You can't look at him for too long without taking away your eyes. You have to look away because that's how much *nūr* [light] he has." I asked her, "Do you think he is a *walī* [saint]?" She replied: "I personally think that he is a *walī*. I know some people say he is the Khiḍr[23] of our time. Some teachers say that Khiḍr never died. So people say that there is a

Khiḍr in every century or every era, and people say that Dr. Umar is the Khiḍr of our era."

As in the account of Yusuf's *karāmāh*, this complete sanctification of Abd-Allah on one level affirms his spiritual authority and the authority of the knowledge he transmits. It enables the integration of seekers in a "traditional" and timeless world. In this (enchanted) world, they have encountered saints. This not only makes that world real but also gives them the potential to also be enchanted and have mystical experiences through their connection to it. They, to use Taylor's notion, become porous. They are vulnerable to the forces of enchantment and a part of the cosmic order. The Qur'anic story of Moses and Khiḍr has long been used in Sufi exegesis to explain the relationship between a spiritual guide and his disciple.[24] Qasim, however, contends that the story of Khiḍr and Moses is sometimes misused in neo-traditionalist spaces. He notes that sometimes it is used to urge seekers that reality is often the opposite of what they perceive it to be. Hence, seekers are likely to doubt what they perceive as the truth in favor of an appeal of esoteric justification whereby the saints know the unseen.[25]

Conditions of Plausibility

Before coming to Rihla, Nermin felt increasingly disillusioned with the hypocrisy of liberal and left-wing culture on campuses, and in the NGO she worked in. Her anthropology class, however, challenged her thinking significantly. "There is this ethnographic study of Paraguayan indigenous communities and their cosmologies," she explained:

> They had strategies and means of engaging with modernity that would be unintelligible to the so-called "leftist allies." The anthropologist who studied these groups said that from an insider's perspective, their political ontology, their view of reality, and what constitutes a "good life" leads them to political strategies that European NGOs would not understand.

Nermin added:

> Before coming to Rihla, I wanted to see what Islam had to say about what "reality" and the "self" were. What I got from Rihla and Shaykh Abdal Hakim was that Islam has a radically different view of reality from that of modernity. It is not that there are different perspectives on reality or multiple realities. It is that what constitutes reality [is different]; the ontology is differ-

ent. The belief that God is in charge of history; that radically changes your political stances.

The retreat opens the seekers to a radical interrogation of modernity as an existential and even a spatial other. Views on science, politics, equality, or gender are thus scrutinized against a metaphysical ideal. This ideal seeker is advised that it may be unintelligible to modernity or modern peoples. However, it reflects the true spirit of the tradition. As such, the plausibility structures that underpin modern living are deconstructed, and the seekers are opened up to alternative and "traditional" plausibility structures. Seekers may have experienced moments of doubt about some of the implications of these changing plausibility structures. However, this doubt is often accompanied by an interrogation of the *nafs* and whether or not it has ascended beyond its modernist disposition enough to realize the truth about the traditional approach.

For instance, Umar Faruq Abd-Allah, in his lectures in Rihla, critiques the hegemony that scientism as an ideology has in dictating even metaphysical positions. He cites the Christian traditionalist[26] metaphysician and mathematician Wolfgang Smith.[27] In 2017, he related a controversial position that Smith puts forward in favor of "geocentrism" as opposed to "heliocentrism." The geocentric model, popular with ancient philosophers, including some Islamic ones, posits the centrality of the Earth in the universe. The heliocentric one asserts that the sun is the center and the planets and the earth orbit around it. Abd-Allah is not entirely concerned with disproving heliocentrism. What is important for Abd-Allah is a change in the conditions of plausibility. For too long, the reign of "scientism" has dictated metaphysical principles.

For the seekers, however, in laymen's terms, the reality of the statement ought to shock their modern sensibilities, but in the space, it does not. Abd-Allah posits that depending on one's metaphysical disposition, the earth, not the sun, could be considered the center of the cosmos. Jamillah recalled that before attending Rihla she had been in another retreat with Abd-Allah:

> I've listened to Dr. Umar before, and he is a big advocate of metaphysics. We went to a retreat with him where we studied *'aqīda*, and he mentioned metaphysics a lot. I read *Science and Myth: What We Are Never* Told by Wolfgang Smith—he is a mathematician. His whole book is based on a scientific basis. I was reading a book by a Christian believer who was also a physicist who also has the same thing we were saying. It gave me a boost of confidence.

The plausibility of "geocentrism," for the seekers in the space, is not an absolute shedding of beliefs in popular scientific principles. Rather, it opens the doors to the possibility of an entirely different way of seeing the world. Outside the physical location of the retreat, they may have to negotiate these radical principles with the modern discourse of science—where Wolfgang Smith is on the margins. Inside the retreat, however, the symbolic authority of the space opens the gates to different potentials; the real and symbolic authority of the shaykhs as transmitters of the tradition makes the possibility of a geocentric view of the cosmos a real possibility.

In another instance, Walead Mosaad stated that the political strategies Muslims employ are opposed to the spirit of the tradition. Mosaad noted that instead of ridiculing Donald Trump—which goes against the spirit of the Islamic tradition—Muslims should instead focus on making supplications to make him a better leader. Mosaad continued to add, imagine if Muslims made supplications for Trump or Netanyahu to become Muslim. This could potentially solve their predicaments. However, Muslims no longer believe in the power of supplications and instead emphasize the power of their actions. This political strategy integrates a religious disposition that connects the believer to his maker. It enables the believer to depend on and trust God for his affairs. As an American citizen but also as a spiritual seeker, Nermin notes that there was some tension. In the space of the retreat, she was open to this kind of intervention as a metaphysical approach unpoliced and unmediated by a modernist political disposition. Outside the retreat, however, she had some doubts. The space's symbolic authority seemingly changes the conditions of plausibility.

The Making of the Ideal Muslim and the Ideal Citizen

Authority is not, however, exclusively or predominantly maintained by this vulnerability to the forces of enchantment. It is maintained by the intellectual rigor of the three shaykhs and their appeal to orthodoxy. In the lectures, seekers often noted being dazzled by the intellectual depth of, especially, Abdal Hakim Murad's lectures. Most of my interviewees, except three, found his discourse exceedingly difficult to understand. They would have to go over their lecture notes many times so that they could understand what he had to say. Meriem joked, when I asked her what the students thought of Abdal Hakim Murad: "They said that he was a genius, but no one understood him. We used to say one was Dumbledore and one was Harry Potter. Who was the genius out of the two?" She was, of course, referring to Abdal Hakim Murad and Hamza Yusuf.

The very appeal to an unapologetic, "undiluted" Islamic orthodoxy is why many seekers chose that space. The nature of Islamic belief is redefined and demystified of presumed "lowest common denominator" spiritualties, such as "cultural" Islam, "political" Islam—in both its liberal and Islamist versions—as well as Salafi claims of orthodoxy. The discourse of orthodoxy develops and is affirmed by the modern–traditional polemic. In a sense, there is a direct relationship between the regulation, adjustment, and requirement of correct beliefs to the condemnation, exclusion, and undermining of incorrect ones.[28] The latter position relates to the modern corruption of Islamic belief systems established by tradition. Seekers often find themselves "rediscovering" Islam in terms of beliefs and practices. For instance, one noted that in Rihla he had discovered that he had been making ablution wrongly his whole life.

The 2017 Rihla program was inaugurated with a set of lectures on Islamic theology—from the Ash'arī creed. Seekers were, first, taught a text by Muhammad Taqi Usmani. This text, which was in their course pack, included questions posed in the Amman Message.[29] The Amman Message is a document outlining the contours of Islamic belief and orthodoxy in order to counter extremism.[30] The construction of the ideal Muslim—in the space of the retreat—corresponds to the construction of an ideal citizen. Although the discourse of citizenship is not always overt throughout the retreat, it is one of the stated aims. The Deen intensive website states, "The programs are designed to enlighten and empower a wide cross-section of students with the basic values of faith and citizenship so that they may live as dignified and upright individuals."[31]

The aura of neutrality that the space of the retreat commands, by being outside modernity, is not fundamentally apolitical. Rather, it allows politics to enter under specific conditions and claims, namely, that the world seen from a metaphysical lens—which I discuss in the next chapter. Correcting beliefs and practices—so that seekers may imbibe the true spirit of the tradition—is in the same vein as an effort to condemn radical beliefs born of Salafism and Islamism. This articulation of an Islamic orthodoxy was very powerful for Ahmed, who was previously a Salafi. "Wahhabi Islam is very modernist. It is a modernist abstraction of Sunni Islam," he explains. He added:

Wahhabis think that every major figure somehow had a deathbed conversion. Things like 'Fiqh-us-Sunna' are a reinterpretation of fiqh based on your projected understanding from now into history. As opposed to the casual build-up of *sharḥ* and commentaries of scholars throughout the ages. But they're inspired by people like Muḥammad ʿAbduh. And I learned that to be the case.

"What is wrong with ʿAbduh?," I asked. "Isn't that the same vein of thought? I know nothing about him, just the idea of reimagining Islamic orthodoxy. Taking it away from the traditional codified Sunni Islam."

For other seekers, finding a personal *madhhab* was both simultaneously meaningful and difficult. Sara explains:

> For the longest time, I thought you didn't need one [madhhab]. It was unnecessary. Allah gave us these *rukhsa*s (religious dispensations) for a reason, you go with whatever's easiest for you. I realized that I had been cherry-picking for the wrong reasons. It was an eye-opener and gave me more respect for madhāhib because it made me think to look at this rich history. We have this rich tradition. We have tolerance. Like all these teachers, these imams were students of one another.

As seekers study the three main components of the Islamic tradition that forms orthodox Islam and other traditional and intellectual subjects of the study, they become acutely aware of a number of things. From the outset, they are aware that they are correcting both beliefs and practices that they previously had. They need to be aware of an incorrect Islamic "other"—not necessarily for sectarian purposes. This Islamic "other" has created forms of deviation in the religion that need to be repaired, and its social manifestations need to be remedied. By studying orthodox Islam, the seekers are primarily correcting their personal beliefs about Islam and their personal ritual practices. Furthermore, they see themselves as correcting the modernist dispositions to which they had been acclimatized. Finally, seekers are not learning a new Islamic method with a revivalist bent. On the contrary: if they are born Muslim, they are simply returning to the true orthodox religious belief system of their forefathers—before the ruptures caused by modernity.

Sufism, as such, becomes central not just to the spiritual lives of seekers but to their political lives as well—making them viable citizens. The rise of extremism, they learn, was a direct result of young people no longer seeing the need for traditional spiritual guides. Jamillah recommended that I watch Hamza Yusuf's lecture on the rise of ISIS. She noted that when she was eighteen years old she saw this video for the first time and took an interest in Yusuf.

As human beings, she explained, we are not always equipped to make sense of the world and its injustices. Human beings need authorities to guide them; unlike what democratic liberal ideas would have you believe, every Muslim needs someone above them. She broke this down further:

> Let us compare this to the Protestant Revolution. Before the Protestant Revolution, the church would have someone who could read the Bible and impose an idea on the whole mass. The Protestant Revolution wanted everyone to have their own Bible. Look now at all the deviations and the different Christianities that have been created. In Islam, we have the right to have a Qur'ān at home and to read alone, but it is too rich for us to be able to absorb correctly. We have this tradition in Islam of having a *sanad*. We have to make the line of *sanad* pure because it goes back to a pure source—that is, someone with good intentions.

Mysa echoed Jamillah's concern. The new generation has no concept of authority, unlike her father's generation. They read books on their own, and they became their own shaykhs. This, she claims, is what gave rise to ISIS. They lack both the spiritual and the religious guidance that comes from being in a part of *sanad*. Here both Mysa and Jamillah affirm the neo-traditionalist shaykhs' contention that the "tradition," and precisely *taṣawwuf*, can be an antidote to extremism and political violence. This contention is salient not just for the seekers of sacred knowledge and the shaykhs but also for policymakers amplifying the importance of Sufism as an antidote to political violence.

As I have shown, the retreat becomes a re-enchanted space that develops and forms new meanings, authorities, and plausibility structures. Through the strategic, physical seclusion of the retreat from the hustle and bustle of the everyday, it had come to represent a physical location outside of modernity and its concerns.[32] Therefore, the neo-traditionalist shaykhs would critique the modern conditions in this space as an existential and imagined other. As a traditionalized space, I have shown, the retreat assumes a sharp boundary between itself and the modern world—in terms of space, values, and, most importantly, its methods of ascertaining truth.

I have demonstrated that by deconstructing the received knowledge or modern narratives on science, sociology, history, or religion, the shaykhs have been able to provide radical alternative accounts. The shaykhs have argued that these accounts were more attuned to Islamic metaphysics and closer to the social approach of traditional people. I have argued that the plausibility of these accounts would be more readily accepted in the space of the retreat than outside it. This is because the closed system of meaning fashioned (closed off from modernity) is clothed by the authority and the charisma of the shaykhs. From the vantage-point of the seekers, their individual bids at meaning-making are a way of locating themselves in the space. The conscious enactment of the tradition is a bid to become traditional. The retreat, as an allegory of the ideal and enchanted pockets outside of modernity, I have noted, presented the space as outside the corruptions of modern politics. In the following chapters, I will examine how neo-traditionalists conceive of politics from a traditional standpoint.

5

THE METAPHYSICAL LENS

In 2016, the Saudi-owned television channel MBC broadcast *Rihla* as a part of its annual Ramadan specials.[1] Eissa Bougary, the creator of the program and a long-time friend of Hamza Yusuf, set out to reintroduce him, the retreat, and the seekers to an Arabic-speaking audience. In the early 2000s, Yusuf—along with Abdal Hakim Murad and Umar Faruq Abd-Allah—was first introduced on MBC in a series that lasted a season. The framing of the program, this time round, was strikingly different. No longer centering on activist youth engaged in a dialogue between East and West, this season was curated meticulously to respond to the Arab Spring, revolutions, and the rise of terrorism—as interlinked phenomena.

In the opening of the first episode, there were striking images of violence and tumult in the aftermath of terrorist attacks in France and Saudi Arabia. The camera then zooms into the lecture hall in Rihla, where some seekers are sitting on the floor while others are on chairs taking notes on Hamza Yusuf's lecture. Yusuf passionately denounces the terrorists and their violent actions, affirming that they have nothing to do with Islam. He enthusiastically responds to critics who laud him for not speaking out against leaders and oppressors. He explains that a Muslim scholar's primary responsibility is to respond to the religious deviation of extremists.

Later in the series, Yusuf further explains a metaphysical approach to the problem of theodicy. He proclaims that believers must understand that the world is an abode of injustice; that is its destiny. Furthermore, believers should internalize that believing in the Day of Judgment means that even if there are sixty years of oppression in the world, there will be infinite justice in the after-life. From a metaphysical lens, this is tribulation; once people cease to see their tribulations through a metaphysical lens, all else collapses. In the following episode, Yusuf delved deeper into the transient nature of worldly injustice. He adds that everyone feels as if they have been wronged or have faced injustice at some point in their life. He declared that people were saying even at some point that the guided Caliph 'Umar ibn al-Khaṭṭāb was unjust. Yusuf then cited Ḥadīth encapsulating the metaphysical truth "As you are (as far as your actions are), so will be the rulers that will soon be set over you."[2]

The creators of the series juxtapose the traditional harmonious beauty that the shaykhs represent with the chaos and destruction instigated by extremism and terror. The same traditional metaphysical lens by which Muslims developed great civilizations also dictated how they ought to act in times of strife. As one of the seekers Bougary interviewed stated, in Rihla, seekers move away from the battles out in the world to fight the battle within. However, internal battles are never too remote from external ones.[3]

The neo-traditionalist shaykhs, from the outset, guide the seekers toward a path of introspection as opposed to political activism. Their da'wa spaces—particularly the religious retreats and conferences—aim to cultivate virtues of the heart. The shaykhs argue that political calamity must be seen from a metaphysical perspective whereby a person sees how he has erred or sees how his heart can stand it and remain unaffected by it. That discursive appeal to introspection over political action lends the shaykhs a reputation of being seemingly unpolluted by the ideological influences of the different strands of Muslim activism. They are concerned with deepening and strengthening the community intellectually and spiritually and rarely advocate a direct form of political dissent. They therefore appear politically neutral, quietist, or even ambivalent. Indeed, some observers point out that taking an "anti-political" stance is a political position. This chapter goes beyond that critique, as I note that the discussion of politics has always been central to their discourse. Politics is embedded both in their conceptions of a normative, traditional Islamic world-view and metaphysics and in their critique of the social order represented by the different forces of modernity. From within the story of Islamic modernity, Islamists represent the foremost cosmic destabilizing force.

For the sake of clarity, this chapter and the next should be considered in tandem. In this chapter, I show the starting point that the shaykhs share in terms of political attitudes based on metaphysical justifications. Having lost their metaphysical perspectives on modernity, Muslims had become vulnerable to a host of political problems. This metaphysical loss is reflected in the way they conduct their activism. Islamists—the inheritors of the postcolonial religion—are at the center of the problem. They were influenced by Marxist and utopian ideas that subsequently led to zealotry and violence, as well as the complete loss of a metaphysical perspective. The solution, therefore, is to be found in the "tradition," which entails retrieving the metaphysical lens and a traditional approach.

Although this is a shared starting point of the three neo-traditionalist shaykhs, their locus of attention and conclusions are somewhat different. After outlining their shared points of commonalities, this chapter will focus on Hamza Yusuf's political articulations. I focused on his political discourse from 2012 onwards, as this was the timeframe in which most of the seekers I interviewed went to neo-traditionalist retreats and engaged with his discourse. That said, although there were fundamental continuities, Yusuf's discourse on politics has evolved as he reacted to and engaged with different political contexts.[4] As Yusuf articulates a metaphysical position in the tradition—which informed different aspects of Muslims' religious, social, and political lives— the importance of stability becomes paramount. This chapter explores the way Yusuf conceives political dissent in different contexts—such as the Muslim majority and minority contexts. It additionally explores how he frames the problems of political activism. In the next chapter, I explore—albeit with a closer focus on Murad and Abd-Allah—how the three shaykhs regard identity politics in terms of cultural, religious, and gender identities. Murad and Abd-Allah share many of Yusuf's concerns and a priori assumptions about the relationship between politics and metaphysics.

Cosmic Legitimations

The boundary between the metaphysical and the political, for the shaykhs, is blurred. They contend that politically-oriented religious movements, which have adopted modernist approaches, caused a decline in metaphysics.[5] This, in turn, entailed a deconstruction of the "metaphysical lens" though which Muslims traditionally viewed their social and political worlds. The socio-political arrangement of this world is intimately related to its connection with the cosmos. Peter Berger explains this link through what he calls "cosmic legitimation." Cosmic legitimation positions and explains how the social world and its institution relate to the cosmos—or "sacred order of the universe."[6] It designates an ontological status for social and political institutions by giving them a location within the sacred cosmic reference.[7] For example, divine kingship and the institutions representing it are a link between the world of men and the world of gods.[8] This cosmization of political institutions endows them with meaning and significance beyond their immediate or material utility.

This also transforms the dynamic of political critique and the conception of political theology. Cosmically significant institutions are essential in providing a link from the social world to the world of gods. This means that the dissent against institutions is not merely a political position but a metaphysical one as well. If one accepts the premise that divine kingship forms a link between the world of man and the world of gods, then dissent against that institution is an affront to both worlds and to the metaphysical link that binds them. The implications of endowing social institutions with a cosmic significance are twofold. Berger explains that social "institutions are always threatened by not only the ravages of time but by conflict and discrepancies between the groups whose activities they are intended to regulate."[9] This is the material reality of political and social institutions. When endowed with cosmic meaning through cosmic forms of legitimation, Berger explains, "[t]he institutions are magically lifted above these human, historical contingencies. They become inevitable because they are taken for granted not only by men but by the gods. The empirical tenuousness is transformed into overpowering stability as they are understood as but manifestations of the underlying structure of the universe."[10] The dynamics and relationships individuals have with these institutions, too, are bound by the recognition of their metaphysical cosmic status. Therefore, political values and forms of action either reaffirm this link or facilitate its withering.

Hamza Yusuf contends that in modern times, forms of political activism marginalized a cosmos-centric view in favor of a purely materialistic one. Following Christendom's path to secularity, modern Muslims have lost their "metaphysical lens."[11] Metaphysics is not used in the strictest sense to refer to 'ilm al-kalām, but is a more generalized notion of metaphysics, as indicated in neo-traditionalists' narrative of modern decline. Yusuf explains that although the knowledge of metaphysics was explicitly held by the spiritual and scholarly elites in the Islamic tradition, it was implicitly held and governed the worldviews of Muslims in the past.[12] The cosmic link enabled people to see their social world through a metaphysical lens. This informed everything from architecture to symbols communicated to them in their *ṭarīqa* affiliations and

Friday *khuṭbas*.[13] Abdal Hakim Murad adds even the splendor of clothing in past times. The beauty of the arrangement of the past was an indicator of the Truth—God. Society was in equilibrium. This metaphysical ordering of the cosmos, Abd-Allah adds, was recognized by traditional Muslims in the past. Human beings and the cosmos fit one another.[14] However, it is not just architecture and clothing that traditionally pointed people to the metaphysical Truth. It was the arrangement of society and government; it was presented through how people reflected on tribulation and how men and women saw their gender identity in contradistinction to modernity, where all of these have been liquidized.[15]

In traditional societies, the result is a sense of harmony. Murad cites the economic crisis as an example. The crisis commenced in 1914; the gold standard crumbled because Germany no longer used it. "In many ways," he argued, "[t]hat is a more fundamental transformation than the beginning of the genocidal mega-conflicts of the twentieth century because wars come and they go, but we are still off the gold standard. What does that mean? From a shariʿa perspective, it means that we are decentered, that meaning is gone and that there is no referentiality. [Gold] is the material to do with the sun. It is to do with the cosmos itself. It's inherently valuable."[16]

Gold in the hierarchy of material reaffirms the centrality of a cosmos-centric vision and therefore maintains the structures of meaning. In contrast, according to this view, money has an imagined worth in symbolic terms without a point of reference. This fragmentation of solid referential truths makes sense to a postmodern state which accepts no objective truths. The view juxtaposes gold (essential to the order and meaning of the cosmos) with "genocidal mega-conflicts" while holding the latter inconsequential. Murad's point is not to belittle the scale of suffering caused by genocides in the twentieth century. Rather, he explains that the material loss of life could be overcome and not disorient one from the coordinates of the cosmos. However, relinquishing the gold standard meant losing the coordinates.

Three Metaphysical Scopes of Analysis

Before approaching the specific case studies in which each shaykh provides cosmic legitimation for political institutions and modes of political action or inaction, one must see how their metaphysical positions translate in the Muslim context. Traditional Muslims accepted and internalized the notion of anthropic realism—the belief that human beings and the cosmos fit together, or with a mutual belonging.[17] Implicitly present in this cosmos-centric vision is the acceptance of a deeper metaphysical reality. This inward knowledge of metaphysics was manifested in *taṣawwuf* and assembled in the structures of *ʿaqīda*.[18] Both the natural and man-made elements exist within this cosmic system, which accepts the metaphysical reality of the necessary existence and power of God.[19] In the tradition, Muslims recognized that the cosmos was organized, layered, meaningful, and had an understanding of recognized authorities.

The notion of authority and hierarchy becomes especially important. They provide a sense of stability—be it the epistemic stability of "orthodoxy"—in the form of the traditional ʿulamā', or political stability by *walī al ʿamr*. Religious authorities, be they the methodological authority of a specific *madhhab* or that of a religious scholar who personifies it, do not derive their authority merely from outward knowledge but also carry a form of gnosis. Umar Faruq Abd-Allah, therefore, defines tradition as the "reception of a rich past, a profound past with metaphysics, theology and law and a deep understanding of civilization that we receive not just in word but in spirit."[20] The scholars, their religious methods, and saintly authority are signifiers of a porous cosmos.[21] Their charismata or *karāmāt* show that the world is open and vulnerable to the enchanted *otherworldly*.

So what went wrong in modernity? First, the loss of the principal metaphysical lens dictates how Muslims ought to act. In the past, Muslims recognized introspection and responsibility foremost as a basis. According to Yusuf, this was the lesson humanity received from Adam and Eve on the responsibility of the viceregency. Adam and Eve took full responsibility for their actions. They did not see themselves as victims. They did not blame Satan or each other. Satan, on the other hand, blamed others for his condition.[22] Yusuf then goes on to tie this conception of the responsibility of Adam and Eve to the political condition of the Muslims. He explains:

> Muslims see themselves as victims. Victimization is a defeatist mentality. It is the mentality of the powerless. Muslims never really had a mentality of victimization. From a metaphysical perspective, which is always a Muslim's first and primary perspective, there can be no victims. We believe that all suffering has a redemptive value.[23]

The victimhood–responsibility dichotomy deeply impacts the stances Yusuf takes vis-à-vis political activism. The main responsibility of the community of believers, according to Yusuf, is to mend their internal states. In the context of political upheaval or tribulations, believers must take responsibility for their hearts and ponder whether they have transgressed in a way to deserve their tribulation. The metaphysical designation of the world is to be an abode of tribulations where there can be no complete justice.[24] Yusuf explains, "When the Mongols invaded the Muslims, they [the Muslims] did not blame them [the Mongols]. They took account of their selves and asked what they had done to deserve the tribulation."[25]

Since there can be no victims, the burden of responsibility falls entirely on the individual and the community of believers. That burden of responsibility does not entail constructing a utopian form of justice—as, he contends, the Islamists try to.[26] Not only is that impossible, but attempting it has begotten more injustice. In the spirit of responsibility, Yusuf dissuades believers from deflecting responsibility for any external or institutional causes of violence. This position was not without controversy. Yusuf was heavily criticized when a 2016 lecture at the Rihla retreat was posted online about the Syrian revolution. In that video, he said:

> Do you know ... the slogan of the Syrian revolution? "The Syrian people will not be humiliated." That was their slogan. They were all shouting it in the streets. Now, all these poor innocent people are begging non-Muslims to let them into their country. They are fleeing across the ocean in boats. Allah can humiliate whomever he pleases. If you humiliate a ruler, God will humiliate you.[27]

After many critiques, Yusuf released another video to clarify his position better, in which he expressed deep regret at the pain the clip may have caused. He expressed the view that although there is no way of truly understanding why tribulations happen, he believes in a tradition in which God is active in history.[28]

The Unholy Alliance: Islam and the Left

The most symptomatic result of the loss of the metaphysical lens is the Muslim internalization of Marxist epistemologies and cognitive frames.[29] Islam has become an ideology.[30] To neo-traditionalists, the notion of ideology specifically relates to a modernist arrangement and a flattening of transcendental meaning so as to set a political agenda. Abd-Allah explains that ideology is a form of artificial social engineering—as opposed to the metaphysical harmony the tradition entailed. Ideologies are predicated on a combative worldview as opposed to the traditional harmonious ordering of the world. Ideology sees the world through the prism of victors and vanquished and is inherently militant and violent.[31] There is a certain blurring of the lines between what constitutes the categories of the "ideological," the "Marxist," and the "neo-Marxist." This blurring enables a certain fluidity in the scope of analysis, if not accuracy itself, which enables the shaykhs to construct meaningful links and ideological designations across a wide spectrum of Islamic and non-Islamic thought. According to the shaykhs, the Marxist framework aims to establish a form of utopia on earth. Essentially, this materialist utopia leaves no space for God. As Murad explains, "Ideology teaches that our actions can have outcomes in a real rather than a conventional way."[32] In the zeal and confidence in human power to achieve material heaven on Earth, this framework requires a revolutionary unsettling of the world.

The basis of the Marxist framework removes from the oppressed any metaphysical dimension to their oppression—the idea that they are being tried by God. Yusuf contends that this constructed oppressed–oppressor dichotomy alleviates the responsibility of those who see themselves as oppressed. They then see themselves as perpetual victims, which bars them from introspection. For Yusuf, the epidemic of perpetual victimhood began with the Islamists. Younger generations have further internalized post-Marxist paradigms such as Foucauldian critique and critical theory.[33] In the RIS 2017, Yusuf wrote a letter cautioning young Muslims in secular universities:

> Our discourse is troubling: They seem to derive from dark luminaries [the oxymoron was intentional] as Derrida, Foucault, and their influence from Karl Marx. We need to know the chain of thought of those we take as our teachers. The current discourse is demonic, yet many of those who espouse it are unaware of that. The modern, secular view known as critical theory deems such a view as "blaming the victim."[34]

Yusuf's unease with the critique of power and institutions was inbuilt from the outset in his narratives of modernity. The first renegade scholars from the Nahḍa movement, not the colonial powers, were to blame for planting seeds of modernity. The Islamists, not the postcolonial nation-states, subsequently entrenched modernist deviations in Muslim societies.[35] This was because their response favored reform and political change over introspection. Yusuf explains this in a joint lecture with the controversial right-wing philosopher

Roger Scruton. He contends that there are three possible responses to colonialism. The first is a Herodian response which concedes the loss of power to colonialism. This is a safe option taken by Morocco and Malaysia. There is the zealot's response, which is a nihilistic fight to the death. In the end, as you fight the monster, you become the monster—as with the case of those who resisted colonialism. The best option is one of self- and cultural preservation. The burden of responsibility, therefore, lies almost entirely on the individual and the community of believers rather than on the structures of power to maintain the cosmic order threatened by the forces of modernity.[36]

The problematic relationship Islam cultivated with the Left in its modern history prompted the shaykhs to argue for a closer relationship with the Right in what they call "the moral majority." Jibril Latif explains that as more Muslims identify with oppressed groups, their identities become reformulated around a discourse of oppression. They find interlocutors among other "oppressed" and "minority" groups, and their Islam becomes reduced to identity in intersectional politics.[37] The shaykhs, consequently, argue that Muslims have more shared values with conservatives in their anti-pornography campaigns, their affirmation of the importance of traditional family values, gender distinction, or even "pro-life" stances.[38] Murad, too, called for a "sacred alliance" of conservative believers.[39] This alliance with the Right becomes especially important in Yusuf's political discourse.

Hamza Yusuf: Political Dissent

Hamza Yusuf considers dissent that threatens order and institutions a cosmically destabilizing force.[40] This is an important starting point for illustrating how the conception of the generalized notion of "metaphysics" informs political positions. Three overarching themes at play produce internal tension in Yusuf's metaphysical, theological, and material conceptions. The first theme is the cosmic significance of order and authority as immutable metaphysical principles—even when unjust (or untraditional, such as modern nation-states). The second theme represents how he contextualizes and reads the "tradition" as a form of cosmic legitimation. For example, what is the political significance of saying that the four Imāms, Abū Ḥanīfa, Mālik, Al Shāfiʿī, and Ibn Ḥanbal, were apolitical? Or what is the theological significance of translating *khurūj* as "rebellion"? Lastly, how does Yusuf identify the burden of responsibility for the decline and fragmentation in modernity? These three themes exemplify how he conceives political dissent as a modern metaphysical fallacy in Muslim-majority countries (as modern nation-states or democracies) and Muslim-minority contexts (even when explicitly Islamophobic).

What is political action predicated on?

In recent times, extrapolating an internal logic or coherence in Yusuf's political discourse vis-à-vis the state might be considered an arduous process. This is not just because Yusuf has changed his view recently, but also because his discourse holds theology, metaphysics, politics, and history in a common discursive space. All these seemingly contradict each other over time, but the shaykh weaves them together. He would make a metaphysical point about victimhood and then evoke a political quietist statement about staying away from rulers because all rulers are oppressive. Then, he would talk about the 'aqīda implications for seekers of rebelling against an unjust ruler; however, the theological, metaphysical, and historical points about the "tradition" form a single discourse and recommendation on how to engage power. Additionally, as the political context changes, so does making political recommendations; still, there is a seeming internal logic tying them together. In different contexts, the political role of the individual is not linked to the nature of the government, regardless of whether it is oppressive or not, Muslim or not. Indeed, Yusuf would argue that the majority of governments are oppressive. For him, this affirms the importance of order and stability in the metaphysical approach of Muslims.

The cosmic designation of the state is founded on the metaphysical knowledge of the nature of the world. Yusuf explains that the nature of the world is that "we live in the abode of injustice. The world is destined to be unjust."[41] From the outset, the political relationship an individual or the community of believers has toward the state is not governed by a material sense of injustice or being wronged. Yusuf explains:

> That's why our 'ulamā' traditionally were opposed to revolution. Not because they thought oppression wasn't wrong or they were trying to keep the oppressors in power. They saw it from a metaphysical perspective first and foremost. That this was 'ibtilā' (tribulation) from Allah. If you remove metaphysics, then the world makes no sense at all. You can tear everything down.[42]

Although Yusuf cites scholars who discuss revolution in terms of fiqh or even in terms of 'aqīda, the point he makes is first and foremost metaphysical. Central to this metaphysical conception is the importance of stability and order. Yusuf laments the decline after the Arab Spring because people did not grasp this point. One of the most popular chants, he explains, is "Ash-sha'b yurīd isqāṭ an-niẓām," which translates as: the people want to bring down the "order." They would chant this at the Police or the Army. Revolutions by their nature herald and legitimize disorder. [43] The distinction here, Yusuf clarifies, is that he does not advocate injustice, or advocates supporting it. That said, given the metaphysical importance of order, it is better to have the injustice that comes with order than anarchy that seeks justice.

Traditional cosmic legitimation: historical sources and the Arabic language

Yusuf uses two forms of "traditional" cosmic legitimation to justify his position on political dissent. First, he usually prefaces his position with a linguistic claim. Second, he uses historical anecdotes to justify and reaffirm his position. While the linguistic argument does serve a rhetorical purpose, it also assumes a certain cosmic designation to the Arabic language—even outside the Qurʾānic discourse. Omar Bajwa argues that Hamza Yusuf's usage of the Arabic language is rooted in the belief that language structures our reality. [44] Therefore, the linguistic root of a word in pre-modern Arabic contextualizes its positioning in the cosmic order. Yusuf explains the etymology of the word *thawra* (revolution), contending that it is derived from the word *thawr* (bull). The word is meant to indicate that revolutionaries act haphazardly, just like a bull, causing chaos rather than acting as rational beings. [45] Yusuf cites historical references from the "tradition" to affirm his point. He made the point that none of the four Imāms—Abū Ḥanīfa, Mālik, Al Shāfiʿī, and Ibn Ḥanbal—ever engaged in politics. He added, "That is the way our religion has to be; free of politics." [46] The example of the four Imāms—albeit historically questionable, as I show below—is meant to demonstrate a traditional archetype for political quietism that modern Muslims need to uphold.

   In these two examples, the modes of cosmic legitimation do not entirely hold up to linguistic or historical scrutiny. For example, before Yusuf, the deposed Libyan leader Muammar Gaddafi made the same linguistic point regarding the origins of revolution. [47] This prompted the Mauritanian scholar Mohamed El-Moctar El-Shinqiti to write an article in response. El-Shinqiti affirms that the pre-modern usage of *thawra* most commonly indicates conflict rather than a "female bull" (a term which is rarely used, since most would opt for using the word "cow" or *Baqarah*). He cites Ibn Khāldūn's chapters on *Thawrat al-Murābiṭūn* and *Thawrat al-Muslimīn b-Sawāḥil Ifrīqiyā ʿalā al-Ifranj al-mutghaalbīn fīha* as examples of pre-modern uses of the term *thawra*—which were positive rather than negative.[48] Similarly, in the case of the four Imāms, they were all involved in some form of passive resistance. Abū Ḥanīfa is very credibly said to have bankrolled the rising of Muḥammad al-Nafs al-Zakīyya.[49] Shāfiʿī is said to have been brought before a judge for his seditious activities before being reconciled to the authorities.[50] As for Aḥmad, even though he was not an advocate of overthrowing the authorities, he has been reported as having prayed for Aḥmad b. Nasr al-Khuzāʿī, who rebelled against al-Maʾmūn.[51] During the reign of the successor of al-Maʾmūn, Abū Isḥāq al-Muʿtaṣim, Ibn Ḥanbal was flogged and interrogated for refusing to accept the creatededness of the Qurʾān.[52] Yusuf's depiction of an unproblematic, unpolitical historical narrative in which the four Imāms did not engage in politics indicates that the unity of tradition requires a degree of historical revisionism. In doing so, it designates a certain metaphysical authenticity and harmony with the past. If modernity and its modes of activism indicate disharmony and rupture, pre-modernity needs to be the opposite of that. To achieve this, Yusuf takes certain liberties in interpreting and rearranging language and history to make that larger point.

Agency and the burden of responsibility

For Yusuf, the state can only represent a point of order; the individual, on the other hand, can be an agent of either order or disorder. The political agency of individuals is multilayered since it transcends the material realities of their condition. Four questions need to be addressed to answer the question of political dissent and agency. First, what constitutes injustice? Second, what is a victim? Third, what are the duties of Muslims in times of perceived injustice? Lastly, who bears the burden of political responsibility?

The question of political responsibility, generally and in times of injustice, requires one to address the nature of injustice and define what a "victim" is. From the outset, justice requires placing things in their rightful place. By definition, injustice would be when things are not in their rightful place.[53] Yusuf uses Naquib Al-Attas's definition as a starting point.[54] Al Attas explains, "Injustice, being the opposite of justice, is putting a thing in a place not its own; it is to misplace a thing."[55] For Yusuf, notions of justice and injustice are connected to the harmony or disharmony of the cosmos rather than individual experience. Experience in nature is relative, while the reality is dependent on universals. He explains that everyone feels at some point in their lives that they have been wronged or that they have faced injustice."[56] Experiences or personal feelings of being aggrieved are, therefore, relative. Political decisions cannot be made on such a tenuous basis.

So, does what it means to be a "victim" of political injustice relate not to experience but to the metaphysical purpose of the world? Yusuf explains:

> The reality is that whatever happens to a person, he deserves it because of his sins and his distance from God, Most High, is far worse ... Imām al-Ṭarṭūshī in Sirāj al-Mulūk said, "As you are, so will your rulers be" (kamā takūnūna yuwālla ʿalaykum) ... The calamity of tribulation (*fitna*) affects both the innocent and the criminal. This is why avoiding *fitna* is the most important of things. *Fitna* is blind; they afflict both the pure and the impure. "Will we be destroyed while there are righteous people among us, O Messenger of God?" [He replied:] "Yes if impurity proliferates."[57]

The calamities facing Muslims result from their sinful state, despite their having innocent people among them. Yusuf further affirms this point by stating, "From a metaphysical perspective, which is always the first and primary perspective of a Muslim, there can be no victims. We believe that all suffering has a redemptive value."[58] If the designation of victimhood is nullified from a metaphysical perspective, what should the afflicted do in time of *fitna*?

The question of the burden of responsibility is the most pressing one here: who bears it? In his book *The Prayer of the Oppressed*, Yusuf explains the basic ideas he expressed in the RIS 2017 speech. The Qurʾānic perspective, he argues, demands that humans see calamities such as human suffering and oppression as "fruits of our own tyranny."[59] He says, "If we have unjust rulers, we must ask ourselves whether we are getting the rulers we deserve?"[60] Before going through the motions and blaming the leader, he argues, "The oppressed must first acknowledge that rulers often time reflect the people they rule."[61] This is the Adamic Sunna which established humanity's viceregency. Adam and Eve took responsibility for their actions even though the devil, too, was to blame.[62] Yusuf here advocates a sense of responsibility. This burden of responsibility requires the believer to do two things: to fix their internal state and live in accordance with the will of God, and to not engage in the *fitna* that political dissent begets.

He explains that engaging in political dissent changes the hearts and conditions of the oppressed. He says:

> Unfortunately, the oppressed also do their part in perpetuating the cycle of oppression. Often, due to the oppressed people's helplessness and frustration in defending themselves against their aggressor, a deep resentment begins to take root in their hearts. This resentment either poisons them entirely or bursts forth in an aggressive attempt to purge the body politic through the redressing of wrongs. Too often, the purging spirals into bloodletting, and the bitter cycle continues. Hate, aggression, and violence beget more of the same.[63]

Anger, prompted by a sense of being wronged, creates a false sense of righteousness. According to Yusuf, it amplifies the sense of self and reliance on experience rather than truth in informing reality. The only remedy for those who feel a sense of being wronged is self-purification. An integral part of that is forgiveness. Through forgiveness, the harmful repercussions of political vengeance can be avoided.[64] Yusuf acknowledges the right for retribution in sharī'a; however, he affirms a grander metaphysical reality, which demands that people see what befalls them as stemming from themselves.[65]

Muslim majority context

Unlike Murad and Abd-Allah, Yusuf has increasingly taken an active role in Middle Eastern politics alongside his Mauritanian shaykh, Abdullah bin Bayyah.[66] In the context of a Muslim majority country, Yusuf translates his metaphysical position on politics as obedience to the leaders and traditional scholars, and affirming the cosmic need for order and stability. In an interview on the Emirati TV channel, he explains:

> By glorifying our leaders and our *'ulamā'*, God will rectify our world and the Hereafter. When we denounce our leaders and *'ulamā'*, we lose the *dunyā* and our Hereafter. Exalting the leaders is the basis for society. How will the people feel secure if the government is not respected and abused? The greatest blessing of Allah onto people is security.[67]

The political role of a Muslim is to glorify the leader, which maintains a semblance of stability, necessary for keeping the cosmos ordered. If that formula is broken by political dissent, security and order are no longer maintained, and political and religious chaos ensues. For that reason, Yusuf argues that Muslims believe in the Day of Judgment. What does it matter if they live through sixty years of oppression when they will have an infinity of justice in heaven?[68] He affirms, however, that there is a limit to obedience. He points out that one of the immutable principles is that one cannot disobey Allah to obey a leader. For example, if the leader demands that you kill an innocent person or drink wine, you cannot obey him.[69]

Yusuf draws a link between the soundness of the internal state of a believer, his political quietism, and the maintenance of political order and stability. He explains, "This is why our scholars said an unjust ruler is better than continued sedition."[70] Yusuf emphasizes the importance of this point in theology, proclaiming:

> We do not accept any rebellion (*khurūj*) against our leaders or our public affairs even if they are oppressive. This is the *'aqīda* of the Muslims ... you are to tell me we have to go out against the government? Our *salaf* said, and they all agreed (you can't)—even if they are oppressive. Why did they put that in there? Because they knew people would say, but they have oppressed us.[71]

Yusuf translates the much-debated notion of *khurūj* in the widest possible way, as rebellion. *Khurūj*, however, is a very specific technical term indicating organized armed rebellion to seize power. In his book *Rebellion and Violence in Islamic Law*, Khaled Abou El Fadl illustrates the boundaries of what could be considered *khurūj*. He argues that the legality of rebellion is highly dependent on the reason for rebellion and on the ways in which one rebels (an armed and organized rebellion to capture power is different from an unorganized or unarmed one), the legitimacy of the leader and whether or not he is just contributing to the scholars' ruling. Additionally, scholars who deemed rebellion impermissible simultaneously stated that it was impermissible for the leader to fight the rebels.[72] However, for history to be "tradition," it must become based on absolutes or universals outside historical and experiential contingencies.

Democracy, nation-states, and monarchies

Hamza Yusuf's problematization of political agency and his simultaneous calls for obedience could potentially constitute a problem in a democratic context. He is not anti-democratic per se; still, the political agency of individuals is strictly limited.[73] During an interview conducted in Singapore and produced by the office of the Mufti and the Islamic Religious Council of Singapore, he was asked about political agency in a modern democracy. He responded, "That question is purely predicated on the context that they're living in. In a place like Singapore where Muslims have access to the political process, it is very important that they engage in it; same in the United States and other places."[74]

Yusuf means that if the system representing order and stability requires political engagement, then it is important for Muslims to engage with the tools legitimizing this system. Here the emphasis is not on the benefit of political engagement itself, but rather on the fact that it allows for the continued order of the system. This point can be further illustrated in terms of how Yusuf conceives the modern nation-state.[75] Yusuf explains that some young Muslims in the Middle East refuse to view the borders drawn in the Sykes–Picot accords as legitimate since they were drawn by colonial forces. These nation-states, even if their legitimacy was questionable at the outset and even if they were the key instigators of the processes of modernization and secularization, are a fact of reality and represent a stabilizing force. Trying to undo that creates greater harm.[76] The stabilizing force of the nation entails that Muslim citizens of these nations show loyalty to it.[77]

That said, while any government is representative of order and stability, Yusuf prefers constitutional monarchy because it balances spiritual authority and temporal power.[78] He explained:

> Kings do not have the susceptibility for corruption that a poor person or the nouveau riche do. Kings are not hungry. They have everything, so they do not need anything. If a king is good, he will raise his children to be good. We have a great example in Morocco. The King in Morocco comes from a good, well-esteemed, and clean family. He loves his people, and his people love him. I have seen the same thing with Al Saud, but bad people often surround them.[79]

He was then asked what he thought about the constitutional amendments that allowed for more democratic engagement. He respectfully responded that it was not his personal preference. The Islamic world is increasingly more volatile and needs quick and swift action that is best served by a king.[80]

Yusuf echoed the same statement in an article he wrote praising Turkish leader Recep Tayyip Erdoğan[81] in the aftermath of the 2016 coup attempt. He said:

The world is, and has always been, a dystopia. There is no such thing as a perfect or flawless government, and any doctrine or ideology that entices people with the promise of a paradise on earth is flawed and demonic; the Devil tempted Adam with a "Dominion that would never end." Democracies, liberal or otherwise, are profoundly imperfect systems. Monarchies are also flawed in many ways, but kings are far less susceptible to corruption, given their vast wealth than elected leaders who often emerge from the petty-bourgeois, with natural predilections to social status and ladder-climbing that invites corruption.[82]

Muslim minority context

In keeping with his metaphysical framing of politics, Yusuf urges Muslims in the West to examine the activist culture as a potentially destabilizing force that upholds a victimhood narrative. Jibril Latif explains, "With Muslims being increasingly persecuted, their embrace of Leftism and progressive social platforms has displayed a tendency to emphasize religion as a liberation theology for the oppressed."[83] Latif argues that there is a pushback against the so-called "grievance-based Leftism," borne by university campuses. This attitude, he contends, finds its basis in Marxist and Foucauldian influences.[84] In an interview on Al Jazeera, Hamza Yusuf cautioned Muslims against going too far with the feeling of victimhood. Despite some transgressions, the United States and its institutions, including the FBI, have done what they could to redress forms of discrimination Muslims may face.[85] He urges the Muslim community to note that Muslims are much better off living in the United States than in any Muslim country. In the Muslim world, day-to-day living is contingent on bribery, making it very difficult for a normal person to survive. As harmful as Islamophobia may be, Muslims are among the most successful immigrant communities. The trajectory of discrimination Muslims face in American history is consistent with every community's story in the United States. It is the story of initiation into the American tapestry.[86]

Yusuf considers the right to dissent as contingent on the context. In the same interview with Riz Khan, he states, "The right to dissent is a fundamental Western right ... Dissent is as American as apple pie."[87] This was during the Obama administration. However, as the situation seemingly became more volatile for Muslims with Donald Trump's presidency, Yusuf changed his tone. He argued that protests were more counterproductive and contrary to the metaphysical lens that Muslims ought to maintain.[88] Yahya Birt contends that Yusuf immensely softened his criticism against the US government after Donald Trump's election.[89] Following on from the metaphysical premise that the world is an abode of injustice, it is natural not to agree with this injustice; however, how you act upon this "dissent" is the marker of your metaphysical state. Yusuf states:

> One, keeping recognition that we have a metaphysical lens with which we look at the world, and always seeing God behind these things. God is in charge: Trump is a servant of God ('abd Allah), just like everyone else. He'll either serve with good or with evil, but he will serve God. And so it's important for us, as people who want and aspire to be servants of god, to be that good in the world so that other people can see that. I am a deep believer in *fiṭra*, in that principal nature of human beings. The *fiṭra* is good, and we should allow people, even the worst people, to change ... Criticism will not build a civilization; criticism tears down a civilization.[90]

After his election, according to Yusuf, Donald Trump's presidency proved to be a trial from God to test the community of believers. When it is unjust, the response to the political order is to see it as a form of tribulation and to try to build up and not break down.[91]

Knee-jerk activism, Yusuf argues, is a result of the influence the Left has had on Muslims. As Birt explains, Yusuf sees that the alliance with the Left was to the detriment of the conservative values of Muslims. Muslims have become unable to engage with their natural allies—the Right. Yusuf adds:

> One of our major problems right now is our inability to speak to the right. I think before 2001, we had a lot of Muslims who were registered Republicans ... That's no longer the case. Millennials have shifted incredibly towards the Left, so we don't have an ability to talk to them.[92]

Yusuf believes that the Left carries so much epistemological baggage that alienates Muslims from the true principles and ethical values of their tradition. The implicit assumption here is that because the Right has specific ideas on gender or secularism, it is closer to Islam and is, therefore, without this baggage. This assumption can, however, only be credibly made if coupled with an ideological ambivalence toward power structures and their impacts—as will be seen in the rest of the chapter. In this section, however, it suffices to pose the following questions. Can the Right be taken without its epistemological and historical baggage? Similarly, can the modern post-Sykes–Picot nation-state in the

Middle East represent the order in the cosmos without considering that it is the major agent of the violent modernization process in the Middle East? As I show in the final chapter, these are the questions that seekers navigate.

Black Lives Matter

For the seekers I interviewed, one of the most polarizing political positions Hamza Yusuf holds is his critique of the "Black Lives Matter" (BLM) movement—particularly in the Reviving Islamic Spirit conference (RIS) in 2016.[93] This section contextualizes his statements on BLM through his overall metaphysical approach to politics. Although his interview with Mehdi Hassan in the RIS first prompted the controversy, this was not the first time Yusuf has criticized the group. Yusuf first addressed the topic of the BLM in a joint lecture in September 2016 with the progressive Catholic intellectual John Sexton, moderated by Rev. Dr. Serene Jones.[94] The lecture topic was "The secular and the sacred in higher education."[95] Latif notes that Yusuf's critiques in the lecture were aimed at helping people overcome themselves so that they might not be consumed by anger and that "the secular voice too easily falls into the *demands* of justice."[96]

In the Q&A section of the lecture, Rev. Jones spoke briefly about the moral problem of mass incarceration and the role of faith in interjecting. Jones then turned to Hamza Yusuf and asked him about the role faith should play in upholding social justice. Yusuf prefaced his response by stating his base metaphysical claim. He explained that injustice has always been a fact of life. He then alluded to his critique of contemporary activism, stating, "There is a utopian fantasy of eradicating injustice." He explained the cycle of oppression among activists today, motivated by hatred, declaring:

> Someone who struggled with my mother in civil rights said at her funeral that we were motivated by a sense of hope, a sense of righteousness and indignation about these things but said ... there wasn't the kind of anger you're seeing today, and that is because of the absence of the sacred ... Nietzsche warned us [to be careful that] in fighting the monster one doesn't become the monster. This is often what happens in these movements. One of the tragedies is seeing a lot of reverse racism ... just from the Black Lives [Matter] movement, which is addressing a very important issue ... I don't think there is any society (and I have been all over the world) that is actively trying to overcome the historical wrongs of the past like this society. The

anti-discrimination laws that have been enacted in this country are unprecedented. If you want to see real racism, and I've lived in Africa and the Middle East, and I've been to Asia, you will find racism that has no redress to these wrongs. I think the fact that there was so many white people involved in the civil rights movement to redress these wrongs … I get the real problems a lot of white people have about white privilege and things. But we need to help people overcome from within themselves not from a place of anger but a place centered and rooted in a spiritual desire. It is the sacred voice that enables this, not the secular one, because the secular voice too easily falls for the demand of justice. We don't just need social justice. We need social mercy. We need a social mercy movement.

In this comment, Yusuf reaffirms his point that the basis of activism is to achieve a utopia. Conceiving a utopian world in its very essence contradicts the metaphysical view of the world—only heaven could be utopian, while this world will remain imperfect. Yusuf then critiques the Marxist basis on which this form of activism is based and legitimized. It allows for a discourse of anger to fester. He views the ontological value of anger in activism as turning the victims into victimizers. Yusuf finds that the discourse of privilege and the structural critiques of racism hinder intrapersonal attempts to forge a movement of mercy. Yusuf's metaphysical view of politics does not allow for structural critique, since structures represent order—even when they are imperfect.

This lecture only resurfaced as significant on YouTube after Yusuf's comments on Black Lives Matter in the RIS conference, or what was later known as "RISGate."[97] The controversy was prompted when Suhaib Webb, another Imam speaking at RIS, posted a comment on his Facebook page criticizing Yusuf for his comments about the BLM movement.[98] Although no one at this point had footage or a recording of what Hamza Yusuf had said, the internet was nonetheless highly polarized. A recording was released later that night. In a Q&A session with Mehdi Hassan, Yusuf was asked what he thought was the responsibility of Muslims in showing solidarity with justice movements such as the BLM movement. Yusuf made the following points. After 9/11, Muslims have become subsumed by their alliances with the Left and are now unable to even reach out to the Right. He reiterated that the United States has some of the best anti-discriminatory laws in the world. Instead of at external focus, the Muslim community should look within. Muslims need to tackle anti-Jewish rhetoric or Arab racism against South Asians. Before tackling the issue of white privilege, Muslims need to address the problem of Arab privilege in their communities.[99]

He then addressed the issue at hand—the Black Lives Matter movement itself. He explained:

> There is not a word in Arabic for racism, which I find fascinating. There are modern words, like *'unṣuriyya*, but these aren't real words in terms of classical seventh-century Arabic. One of the things that the Arabs understood was that they called it ignorance. It is *jahl*. And the beauty of identifying it as bigotry or ignorance is that ignorance is not essential to human beings. Accidents can be removed.

Yusuf then went on to cite statistics on the topic of police brutality and "Black-on-Black" crime to show it as the bigger problem. The BLM activists, Yusuf added, are mistaken in thinking that all police are racist. He contends that twice as many white people have been shot by the police as Black. He then mentioned that out of 15,000–18,000 homicides a year, 50 percent are Black-on-Black crime.

The recording stirred controversy on social media. Some were indignant, while others jumped to his defense, stating that they knew the shaykh was not a racist. The first group called for accountability, while the latter condemned the state of the community that did not give him the benefit of the doubt or *ḥusn dhann*. The next morning, Hamza Yusuf gave a speech to clarify his intention and to apologize to anyone he might have offended. In this speech, he made several important points central to his metaphysical view of politics. He prefaced it by stating that in his life, very few of his friends would fall into the category of "white." He had married an indigenous Mexican woman, and his surrogate father was African-American. The category of "white" to him was, therefore, merely descriptive—not ideological or political. He added:

> My point, and it was lost in translation, [was that] the biggest crisis facing the African American community in the United States is not racism; it is the breakdown of the Black family … To rebuild a family is very difficult. The Black Church had a role in maintaining the Black family, and religion is the only thing [maintaining it] … We have to be careful as a minority community not to fall into the agendas of other people. There are people in the United States who would like to see a race war who would like to

see violence in our communities ... We have anarchists who want to see a complete breakdown of society. If we fall into these people's agendas without knowing where they are coming from or what they are about, we would do what the Muslims have consistently done for a long time—being a pawn in other people's games.[100]

There are discernible themes in these statements consistent with Yusuf's political discourse. Yusuf highlights the tension between the metaphysical perspective, which recognizes the imperfection of the world, and the Marxist drive to create a utopia on earth. The activist drive has three implications. If the metaphysical perspective is marginalized, the world's objective reality becomes open to the relative and emotive experiences of people. The anger then traps young people in a cycle of self-perceived victimhood, keeping them from any sense of introspection. This finally propagates deep fragmentation and upheaval in society, which could almost be considered a race war. Hamza Yusuf conjures classical Arabic as a form of cosmic legitimation. Racism is ignorance; it is cosmically nonessential. This point informs an ideological (not an accidental) ambivalence regarding the role structural powers play in racism and fragmentation.

Consistent with his metaphysical perspective on the nature of the world, Yusuf prefaces any discussion on social justice with a cardinal truth about the nature of the world. It is an abode of injustice; it always has been and will always be. This metaphysical claim from the outset contextualizes how he views the positions of the political "other." This political "other" tends toward a left-wing, combative, anarchistic, and nihilistic philosophy, as opposed to his own, which is an ordered, harmonious one. According to Yusuf, people on the Left lack an understanding of the nature of the world, which leads them toward utopian tendencies. As he explains, the utopian fantasies of the Left are flawed for two main reasons. First, they seek to accord this world with what is meant for the heavens. Secondly, this utopia fundamentally reshapes how people identify. It constructs the categories of oppressor and oppressed. Instead of achieving a harmonious resolve, activists feed off an anger that will only reproduce cycles of bloodletting and injustice.[101]

In his first speech with Sexton, Yusuf describes how the politics of anger has today changed the pristine movement of the civil rights era. The sense of righteous indignation disappears in a cloud of anger. The BLM movement, like other left-wing activist movements, for Yusuf fashions an identity out of anger. In doing so, it breaks down the world into oppressor and oppressed. Those who were once oppressed become the oppressors. He adds that one of the tragedies of the BLM movement is that it now allows for much reverse racism. Its radical utopian (anarchist) activism becomes instrumental in fragmenting the order of the world. Muslims, Yusuf argues, need to take heed not to internalize these ideas nor be dragged into a "race war"—as the BLM movement would have them do and be.

Yusuf contends that the nature of racism ought to be understood differently from how left-wing activists conceive of it. He argues that there is no equivalent of "racism" in classical Arabic. The only Arabic equivalent is modern. Traditionally, racism was known as ignorance, and since ignorance was an accident it could be removed, whereas racism is a character description; if you call someone a racist, they are less likely to transcend that category. This enables activists to create a clear and unbridgeable gap between people. Yusuf's usage of classical Arabic as a form of cosmic legitimation reflects the role "tradition" plays in informing reality and politics, in extension. This again raises the question of traditional truth and universal, immutable metaphysical principles instead of experience dictating reality, thereby disembodying it. There are two levels of cosmic legitimation at play here. Such legitimation, firstly, contextualizes the limits and uses of racism as *jahl* in the cosmic order, the second level being the inherent destabilizing force of modern activism. The problem, therefore, needs to transcend individual or communal experience. As tradition diagnoses the problem, it could also, therefore, provide solutions to it.

Yusuf is attempting to discount from the contemporary understanding of racism, using classical Arabic as a form of cosmic legitimation, the element of power—institutionally or in the form of white privilege. The ambivalence of the overarching structural form of racism is in line with the metaphysical starting point. The power structures cannot be problematized to the point of deconstruction, even if they are unfair, for they maintain order. Yusuf goes a few steps further. The United States, he contends, has worked on redressing the wrongs of the past more than any other society in the world. He adds that it has some of the world's best anti-discrimination laws. From this perspective, if the system attempts to reform itself, dismantling it (as BLM and other left-wing activists would like) only brings more chaos and injustice. In contrast, he makes the point that in Africa, Asia, and the Middle East the, racism is much worse, with no redress. Yusuf here is reaffirming the ambivalence

146 | NEO-TRADITIONALISM IN ISLAM IN THE WEST

toward the power dynamics at work in the forms of racism in Africa, Asia, and the Middle East. Besides the point of sensitivity to nuances in discussing a wide range of places, Hamza Yusuf discounts colonial responsibility in forming legal systems in many postcolonial states or enshrining racist structures and ideas.

Discounting power dynamics, again, raises the question essential to his discourse. Who bears the burden of responsibility in maintaining cosmic order? In the past, Yusuf contends, the Black church and the family structure maintained the semblance of order and community for Black people. The fragmentation of the Church and family disoriented the Black community in many ways. The decline in the sacred, which maintained a semblance of order, is a moral and spiritual concern. As in the case of dissenters in Muslim majority countries, the individual and community's ambivalence to their spiritual states allowed for fragmentation in every way.

Yusuf contends that the loss of the sense of sacred gave way to the form of secular resistance predicated on anger alone. Some argued that Hamza Yusuf fundamentally misunderstood the structural reasons for the breakdown of the Black family.[102] However, structural critique is outside his scope in keeping with his political metaphysics. The burden of responsibility for the community's state of being again falls on itself. This could be deduced from the statistics Yusuf cited on the so-called problem of "Black-on-Black crime." The statistics also echoed the discourse of certain commentators on the Right, which raises the question (that will be dealt with in the next chapter) of the impact of the Right in forging the agendas and ideologies of the neo-traditionalists.

In this chapter, I have shown that Hamza Yusuf believes that political difficulties facing Muslims—both in the Muslim majority and minority context—ought to be seen through a metaphysical lens. He has argued that ideologies borne of modernity heralded a decline in the traditional metaphysical view of the world and its tribulations. In this view, believers understood their cosmic role and designation in times of tribulation and injustice: that is, to seek spiritual elevation and to show forbearance. I have noted that political stability in Yusuf's discourse is central to the order and equilibrium of the cosmos. I have also shown that Yusuf deploys tradition to mitigate structural critiques of power—which, he contends, have a modernist basis. I have demonstrated from pro-democracy activism after the Arab Spring to Black Lives Matter protests, Yusuf has stressed that modern political activism is both nihilistic and unproductive. In the next chapter, I examine how Abdal Hakim Murad and Umar Faruq Abd-Allah use metaphysics to make social and political interventions on race and gender. I will show that the wider metaphysical critiques present a view of tradition that shares the same concerns as those of the religious Right.

6

RACE, GENDER, AND BELONGING

Abdal Hakim Murad introduced his essay "On Migrating to Lands of Melancholy" in The Journal of Zaytuna College, *Renovatio*, by relaying verses from Matthew Arnold's "Dover Beach:"[1]

> Pebbles which the waves suck back, and fling,
> At their return, up the high strand,
> Begin, and cease, and then again begin
> With tremulous cadence slow, and bring
> The eternal note of sadness in.

The poem is a melancholic depiction of Christian England slowly losing its Christianity to the intrusive forces of "science and the critical study of scripture."[2] Murad goes on to add:

> Dover's shingled beach is still there, of course, but it has become, in our traumatized and unsteady twenty-first century, the site of a different and unexpected wave, this time of distressed refugee humanity ... It is an irony and a calamity of our times that ninety percent of those who complete this odyssey and stagger up the beach are Muslims. The great symbol of a departing Christianity seems to have become an emblem of an arriving but destitute Islam.[3]

Murad hence suggests a parable. The story begins with a Syrian refugee he calls Ishmael (an allegory of the Ishmaelite people or the Muslims) arriving on Dover Beach (an allegory of the fading Christendom). Ishmael—in contradistinction to the society he found himself in—is virile, confident in his masculinity, and plans to become a patriarch of a traditional family. On the other hand, Europe is facing a demographic collapse, an aging population, and needs a virile new principle. Murad goes on to add: "Our Ishmael is unlikely to admire the mean and brutal culture of abortions or the new hyper-liberal doctrines of gender plasticity that he will learn about beyond the cliffs; still less will he respect the fanatic modern assault on 'toxic masculinities'; he is not 'woke' and he is unlikely to become so."

Murad depicts a doleful post-Christian and postmodern Europe. With the glaring void left by the departing Christianity and the modernist hope of crypto-religions and failed utopias (such as Marxism), he adds: "The man of the future will be neither dynamically creative nor passively inactive; he will be a brilliant mediocrity constrained by an ontological negativity, a melancholia, a producer-consumer dimly but fatally conscious of the lost depth of the past and the flat horizon of the secular new."[4] If Ishmael can truly hold on to tradition—rather than be seduced by the grievance-based fundamentalism of Islamists—he can be a beacon, a rejuvenation of a theology of optimism in a dying Europe.

Murad concludes the essay with a note that for Muslim immigrants to truly embody a counter-liberal theology of optimism; immigrants must migrate with good intentions, that is, the intention of healing and forgiveness. To illustrate this, he cites a story in Sufi exegesis about Joseph and Potiphar's wife, Zuleikha:

> In the old Muslim stories, Potiphar's wife Zuleikha seeks to tempt Joseph, but through his self-mastery, he finally converts and marries her, and their fruitful union revives all of Egypt, and this he has only been able to achieve by finding the strength to forgive her sexual harassment and continuing to value the wounded humanity that always lay beneath. Hating the seducer— whether it be an alien world or the world in its worldliness—is a frequent theme of modern Islamism, but it is foreign to Ishmael's best inheritance.

This parable illustrates forgiveness as a higher moral and ideal. For that purpose, Murad invokes the claim—highly disputed in Islamic sources—that Joseph forgave and married Potiphar's wife Zuleikha.

This chapter examines many of the themes analyzed in the previous chapter, namely how the neo-traditionalist shaykhs conceive of a metaphysically sound social and political life. Considering the scholarship and discourse of

Abdal Hakim Murad and Umar Faruq Abd-Allah on race, belonging, and gender, this chapter explores the issues they deem pertinent to the development of Islam in the West. To them, the foremost impediments to developing an indigenous Islam that is both orthodox and spiritually sound are religious attitudes born out of a lack of a metaphysical perspective. This chapter deals with the cosmic legitimations Umar Faruq Abd-Allah and Abdal Hakim Murad make. That is to say: in a sense, this chapter will explore how they link metaphysical positions to social phenomena, thereby producing a metaphysically sound social and political perspective. They illustrate a postmodern dystopia in the West, whereby the loss of the sacred begot a loss in aesthetics and beauty and left Western civilization thoroughly secularized and adrift. As such, they seek to culturally reframe Muslim presence in the West away from the baggage of the postcolonial religion of immigrant Islam. Also, moving away from the left-wing formulation of identity politics, the shaykhs contend that Muslims' real concerns are moral, much like those faced by Christian and Jewish believers in the West. In doing so, they highlight the concerns these believers have regarding the loss of traditional values, particularly changing gender dynamics.

Locating Islam in a Post-Christian Story

In the spring of 2017, Umar Faruq Abd-Allah convened a "Foundations of an Islamic Worldview" class at Bayan Claremont Islamic College.[5] The class aimed at synthesizing the metaphysical, legal, and ethical dimensions of the faith with Muslim life in the modern world. The syllabus included the works of Christian theologian William Craig, Christian scientist and philosopher Robert T. Pennock, Catholic, Perennialist metaphysician and mathematician Wolfgang Smith, and conservative scholar Richard Weaver as primary required reading. Abd-Allah often-times begins his critiques of modernity by citing the works of Wolfgang Smith and Richard Weaver. Weaver, in particular, critiques the implications of the modern condition. In class, seekers study chapters from his magnum opus *Ideas Have Consequences*.

From the outset of the book, Weaver cautions the readers, "This is another book about the dissolution of the West."[6] Indeed, Weaver conveys the conservative anxieties dominant in the aftermath of the Second World War regarding the "civilizational crisis" facing the West. This, he notes, began with the rise of nominalism in Christendom. In fact, Hamza Yusuf's polemics against nominalism appears to be derived from Weaver's (and other Catholic conservatives') narrative on nominalism and modernity.[7] Weaver explains that nominalism inadvertently led to the decline of a source of a higher truth independent of man and his experience.[8] He mourns the loss of universals and the ideals they represented, such as nobility and chivalry: the romantic conservative lost causes. Samuel Goldman explains that the book promoted a discussion among conservatives as to whether "the catastrophes of the twentieth century—including the world wars, the rise of communism, and the Holocaust—had been permitted, or even caused, by the corruption of aesthetics, epistemology, theology, and political theory." The decline in the metaphysical arrangement of the traditional worldview with modernity's advent instigated not only cultural decadence and loss of meaning, but horrific wars as well.

Weaver presents a moral, traditional critique of modernity. Modern man has lost the knowledge of his forefathers. The subsequent triumph of relativism over the world based on metaphysical universals is the root cause of degradation.[9] This epistemic anarchy is consequently predicated on eradicating what he calls the "metaphysical dream." A metaphysical dream is a form of unrefined intuition that amalgamates all ideas and beliefs to provide context and meaning to the world. The metaphysical dream, in the past, was organized and ordered around the universal conception of truth. The decline of intrinsic universal principles has normalized debauchery in society and caused moral decay. This, furthermore, has been represented in the decline of social hierarchies and distinction—leading to a fragmentation of order.[10] Essentially, social forms like family and relationships become a liability in a relativistic world where the individual is the measure of all things.[11] This collapse heralded the collapse of higher ideals of nobility. Weaver argues that as long as the West could hold on (as in the past) to a gentleman class, there was some protection for the transmission of tradition and culture. If their ideal was imperfect and not always realized, the very existence of such a class as an ideal outweighed any of its disadvantages.[12]

Weaver was, in fact, a pioneering, albeit by no means a lonely, voice, cautioning society from the impending "civilizational crisis" in the West. The "civilizational crisis" genre emerging after the Second World War—that mourned the loss of aesthetics along with traditional ideals—proceeded from the white crisis genre of 1890–1930.[13] White crisis literature was concerned primarily with the "lower races" overtaking white society. Alastair Bonnett noted that despite the prevalence of white crisis literature before the 1930s, white solidarity was an intrinsically fragile formulation. Civilization did not belong to all whites; it was the domain of the cultured few or the elite.[14] After the Second World War, Bonnet argues, "The idea of the West did far more than simply erase the embarrassment of race. More specifically, it could evoke a set of political principles and values that could be both cosmopolitan and subtly ethnocentric, potentially open to all but rooted in the experiences and expectations of narrow social strata."[15]

While the idea of civilizational crisis did not just emerge from the literature on the white crisis, they overlap in many ways and convey similar anxieties about the dissolution of a world order restrained by hierarchy. Cory Robin argues that the primary preservation instinct of the conservative movement, which laments a loss of distinction, is, in fact, to mourn a loss of power. This is born out of a belief that the social order, with its established hierarchies, maintained a sense of harmony. In turn, the revolutionary unsettling that came out of different emancipatory movements, from anti-colonial movements to civil rights and feminist movements, caused a radical unsettling and subsequent decline in beauty, harmony, and aesthetics.[16]

For Richard Weaver, the higher ideals, arranging the metaphysical dream, existed because the world, prior to modernity, understood the importance of distinction and hierarchy. Here one can trace a parallel defense of forms of aristocracy and a critique of democracy present in Traditionalist metaphysics.[17] In his metaphysical dream, Weaver argues that the good man, the man of virtue, recognizes and trusts "natural" authorities.[18] These authorities are natural in that they intrinsically maintain the orientation of the cosmos. He explains that the process of social and hierarchical disintegration, beginning in the fourteenth century with the Renaissance and culminating in the nineteenth century, decentered the cosmos from transcendence. This process has culminated in modernity with the rise of socialism.[19] He explains:

> The consumer has the power to destroy utterly that metaphysical structure supporting hierarchy. Let us remember that traditional society was organized around king and priest, soldier and poet, peasant and artisan. Now distinctions of vocation fade out, and the new organization, if such it may be termed, is to be around capacity to consume.[20]

The distinctions removed are not just classist or vocational; the distinction between genders, too, withers. With calls for gender equality, the hierarchy of the family disintegrates. With the withering away of the "gentleman," the conception of the "lady" too had to go. In losing their metaphysical positioning as "ladies," women lost the structures that protected them. The repercussions of this are twofold. Firstly, this bid for equality destroys the family unit. Secondly, the removal of distinction between the sexes in role, conduct, and dress only initiates women into the drab realities of modernity in which men now reside.[21] Weaver's whole system of cosmic legitimations is based on a single epistemological claim: in modernity, truth is predicated on individuals' respective experiences (often emotive), whereas prior to modernity it had been based on universals and truth. That was the metaphysical dream.[22]

Abdal Hakim Murad: Post-Christian angst

Likewise, Abdal Hakim Murad posits that for Muslim life to flourish in the West, it needs to redirect its focus. The story of Islam in Britain, Murad contends, is too often told from the vantage of the "race relations" paradigm, which assumed a "generic whiteness" to be axiomatic. The story is thus more complicated when one accounts for religion rather than race. He explains:

> Understanding the journey British Muslims have made from the 1950s and earlier, to the current decade, cannot properly be attempted unless we recall that British religiosity and the value system it supported have changed almost beyond recognition. At the beginning of this period, Muslims found themselves in a largely churchgoing society ruled by Mrs Miniver, where queers were in the closet and nice girls said no.[23]

Murad's depiction of an idyllic churchgoing society in 1950s Britain affirms not only the orthodox practice of conservative believers but also the cosmic link it produced in terms of wider morality. This morality, that restrained and restricted society, furthermore created the social mores around the traditional structure of a family and sexual politics. As a result, Murad depicts a form of harmony or symmetry between a Christian Britain and the values of Muslim immigrants.

For Abdal Hakim Murad, the problem begins with the framing of the context. Although the realities of Islamophobia make the lived experience of Muslims harder, the more fundamental problem is the deconstruction of the sacred in modernity and its complete collapse with postmodernity. This is a reality Muslims share with Christians and other believers. The decline in religion, and consequently metaphysics, left people searching for certainty. Postmodernity has dissipated the ancient "mind–body–spirit" equilibrium, allowing only the body to reign supreme. As a result, he notes, "we inhabit an age preoccupied by tattoos and cosmetic surgery, of dieting and fat-shaming." He goes on to add:

> Craving certainties and codes to define in- and out-groups, and lacking the possibility of metaphysics, late modern society is turning the body into a credal object, so that entire human identities seem to radiate from it. Some of the more recent body beliefs are handily weaponized by identitarian social justice warriors in order to demonise traditional religious groupings in society, which are often unsure how to respond.[24]

This dissipation of traditional sources of certainty, which leads people to alternative forms of false certainty based on the body, not spirit, produced the sexual politics of the day. For example, Murad laments, "In 2014, Facebook offered new users the choice of fifty different genders."[25]

Murad explains that when the first waves of migrating Muslims landed in the UK, they found themselves in a society that was mostly Christian and where most people still went to church. The cultural values and institutions that existed in the country reflected that very belief in God. Slowly, as they withered, so did the meanings they entailed. Postmodernity had no conception of a fixed essence. Essential meanings of gender or monarchy, for example, were secularized and reduced to a form of materialist functionalism. The Church itself has been transformed into the secular angst to manage pluralism. Murad contends that even the liturgy cannot assume a religious commitment on the part of the bereaved, so prayers have become generic. The deconstruction of essences (or essential metaphysical principles) is only possible when Truth[26] is no longer a concern. It is no surprise with postmodernity and the devolution of essential meanings, Murad argues, that researchers were more concerned with framing the presence of Muslims within the older paradigm of the study of "race relations" than with the backdrop of the decline of religiosity and value systems in Britain.

The structures that governed, restrained, and restricted society (in Western Christendom) have disappeared with the departure of ontology, metaphysics, and ethics.[27] This was a direct result of the disintegration of religious and imperial narratives. With the amplified concern over identity in modernity, so confusion over meaning is amplified too. These cosmic legitimations have become secularized to a degree where the link between this world and the cosmos can no longer be seen as it was in the past. Most symptomatic of this void is that the art that once indicated some metaphysical meaning or essential truth is now being replaced by meaningless modern art. Truth, meaning, symmetry, and beauty are all replaced with confusion and relativism.[28] Murad explains that naturally, "Europeans feel disempowered by impersonal global forces, and denuded of meaning and context by the new digital and multicultural environment."[29] Building bridges that seek to understand and validate this angst, for Murad, is thereby more productive than activism based on negation.

Still, Europe must contend with its historical chauvinism if it seeks to transcend its postmodern malaise. Murad explains that many of the current roots of Islamophobia lie in the cultural jealousy of a secularized Europe regarding the self-confidence Islam seems to exhibit over gender identity and the desire to continue traditional family life.[30] This chauvinism is now denoted as Islamophobia in an effort to racialize bigotry. Murad explains that, rather than "importing baggage from older race-relations paradigms for polemical purposes" by defining Islamophobia as a "type of racism," Islamophobia ought to be defined as "an emotive dislike of the Islamic religion as a whole, rather than of its extreme interpretations; or rather, we might more usefully define it as the assumption that extremes and aberrations favoured by some Muslim adherents have normative status."[31] Murad noted that when Islamophobia is defined as a type of racism, the definition seeks to exclude white Muslims. Furthermore, the racism narrative is complicated by the additional fact that racially-marked individuals—such as the Somali-born Ayaan Hirsi Ali—often promote vitriolic Islamophobia.[32]

Instead, Murad encourages interlocutors to adopt another "more indigenously Islamic term" to denote Islamophobia: Lahabism.[33] By Lahabism, Murad alludes to a framework of hate based on the Prophet's paternal uncle Abū Lahab. Initially, Murad notes, Abū Lahab had promised the community of believers protection under tribal honor codes, but was angered by their increasing numbers.[34] Like Yusuf, Murad posits a less "ideological" definition of this form of bigotry. Power dynamics aside, he contends that Lahabism is a sin—the greatest of the seven deadly sins—for it reflects a form of arrogance at its heart.[35] From the outset, religious normativity plays a central role in how he argues for the pushback against Islamophobia. Thereby, the political problem of Islamophobia could be rectified with a normative theological response. The racial and cultural elements are marginal to the question of religion in the metaphysical and not the theological sense. This entails a political approach that is both in harmony with an Islamic prescription on how to act in times of *fitna* and would, also, reflect a conception of Islamic subjectivity.

Murad posits that by resolving the question of identity, Muslims can lead a positive life in Europe. The Muslims' forms of belonging, as Christopher Pooya Razavian notes, see Islam as a "natural progression" or extension of British values.[36] As Murad explains:

> My own belief is that the future prosperity of the Anglo-Muslim movement will be determined largely by our ability to answer this question of identity … Our thinking about our own position as British Muslims should focus on that fact and quietly but firmly ignore the protests both of the totalitarian fringe and of the importers of other regional cultures, such as that of Pakistan, which they regard as the only legitimate Islamic ideal.[37]

Murad's vision of a British Islam puts itself in opposition to the cultural particularities of immigrant Islam. His reading of Islam's universalism makes it the most suitable faith for Britain, as "its values are our values."[38] The contrast here is between the Pakistani cultural particularity, which breeds extremism and exclusion, and British universality in its traditional form, which is tempered and moral. This reading of postcolonial Islam, as too culturally and politically burdened and unable to develop mechanisms for acclimatization in British society, naturally renders it unfit to find adequate solutions to Islamophobia.

Murad claims that the postcolonial Muslims who migrated to Britain, particularly from South Asia, on the precipice of the breakdown of the British empire did not come with the intention of seeking God's favor. Instead, Murad argues, they came seeking the *dunyā* (the material world). These migrants, he argues, came and stayed with materialistic and pragmatic intentions—namely "the continuing economic failure of their countries of origin, usually resulting from secular or carceral-Islamist mismanagement."[39] They did not consider the *Sharīʿa* implications of their migration. He continues:

> "This defect of intention (*niyya*) is one reason why the second and third generations, to whose spiritual and moral formation the first generation gave no careful thought, now often manifest ugly and growing dysfunctions, including tone recruitment, drug addiction, the predatory grooming of underage girls, and large-scale criminalization. The older generation threw their babies into the melting-pot, hoping for the best, and failed to give their growing children a theology of belonging, with the result that the youth were not securely established in a consistent cognitive frame or an attendant compre-

hensive morality. As their misfortune unfolded, the ambient society either ignored them, queried their presence, or treated them according to social science paradigms rooted in the incongruous "race relations" philosophy. An Islam whose articulation belonged overseas proved only weakly capable of claiming the deep loyalty of a new generation Europeanized by the schools and confused about its identity. In Britain the Dār al-ʿUlūm seminaries, mostly determined to replicate Indic scholarly and cultural forms, tended to produce graduates who are, as the sceptics claim, "mango trees planted in Lancashire."[40]

Murad makes a similar critique of North African immigrants in France. "Most Muslims in France," he argues,

> migrated in order to eat more tagine or to seek a EU passport, but this, in Sharia terms, did not usually comprise a good reason for *hijra*. "Whoever's migration is for some worldly thing, or to marry a woman, then his migration is accordingly for that." As we have already observed, those who were led by such an intention are likely to find themselves watching their children being ensnared and stressed even more intensely than they themselves are by possessions and desires. Their intention must now be consciously and decisively changed to embrace what is usually the only real Sharia legitimation for leaving their ancestral hearth: the summons to al-Raḥmān.[41]

While Murad reserves somber respect for the reactions born of the post-Christian angst and presents it as axiomatic and universal, he has less sympathy for the postcolonial story. The story of postcolonial migration becomes a cautionary tale of materialism and greed, rather than survival. The post-Christian story, paradoxically, is relieved of its imperial blunders, seemingly an accident of its history rather than its core.

Although the problem with immigrant Muslims, according to Murad, began with a deficiency in intention, this was not the only problem. Murad adds:

> Many migrant-origin Muslims have roots in weakly-educated cultures, their imams and community leaders having little acquaintance with the higher discourse of classical Islamic scholarship; they suffer likewise from a poor understanding of the European environment and the immensely complex promises and threats which it presents. Many opportunities for entrenchment and growth have been lost due to this twofold incapacity.[42]

As a result, their children, who are the inheritors of the postcolonial religion, second- and third-generation Muslims, internalized a left-wing framework reducing Islam to a racial identity. Islamists, Murad argues, were the first to initiate Muslims into a leftist framework. They reduced religion to a vocabulary to fit into their framework for identity. The victimhood paradigm overstated the boundary between the self and the "other." This amplified sense of self derived meaning from a historical sense of wrong or anger. This resulted in a "steady draining-away of religiously-inspired assumptions concerning the universality of notions of honour and decency."[43] By this, he is referring to essential universals in the traditional metaphysical arrangement of the cosmos no longer recognized in modernity.

The external pressure on the community alongside the political prevalence of leftist and Islamist conceptions of the self, Murad argues, has disoriented the Muslim subject from their position in the cosmic frame. Murad explains that in the "traditional, indigenous understanding of how sharī'a should be," there is no equivalence to the concept of identity.[44] Murad points out that since "identity" is essentially a modern imposition, an increased focus on it as a category comes from the withering away of the traditional order. He explains, "We are all so atomized by modern consumerism, individualism, and menu of endless choices we have become insecure, rootless. We are no longer confident about who we are, what we are, who our neighbors might be. Everything now is a matter of choice."[45] The root of the problem for Muslims, like non-Muslims in the West, is that the traditional semblance of order no longer exists. Modernity has created a paradox. It fragments meaning inherent in the position of all things, including the human subject, by disrupting its metaphysical link between the world and transcendence.[46] Essential meanings are fragmented, and people are given the power to construct their personal meanings, but this paradoxically leaves them not knowing who they are or where they are.

Murad explains that Muslims have been subsumed in an "atmosphere of grievance and complaint."[47] This has partly been in response to the increased hostility of Western governments and Islamophobes. Still, more importantly, these responses were shaped by the encroachment of Islamist and left-wing ideologies. Murad contends:

> The race relations industry has a language that we have internalized in our own community, so that we may play the game of identity politics. The

basic sense of ourselves, the core of ourselves, is that we are historical, under-
estimated, put upon, aggrieved, and we need to get our own back so we
can claim our place in the sun. The civil rights in America is an example (of
success). It's rooted in this idea that communities have at the core of their
identity a sense that historic wrongs have been done to them. I think that's a
dangerous basis for a religious community and I don't find it in the Qur'ān
and the *sunna*.[48]

As Yusuf pointed out, fashioning a political ideology out of a sense of grievance or victimhood represents a fundamental misunderstanding of the metaphysical purpose of the world. Murad further outlines that this ideological
rearrangement of the Muslim subject only amplifies his sense of alienation.
In this case, following the example of the civil rights movement and the "race
relations" industry, Muslims internalized a language alien to their religious
worldview. This condemned them to construct a faux reality. Murad suggests
that the whole raison d'être of Islam is to deconstruct identity politics. He
likens the notion of "victimhood"—in this formation of identity politics—to
tribal vengeance in pre-Islamic *jāhiliyya*.[49]

Murad posits a dual authenticity paradigm to resolve the problem of Islam
in Britain—a traditional Islamic authenticity and a European authenticity.
Traditional Islam is thus theorized in contradistinction to the authenticity
of "identity politics"—a term racially coded to indicate non-white identity
politics—and Islamism. He therefore contends that traditional Islam opposes
identity-religion, which is inherently egoist and a declining reference to transcendence (meaning secularity).[50] This authenticity is aesthetically grounded
and prioritizes beauty instead of the Islamist other. He adds: "Yet if the soul
has been misshaped by the ideologies of the Fearful it will disclose only ugli-
ness: the disorder of a self wracked by stress, disharmony and ill-controlled
desires (*ahwā'*) ... Nothing is more subversive and obstructive of God's cause
than offering an ugly manifestation of the self and claiming it to be Islamic.[51]
He notes that in the postcolonial Arab dystopias, for example, there has been
a decline in music therapy and the *maqāmāt* tradition, whereas in Turkey
the culture of sacred music continues to thrive. This, he notes, is "one of the
several reasons for the lack of rage-based radicalism in Turkey."[52]

Murad urges Muslims to adopt the second mode of authenticity, a form
of European authenticity. To live faithfully as Muslims committed to *da'wa*
in Europe, the immigrant community must shed its cultural traditions. He

contends: "Amsterdam Muslims who wear Indonesian apparel, eat Indonesian food and maintain an Indonesian outlook, cannot expect to spread their faith to their neighbours, who naturally will not be enabled to envisage how Islam might be for Dutch people."[53] Furthermore, Muslims need to master the languages of Europe. He adds:

> Mawlids and other literatures are frequently composed in the vernacular, and as they appear in European languages they will ennoble them and give Islam a voice that vindicates it as a universal rather than a foreign faith. When the majesty of Muslim monotheism and the beauty of its narratives appear in worthy English, or French, or Danish verse and prose, the defences of anti-immigrant zealots and "counter-jihad" protestors will be crucially enfeebled.[54]

In the post-Christian context, Muslims should engage the dissident voices from within modernity and reflect on their state. In one of his most popular online lectures, *Riding the Tiger of Modernity*, Murad introduces the Italian fascist metaphysician Julius Evola. He contends that most Muslims, who have little knowledge about modernity, let alone the dissident voices opposing it, would not know Evola or the school of thought he comes from. Murad explains that although Evola's legacy is taken up solely by xenophobes, many Muslims could benefit from him.[55] Evola's intervention meant to pose for Muslims inhabiting modernity an approach to the question of how to dissent against the modern world. As Evola's subtitle suggests, Murad asks if Muslims represent "aristocrats of the soul." Murad clarified this as follows:

> He [Evola] believed, drawing on what he called along with Guenonians[56] tradition capital T that we inhabit some sort of cosmic endgame, that the signs of the hour are upon us ... The current breakdown of tradition, monarchy, order, natural hierarchy, and a sense of the sacred is an inevitable end predicted presaging of the last days, the *turba magna* ... So this is the dark age; the age of iron, the age of dissolution of hierarchy, family, of priesthood, of the sacred, pilgrimage ... all the things that historically shaped and defined the guiding priorities of normative humanity. We are according to Evola now inhabiting that age of darkness.[57]

Inspired by René Guénon's critique of the disorder brought on by liberal democracy, Evola's metaphysical view imagined an ordered, meaningful, and layered cosmos. Prior to modernity's rupture, the innate metaphysical principles positioned everyone in their appropriate place. So "race," "gender," and "class" all meant something deeper. Like others of his time, Evola was concerned by the hegemony that science had in meaning formation and reconstructed metaphysical alternatives.

Evola's metaphysical standpoint, Murad accepts, could be seen as inimical to a Muslim worldview. He adds that, despite accepting certain aspects of the race theory of his time, Evola can at least represent a "pause for thought" for Muslims in how to dissent against modernity from within modernity.[58] Murad was quite modest in his depiction of Julius Evola. In his time, Evola was deemed too "radical" even for Mussolini's Fascist party. Subsequently, he traveled to Germany, where he lectured to the SS.[59] In his philosophy, metaphysics replaced fascist pseudo-sciences in outlining racial and sexual categories and hierarchies. For Evola, the racial distinction had an esoteric and metaphysical meaning and positioning. "Evola described a metaphysical Aryo-Vedic tradition that allegedly governed the religious and political institutions of archaic Indo-European societies. He traced the accretion of golden age myths relating polar symbolism and the Arctic origin of the white Aryan race through ancient Indian, Iranian, Greek and Amerindian texts."[60] Many fascists in Italy were not convinced of his metaphysical essentialisms. He, in turn, said the Italians were not ready for fascism.[61]

In this lecture, Murad amplifies the tension in modernity. Essences and the institutional coordinates they entailed in modernity have been stripped of their meanings. This is a reality, Murad explains, that Muslims share with Christians as well as with other believers. Evola represents a form of dissent from within modernity. Unlike the Muslim dissent, which is exemplified by their discourse on identity, this dissent reflects a concern for something larger and more intrinsic. It is a concern for meaning. That said, Murad concludes that Evola's response to modernity's metaphysical crisis is not one Muslims should seek to emulate. "Riding the tiger of modernity" implies that one can tame modernity by engaging it. He gives the example of Islamic finance as a Muslim attempt to tame the tiger of modernity, which is not much different from other forms of modern financial transactions. In the *turba magna*,[62] he concludes that Muslims should reflect on a principle from the Naqshbandi Sufi order—*Khilwat dar anjuman*.[63] This means solitude in the crowd; inhabiting the modern world without taking on its base assumptions.

This post-Christian narrative contends that Islam reflects the true traditional essence of the West left vacant by modernity. This narrative fixates on the shared values and meanings deconstructed by modernity. It is the same concern as is shared by conservative believers. By positioning Muslims in this narrative and giving them the same access and a vested interest in the traditional story of the great British past, Muslims can then be unburdened by the postcolonial story and its baggage. They can then privilege the shared morality over political activism and even develop a vested interest in the notions of order, hierarchy, aristocracy, and distinction in the traditional story of the West. As Kate Zebiri notes, "Abdal-Hakim Murad has expressed the view that Muslims should seek to make alliances not with the left wing, whose social policies may conflict with Islamic teachings, but with those who are more socially conservative and religiously inclined such as orthodox Jews or traditional Catholics."[64]

Murad presents an attitude both of accommodation and subversion. On the one hand, he commends Muslims to be polite "guests" in their "host" countries.[65] On the other, he argues for a synchronistic reading of the Islamic narrative through the wider post-Christian context. For example, Kate Zebiri notes that he goes further than most Islamic figures in the UK to harmonize a sense of British nationalism with Islam—even using, at times, esoteric Christian themes to explain the harmony between Islamic identity and an English one.[66] Murad has actively worked to revive British Muslim heritage, such as reviving the traditional English songs composed by the nineteenth-century English convert Abdullah Quilliam, sung at times as Anglican hymns.[67] Murad is giving Muslims access to the traditional Western story, and consequently to its anxieties about what it had lost from its traditional values in terms of its esteem, prestige, and power. This new story also decouples Muslims from postcolonial baggage by privatizing the system of belonging. The religious-political need for Pan-Islamic *ummah* solidarity is trumped by the need to develop British Muslim communities.[68]

One of the success stories of this *alliance sacrée* (or sacred alliance of conservative believers) is the conversion of Joram Van Klaveren. Van Klaveren was a senior politician in the far-right Dutch nationalist Party for Freedom who converted to Islam after corresponding with Abdal Hakim Murad.[69] In 2019, he published his book *Apostate: From Christianity to Islam in Times of Secularisation and Terror*, about his conversion, with forewords by both Hamza Yusuf and Abdal Hakim Murad. In this book, Van Klaveren seems to weave a neo-traditionalist critique of modernity, an affirmation of the tradition through *fiqh*, *'aqīda*, *and taṣawwuf*, and still his suspicions about Muslim immigrant communities and claims of Islamophobia. In the book he points out: "Recently, it turned out that Kuwait is spending millions on the financing of certain mosques in the Netherlands, while in Amsterdam extremist committees manage nearly half of all Moroccan mosques."[70]

According to Van Klaveren, this resulted from the prevalence of Wahhabism in Europe.[71] By contrast, traditional Islam is associated with conservative values in post-Christian Europe. He relates:

> In an exceptional dialogue between British conservative Sir Roger Scruton and Shaykh Hamza Yusuf, the kinship between traditional Islam and conservatism (in line with Edmund Burke) becomes clear. What affected me in my research in this regard was the analysis that both visions carried within them a theoretical aversion to "modern blueprint ideologists" who have immersed themselves in the concept of the malleability of society and the postmodern notion that Truth does not exist.[72]

His engagement with Yusuf and Murad—in which they validated and shared his anxieties over the atomization of meaning—prompted his conversion.

Umar Faruq Abd-Allah: Islam and the Cultural Imperative

Umar Faruq Abd-Allah, in his essay "Islam and the Cultural Imperative," likens Islam to a river whose water is clear, sweet, pure, and life-giving. The water is colorless and neutral but reflects the culture in which it is found.[73] For example, he mentions that Islam in China was Chinese but in Mali was African. He explains, "Islam does not merely encourage but requires the creation of a successful indigenous Islamic culture in America and sets down sound parameters for its formation and growth."[74] Abd-Allah's discourse of indigeneity—at least on a discursive level—is culturally pluralistic. To be indigenous is to have a sense of true belonging. He adds, "Islam in America becomes indigenous by fashioning an integrated cultural identity that is comfortable with itself and functions naturally in the world around it."[75]

In her ethnographic study of Abd-Allah's students in Chicago, Justine Howe notes that this discourse of indigeneity is racially coded. As one of the seekers explained to Howe, "many other immigrant imams often impose the cultural values of their ethnicity or of where they are from. Dr. Umar is there to tell us that it's ok if your pants aren't above your ankles and it's ok that you shake hands. It's the cultural norm here; it's inappropriate if you don't."[76] Howe explains that Abd-Allah, via his "unmarked racial identity," represents "a universal American culture free from the constraints of race and ethnicity."[77]

For Murad and Abd-Allah, rooting Islam in the West requires an assessment of the historical baggage and subjectivities developed due to the postcolonial religion, including how Muslims self-define in the age of Islamophobia. In contradistinction, Abd-Allah posits that the cultural imperative of Islam is to produce harmony and continuity.[78] For the shaykhs, Islam should read its story within its Western context and address its problems from that perspective.

The tension between ideological visions of Islam and a metaphysical one is therefore reflected in the conception of culture and subjectivity. Umar Faruq Abd-Allah argues that the main problem with the conception of Muslim identity in the West is based on Islamist premises. It is ideologically combative and ultimately devolves to what he calls a "culturally predatory" outlook. The Islamist worldview, Abd-Allah contends, is based on a form of negative politics. It cannot comfortably have a location or embrace cultural norms. This has been the main hindrance to the development of Islam in the United States and Europe. Therefore, the project to root Islam indigenously ought to be a conscious project.

Abd-Allah goes on to explain that the purpose of any culture, Islamic or not, is to ensure stability and harmony. He explains, "Culture—Islamic or otherwise—provides the basis of social stability but, paradoxically, can itself only flourish in stable societies and will inevitably break down in the confusion of social disruption and turmoil."[79] Political instability, he contends, will result in cultural decline. Cultural harmony is disrupted when traditional continuity is ruptured. For example, Abd-Allah explains that in the Muslim world, the rupture of tradition and instability caused a fundamental cultural decline. People in these societies can no longer comprehend the hidden wisdom in what little remnants of traditional culture survive. With the rupture of traditional wisdom and political instability, Muslims no longer have access to wisdom in the older cultural forms.[80]

The cultural problems Muslims face in Muslim majority countries and the West result from the Islamist framework of cultural objectification and reduction. Abd-Allah defines Islamism in terms of "highly politicized twentieth-century revivalist movements with essentialist interpretations of Islam, generally advocating particular state and party ends as Islam's chief or virtually unique focus."[81] Islamists essentially take the cultural outputs of modernity as epistemically neutral, and they therefore inadvertently accept their underpinnings and expectations. As was shown in the previous chapter, Abd-Allah and the neo-traditionalists contend that the Islamists have internalized Marxist frameworks in constructing their ideology. Like the Maoists, their call for unity eventually degenerates into a culturally predatory program for uniformity.[82] This crushes indigenous cultural forms and positions a specific cultural form as inherently superior. In the case of Islam, this is often a form of Arab superiority. Abd-Allah then argues that to be Muslim, you do not need to be a cultural "apostate" or be subservient to the Arab culture.[83]

The Islamist framework creates a cultural understanding alien to the Islamic tradition. Abd-Allah juxtaposes an Islamic "ancient cultural wisdom" with the modernist Islamist rhetoric.[84] He argues that a "Western revolutionary dialectic has heavily influenced the Islamists." They reinterpreted the corpus of religious scriptural texts to fit within that framework. This has instigated the "instability" that caused the present cultural decline in the Muslim world. In the West, their insecurity about being a minority, supplemented with ignorance of the "dominant" culture, only amplified the politicized reading of their context. The Islamists then conjured their "selective" and combative reading of the religious tradition and presented it as an Islamic framework.[85] The Muslim identity, therefore, becomes a mere negation of the dominant culture.[86] This negation can only exist when the boundary of the self is marked and defined in opposition to the other. This self–other dichotomy is predatory, in that it believes it must eliminate the other, so it can never foster an environment of belonging to the Muslim subject.

Curing the cultural ailments caused by the Islamist framework requires a metaphysical and practical response. A cultural framework, Abd-Allah explains, cannot be constructed if it does not create an environment of continuity of cultural and traditional practices. This requires it to be rooted in transcendental Islamic values and to have an understanding of the universal Islamic values or first metaphysical principles.[87] In practice, the mosque would become a sacred American space in harmony with an indigenous ethos and normative aesthetic sense.[88] Political stability only reflects internal spiritual stability and consistency. Therefore, metaphysics and the knowledge of the transcendental center is essential for harmonizing reality in any given context.

Abd-Allah contends that in the West, different Muslim groups, including culturally predatory ones, compete over cultural production. For that reason, constructing an indigenous Muslim culture in the West needs to be consciously directed. He explains that this is essentially the raison d'être of neo-traditionalist discursive spaces, as seen in Zaytuna College or the Ta'leef collective.[89] These institutions create a truly indigenous American space where

Muslims belong regardless of their cultural backgrounds. Unlike the Islamist framework that inadvertently became subsumed into an alien framework, this cultural production needs to be intentional, with a concrete vision. He explains: "We [Muslims in the West] are inundated by language, symbols, ideas, and technology, none of which is neutral. We must define where we stand with regard to them and adopt appropriate intellectual and behavioral responses."[90] This could only be done by recognizing the traditional Islamic wisdom that can deconstruct the Islamist paranoia.[91] It is important to note that, consistent with neo-traditionalist political metaphysics, the discussion on the forging of Islamic identity is ambivalent as regards the question of power.[92]

Metaphysics of Gender

In the late 1940s, the conservative thinker Richard Weaver reflected on the changing role of women. He pondered: "With her superior closeness to nature ... how was she ever cozened into the mistake of going modern? Perhaps it was the decay of chivalry in men that proved too much."[93] Weaver describes an age in which the bid for female equality effectively masculinized women.[94] The moral order before the Second World War had an arrangement whereby the metaphysical place of the sexes was reflected in their material gender roles. This is the traditional story the shaykhs reflect upon. Murad notes, "Back in the 1950s and early 1960s, British family values were still recognizably derived from a great religious tradition rooted in the Society and politics family-nurturing Abrahamic soil."[95]

Abdal Hakim Murad and the Crisis of Masculinity

In his lecture "Star Wars and the Crisis of Modern Masculinity," Abdal Hakim Murad adds to Weaver's claim that feminism masculinized women and feminized men.[96] He cited the popular—albeit controversial—*Star Wars* sequel *The Force Awakens*. The film incited much controversy and discussion among avid fans. The film's new director, J. J. Abrams, had a different vision for the film from that of its original creator, George Lucas. Lucas's original vision for Star Wars was heavily inspired by the novelist Joseph Campbell, author of *The Hero with a Thousand Faces*. The film explored many mystical themes inspired by Campbell.[97] Campbell was, in turn, influenced by Carl Jung, who contended that myths from different religious traditions were built on elementary ideas or "archetypes," meaning human beings shared a "subconscious model of what a 'hero' is, or a 'mentor' or a 'quest.'"[98] On this basis, George Lucas constructs a quasi-religious and mystical narrative of the male archetype—through the figure of Luke Skywalker—that undergoes a process of initiation into manhood to save the galaxy.

The new sequel, directed by J. J. Abrams, represented a changing vision. The story of traditional male heroism, wisdom, and religion was replaced with explicitly feminist interjections. Abrams emphasized the female characters' power and presented the declining role of the male protagonist.[99] The film elicited debates between two contending visions of Western civilization: that is, a vision of traditional masculine archetypes, put forward first by Joseph Campbell and later (as Bishop Robert Barron contends) by figures such as Jordan Peterson, and a liberal feminist vision.[100] Barron adds that the function of the myths elicited by the first camp is to revive the male archetype from a state of complicity to one where this archetype actualizes his role.[101] Indeed, the film was critiqued for reversing these roles. The sexual politics surrounding the controversy in *The Force Awakens* reflects a wider debate on the seeming decline of the patriarchy and the rise of the right-wing "meninist movement."[102] On the other side, the celebration of the female archetype also indicates a changing discourse in the media that celebrates a specific narrative of "girl power" femininity.[103] It is from within that story of the loss of gender roles, distinction, declining patriarchy, and the simultaneous rise of a secular feminist discourse that Abdal Hakim Murad addresses the problem of modern masculinity.

In this *Star Wars* example, Murad evokes a notion of manhood pervasive in all traditional societies.[104] This manhood displayed a metaphysical character. Through initiation, young men become disciplined and recognize their role and duty. This role is both sacred, as a part of the cosmos, and secular—as a cosmic legitimator. The metaphysical ordering of the world entails the genders' roles being complementary: the woman has her place, and the man has his. This is quite similar to Weaver's claim that, with the loss of the notion of the "gentleman," the figure of the "lady" too had to go, resulting in the breakdown of the family. Murad shows that in *Star Wars*, as it reflects the popular mood in modernity, man is no longer the patriarch and warrior. In the story of a male becoming, men are made to make peace with "taking responsibility" for what they are and to tame their negative qualities so as to transcend themselves and play the cosmic role of leader. With this initial rupture in traditional forms, men have lost their place in the traditional ordering of the cosmos. In the same way, women have lost their position in the cosmos. Whereas men traditionally needed initiation, women in the modern world assume a place of male strength without even needing this taming. The trope of the strong independent female who can "do it all," so prevalent in modern society, disturbs the traditional equilibrium of the ordering of gender.

Murad introduces the *khuṭba* by citing an article in *Atlantic Monthly* called "All the Single Mothers," on the disappearance of marriageable men or the disappearing father. He posits that this results from the rise of "second wave" feminists and their morally-driven social engineering projects trying to shift the historical norms of the family, society, etc. This caused a breakdown or fragmentation of the family structure. He then cites further statistics on the impact of fatherless families on the mental well-being of the children and their propensity for crime. Murad then explains the new *Star Wars* films to show how the decline of the metaphysical perspective caused a transformation in both genders' social and political roles, subsequently causing a fundamental crisis.

The transformation in the motifs of *Star Wars: The Force Awakens* from earlier films in the series, for Murad, is symptomatic of the crisis of modern masculinity. The film presents the collapse of the male hero archetype and his replacement by the notion of the "autonomous woman who is beyond reproach." By contrast, Luke Skywalker is no longer a heroic figure. Murad explains, "[He is] sulking at the edge of the galaxy somewhere. He is not being a hero and dealing with the evil empire. He is licking his wounds and being a bit of a loser." Murad contends that this is the form of broken masculinity that appeases certain extreme feminists. As Murad describes through the figure of Luke Skywalker, modern men are broken, eternally children, "touchy-feely," "quite tearful," and wholly unable to deal with their masculinity. The reversal of roles in the modern world, where the rise of the powerful woman has essentially dethroned masculinity, has left men questioning their role.

Murad makes three important assumptions about tradition, modernity, and the essential nature of the genders. Firstly, he ascribes an essential feebleness to the female in the tradition. This feebleness can reflect their role in society and the family; still, the point he is making here relates to their essence. Secondly, he shows that Luke Skywalker is almost alienated from his masculinity. The essential meaning of maleness is to not be tearful, not to be weak, but to overcome this and become the "hero" or the patriarch. Lastly, he suggests a direct correlation. If women were to be strong, that would automatically reflect a weakness in men.

Abdal Hakim Murad expands on this: "The power of the female and the uselessness of the male leaves them questioning: Where does this leave young men who still have the physiology of their ancestors and are looking for forms of initiation and a definition of gender? What is it to be growing into manhood?" In this cosmological ordering of gender, gender archetypes of the heroic male and the female who receives this heroism maintained the structuring of the family and wider society. Feminism disrupted this cosmic ordering. By instigating projects of "social engineering," they deconstructed the metaphysical meaning of gender. This in itself is part of the modern project which disrupts the metaphysical worldview and denies any form of cosmic legitimation, including gender. Murad explains that this caused a decline in the stable coordinates. He adds: "Nobody any longer belongs unambiguously to a particular set of coordinates … young people are given very few landmarks. They are not told what it means to be male any longer or to belong to a particular city, or country, or social class; everything is in flux or negotiable."

This decline in order and distinction, which resulted from the West's dissolution, which Weaver had lamented in the early 1950s, is being evoked again by Murad as the Muslim story. He explains: "As a result, many people are breaking down … Gender is not a random genetic outcome but has a deep significant meaning … this is why we need to adhere to the *sunna* and not attempt a radical reconfiguration to try to bring Islam and its often detested gender beliefs aligned with the current beliefs of the modern world."

Murad contends that the story of the original *Star Wars* films reflects the metaphysical understanding of gender known to all traditional societies. Abdal Hakim Murad explains that George Lucas, the original *Star Wars* writer, was telling an ancient story to a modern audience. A story that could be found in the Chinese, Indian, and Islamic traditions—a form of universalized metaphysical view. Indeed, both Campbell and Lucas believed that all ancient traditions tell the same story, notwithstanding their external forms:[105] the story of the masculine hero overcoming himself, finding harmony with the feminine principle. He grows into "sacred warriorhood." Before attaining the position of the sacred warrior and the patriarch, he needs to be initiated into maleness; this is a form of sacred initiation into being a hunter, provider, and warrior—as Murad explains. Men were taught the gender role they were to undertake, as is reflected by the cosmic meaning of maleness. Murad goes on to explain that this is primordial, but since metaphysics has been done away with, so has the notion of essential maleness in need of initiation. "Instead," he says, "we have eternal childhood or eternal temper tantrums among the males."

For seekers, engaging in the critique of feminism which posits a radical displacement of metaphysics opens the doors to other traditional stories coming from conservatives in the West. The most popular figure exemplifying this is the Canadian psychologist Jordan Peterson, whom Murad commends in his book *Travelling Home: Essays on Islam in Europe.*[106] Peterson contends that the crisis of masculinity is a result of it coming under attack from feminist movements. For Peterson, this displacement of masculinity has caused men to feminize.[107] I discuss the impact of Jordan Peterson on the community of seekers in the last chapter.

Umar Faruq Abd-Allah and Modern Feminism

Umar Faruq Abd-Allah notes that the predicament associated with gender in the modern world results from a real sense of injustice and a perceived one. He first defines what constitutes an injustice in order to distinguish the real from the perceived. He explains that *zulm*, or injustice, is positioning things in their wrong place. Muslims must put things in their right place.[108] The problem people face (both non-Muslims and Muslims) regarding gender roles and gender identities is entirely caused by the disparity in the way people position their gender identity (with all its economic, political, and sexual dimensions) in relation to the cosmos. This disequilibrium in the cosmos—or rather the disequilibrium in how people position themselves vis-à-vis the cosmos—is not an accident of history. The modern breakdown of gender essence, as it was known and understood by traditional people, resulted from the modern project. It is not merely a biological or sexual category, although biology and sexuality relate to metaphysics. Abd-Allah explains that in Islam, gender cannot be understood without understanding the metaphysics of gender. For that reason, he points out that, unlike with neo-Marxist feminist perspectives, gender roles are not based on economic or material values but rather on metaphysical principles.

The feminist project, Abd-Allah explains, has its genealogy of ideas. He presents the evolution of knowledge as a form of *isnād* that runs from Descartes to Judith Butler. Abd-Allah locates the starting point of this modern project of gender neutrality in the Cartesian dualism of mind and body. As the mind is gender-neutral and sexless, Cartesian dualism as an epistemological framework deconstructs the metaphysical principle of the gender binary and complementarity in the cosmos. It reduces it to a material and physical reality, not a metaphysical necessity.[109] The next important step in deconstructing the cosmic significance of gender comes from Karl Marx and Friedrich Engels—who wrote *The Origin of the Family, Private Property and the State*.[110] At the root of Marxist thought is the destruction of essential and intrinsic truths. Therefore, metaphysics is replaced by dialectic materialism, as the family, one of the foremost economic institutions, needs to be overthrown. Abd-Allah explains that Marxism aimed to overthrow the family, the "reign of hetero-sexuality," and ultimately the "reign of God." For that reason, he explains, marriage was abolished when the Bolsheviks took power. Ideology became the basis of social engineering, and for this reason, the USSR attempted many projects of gender engineering.

Marxists attempted to dislocate gender from its cosmic significance from an economic perspective; Sigmund Freud and his interlocutors viewed this from a psychosexual standpoint. While Marx saw the nuclear family and, therefore, female sexuality as subject to economics, Freud started with a sexual reading of gender. Building on Freud, Abd-Allah explains that his student Wilhelm Reich advocated the breaking down of all barriers to sexual expression. He argued that a sexual revolution was needed to produce a classless society. The sexual revolution is not just a metaphorical revolution, as Reich intended to overthrow the reign of heterosexuality and even remove the taboo of incest. Abd-Allah explained that to Reich, heterosexuality was the basis of class distinction. The next link in the chain is Herbert Marcuse. Marcuse was the foremost figure in the 1960s sexual revolution. He argued that the pleasure principle is the basis of a free society. It is essential to deregulate sexuality. The culmination of the genealogy of modern feminist thought is with Judith Butler. Judith Butler contends that gender is in itself a social construct. The key to deconstructing and overthrowing heterosexuality is recognizing that there is no real male or female category.

This is the contextual backdrop against which Abd-Allah begins to outline the metaphysics of gender. It is worth noting that this story of feminism is very specific. It is contextually framed in his wider narrative of modernity. It fails, however, to engage with or critique other stories of feminist movements that are arguably more nuanced and more representative of a non-male-centric or Eurocentric approach, or even to engage with the work of Muslim feminists. Positioning this narrative as the central critique reflects the anxieties the neo-traditionalists are responding to. As with the way in which Abdal Hakim

Murad posits post-Christian modern angst as context, as described in the previous section, the context of the problem informs the solutions posited.

This critique of modernity represents a failure to engage with the intellectual work produced by postcolonial thinkers in Asia, Africa, and the Middle East—or even their Western Muslim counterparts.[111] The appeal of this metaphysics lies in the unity it offers. It provides a completely ordered system of meaning at a time of apparent meaninglessness and fragmentation on all levels—the political, the social, and the religious. The main claim it makes is that it is not an exertive act of interpretation subject to historical context. After all, the tradition represents "an uninterrupted transmission, through innumerable generations, of the spiritual and cosmological principles, sciences and laws resulting from a revealed religion: nothing is neglected, from the establishment of social orders [to] codes of conduct."[112] That said, the critique that Abd-Allah presents displays an obvious historical and cultural positioning, his observations on metaphysics and the critique of modernity reflecting a post-Christian anxiety.

From this perspective, Umar Faruq Abd-Allah begins to outline the traditional metaphysics of gender. Although it is presented as normative, as most features of the "traditional" outlook are deemed to be, it is based on Sachiko Murata's sourcebook *The Tao of Islam*, and seemingly appropriated Jungian psychological principles.[113] Despite being an innovative interjection, it is by no means orthodox. Abd-Allah explains that the whole cosmos is engendered. There is nothing in the cosmos that is without gender. The equilibrium of the cosmos is based on gender complementarity. Equality is, therefore, a metaphysically null concept. Despite modern sensibilities, it is essential to understand that the cosmos is organized through hierarchies. This is not to say that the male or the female is superior, but only that the complementarity of their roles entails a certain ordering. In the cosmos, Abd-Allah explains the complementarity of the male principle and the female principle. This does not completely correlate with the gender of the person. Men possess male and female principles—although the male principle will be dominant. Likewise, women possess female and male principles—although the female principle will be more dominant.

Gender, therefore, needs to be understood in terms of how it fits in the cosmos. From the female and male principles, there are both positive and negative male and female principles. The positive female principle is equivalent to the *yin* and the positive male principle to the *yang*. The throne of God has a male principle in relation to the human world—as it stands in majesty toward it. However, it possesses the female principle in relation to God. For that reason, Abd-Allah explains, Ibn 'Arabī says that you cannot reach any spiritual attainment if you do not speak to Allah with a feminine voice.[114] These principles, he goes on to add, are metaphysical absolutes. The crises in the world occur when negative male and female principles dominate each other. The ecological crisis, for example, is a result of the triumph of man's negative male principle. For that reason, Muslims should aspire to the patriarchy and the matriarchy of positive male and female principles. These metaphysical essences shape gender identity in the way it ought to relate to the cosmos. Metaphysics is thus the basis of gender roles, and not social construction.

As I have shown in this chapter, Murad and Abdullah paint a somber picture of the decline of Western civilization and traditional Muslim societies. They reflect on the anxieties of a post-Christian society that purportedly fell into dissolution with the departure of metaphysics, aesthetics, epistemology, and social and political distinction. As I argue, Murad posits both pitfalls and possibilities for Islam to indigenize itself in the West. He has argued that the postcolonial condition—which he depicts as predatory and theologically adrift—has failed to make Europe home and has developed pathologies in Muslim communities. In turn, he presents the post-Christian angst—particularly on gender as a marker for "traditional values" to be axiomatic. Thus Muslim virility and masculinity are set to save an ailing West. Therefore, I have shown that the shaykhs' discourses on race, gender, and belonging are closely interlinked. Feminism—like Islamism or Marxism—according to the shaykhs has instigated great upheaval in society and unsettled the metaphysical arrangement that entailed gender harmony in the past. While these metaphysical principles appear almost esoteric, I show in the next chapter that they are not immutable principles but are responding to and being shaped by very concrete political conditions and power interests.

LOCATING NEO-TRADITIONALISM IN MODERNITY

7

THE SUFI, THE PALACE,
AND THE PEOPLE

In 2014 in Abu Dhabi, Hamza Yusuf delivered an impassioned speech on stage at the first annual conference of the Forum for Promoting Peace in Muslim Societies (now known as the Abu Dhabi Forum for Peace).[1] In front of him sat his shaykh and president of the Forum, Abdullah bin Bayyah, and the Minister of Foreign Affairs of the UAE and patron of the Forum, Abdullah bin Zayed Al Nahyan. The topic of the speech was scholars, the media, and the imperative for promoting peace. Yusuf began by raising a number of addendum questions to the topic at hand. If there is now an imperative for scholars to promote peace, have scholars been promoting conflict all along? And since Muslims are not materialists, what then are the metaphysical dimensions and consequences of conflicts?

Yusuf traced the source of conflicts to the dual deconstruction of scholarly authority and legitimate political power. The internet, while revolutionizing information, also caused religious havoc, allowing for common people ('awām) to make rulings and give fatwās. An unlearned class emerged to usurp authority from established scholars and to usurp political power. The UAE, he commended, has given special attention to this predicament. Alluding to Islamists, he noted: "The core problem of conflicts is that the assailant presents himself as the sole representative of Islam ... and the inheritor of tradition." He went on to add:

He who looks unto history will find that it is from the duties of the *ummah* to respect the leader (al-sulṭān). We should not obey them if they compel us to drink wine or to kill a human soul ... but this is the principle. The leader (al-sulṭān) is the shadow of Allah. Qāḍī Abū Bakr al-Ṭarṭūshī in *Sirāj al-Mulūk* used to say: I heard people say, 'As you are, so will your rulers be (Kamā takūnū yuwala ʿalaykum).' And then I found this axiom in the Book of Allah: In this way, We make some evildoers have power over others through their misdeeds. [6:129]

Yusuf explained, "People in the past held this belief to be true: our calamities are a result of our sins. However, we lost this great monotheistic (*tawḥidī*) tradition ... Our *salaf* used to say, 'An unjust ruler is better than continued sedition' and 'Sixty years with an unjust ruler is better than one hour of anarchy.'"

At the end of the panel, Yusuf stepped off the stage, shook hands with his shaykh, Abdullah bin Bayyah, and kissed Abdullah bin Zayed. The optics of the speech were particularly significant. It had been less than four years since the beginning of the Arab Spring. Fearful of the marginal electoral success of the Islamist factions, the UAE had taken a corrosive interventionist and counter-revolutionary role in the region. Yusuf stood before some of the most powerful forces in the region, proclaiming that the leader is the shadow of God—consequently sanctifying their actions and interventions.

The Forum had, since its inception, positioned itself as the authoritative religious voice advocating for peace and non-violence. A year after Yusuf's seminal speech, the Forum invited the Syrian Muslim scholar and long-time advocate of non-violence Jawdat Said to receive an honorary award. In response, Said sent a strong letter of condemnation to the President of the Forum, Abdullah bin Bayyah. Jawdat Said resolutely stated:

> Intellectuals and scholars are responsible for our current crises: whether it is things they have written, a sermon they presented, ideas they have disseminated, or even issues they chose to be silent about. For that reason, I would like to speak earnestly to the degree that might be inappropriate: it is a great scam and fraudulence for Muslim scholars to be gathered like this and pretend to be saviors. It is more appropriate that they come as criminals seeking repentance, radical self-criticism, and transformation.

He added:

> Scholars and jurists have long deemed it impermissible to go to *ḥajj* in a car or use a cell phone. Still, many today deem it impermissible for a woman to

drive or deny even the basics of ḥadīth scholarship. This only goes to show how far they are from reality. It also shows the extent to which such scholars are co-opted to the point that they are silent in the face of corruption and oppression. They accept the privileges given to them, and whenever politicians summon them, they just tell them what they want to hear, not what should be said. The jurists legitimize coups against democracy, legitimate rule, and the consensus of the masses in one place while claiming they support legitimate rule in other places.

Finally he concluded:

> Although I am pleased with your kind gesture, the reality confirms that I do not deserve it. I apologize; I cannot accept it, and I will not be attending. I thank you for your trust, and I hope that God will produce from our loins a generation that will serve this religion and elevate the message of his Prophet.[2]

Said's strong words to Bin Bayyah reflect the controversial role that the Forum for Promoting Peace played in the wider religious and political contexts. Alluding to the counterrevolutionary role the UAE has played in the Middle East after the Arab Spring, and in particular the support for the military coup in Egypt, Said places the blame squarely on religious scholars whom he believes are co-opted by political power.

In the previous two chapters, I have examined the neo-traditionalist shaykhs' metaphysical interventions in disembodied form, outside the political contingencies of time; now, I would like to explore the more concrete and practical form. The preceding vignettes illustrate the fraught relationship between religious scholarship and the policy agenda of the UAE government, and in particular the policy implication of Hamza Yusuf's seeming quietist stances. This chapter contextualizes Yusuf's metaphysical claims regarding politics. The locales of power in which he operates are not only state actors—as in the case of his work in the UAE. They also include their relationship with right-wing conservatives. This often filters down into discussions of race, gender, and the conditions of belonging in the West. This highlights the fragility of "traditionalism" as a construct, especially when engaging with the question of modern power, or the different meanings and shapes it takes in engaging other locales of power.

Political Contexts and Locales of Power

The 9/11 attacks were the first and most significant political challenge to the young neo-traditionalist network. There was a tangible transformation in the religious and political discourse of Hamza Yusuf. In the 1990s, Yusuf was known in Muslim communities for his critiques of American imperialism, capitalism, and despotic Muslim regimes. His religious discourse sometimes bordered on revolutionary anti-modernism with messianic undertones.[3] These undertones were consistent with the revolutionary messianic discourse of the *Murabitun* movement of which he had been a member for many years. By the late 1990s, a subtle change in discourse had occurred. In an interview with Yusuf and Abdal Hakim Murad, Yusuf's discourse appeared to be already mellowing. Although neither Murad nor Yusuf advocated quietism, Murad recognized the legitimacy of the Bosnian fighters, for example. In criticizing the supposed anarchistic tendencies of Muslim activism, they offered what they deemed the "traditional" view of deference to the scholars and a path of traditional scholarship instead.[4] Similarly, Umar Faruq Abd-Allah seemed to have transformed his position of dissent toward political Islam, although the timeline is not entirely clear. In 1983, he published a book titled *The Islamic Struggle in Syria*.[5] The book provides a detailed and sympathetic study of the Syrian Muslim Brotherhood. After 9/11, the neo-traditionalists, like every Muslim institution, religious trend, or individual residing in the West, underwent transformations.

The "War on Terror"—knowingly or unknowingly—presented Muslim communities as suspect. Streams of media reports about potential terror within Muslim communities, or questioning the community's allegiances, were a staple in the wake of the War on Terror.[6] The Muslim community in America was put under increased surveillance.[7] This was not a unique condition for Muslims in America: similar law enforcement measures were taken in many parts of the Western world. Media channels, politicians, and even scholars raised the question of integration with a degree of urgency. Their concern over integration was framed as part of a larger concern with the question of radicalization. The nature of Islam as a religion became a focal point as Bush set the tone for a war between good and evil. As Mahmood Mamdani explains, "President Bush moved to distinguish between 'good Muslims' and 'bad Muslims.'"[8] "Bad Muslims" are religious extremists with a political project who are to blame for terrorism. "Good Muslims," on the other hand, need to clear their name of the crimes committed by their co-religionists. They need to be "with us."[9] This narrative was not implicit, nor simply deduced by media pundits. It was a basis for policy production in both the United States and the United Kingdom. As Peter Mandeville and Shadi Hamid explained, in the aftermath of the War on Terror, "once Islam is inserted into public debates, how citizens interpret their religion becomes, in effect, a matter of national security."[10]

In 2003, two neoconservative policy think tanks, the RAND Corporation and the Nixon Centre (now known as The Centre for National Interest), produced reports on the most suitable form of Islam as an ally in the War on Terror.[11] This marked the beginning of the political role some Sufi and neo-traditionalist figures and institutions would play in the Muslim world and the West. The Nixon Centre report, for example, was drafted from a conference that brought together scholars and academics from different regions with significant Muslim populations to show the ways in which Sufism can counteract "radical Islamism." The keynote speakers at the conference were the famed orientalist historian Bernard Lewis[12] and Shaykh Muhammad Hisham Kabbani, the deputy leader of the Naqshbandi Haqqani Sufi order.[13] The report states: "On October 24, 2003, the International Security Program of the Nixon Centre hosted a conference in Washington to explore how Sufism—the spiritual tradition within Islam—relates to US foreign policy goals. The purpose of the meeting was to introduce US policymakers and the policy community to this neglected part of Islam, often referred to as 'Cultural Islam.'" Sufism is practiced by millions of people around the world, including in the United States.[14]

From the outset, the discrepancy between the two visions of why *taṣawuuf* is an antidote to radical Islamism is apparent. For Lewis, most forms of Islam constitute a problem, with some Islamic forms being worse than others.[15] Some forms of Islam may be considered tolerant, but only in a passive sense. It is only in the tradition of Sufism that one can find what is more than passive tolerance. Lewis explains, "It is not just tolerance; it is acceptance. There are poems by Rumi, by Ibn Arabi in Persian and Turkish, which indicate that all the religions are basically the same: All religions have the same purpose, the same message, the same communication, and they worship the same God."[16] In this sense, Lewis's view of Sufism as a universal religion meant that it is far more amenable to secular citizenship. Kabbani did not contradict Lewis. Rather, he posited a different view of Sufism's amenability to secular citizenship. Sufism is traditional, orthodox, and moderate, as opposed to the inauthenticity of "radical Islamism."[17]

From this point onwards, Sufi and neo-traditionalist policy initiatives aiming to counter Islamism took two nodes. The first was interfaith initiatives aimed at promoting the universal ideals of all religions, tolerance, and building a blueprint of citizenship (illiberal as that may be). This included initiatives such as A Common Word Between Us and You (2007), the Marrakesh Declaration (2018), the Document on Human Fraternity for World Peace and Living Together (2019), and the Abu Dhabi Declaration of Inclusive Citizenship (2021). The second policy initiative concerns itself with affirming orthodoxy, showing its parameters, or correcting the Islam corrupted by "extremists," as exemplified by the Amman Message (2006), the Mardin conference (2010) or the "Who Are They, the Followers of Sunna?" conference in Chechnya (2016).[18]

Epistemic Communities

As the political demand for religious allies increased, neo-traditionalists formed a loosely knit epistemic community. According to Peter Haas, an "epistemic community" denotes a network of professionals with recognized expertise and competence in a particular domain and an authoritative claim to policy-relevant knowledge.[19] The term is often used to denote scientific communities that share some epistemological criteria relevant to policymakers— and Islam had become such a community after 9/11. Epistemic communities are often transnational networks with shaykhs in the West like Hamza Yusuf and shaykhs in the East like Habib Ali Jifri and Abdullah bin Bayyah. The knowledge they produce is additionally transmitted across geographical locations. This knowledge is conveyed to state and non-state actors and the wider society—in this case, to the seekers.[20]

Emanuel Adler explains that "the community members share knowledge about the causation of social and physical phenomena in an area for which they have a reputation for competence, and they have a common set of normative beliefs about what will benefit human welfare in such a domain."[21] For a neo-traditionalist community, the relevant phenomenon is religious extremism under the umbrella of political Islam. This community of shaykhs and scholars derive a shared methodology for diagnosing this problem. As Nukhet Ahu Sandal points out in her study of religious epistemic communities involved in conflict resolution in Northern Ireland, they often represent a leading religious discourse countering another religious discourse,[22] meaning their authority and frame of reference is exclusively religious.

The last feature of an epistemic community, as outlined by Haas, is that it shares a common policy enterprise.[23] This sets it apart from other knowledge-based or cognitive communities. Epistemic communities are often called upon by policymakers in times of uncertainty or a post-crisis situation—whether after terrorist attacks or, as I will show, after the Arab Spring.[24] For policymakers to "hire" a specific epistemic community (which they can also "fire"), they must have a common understanding of what the problem is.[25] In this case, the problem, stated loosely, is the rise of political Islam or "extremism." Everything else is negotiated, with policymakers having the obvious upper hand. Once an epistemic community has identified causality, it can then assume its role in formulating a solution. The solution is filtered through the internal epistemological dynamics of the community and goes through a negotiation process with policymakers. Like epistemic communities, policymakers have their own internal tests. Therefore, "it is not necessarily the best-fitted ideas that were selected and turned into policies, however, but those which best fit the interests of policymakers."[26] Hence, "epistemic communities create reality but not as they wish."[27] This could be seen in Hamza Yusuf's affirmation of the nation-state model, as shown in Chapter 5.

The anti-Islamist and quietist discourse of the shaykhs, albeit consistent, took on different forms and meanings. The Radical Middle Way (RMW) project was perhaps the clearest policy-driven project that brought together the three shaykhs. Issa, a British Bengali seeker, had been involved in RMW since its inception. He explained that it constituted a large paradigm shift for many hopeful seekers of knowledge: "When we were younger, we were taught that speaking out against a corrupt ruler was the best Jihād. This was now being inverted. Speaking out against the ruler now causes *fitna*—even if the ruler was evil. That made some people quiet." Issa had been a seeker for over a decade and looked up to the shaykhs for guidance. In RMW, he noted, the shaykhs affirmed the utmost centrality of their authority as traditional teachers. Seekers, therefore, looked up to them not only for guidance in their daily lives but also for how to engage with democracy and politics.

Although the shaykhs' quietist discourse disheartened Issa, he pointed out that at least they were true to their quietism. They did not engage in power. However, RMW instigated his disillusionment with neo-traditionalism. It held a conference, Issa explained, called "Eyeless in Gaza," during the Israeli war on Gaza of 2008–9. He added that most of those who attended the conference were South Asian and did not come from politically quietist backgrounds. They "were very despondent because the message we got was this is bad. But there is nothing you can do about it. Politics is for the people of *dunyā* (the world); we are the people of *akhirah* (afterlife)." I asked Issa how that made the audience feel. He responded, "You have to understand that at the time, you might feel disappointed, but you look up to the ʿulāmaʾ so much. You immediately make an allowance for them or think, 'maybe I am wrong.' It is the beginning of the seeds of disquiet that have now bloomed as I am speaking to you. You start to question, but you don't entertain the questioning too much."

Since then, Hamza Yusuf—more than Abdal Hakim Murad and Umar Faruq Abd-Allah—has been actively involved in policymaking projects alongside his shaykh, Abdullah bin Bayyah. He actively operates in neo-traditionalist Arab networks that aim to counter Islamism and promote political quietism. Even though Abdal Hakim Murad is even more unapologetic in his critique of political Islam as a precursor to violent extremism, he has been less involved in policy-driven projects. Rather, he works more on interfaith and public-facing programs. Unlike Yusuf, his work is much less transnationally located. He indeed has an international following. Still, his work mainly consists of forming an "English Islam"—which entails forming categories of belonging and views on gender. Likewise, Umar Faruq Abd-Allah focuses on what belonging to American Islam entails, as well as forming traditionalist, essentialist gender categories.

That said, the three shaykhs—along with Abdullah bin Bayyah—have collaboratively advised the former Prime Minister of Pakistan, Imran Khan, in founding Al-Qadir University near Islamabad. In 2019, Umar Faruq Abd-Allah traveled to Pakistan with his shaykh, Muhammad Hydara Al-Jilani, to discuss Khan's plan to build the university.[28] The university's mission statement expressed lofty goals such as "To carry out research in traditional Islam, and establish its importance and relevance to challenges we face today" or "To be a thought leader in traditional responses to modern challenges."[29] While the university seems to only offer a BS (Hons) in Management, it has a "Centre of Islamic Spirituality" that aims to merge classical Sufi literature and the field of self-development.[30] The university's global advisory board includes several neo-traditionalist and Traditionalist shaykhs and scholars, including Seyyed Hossein Nasr, Hamza Yusuf, Abdal Hakim Murad, Firas AlKhateb, Recep Senturk, and Amin Kholwaida.[31] In 2021, Khan hosted many of these figures in public-facing sessions where he asked them to provide an ethical and Prophetic framework for governance.[32] They provided a shared ethical vision representing overarching neo-traditionalist ideals on the symbiosis of religion and science, morality, and patriarchy.[33]

The Arab Spring

In 2011, waves of protests erupted all over the Middle East and North Africa. They called for the end of long-standing autocratic regimes in the region. Since 9/11, the policy agenda of Western governments—concerned with fighting the War on Terror—has favored the stability of secular authoritarian governments over democracy in the region. As such, authoritarian governments habitually use terrorism as an excuse to clamp down on dissent. These revolutions successfully overthrew longstanding dictators in Tunisia, Egypt, Libya, and Yemen. The aftermath of the Arab Spring witnessed the short-lived electoral success of Islamist political parties in places like Egypt, and subsequent violent military repression.[34] In other countries like Syria or Libya, civil wars ensued due to the violent repression of peaceful protests by the regimes.[35] In Yemen, a brutal war raged between local fighting factions and a Gulf coalition led by Saudi Arabia and the UAE. This coalition has since been criticized for its excessive use of violence and its targeted attacks on civilians.[36]

Hamza Yusuf seemed enthusiastic and sympathetic in the immediate aftermath of the Arab revolutions. This initial enthusiasm confused many given his decisively anti-revolutionary discourse less than a year later. After the Tunisian revolution deposed the regime of Zine El Abidine Ben Ali, Yusuf wrote a sympathetic blog post. Yusuf lauded Mohamed Bouazizi, the young Tunisian street vendor whose desperate act of self-immolation sparked the Tunisian revolution and subsequent Arab Spring. Yusuf even recalled an unpleasant encounter with the Tunisian secret police to fortify the legitimate sense of injustice. However, even this initial enthusiasm was tempered by his general skepticism regarding the efficacy of revolutions. Yusuf pointed out, "This seems to be the great lesson of revolutions and coups: with rare exceptions, they bring in new governments that are as bad or worse than the ones they ousted."[37] This was especially clear with the Arab republics that replaced longstanding monarchies. In his standard defense of monarchies, Yusuf explained, "Monarchs of old practiced the tradition of benevolence. They were not always benevolent but were raised with the understanding that they were there to serve the people."[38]

For Yusuf, the seeming "lack of ideology" in the revolutions was the most promising aspect. This was a sentiment he echoed again in an article he wrote one month after the Egyptian revolution.[39] For Yusuf, the power of these young Egyptian revolutionaries lied in that they were probably "more inspired by Bob Marley than by their local imam quoting Sahih al-Bukhari."[40] The visible absence of political Islam and the possibility of a secular government was the most redeeming quality of this revolution. He asserts:

> The lack of an ideology, for me, is the most refreshing aspect of this uprising. The stale rhetoric of "Islam is the solution" that has marked countless demonstrations for decades is absent ... Islam is not a political ideology and hence does not offer a political solution per se; basic morality in politics is the solution. Most Muslims would be content living under Finnish or Swedish forms of governance, with a few adjustments to the sexual liberties in those countries and feel as if it were the time of Saladin.[41]

Despite Yusuf's seeming optimism about the revolutions, he expresses clear reservations that would shape his anti-revolutionary and quietist discourse soon after. First, perhaps most importantly, he takes a resolutely anti-Islamist/anti-Muslim Brotherhood position. Yusuf expresses a clear preference for monarchies over republics and secular (albeit socially conservative) governance over Islamism. Second, he expresses the need for deference toward Eastern neo-traditionalist scholars, such as Ali Goma, in this article, and later people like Habib Ali Jifri, as the foremost source of political guidance. Lastly, even at this early stage, we can see a constant reference to the secular Western nation-state model as a political ideal, although not necessarily "democracy." Yusuf cites the American and French revolutions as the benchmark for the social contract, but also notes that democracy is "not only improbable but more likely a destabilizing factor that results in life becoming even more unbearable."[42] It is, therefore, not a surprise that Yusuf's faith in the secular Egyptian revolution would wane when the Muslim Brotherhood candidate Mohamed Morsi won Egypt's first presidential election in 2012 by a small margin.[43]

Usaama al-Azami notes that Yusuf was already disillusioned with the Arab Spring by August 2011. In an interview with the Saudi presenter Turkī al-Dakhīl, Yusuf stressed his support for Saudi, Moroccan, and Emirati royal families and the nobility they represented.[44] At that point, Yusuf's anti-revolutionary quietist discourse took form more as a caveat against instability and the fragmentation of order. The revolutionary chaos that ensued seemed to dethrone and disrespect all forms of hierarchy—including that of the 'ulamā'. On this basis, he advised seekers to forgo direct activism and focus more on introspection. Yusuf advocated obedience to the rulers and stressed that opposing the government is not permitted in the Islamic tradition.[45] This coincided with and possibly resulted from a political shift his shaykh, Abdullah bin Bayyah, underwent.

Abdullah bin Bayyah is somewhat of an enigmatic figure. To young Muslims in the West, he is known primarily and almost exclusively as Hamza Yusuf's shaykh.[46] The fragile-looking learned scholar embodies the symbolic authority of the land of Mauritania, the spiritual authority of a saint, and the depth and knowledge of an orthodox ʿālim. These qualities give him the wisdom of the tradition that can deal with and even circumvent modernity.[47] For those with knowledge of sharīʿa, he is known to be a scholarly genius in the field of ʾuṣūl al-fiqh. Bin Bayyah is, however, less known for his long political career. From the very beginning, following Mauritanian independence from France, Bin Bayyah gained prominence in the then ruling Mauritanian People's Party, where he was a Permanent Trustee for the Party and a member of its Cabinet and Permanent Committee from 1970 to 1978.[48] He quickly rose to political prominence in the country. There he held the following positions: Judge at the High Court of the Islamic Republic of Mauritania, Head of Shariah Affairs at the Ministry of Justice, Deputy President of the Court of Appeal, Main negotiator on Religious Affairs in the Republic, First Minister for Islamic Affairs and Education, Minister of Justice and Official Holder of the Seals, Minister of State for Human Resources—along with the positions of Deputy Prime Minister and Minister of State for Directing State Affairs, Organizations and Parties (which included overseeing the Ministry of Information and Culture, the Ministry of Youth & Sport, the Ministry of Islamic Affairs, and the Ministry of Postal Services and Communication).[49]

In 2004, Bin Bayyah became a founding vice-president of the International Union of Muslim Scholars (IUMS), with the Qatar-affiliated and pro-Muslim Brotherhood scholar Yusuf al-Qaradawi as a founding president. In that period, the two scholars worked closely together and shared a similar theological vision. Like Qaradawi, Bin Bayyah was influenced by Rashīd Riḍā. David Warren explains:

Qaradawi's and Bin Bayyah's points of departure for their intellectual thought are very similar and draw upon Rida's model and the *wasaṭiyya* outlook. Riḍā's influence extends beyond those who explicitly lay claim to his legacy, like Qaradawi, and includes Bin Bayyah, who also utilizes Riḍā's model of reviving and centering once marginal legal concepts to articulate reforms. However, Bin Bayyah and his staff have expended substantial effort to differentiate him from Qaradawi by foregrounding his attachment to the Maliki legal school and sympathies for Sufism.[50]

Qaradawi and Bin Bayyah's shared understandings of *wasaṭiyya* (centrism or moderation) and other principles, such as *fiqh al-wāqiʿ* (jurisprudence of reality), were a result of years of collaborative work. In 2004, Warren notes that "Bin Bayyah said it was Qaradawi who best exemplified the wasaṭī approach."[51]

In 2011, the IUMS and its president Yusuf al-Qaradawi took a resolutely pro-revolutionary stance. Bin Bayyah, on the other hand, while not wholly opposing the revolutionary upsurge, had some reservations. Al-Azami reports that on February 2, 2011, one week into the protests in Egypt, Bin Bayyah shared a lecture he presented with the Radical Middle Way entitled "From Protest to Engagement."[52] He explains, "As its title suggested, the lecture argued that Muslims needed to engage more constructively with their interlocutors rather than adopt a posture of opposition and criticism."[53] One month later, Bin Bayyah released a shorter clip—in which Hamza Yusuf served as his translator—in which he warned of "dangers inherent [in] the activities of the uneducated masses [the "ignorant" and the "foolish" in Yusuf's translation] who needed to be restrained by a society's elites to prevent disaster."[54] Bin Bayyah, still an affiliate of IUMS at the time, remained cautious.

In 2012, the marginal electoral success of the Muslim Brotherhood candidate in Egypt, Mohamed Morsi, signaled a challenge to many regional powers. With the covert financial backing of the UAE, General Abdel Fattah al-Sisi overthrew Morsi in a military coup. In August 2013, the Egyptian military killed 1,000 anti-coup protesters in Rabaa Square. Throughout the events of the coup and massacre, Qaradawi expressed anger and condemned the massacre. Bin Bayyah, on the other hand, remained silent. Less than a month later, on September 7, 2013, Bin Bayyah resigned from the IUMS.[55] Bin Bayyah briefly explained that "the modest part I am attempting to play in the pursuit of reform and compromise (muṣālaḥa) ... requires a discourse that is not compatible with my position at IUMS."[56] Upon his resignation, Bin Bayyah founded a rival organization to IUMS—the Forum for Promoting Peace in Muslim Societies (FPPMS) under the auspices of Abdullah bin Zayed (the Emirati

Minister of Foreign Affairs and brother of the crown prince Muhammad bin Zayed Al Nahyan).

Bin Bayyah, however, was being courted by the Emirati royal family before his resignation. On February 24, 2013, Abdullah bin Zayed visited Bin Bayyah in his home in Jeddah to discuss "the state of the *ummah* and the possibilities of its revival."[57] Two months later, Bin Bayyah met the UAE's crown prince, Muhammad bin Zayed (MBZ), at the Global Vaccine Summit.[58] In July 2013, Bin Bayyah traveled to Abu Dhabi to give a lecture in honor of the founding emir of Abu Dhabi, Zayed bin Sultan.[59] This was sponsored by the General Authority of Islamic Affairs and Endowments.[60] This visit was scheduled two months after the UAE and other Gulf states had pledged $12 billion to the leaders of the coup in Egypt and later an additional $4.9 billion stimulus package.[61] In seeking to challenge Qaradawi, the IMUS, the Muslim Brotherhood, and pro-revolutionary religious discourse, the UAE successfully courted Qaradawi's erstwhile deputy, Shaykh Abdullah bin Bayyah.

The role Bin Bayyah and Hamza Yusuf played under the UAE's auspices after 2013 has been part of a much larger policy project that goes back to the year 2004 after the passing of Shaykh Zayed Al Nahyan, the ruler of Abu Dhabi. The new rulers of the UAE cultivated a relationship with Sufi "neo-traditionalist" networks. The newly pronounced Sufi orientation of the state allowed the country to differentiate itself from its Wahabbi Saudi counterpart on the one hand, and from the pro-Muslim Brotherhood Qatari establishment on the other. The UAE invited prominent Sufi figures to establish research centers to expound the Sufi history of the country and give counter-terrorism recommendations. In 2005, Habib Ali Jifri founded the "Tabah Foundation."[62] This brought together both Arab and Western neo-traditionalists.[63] In 2009, Tabah took on a more politicized role focusing its discourse on countering jihādī movements, Salafis, and political Islam/Islamism.[64] In 2009, the Libyan politician Aref Ali Nayed established the Kalam Research and Media Center in Dubai.[65] Neo-traditionalist networks, at this point, played a significant role in the UAE's foreign and domestic policies.

From the outset following 9/11, the UAE had been a strong ally in the "War on Terror." This unqualified support came after it was discovered that two of the hijackers had been Emirati citizens and most of the others had flown directly from Dubai. Furthermore, the 9/11 Commission found that the operation's financing had gone through the unregulated UAE *ḥawāla* system and bank transfers. According to Richard Clarke, the then US

National Coordinator for Counterterrorism, MBZ, who was not yet crown prince of the UAE, convinced his father to arrest 200 Emirati nationals and 1,600 residents on terror charges.[66] After his father's death in 2004, MBZ slowly consolidated his power by marginalizing his brother Khalifa bin Zayed Al Nahyan, the effective ruler of the UAE. In 2007, most of the executive powers were transferred to MBZ, and he became the de-facto ruler. University professors and schoolteachers with purported Islamist sympathies were subsequently terminated from their positions or were sidelined.[67] MBZ boasted to an American diplomat that the government had closed down 80 percent of so-called "extremist" Qur'an schools.[68]

Before he consolidated his power in 2003, Muhammad bin Zayed attempted to convince the leadership of the loosely liberal Islamist "Al Islah" Movement to disband their political activities. After they refused, the crown prince lent his support to neo-traditionalist figures. After the Arab Spring, MBZ felt the need to consolidate his power. On March 3, 2011, 133 Emirati intellectuals—including journalists, prominent judges, and university professors, both Islah and liberals, presented a petition to the government calling for modest political reforms.[69] This threatened the political system of absolute monarchy. Five of the signatories were arrested but were later released. Subsequently, seven other signatories were stripped of their citizenship and were arrested on terrorism charges.[70] This was again followed by a series of arrests, that included ninety-four Islah members who were charged with attempting to overthrow the state and "forming and running an illegal political organization that sought to oppose the basic principles of the UAE system of governance," and with "seeking to turn public opinion against the leadership by fabricating reasons for government action taken against them."[71] Warren explains: "since 2011 'the Muslim Brotherhood' has become the Al Nahyan's generic term for extremists, 'part of a pattern' of 'extreme rhetoric' about the group as Abu Dhabi has advocated for repressive measures against the MB both at home and abroad."[72] In addition to their clampdown on dissent, MBZ and Abdullah bin Zayed set up several counterterrorism forums in their War on Terror, such as Hedayah or the "Guidance" Center in 2012 and the Sawab or "Right Path" online forum in conjunction with the US government.[73]

In another major regional shift in terms of both politics and theological discourse, the former Saudi defense minister and son of King Salman al Saud, Muhammad bin Salman (MBS), was made crown prince of Saudi Arabia in

June 2017 after deposing Crown Prince Mohammed bin Nayef (MBN) in a palace coup. He has since been the de-facto leader of Saudi Arabia.[74] He had become Muhammad bin Zayed's closest ally in the region. MBS has had a mixed legacy. He consolidated his power first by eliminating opposition to his rule, by imprisoning twenty of the country's richest princes in the Ritz Carlton hotel.[75] In the West, he was first hailed as a reformer for finally allowing women in the Kingdom to drive, albeit he also imprisoned the feminist activists who had campaigned for this reform.[76] Still, it seemed things were changing in Saudi Arabia. The crown prince, at least in the media, appeared to be neutralizing Salafi discourses in favor of a more "moderate Islam."[77] It is unclear whether this "moderate Islam" represents an overturning of the religious Salafi narrative or merely liberalizes it, although the latter seems more likely. MBS's image as a young benevolent reformer was quickly tarnished after the dissident journalist Jamal Khashoggi was lured into the Saudi embassy in Istanbul and brutally murdered.[78] MBS's relationship with the UAE reached its apex when it decided to place an economic embargo on Qatar in 2017.[79] Together MBS and MBZ formed a coalition to counter any potential rise of political Islam in the region.

The narrative of reform—religious, social, or otherwise—was put at the front and center of Muhammad bin Salman's reign. To gain power, however, MBS had needed to oust the then crown prince Mohammed bin Nayef. There was no love lost between MBN and MBZ. MBZ once told a group of American diplomats that MBN's father "had a 'bumbling manner,' which proved 'Darwin was right.'" [80] MBN was reportedly concerned and tried to warn King Salman of a UAE-sponsored coup in Saudi Arabia. According to Christopher M. Davidson, MBN purportedly wrote a letter to the King stating that "we are facing a dangerous conspiracy ... an Emirati plot has been exposed to help aggravate the differences within the Royal Court."[81] "One American official and one adviser to a Saudi royal said Mohammed bin Nayef opposed the embargo on Qatar, a stand that probably accelerated his ouster."[82] Bin Nayef may have had a different vision of regional alliances from his successor. A security think tank affiliated with the then crown prince Mohammed bin Nayef produced a document in Arabic and English called "Abu Dhabi's Network of Political Sufism: and Its Implications on the Security of Saudi Arabia." This was then disseminated on a website called "Shu'ūn Islāmiyya." According to a former employee, the think tank and the website have since been shut down.[83]

The document provides a detailed, albeit not always accurate, account of Sufi and neo-traditionalist networks operating within the UAE. It cautions Saudi Arabia against this seeming threat. It seems to have some Salafi and pro-Islamist undertones. As per anti-Shia and anti-Iranian Saudi policy, it stresses the doubtful Shia and potential Iranian link through the figure of Sayyed Hossein Nasr. The document has three chapters. The Introduction warns of Muhammad bin Zayed and the UAE's attempts to circumvent Saudi Arabia both politically and religiously.[84] It states:

> One of the most important positions Mohammed bin Zayed has occupied is his role as the advisor to the Head of State for National Security. Over the past ten years (2004–14), he has worked on incorporating religious affairs with national security as part of a joint policy approach, considering the Sunni Maliki Madhhab and Sufism as integral parts of the national identity of all the UAE.[85]

The Introduction describes the policy initiatives undertaken by the US government to promote Sufi and neo-traditionalist networks—such as the RAND and Nixon reports. It discusses the political motivations and uses of *taṣawwuf*: from US post-9/11 interests to standing up to political Islam and reaffirming the power of the UAE, and forging an alternative religious authority.

The second chapter, entitled "The Political Role of the 'New Dervishes,'" goes through the profiles of neo-traditionalists focusing on their political networks and their anti-Salafi, anti-Islamist stances. Among the Arab neo-traditionalists mentioned are Ahmed al-Tayeb, Abdullah bin Bayyah, Habib Ali Jifri, and Ali Goma. The Western neo-traditionalists profiled include Hamza Yusuf, Abdal Hakim Murad, Zaid Shakir, Musa Furber, and Jihad Brown. Yusuf's profile in the document misrepresents his religious affiliations. Interestingly, though, Murad and Zaid Shakir's profiles present them less negatively. The last chapter warns of a security threat to the "long-established religious authorities in the kingdom" while simultaneously urging the kingdom to change its relationship with Islamic movements (Islamists).[86] It is unclear whether Bin Nayef himself was sympathetic to a reconciliation between the Saudi state and Islamists or whether he only allowed for these voices. Either way, after his ousting by Muhammad bin Salman, it was clear that the Kingdom's religious policies would be resolutely anti-Islamist.

With MBS in power from June 2017 to 2020, a regional crisis ensued when Saudi Arabia, the UAE, Egypt, Mauritania, and other countries cut diplomatic ties and blockaded Qatar. This coalition, led by Saudi Arabia and the UAE, claimed that Qatar was aiding the Muslim Brotherhood and other "terrorist organizations," causing regional unrest. This signaled the beginning of an even closer diplomatic alliance between Turkey and Qatar and greater Turkish mistrust of the UAE/Saudi camp. After the Saudi journalist Jamal Khashoggi was killed and dismembered by an assassination team sent by the Saudi government to its embassy in Istanbul in 2018, this cold war reached its apex. This put Yusuf in an uncomfortable position. Yusuf had long been an admirer of Turkey and its leader, Recep Tayyip Erdoğan, and has publicly defended the government's response to the 2013 Gezi Park protests and the 2016 coup attempt.[87] In turn, Erdoğan had long supported Yusuf and other neo-traditionalist figures—even attending the opening of Cambridge Mosque founded by Abdal Hakim Murad.[88] The Rihla retreat was, in fact, held in Turkey between 2011 and 2016 with the support of the Turkish government. The relationship between Erdoğan and Yusuf subsequently soured—especially after the American Muslim boxer Muhammad Ali's funeral, where the Turkish president was denied an opportunity to speak, for reasons that are still unclear. The next year, Rihla was held in Malaysia.[89]

Policy Initiatives

Before the inauguration of the first annual Forum for Promoting Peace in Muslim Societies in 2014, Abdullah bin Bayyah and Hamza Yusuf led a number of policy enterprises. From the outset, these enterprises seemed squarely concerned with interfaith dialogue, the plight of minorities, citizenship, and disassociating Islam from extremism. However, the underlying problem of causation that the members of the neo-traditionalist epistemic community spearheading these initiatives seem to share with policymakers is the concern over political unrest or revolutions in the Middle East, Islamist politics, the contestability of the authority of the leader and state, and radical extremism (sometimes overtly linked to Salafism, sometimes not). The first type of policy enterprise includes interfaith, with a particular focus on non-Muslim minorities in Muslim-majority countries, for example "A Common Word Between Us and You" (2007, under the auspices of the Kingdom of Jordan) and "The Marrakesh Declaration" (2016, under the auspices of the Kingdom of Morocco and the UAE). The second type of policy initiative is framed as a concern for defining the parameters of orthodoxy to counter the heterodoxy of religious extremism. These are initiatives such as "The Amman Message" (2004, under the auspices of King Abdullah II bin Al-Hussein of Jordan), "A Letter to Baghdadi" (2014), and the "Mardin Conference" (2010, organized by the Global Center for Renewal and Guidance). They are framed as a form of religious corrective approach by which authentic traditional scholarship can mend the religious understandings that led to the aforementioned problems of causation.

These initiatives, as Warren argues, are a part of a larger trend of "state-branding" following the War on Terror.[90] As such, the political utility of these enterprises serves more than their stated goal. It is also not entirely cosmetic, as some have noted.[91] In the case of "A Letter to Baghdadi," "Amman Message," and the "Mardin Conference," each establishes religious edicts that ascertain that terrorism is, first and foremost, caused by heterodox belief. Furthermore, it is caused by the declining authority of religious leaders—which they themselves represent. After all, the knowledge production of epistemic communities requires them to be authoritative to be effective. Indeed, as Hamid and Mandeville note, these initiatives solidify the religious claims of states—which are often monarchies.[92] Although these states often use Islam as a legitimizer, it is not often the basis for governing. The policy-driven concern for orthodoxy is, therefore, less related to the actual policymaking process and more to delegitimizing the "heterodox" religious "other." It essentially constructs the parameters and conditions under which an Islamic discourse could be dealt with as authentically Islamic.

In the Mardin conference, for example, Abdullah bin Bayyah asserted that European Muslim terrorists conducted terror attacks based on a mistranslated *fatwā* made by Ibn Taymiyyah. Bin Bayyah claims to have uncovered the original manuals, to find that it was all based on a simple error.[93] Yusuf cites this conference in public lectures and to seekers as a way of theologically debunking terrorism and affirming the authority of the shaykhs.[94] Seekers are stunned at how seamlessly Bin Bayyah can refute a *fatwā* on which many terrorist attacks were premised. Yahya Michot and Ali Bardakoğlu, the Head of Turkey's Directorate of Religious Affairs, were not so sure. Bardakoğlu argued that it is a futile endeavor to try to place the responsibility for modern political wars and insurgencies that have come out of specific conditions merely on a *fatwā* issued in the past.[95] Michot argues that the contested figure of Ibn Taymiyyah and his *fatwā* are signifiers for a modern contestation of authority,[96] that is, the authority of neo-traditionalist scholarship versus that of the

Salafis. Additionally, correcting the Mardin *fatwā* as containing a "typo"—as Yusuf calls it—did not deter ISIS years later.[97]

The second mode of policy-relevant initiatives, that of interfaith initiatives, unearths another important locale of power: the modern nation-states and, by extension, the regimes that represent them. Much like the "orthodoxy" initiatives, these initiatives are constructed as an antidote to extremism.[98] The first of them was the 2016 Marrakesh Declaration, held under the joint sponsorship of the King of Morocco, Mohammad VI, and the Forum for Peace (FPPMS) under the patronage of Shaykh Abdullah bin Zayed. Bin Bayyah, alongside Hamza Yusuf, drafted recommendations to develop notions of citizenship based on the Charter of Madina as a template.[99] In the Arab world, this received little attention. It was seen as an idealistic or cosmetic call for interfaith unity that would be less likely to cause tangible change.[100] The Marrakesh Declaration sought a change, but not necessarily just to the conditions of religious minorities. Its locus of attention was directed to the plight of minorities at the hands of non-state actors. The context the "Marrakesh Declaration" posits regarding its emergence is the rise of armed struggle as a way of settling conflicts, the weakened authority of legitimate governments, and the distortion of the fundamentals of religion.[101]

Unlike the "orthodoxy" initiatives, however, the Marrakesh Declaration is not a simple restatement of the boundaries and limitations of what is deemed true rather than false. In Zaytuna College, Hamza Yusuf lauded Bin Bayyah for this initiative as a "creative traditionalist."[102] The traditionalist/modernist hybrid of the Marrakesh Declaration sets the methodological tone for the later concerns of the Forum for Peace in Abu Dhabi. The starting point of the declaration is the dual decline of the political authority of the states and the religious authority of the traditional scholars (or, as Bin Bayyah notes, "al-rāsikhūn"). Methodologically, however, centering the project around the nation-states paradoxically places them on a par with their Islamist opponents. It is, in fact, not new for thinkers to argue for a jurisprudence of citizenship based on the Charter of Madina. Islamist scholars and thinkers such as Yusuf Qaradawi, Abdul Majid Najjar, and Rashid al-Ghannoushi had made this point much earlier.[103] The main difference becomes the appeal to authority and political conclusions. Deriving the foremost authority for stability from the nation-state essentially requires neo-traditionalists to negotiate their epistemic criterion with the needs of the state.

The Forum for Promoting Peace in Muslim Societies

The Forum for Promoting Peace in Muslim Societies, with its institutional and financial center in Abu Dhabi, synthesizes all the aforementioned elements. It affirms the authentic authority of the scholars present. It explicitly centers on the legitimacy of a religious methodological narrative around the modern nation-state, as represented by liberal autocracies in the Middle East. The nation-state becomes more than a by-product of colonial modernity, to become the guarantor of stability in a fragmented world.[104] For the sponsors of the Forum, Abdullah bin Zayed and Crown Prince Muhammad bin Zayed, it represents a much-needed scholarly response to those who advocate "civil strife."[105] In fact, the Forum supports the policy agenda of the Emirati government in several ways. Since the inauguration of the Forum, promoting "religious tolerance" has been the cornerstone of the UAE's public image[106]—so much so that, in 2016, the UAE established the Ministry of Tolerance and Coexistence and declared 2019 the "Year of Tolerance."[107] In turn, the Forum provides religious sanction against dissenting voices as an affront to said tolerance. Furthermore, it brought together Christian and Jewish leaders, as a part of its religious diplomacy project, culminating in the Abraham Accords of 2020.

In 2014, Abdullah bin Bayyah gave the keynote speech as the forum president. In it he stated:

> In societies that are not ready, the call for democracy is essentially a call for war. Since the human and financial costs of establishing democracy may be very high in societies without common ground, justice in its Islamic sense must be established as a foundation for peace and security ... our tradition teaches us that reform is preferable to revolution, as revolution brings destruction without offering solutions.[108]

He continued to explain that the importance of obedience is stressed in the tradition so that society may avoid bloodshed and ensure peace. Bin Bayyah adds that obedience should go beyond merely following the laws of the state, but "may also be expressed by waiving one's rights"—this earns one respect and makes others reconsider their positions.[109] Bin Bayyah advocates a political position, which Yusuf echoes: that peace is the necessary requirement for justice, and is necessary even in spite of it. In this sense, the notion of citizenship lacks both traditional rootedness and the modern implications of democracy. What remains is that the nation-state is accorded primary importance.

In 2018, the Emirati government established the "UAE Fatwā Council" to "ensure that religious scholars advocate moderate Islam and eliminate any source of conflict among existing and future fatwā," with Abdullah bin Bayyah as president and Hamza Yusuf as a member.[110] In an interview Yusuf gave to the *Emirati Nation News* website, he explained:

> It is important to note that the UAE has been active in addressing the crises of the fatwā. Sheikh Abdullah bin Bayyah's approach is the only one that will enable Muslims to navigate the modern world without losing their way by going from one extreme, which is the violent extremism, to the other, which is losing the religion altogether.[111]

The trope of the "chaos of *fatwā*" has been a salient concern for both Yusuf and Bin Bayyah throughout, including before the Forum. Warren notes:

> Bin Bayyah's concept of chaos, be it the chaos of the fatwā or religious discourse, is central for contextualizing his decision-making. He is deeply concerned by the perceived erosion of the 'ulamā''s authority and their consequent inability to combat charlatan muftis whose nefarious fatwās are, in his view, behind every act of terrorism.[112]

The direction that the Fatwā Council has taken since has garnered criticism. In 2014, the UAE government designated eighty-two organizations and figures, including Yusuf al-Qaradawi, Al-Islah, the Muslim Brotherhood, the Islamic Association in Finland, the Islamic Association in Norway, the Islamic Relief Organization in the UK, the Cordoba Foundation in Britain, the Muslim American Society (MAS), the Union of Muslim Scholars, the Union of Islamic Organizations in Europe, the Union of Islamic Organizations of France, the Muslim Association of Britain (MAB), the Islamic Society of Germany, the Islamic Society in Denmark, and the Islamic Society in Belgium terrorist organizations.[113] After Donald Trump's election, it emerged that he too was moving toward designating the Brotherhood a terrorist organization. In early 2017, the Republican Senator Ted Cruz planned to introduce the Muslim Brotherhood Terrorist Designation Act, which aimed to criminalize mainstream Muslim organizations such as the Council on American–Islamic Relations (CAIR) and the Islamic Society of North America (ISNA).[114] In 2020, the UAE Fatwā Council released a statement addressing the UAE's 2014 designation, that read: "The position of the council regarding the groups and organizations is the same position of *walī al-'amr*."[115] Bin Bayyah points out that jurists cannot encroach on a ruler's decision-making since they cannot know the reality behind a particular situation.[116] This meant not only the ratification of mainstream Muslim organizations as terrorist organizations, but also the ratification of Bin Bayyah's long-time interlocutor and companion, Yusuf al Qaradawi, as a terrorist.

After announcing 2019 as the "Year of Tolerance," the UAE took multiple steps to foster its image. In February 2019, Pope Francis participated in an interfaith conference in the UAE and said Mass for 120,000 worshippers. In September 2019, the UAE legalized churches and temples. In November 2019, it was announced that Israel would participate in Dubai's World Expo in 2020 (delayed due to Covid).[117] It was also announced that a new "Abrahamic Family House" would be inaugurated in 2022.[118] This would include a mosque, a church, and a synagogue. The following year (2020), Abdullah bin Zayed, the Bahraini foreign minister Abdullatif bin Rashid Al Zayani, the Israeli Prime Minister Benjamin Netanyahu, and US President Donald Trump signed the Abraham Accords. These normalized relations between the UAE, Bahrain, and Israel (Sudan and Morocco normalized later on). They were framed as an extension of the interfaith projects, and named after the patriarch of the three monotheistic religions. Hae Won Jeong explains:

> The Abraham Accords Declaration has strong idealistic overtones imbued with motifs of peace, religious freedom, prosperity, and human dignity. The treaty explicitly aims to promote interfaith and intercultural dialogue and suggests that religious tolerance is the way to break the political impasse in the Middle East peace process.[119]

The Forum for Promoting Peace in Muslim Societies subsequently released a statement following a meeting with its members on August 15, 2020. The statement commended Muhammad bin Zayed for his efforts in "pursuing a just and permanent peace in the Middle East, and expressed the wish that this initiative would pave the way to peace and promote stability in the region and the world."[120] Bin Bayyah commended the treaty, as it "safeguards one of the fundamental goals of Islamic law and will benefit humanity."[121] As a result of the Forum's statement, Yusuf was heavily criticized. In response, he wrote, "The recent reports alleging my political views were fabricated and erroneous … My allegiance is and has always been with the oppressed peoples of Palestine, whether Muslim, Christian or otherwise. Anyone who says differently is a liar."[122] Yusuf blamed the media for spreading false reports and not seeking clarification. Seemingly, however, it was the media office of the Forum that put out the statement. As a result, Aisha al-Adawiya, another member of the Forum, announced her resignation from the Forum. She wrote on her Facebook account, "In our last board meeting of the Forum, there were no discussions surrounding the topic of Palestine or the UAE's relationship with Israel. Hence, there was no agreement on support for the UAE's deal with Israel."[123]

Alliance of Virtue

Another important by-product of these interfaith initiatives has been a greater convergence between neo-traditionalists and right-wing conservatives. In the previous chapter, I showed that neo-traditionalists have tried to forge intellectual links with conservatives by theorizing about a new continuum that harmonizes Islam with a nostalgic Western past. This discursive shift is not exclusively intellectual. From the outset, Yusuf located Muslim morality as part of the "moral majority"[124]—possibly an overcorrection from the perceived Muslim–left-wing alliances that have skewed their "metaphysical lens." For Hamza Yusuf, this alliance is both political and moral. Yahya Birt notes the dual dimension of this relationship.[125] Religiously, his moral interlocutors have been concerned with the conditions of Christian minorities and anti-semitism in the Muslim world.[126] They are additionally concerned with the rise of political Islam as a force. Politically, these fears are mitigated through the interfaith initiatives undertaken by Hamza Yusuf and Abdullah bin Bayyah with the Forum for Peace.[127] Morally, these groups are united in their fight against pornography, their concerns about homosexuality and LGBTQ rights, the integrity of "traditional marriage," and anti-abortion stances.

In December 2019, the Forum announced the release of the Charter of the New Alliance of Virtue (ḥilf al-fuḍūl) in Abu Dhabi. This call for an alliance of virtue has evidently been a long-time project for Abdullah bin Bayyah and his student Hamza Yusuf. In fact, the founding of the Radical Middle Way project was partly inspired by Abdullah bin Bayyah's call for an "alliance of virtue."[128] This interfaith charter was based on a seventh-century pre-Islamic agreement that Muhammad and his companion Abu Bakr were a part of—in which Quraysh agreed to resolve their problems justly. Muhammad continued to consider this agreement positively after he started to receive revelations.[129]

Martino Diez points out that unlike in the Marrakesh Declaration—in which the framework for citizenship was based on the Charter of Madina—the origin of the alliance of virtue is pre-Islamic. As such, the Charter of the New Alliance of Virtue does not appeal to revelation; rather, it has a "natural understanding of justice." He continued to add, "Staying clear from any reference to this medieval debate, the extensors of the Charter presented in Abu Dhabi chose to implicitly move towards a reactivation of what Catholic thought would call 'natural law.'"[130] The Religious Freedom Institute, a conservative DC-based organization on whose Board of Advisors Hamza Yusuf sits, helped formulate the final text of the charter. Kent R. Hill, a member of the Institute, explains: "Among RFI's contributions was an affirmation of natural rights ... The Charter also acknowledges the importance of *Dignitatis Humanae.*"[131] *Dignitatis Humanae* is a declaration on religious freedom promulgated by Pope Paul VI in 1965.[132]

This Charter of the New Alliance of Virtue was a culmination of several interfaith initiatives instituted by the Forum for Promoting Peace in Muslim Societies—beginning with the Marrakesh Declaration in 2016, and followed by the "American Peace Caravan" in 2017, and the Washington Declaration in 2018.[133] The first order of business of the Trump administration's State Department Ambassador-at-Large for International Religious Freedom, Sam Brownback, after he was appointed was the unveiling of the "Washington Declaration," organized by the Forum and spearheaded by Bin Bayyah. Brownback commended Bin Bayyah and the efforts of the Alliance as follows:

> The Marrakesh Declaration initiative of Shaykh Bin Bayyah and all of his partners in the global Islamic scholarly community is a great example of how civil society leaders can play a tremendous role in helping to set the tone for protecting human rights, including those relating to citizenship of religious minorities. It's not only a tone but a theological basis that it can exist with.

He added: "Most importantly, I will seek your guidance on how the U.S. government can be more effective in promoting international religious freedom in all corners of the globe."[134]

For years, Yusuf has been cultivating relations with Christian and Jewish conservative leaders as a response to the seemingly growing alliance between young Muslims and the Left. In a Princeton Mawlid event, Yusuf decried young people's shift toward socialism. Although he had been consistently critical of free-market capitalism himself, Yusuf now stressed: "The Prophet was the ultimate free-market advocate ... To see Muslims talking about socialism?

Now young Muslims are completely drinking this kool-aid! Private property is one of the six universals in the Islamic tradition; it is protected. Socialism is a crime against private property."[135]

While expressing some distaste for Donald Trump, Yusuf grew closer to the Right after Trump's presidency. In February 2017, following Trump's victory, Yusuf attended the National Prayer Breakfast, where, according to Birt, "Trump strongly advocated for his version of religious nationalism."[136] Yusuf subsequently urged Muslims not to get involved with the protest movements and to focus on building institutions.[137] In 2019, Mike Pompeo, the Trump administration's Secretary of State, appointed Hamza Yusuf as a member of the Commission on Unalienable Rights.[138] This commission was criticized by progressives and human rights organizations, including Human Rights Watch. Kenneth Roth, the Executive Director of Human Rights Watch, argued:

> The commission seems to favor an a la carte approach to rights: the US government will pick the rights it wants to observe, and others can do the same. That approach would be music to the ears of the world's autocrats, and many will happily take the opportunity to trample on certain basic rights that Pompeo himself has rightly defended in places like Hong Kong.[139]

Regardless, this appointment was welcomed by Bin Bayyah. He commended his colleagues, as they "serve as global ambassadors who portray a bright image of the UAE, which has become a model for tolerance and a generous aid donor thanks to the directives of President His Highness Sheikh Khalifa b. Zayed Al Nahyan for promoting and upholding human rights and fostering inter-cultural dialogue."[140] Indeed, Yusuf has been adamant that the main way Muslims can erase the suspicions that conservative Christians have of Islam is to highlight the commonalities they share. To do so, he engaged with conservative intellectuals such as Robert P. George and Roger Scruton.[141] Scruton was an English conservative philosopher. Much more controversial than George, Scruton was criticized for his Islamophobia, misogyny, and belief in eugenics.[142] It would naturally seem that Yusuf and Scruton would have little in common. If one looks more closely, however, one can note some convergence and signifiers of Western decline in a post-Christian context. In a lecture on "The Future of European Civilization: Lessons for America" given at the Heritage Foundation, Scruton argued:

202 | NEO-TRADITIONALISM IN ISLAM IN THE WEST

The rights idea leaves everything that is most important in the life of a Muslim without official endorsement. Everything has to do with sex, marriage, and the family in the operation of the law ... The Muslim heart is at odds with the new official Europe. Had Christianity retained its status as the foundation of domestic custom and public law, it would have been easier for a Muslim to accept the European order. Our way of life would have seemed like a form of obedience.[143]

Yusuf's most recent activism against abortion is the strongest point of commonality he shares with other religious conservatives. In October 2020, Yusuf gave a lecture at Vita et Veritas, a Yale-based Pro-Life group.[144] The talk was loosely based on an article he wrote two years previously in *Renovatio*, "When Does a Human Fetus Become Human?"[145] Yusuf argued against the allowances scholars have made regarding terminating pregnancies and stated that they were marginal positions. He noted that their understanding of ensoulment was based on erroneous science and that Islam has clear prohibitions against infanticide—a term he used interchangeably with abortion. He went on to take the extreme position of prohibiting in vitro fertilization because "a woman is not permitted to expose her nakedness to a physician unless it's as an absolute necessity or a dire need." He defers, however, to the UAE Fatwā Council, which he is a part of, for a formal *fatwā*.

Yusuf then went on to clarify his role on the Commission for Unalienable Rights. He said:

I was recently on a Commission for Unalienable Rights which was trying to get back to what are those fundamental, unalienable rights? The first of which is life and people, a moral choice when they engage in sexual behavior. They have a moral responsibility to understand that first and foremost, we are biological creatures.

Yusuf went on to explain that although pleasure is important, in the Abrahamic traditions, it is considered "a divine trick to bring about children." Yusuf then expressed his view on a new platform for interfaith relations. He stressed:

I sincerely believe that Muslims should be more active in this [the pro-life movement]. I think it's an area where we'd have a much better chance of removing some of the suspicions and concerns that many Christians have about Islam, especially the more traditional Catholics and some of the more traditional Protestant iterations of Christianity.

Yusuf's squarely conservative views on gender and sexuality are a far cry from Geneive Abdo's and other policy experts' early depiction of Yusuf as the young Californian reformer fighting the conservative immigrant mentality of the "old country."[146] In fact, as David Warren eloquently explains, "Whereas in previous decades Qaradawi's social conservatism in matters of sexuality prompted outcries on his visits to the West, now Bin Bayyah and Yusuf's social conservatism is viewed as part of a shared Abrahamic moral majority that the US government is keen to foster."[147] It seems unlikely to suggest that public life in the UAE is in any way harmed by Yusuf's critiques of modernity and secularity. In what Christopher Davidson dubbed a campaign of "liberal engineering," the UAE saw greater efforts at secularization, including changing the weekend to Saturday and Sunday instead of Friday and Saturday, changing the laws of cohabitation to allow non-married couples to live together, and greater allowances regarding alcohol and pork consumption.[148]

Following the metaphysical principles presented as the traditional basis for navigating politics, this chapter has explored Hamza Yusuf and Abdullah bin Bayyah's role in global and domestic politics. It has looked at his role, from his advisory position with George W. Bush's government to his current role in the Fatwā Council in the UAE and the Forum for Promoting Peace in Muslim Society, also sponsored by the UAE. After the "War on Terror," two right-wing think tanks, the RAND Corporation and the Nixon Centre, released reports on how to forge links with different Muslim religious trends as allies. In the United States and the United Kingdom, neo-traditionalists, among other Sufi groups, were used as a tool for soft power. It was not only Western governments that were interested in cultivating neo-traditionalism as a moderate alternative to political Islam. Particularly after the Arab Spring, there was a fear of the rise of political Islam. Arab governments, especially the UAE's, worked closely with Hamza Yusuf and his shaykh, Abdullah bin Bayyah, to develop an alternative religious discourse by establishing the Forum for Promoting Peace in Muslim Societies. Bin Bayyah and Yusuf urged young Muslims to privilege the path of peace over justice and not to be consumed with the discourse of victimhood. This relationship with the UAE sparked controversy due to the country's role in the region—such as the detrimental war on Yemen and its support for counterrevolutionary autocrats.

8

THE SEEKERS, POLITICS, AND POWER

In the age of liquid modernity, where certainties—be they regarding religious criteria, spiritual authority, nationhood, or gender—appear to dissipate, neo-traditionalism posits a sense of certainty and stability for its seekers. The phenomenon of neo-traditionalism exists in ambivalent spaces transnationally. It recreates itself in modern settings of Europe and the US. Still, it continuously seeks external validation by periodic references or visits to distant places in North Africa and the Middle East, seemingly untouched by modernity. These places act as naturally existing "enclaves" of pure-unchanged "Islam." In the neo-traditionalist discourse, both sites, though existing in different contexts, are projected as a meaning-continuum of each other. This discourse positions itself in contradistinction to postcolonial or Black American Islam. Presumably, it does not carry the historical baggage of power struggle and its induced religious and political heterodoxies. Neo-traditionalism, in this sense, encourages seekers to disassociate their religion from the cross-pressures of the different locales of power. Instead, they ought to locate themselves within the metaphysical certainties of the tradition. This affects everything from national and global politics to race and gender.

In traditional spaces, the coherence of tradition is maintained by the charismatic authority of the shaykhs and the enchanted space of the retreat. In a sense, modernity does not intrude. Outside the enchanted space of the retreat, matters become more complicated. As I have shown in the previous chapter, it becomes increasingly apparent that the "traditional" claims of the shaykhs are politically situated and permeable to the imperatives of power. Seekers contextualize and grapple with this aspect differently. Some contend that the shaykhs can be a "little out of touch." By this, they mean that the shaykhs operate in a spiritual realm of reality that cannot account for the impure dimensions of politics. Still, some seekers find themselves at a crossroads as regards the shaykhs' simultaneous proximity to power and their denial of it. Suppose the space of the retreat provides a post-racial, anti-political location where the cross-pressures of Islamophobia and geopolitical concerns do not intrude. In that case, protection is not provided outside this space. The seekers' personal histories, modern subjectivities, and the pressures from different locales of power require them to adjust how they navigate the tradition's ever-changing criteria in their everyday lives. It seems that, increasingly, living in the modern world, and with the racialized, as opposed to the neutral and essential, traditional Islam, leads some seekers to a sense of displacement. Of course, not everyone feels that way.

As I show, there are three ways in which seekers make sense of this. For some, upon their reaching a breaking point, the neo-traditionalists' epistemic claims and authority are put under complete scrutiny. There is a sense of spiritual melancholia and homelessness. As John R. Hall notes, "absence of a shared myth seems to spell certain doom, but a highly developed myth may also prove inadequate for marshaling commitment."[1] The spiritual claims of religious authority become bitterly contested—as much as or even more than their locational proximity to power. The second, and perhaps more common, way seekers navigate this is through keeping religious beliefs in the private spheres of their modern lives. The spatial boundaries which indicate modern/traditional spaces allow for this privatization. For example, it is a requirement in the space of the retreat for women to wear a full *hijab*, even for those who do not normally wear it. Some seekers noted that they would have liked the retreat organizers or the shaykhs to have explained the significance of the *hijab* instead of just making it a requirement. Outside the disciplined space of the retreat, the various psychological, social, and religious factors make the *hijab* a more complicated choice that is not always opted for.

Similarly, other traditional values can be privatized, whereby seekers accept their validity; however, they retain their modern subjectivity—including their political beliefs and dispositions. In a sense, one can be both politically and actively left-wing in one's secular, modern life and still show sympathy for the right-wing views of the shaykhs after their lectures. Such views reflect different religious–secular realms. As Jose Casanova notes, in modern religion, the individual worships in a marketplace of multiple religious and secular value systems, reserving the right only for themselves to denominate what that form of worship would entail.[2] The discrepancies are mitigated in different ways, as will be described in this chapter. The last is complete acceptance. Strikingly, this appears to apply to a very small minority of the seekers I have interviewed—representing only four out of forty. Three noted that the shaykhs' contentions regarding the different locales of power represent a continuity in terms of their religious beliefs and upbringing. Only one noted a complete change in her position.

Space and Politics

On the third day of the Spring Lodge retreat in Nottingham (April 5, 2015), I sat among the seekers listening to Habib Ali Jifri's lecture. It had been a long day. After *fajr* prayers, we sat reciting from the litanies of the Ba'alawī ṭarīqa. Although it had been very early, the marquee where the shaykhs would present their religious sermons was packed. Men sat on one side of the floor and women on the other. That day, Habib Ali presented three different sermons. The first was from a classical text on the "Shamā 'il al Muḥammadiyah," or attributes of the Prophet. In the second sermon, he explained the fallacies of Islamism and how it had been based on the Kharijite doctrine. The third sermon brought Habib Ali Jifri along with Habib Kadhim as-Saqqaf and Shaykh Abdurrahman ould Murabit al-Hajj. The three Eastern scholars sat on stage. Beside them was a Western shaykh translating for them. The shaykhs thought it necessary that they advise seekers on how to engage with modernity and politics in times of turbulence. Although the three shaykhs seemed to agree, Habib Ali Jifri and Habib Kadhim appeared to be more enthusiastic about the importance of their political message than Shaykh Abdurrahman ould Murabit al-Hajj.

The two Ba'alawī shaykhs stressed to the seekers that they should not trust the media. In modern times people feel a sense of urgency to act, as they see images on the screen of oppression and violence worldwide. The shaykhs explained to the seekers that action is neither their religious duty nor their concern. For a Muslim, the soundness of one's heart should be the primary concern. Habib Ali then cited an example he is familiar with—Egypt. He explained that there had been images on television from Egypt of intense police brutality. Seditious news channels, Habib Ali contended, have shown images of burnt bodies from the Rabaa protests claiming that the Egyptian army and police were responsible. He added that the media did not say that it had been the protesters who had burnt the bodies to frame the Egyptian army. He then explained that the senior Egyptian scholar Yusuf al-Qaradawi had issued a *fatwā* which had led to the Syrian Shaykh Ramadan al-Buti's murder in Syria. On stage next to him, Shaykh Abdurrahman ould Murabit al-Hajj looked stunned. He asked Habib Ali if this was indeed true, and Habib Ali confirmed it. At this, Shaykh Abdurrahman shook his head in disbelief, mouthing the words "lā ḥawla walā quwat illā bi Illāh"—there is no might nor power except in Allah.

Although I was shocked at Jifri's massacre denialism, I was adamant about recording the seekers' impressions directly after the sermon inside the marquee. Most were unfamiliar with the events Jifri referred to but appealed to his charisma and traditional authority. They highlighted the perennial wisdom of the tradition as embodied by Jifri. Unlike Salafis, they noted, Habib Ali was always smiling. As one girl noted, this was what it meant to personify the Sunna of the Prophet. I then asked a more specific question: whether they agreed with the political message that Jifri was making. Interestingly, there was no definitive agreement or disagreement. Rather, seekers opted to explain what Habib Ali really meant—to dispel any confusion on my part. The message was understood simply to say that we cannot possibly know the truth, and since the media have a habit of lying, it is of the soundness of one's heart not to engage in politics.

In the interviews I conducted with seekers outside the space of the retreat, there was less meaning-making involved in their reflections and more questions and uncertainty. These uncertainties are not related to the efficacy of the notion of tradition or the shaykhs' authority but rather the implications for their religious journey. Indeed, it is because of the significance of the authority of the tradition and the shaykhs that seekers find it difficult to grapple with these contentious issues. Can the higher disembodied ideals of tradition encapsulate or rehabilitate their modern realities? Can the seekers' subjectivities escape historical and political contexts and achieve the neutral metaphysical disposition of the tradition? What happens when the shaykhs' political stances do not make sense or are seen as problematic, as in the case of Hamza Yusuf's discourse on race?

Hall explains that when the myth of the group is being called into question, interpersonal difficulties can often lead to pluralism, that is, the preservation of relationships despite the myth.[3] This is true in the case of many of

Hamza Yusuf's interlocutors, such as Zaid Shakir, Dawud Walid or Abdal Hakim Murad, who implicitly indicated that they do not agree with some of his political stances and believe that they have gone beyond traditional notions of quietism.[4]

With seekers, the situation is more fragile. Unlike in communal groups, they leave the enchanted spaces of the retreat and go back to their material realities. As Hall remarks, "participants must effectively deal not only with their own social and material situations but also with constraints of the encompassing society from which they hope to withdraw."[5] I assess the reflections seekers have on neo-traditionalism, their religious faith, and material reality in relation to three main linked themes: race and racialization, political quietism and the Arab Spring, and the authority of the shaykhs themselves.

Race and Racialization after the "War on Terror"

The seekers I interviewed, mainly young people aged 18–34, grew up in a post-9/11 world. Regardless of their religious upbringing or race, except for recent white converts, the discourse of the War on Terror was inescapable. Younger seekers, particularly those born from the mid-1990s onwards, only knew of a post-9/11 world. On the other hand, older seekers could remember the event and were hyper-conscious of how their realities had changed after 9/11. In this sense, the younger seekers were only acutely aware of Hamza Yusuf's "famed" transformation post-9/11; however, they did not experience this transformation first-hand. For them, it is more of a fable told by the older generation. For older seekers, the transformation Hamza Yusuf underwent was, in many ways, a part of their own religious story. They knew Yusuf's revolutionary, anti-Western, messianic discourse in the 1990s, so his change took its place among many other changes and a part of the reality they had to grapple with.

Hamida had taken a year off from university to study Islam in Malaysia. Before embarking on her studies there, she decided to go to Rihla. When she was growing up, she explained, her parents would bring her and her siblings Islamic cassettes to listen to. "Growing up, we listened to his [Hamza Yusuf's] lectures," she explained. Hamida paused for a few seconds, and then she said:

> but I do remember a time when my parents stopped playing his lectures. I think he did something political, and it ticked my parents off ... I remember it was 2001—after 9/11. I remember he made some statements to the point where some Islamic bookstores removed his books and his lectures from

their bookstores. Like in Newark, there is a bookstore that I grew up going to. An owner is an Arab man—a Sunni man. I remember that after 9/11, my parents told me that Shaykh Hamza Yusuf made a statement that caused a lot of Muslims to be very upset, and I never really looked into exactly what he said.

The vague invocations of 9/11 by other younger seekers like Hamida represent the fact that the magnitude of the event was felt differently by seekers of different ages. For some, the post-9/11 national and religious politics were the only worlds they knew. They therefore navigated these as such. The War on Terror and its framing of Muslim identity in the West represented a norm. Subsequently, the debates on how scholars and shaykhs related to power at the time only matter in terms of their current engagement with counterterrorism and surveillance initiatives. For older seekers, the neo-traditionalists' securitized discourse on Islamic identity between moderate Islam and radical Islam was a paradigm shift they had to grapple with.

In his auto-ethnography *Radical Skin, Moderate Masks*, Yassir Morsi explains his transformation. Morsi's journey, in many ways, resembles that of Issa. Both Morsi and Issa were teenagers at the time of 9/11. Coming from immigrant backgrounds, they represent two nodes of "postcolonial Islam." Morsi, originally British-Egyptian, relocated to Australia at a young age. Issa has a British-Bengali background. For Morsi, who grew up in Australia, his primary reference to counterterrorism and post-9/11 religious discourse was Yusuf and the offshoot neo-traditionalist community in Australia. For Issa, Yusuf is also an important figure; however, the British Muslim neo-traditionalist community relates more to Abdal Hakim Murad.

Yassir Morsi explained Hamza Yusuf's appeal as follows:

An enjoyable philosophical tone inflected his speeches and attracted me. Even better, Yusuf represented a rich Islamic past ... He helped me separate the War on Terror's account from an intellectual, forgotten but brilliant Islam. My anger sublimated into enjoying a seductive daydreaming about life in a lost civilisation full of Islamic art and manners. I am not suggesting Yusuf encourages this. No. Again, by whatever design, upon my reflection, he came to represent to me my own practice of splitting Islam into good and bad.[6]

In the years following 9/11, Morsi noted an internal struggle. Like many seekers, he enjoyed Yusuf's philosophical invocations. When it came to politics, however, he had to pretend that he could not hear what Yusuf was saying. He felt that his anger was being "managed."[7] Morsi became increasingly disillusioned with Yusuf's framing of the problem of terrorism. Reading Hamza Yusuf's "A Time for Introspection," Morsi felt alienated.[8]

Disagreeing with Yusuf's framing of the 9/11 attacks as a form of Islamic exceptionalism, Morsi noted how the perpetrators' violence was explained in terms of their innate disposition. He contended:

> He [Yusuf] talked about vile creatures who lacked poetry. What purpose does this serve other than to reaffirm that Islamist violence comes from uncultured thugs. Will the racists make Yusuf's distinction between the good and poetic Islam and the rest? Or does it just reaffirm the underlining point of the discourse: them—"them" is the problem. All that Yusuf is disputing is who exactly "them" is. My concerns began as a whisper but grew into a worry. I so badly wanted an authentic Islam that I would ignore the irrelevance of Yusuf's contrasting Muslims today against a noble poetic and abstract Apollonian past, which comes without a proper and sustained reading of politics or the Dionysian we've inherited. His views all sounded like my identity as a Muslim—once again—was measured by what culture I lacked, and the more I lacked the more I wanted the real thing.[9]

Issa notes a similar transformation in light of Abdal Hakim Murad's counterterrorism discourse, although his journey was much longer and more complicated than Morsi's. He told me he had concluded that neo-traditionalists perpetuate the narrative of the "uncultured," "ethnic" Muslim with a propensity for extremism. This is juxtaposed against the learned Anglophile Muslim who studied with the masters of the "East" in Syria and Yemen. Issa argues that in Abdal Hakim Murad's political and religious discourse, there is a conscious erasure of the postcolonial story—specifically regarding British South Asians. He presents it as a kind of unnecessary baggage that condemns South Asian Islam to political violence and religious heterodoxy. Issa had concluded that following Abdal Hakim Murad's claims, he had inadvertently internalized many racist tropes about himself. He added that this was, in fact, true for many seekers—even if they had not yet realized it.

Reflecting upon the apolitical discourse perpetuated by the "Radical Middle Way" project, Issa contends that this allowed for a culture to develop where young Muslims cared only about the boundaries they lived under. In the postcolonial waves of migration, Issa explains, British Asians were very aware of their political context. They were additionally aware of their political positioning as a part of a global Muslim community. However, Issa explains, "they created a group of people who looked down on their Asian heritage and were not engaging politically. There was an internalized racial hierarchy where they saw themselves as down and low. They took on certain behaviors, and they also took on certain political views." That hierarchy centered on the Western white shaykhs and their Syrian, Moroccan, Yemeni, and Mauritanian counterparts as superior to others.

In the context of the War on Terror, the neo-traditionalist project disciplined the boundaries of "Britishness" to exclude the postcolonial story—for its political and religious implications. Issa explains:

> Abdal Hakim Murad has a view of Britain that is Anglocentric. He forgets that this country has colonized the world for four hundred years. Muslims at that point were looking at this group of 'ulamā' [the neo-traditionalists]— saying the state is oppressing us. They are creating racist narratives against us. They are using state instruments to oppress us—you are our leaders! And they had nothing to say. It impacted me in a very profound way. I realized there were so many racist narratives about myself that I had internalized.

For Issa, the neo-traditionalist project that he had been a part of for over a decade has negatively impacted his community in the same way that Salafis had. They perpetuated a narrative whereby South Asian Islam was burdened with its "cultural," "unorthodox," and "postcolonial" baggage. He explains:

> They said your tradition that you're following back home, there is something faulty with it. You have to come up with a more traditional form of Islam—a more authentic form of Islam. You had more Asian people suddenly wearing Moroccan *thawb*, more Yemeni *thawb*, more Syrian clothes as a more authentic expression of their faith—as if there was something wrong with their *Shalwar Kamiz*.

Some seekers felt ambivalence concerning the fact that neo-traditionalist discourses on race reached their apex after Hamza Yusuf's controversial comments on the Black Lives Matter movement at the Reviving Islamic Spirit (RIS) conference in 2016. For some seekers, this represented a breaking point in their commitment to the community. For others, it provoked questions and concerns about the core epistemic commitments that the neo-traditionalist shaykhs typically emphasize.

Nermin, who had initially gone to Rihla searching for Muslim alternatives to left-wing strategies of resistance and epistemic frames, noted her uncertainty. She explained that the shaykhs are obviously not naïve about modernity and its instruments of control and power. "At the same time," she added, "it is almost as if you can extract the Muslim from the wider context so they can cultivate virtues and transcend their modern self and [the] modern context of oppression." She then went on to address Yusuf's speech in 2016 more explicitly: "Yes, we can say that not all policemen are bad, but the police as an institution—from its inception—was founded to protect the modern state. It was a tool of oppression. It is a modern institution, not an Islamic creation, and so it is extremely problematic to engage with it as though it carries our epistemic assumptions."

Before coming to Rihla, she had entertained the idea of a new alliance of conservative believers with an open mind. However, she reached the conclusion that this relationship was as problematic, if not more so, than the one with the Left. Hamza Yusuf, she explained, started from the point of view of a "political survivor" needing to make alliances. For example, Robert P. George, who had previously supported the Bush administration, is very close to Yusuf. Nermin added that Yusuf finds, on the Right, intellectual and moral commonalities, such as their critique of postmodernists like Foucault and Edward Said, as well as agreement on issues like outlawing pornography, defending "traditional" marriage over gay marriage, and opposing abortion.

Nermin agreed that Muslims might be conservative on issues such as the family, making it seem as if the Right is a natural ally. Allying with the Right, however, comes with its epistemological baggage—just as the shaykhs argue when it comes to the Left. On the surface, Muslims may seem to agree with conservative values. However, Nermin explained:

> the assumptions with which they approach these issues are different from ours. American conservatives want to maintain this pre-1960s American suburbia. They have this inbuilt belief in American exceptionalism and the nuclear family. You know the idea of the "good life" is not one we share—at least to my understanding.

The notion of the "good life" on which their traditionalism is premised, Nermin noted, would have excluded most Muslims—not only for their religion but also for their race.

This, too, was the American scholar Donna Auston's critique of Yusuf's comments in RIS. In an interview with Sylvia Chan-Malik, she asked:

when you say that racism isn't the problem, but the breakdown of the Black family is … how do you disentangle a story like that? Because in spite of the fact that Black marriage was illegal according to US law for so long, my mother and her husband still formed a sacred bond of marriage; but this did not protect them against structural racism. The law of the land interferes and intervenes in Black lives in a way that stacks the deck against the stability of families. It is dangerous to trade out these more nuanced conversations about what the breakdown of the Black family actually means, in terms of lived experience, and instead, roll out these easy tropes of Black pathology as the natural order of things.[10]

Many Black Muslim scholars responded to Yusuf in the immediate aftermath of RIS 2016. The Black Muslim Psychology Conference official website—an initiative founded by Kameelah Mu'Min Rashad—collected the responses to the RIS controversy by shaykhs, activists, and academics.[11] At the same time, some of his colleagues came to Yusuf's defense, like Zaid Shakir or Abdullah bin Hamid Ali. Both have explained that people may have difficulty dealing with Yusuf's personality and that he may have erred, but that he was not a racist.[12]

For others, however, Yusuf's cited proximity to people of color—be it his wife, who is Mexican, or his surrogate father, who is Black—does not exempt him from delving into "Black pathology."[13] Ubaydallah Evans explained:

Black pathology is the idea that black people are inherently incapable of thinking and behaving correctly, and it is often used to explain systemic racism. In other words, it's not that bank redlining and intentionally racist public-housing redistricting policies keep economically depressed black communities confined to areas without jobs; they're just lazy. It's not that extremely punitive sentencing for low-level, non-violent drug offenders have wreaked havoc on black men; it's just sexual irresponsibility that has led to the dissolution of the black family.[14]

Evans' contention was shared by many, including Nadirah Angail, who wrote an article titled "Hamza Yusuf and the Dangers of Black Pathology." Evans and Angail contended that while a sincere apology would have sufficed, Yusuf delved deeper into Black pathology instead. Angail explained that it is impossible to speak of the breakdown of the Black family without centering on structural racism. She explains, "Otherwise, you end up sending the message that black men and women are being incarcerated at alarming rates just because. That's black pathology."[15]

The seekers responded to Yusuf's comments and the general neo-traditionalist discourse on race in three different ways. Some noted that there is a conscious erasure of their racial identities. The second group finds the conversations around race troubling, especially in light of the *fitna* created by the RIS scandal, so they refuse to talk about it. The last group finds that neo-traditionalists provide a viable and rooted alternative.

Hamida contemplated her experience in Rihla as a member of the Nation of Islam. Her parents and religious community were very encouraging of her decision to go to Rihla and study Islam in Malaysia. She explained that she was passionate about building bridges between the Nation and Sunnis. I asked her about her impressions after the retreat was over. She had mixed feelings. She was seemingly at a crossroads: was it that the things she grew up believing her whole life were simply wrong? Does that reconstruct everything in her life? What if they (the neo-traditionalists) have it all wrong? One thing she noted was that in Rihla, there weren't any Black Muslim scholars.

When applying to Rihla, she told the organizers that she was from the Nation of Islam. She maintained that she loves being in different spaces with different views. However, the only narrative posited about the Nation of Islam is one of overcoming heterodoxy to achieve Sunni normalcy and orthodoxy. She found it easier not to mention her background or have these conversations. It was not just the orthodoxy narrative she found troubling. This historical erasure, she notes, is common in Arab and Asian Sunni communities, even among left-wing activists like Linda Sarsour. She found the discourse on race generally disquieting, especially in its framing of political activism.

Hamida decided to go to Rihla despite how offensive she found the comments. Other seekers approached the matter differently. Jamillah, for example, noted that she heard people speaking about the "Black Lives Matter" controversy, and it was Allah's protection that she did not follow what had happened lest she would fall into *fitna*. For Amine and Junaid, Yusuf's critique of BLM was not racially motivated. The group has within its ideology aspects—such as its support for the LGBTQ movement—that go against Muslim values. Amine, in particular, noted that, as a British-Moroccan, he is not concerned with what happens politically in the United States.

The seekers, however, ruminated not just on Yusuf's comments in RIS but on the wider neo-traditionalist critiques of anti-racist activism in particular and activism in general. Nermin gave an example from something Abdal Hakim Murad said during a class that had troubled her. Murad's traditionalism seemed to fall into the same traps of imagination as Yusuf's:

> When Murad said [that] from amongst the things we lost in modernity is what it means to be a part of a race, a nation, and a gender, that made me cringe. I was like, what are you saying? What does it mean to be a part of a "nation" and "race," and "class"? That's exactly what I was talking about, these alliances with these conservatives. We can agree on pornography and stuff. But not their assumptions about the kind of societies they are trying to maintain or create. These are societies where we wouldn't survive. Things like that aren't part of Islam at all. For things like race or even gender, people were vaguely aware that they were men and women. Like people identify themselves by virtues like you're a "good" man. Now we're solidifying race and class as meaningful categories?

She added:

> In a lecture, I heard Abdal Hakim Murad say—and I am paraphrasing here—if only Palestinians would stop throwing rockets at Israelis and suicide bombing and approach them with the path of da'wa. That would be better. I just can't get behind this statement. In a way, as Palestinians should be able to transcend that context of oppression and anger to cultivate virtues that like forgiveness and forbearance to attract Israelis to Islam and find a peaceful solution instead of conflict. I feel like you're taking people out of the context that made them what they are. I really have an issue with that.

Sabrina had an entirely different way of seeing this. She explained that she and her husband used to be big activists in her university. "We saw that as a channel of imparting good, defending the oppressed and all that in Palestine, Gaza, and Lebanon," she adds. The seemingly "anti-imperialist," left-wing approach to activism that allows for supposed *ummah* solidarity in response to Western hegemony has convinced Muslims of the faulty notion of equality:

> In Islam, people are at different levels. We are so uncomfortable with the idea of hierarchy now. We've been taught to hate hierarchy without examining what that means or what the implications are. Being an activist, of course,

I've always been anti-hierarchy. God told Musa to approach even Pharaoh in a gentle way, but Muslims have lost that.

The appeal to introspection and self-development guards the boundaries of Pan-Islamist notions of *ummah* solidarity. This appeal is personalized but also nationalized. Each individual should be concerned with their personal spiritual state, and each community should be concerned with its moral state. This essentially privatizes the imaginaries of Muslims in the West away from *ummah* concerns to national ones. This is prompted by changing the different Muslim narratives that different communities have. The neo-traditionalists are, additionally, attempting to correct Muslims' focus from politics to morality—by establishing an intellectual or physical alliance of conservative (right-wing) believers.

Neo-traditionalists and Gender

In recent times and especially during Rihla, the neo-traditionalist shaykhs have tended to focus on providing a traditional "metaphysical" critique of modern ideologies such as feminism. They had been especially concerned with the fragmentation of gender binaries and the seemingly modern attack on heterosexuality. Especially for Abdal Hakim Murad and Umar Faruq Abd-Allah, gender has always had a metaphysical dimension and an essential meaning. It is the metaphysical essential meanings of gender, rather than the materialist historical conditions of patriarchy, that have traditionally informed male and female relationships. The LGBTQ movement is therefore detrimental not just because of the Muslim prohibition of certain sexual acts but also because a modern person is so far removed from their essential nature that they can therefore choose their sexual orientation. Most seekers were astounded by this critique of feminism and the LGBTQ movement. As with all the metaphysical points the shaykhs make, this was said to be self-evident and known to all Muslims traditionally. It therefore becomes a marker between what it traditionally meant to be a man or a woman and what it means now in modernity. None of the seekers I interviewed in Rihla 2017 had ever heard of this critique of feminism before. Nor did they know what "metaphysics of gender" entailed before coming to Rihla. However, they were, for the most part, convinced by it.

Mysa, a Syrian American student, explained that she had never heard that the *fiṭra* was gendered. "I mean, this is something that is super different. I definitely believe it, though. I asked my dad; he had never heard it either, but he said to me it kind of makes perfect sense." As a student in a mixed environment, she struggles between her empathy with people from the LGBTQ movement and her faith. In Rihla, it became clear that modernity has caused a disruption in gender identity. The modern rejection of essences has caused a sort of displacement on the level of men and women. Men lost what it meant to traditionally be a man. Women lost what it traditionally meant to be a woman. This was all a result of the disjuncture between essential meanings of gender and their material manifestations in terms of gender roles and gender identities. For Mysa, this explains much of the malaise felt by heterosexual men and women, and by people who are questioning their sexuality. Human beings need to be attuned to their *fitra*, and the *fitra* is gendered.

Ashely, the recent American convert, found that the critique of feminism struck her sensibilities more than anything else. She explains that she grew up with a "girl-power" type of feminism. A girl can do anything a boy can, and no one can say any differently. When she went to graduate school, she was introduced to Judith Butler's writing and work. She explains, "I felt so condensed in a way, as though I was 'told' I was a girl. I was 'treated' like a girl. I was 'dressed' like a girl. All of a sudden, my whole identity was problematic, and in some way, I needed to push back against it and try and deconstruct everything." Abd-Allah's class on gender, she argues, shows that in Islam, there is a perfect harmony between the human essence and the material manifestations of that essence in terms of roles and identity, unlike feminism, which was always combative in nature.

For seekers, especially the females, this claim becomes more difficult to accept as the shaykhs elaborate materially on what gender essences would entail. I asked Ashely if there was anything in Rihla that she had difficulty accepting. She explained that Abdal Hakim Murad had presented the metaphysics of gender in traditional societies. "I didn't like it when he said all of that stuff about purity and virginity."[16] Ashely mitigates her seeming discomfort by stating that perhaps she is not at a place in her spiritual journey where she can be receptive to this. After all, the shaykhs are on a different level. For male seekers, the disjuncture between essence and material is one of the problems of feminism. They are initiated into the traditional imaginary that Abdal Hakim Murad posits, whereby the male patriarch knew what it meant to be a man and where women did not have to take on traditionally masculine roles.

Malika, a 19-year-old African-American student, notes that this discourse created a new culture of Muslim anti-feminism in the virtual world. She adds,

"I just don't understand how these people are extracting these extreme ideologies from Hamza Yusuf and Abdal Hakim Murad; it is so weird." She notes that young Muslim women of her age identify with feminism only because it allows them to address issues that the Muslim community will not. She repeatedly affirmed that she might not know as much as the anti-feminists online, but she nevertheless finds their discourse harmful, especially to women. They cite metaphysics of gender on the one hand and right-wing anti-feminists like Jordan Peterson on the other hand and invalidate the claims of women. She presented her dilemma passionately:

> The traditionalists on Twitter or Sufi incel types are shameless. I am just really trying to live my life and not be grounded or be overtaken by it all. Incel Sufis lack compassion and are very aggressive: they talk about epistemology and super intellectual bubbles, which doesn't help anybody. I've seen them quoting Peterson. They really echo a lot of conservative rhetoric, and I saw them supporting conservatives because of the LGBT. Especially as a Black person, it's super uncomfortable for me to see them support these openly racist conservatives because of how they feel about abortion. That's not the answer. The more they get into Jordan Peterson and Ben Shapiro, the more incel stuff comes out.

For Malika, her frustration stems from the fact that they derive their authority from a seeming intellectual depth. Any debate or discussion will be reduced to the fact that she speaks from an emotional standpoint while they speak from a place of intellectual authority. The neo-traditionalists on the internet discuss all themes relating to modernity and a liberal intrusion on Muslim values. The clear-cut separation between Islam and notions of modern subjectivities has opened up a space for a degree of policing. The neo-traditionalist intellectual policing culture, often carried out by men but not exclusively, reinforces the authority of some who are deemed more learned. On the other hand, it causes melancholic disenchantment for others. They are asking people to disavow their modern subjectivity while disregarding the fact that modernity is both institutionally and structurally situated, which causes a lot of despair. It relegates the burden of responsibility exclusively to the believer, not the power structures. Malika expressed this to me as follows: "Their unrelatable arguments on Twitter drive people from faith: it's a kind of you 'can't sit with us' Islam. Some people don't even know that God loves them; I've been there. Sometimes I am still there." Seemingly the proximity or the access a seeker may have to power entails that their subjectivities are less problematic since they do not face as many pressures in modernity.

Political Quietism and Geopolitics

For younger seekers, 9/11 is not an immediate context but a marker of the era in which they grew up. This era begat its own contrary religious and political dynamics. For example, how does one simultaneously disavow religious extremism but at the same time remain unapologetic? At a time when "countering violent extremism" projects (CVEs) seemingly innately politicize the very existence of Muslims in the West, how can young Muslims escape politics as a form of liberation? For seekers, there is difficulty in navigating politics and making sense of the neo-traditionalist political discourse. For neo-traditionalists, the soundness of faith is predicated on a specific way of engaging in politics (i.e. forms of quietism)—radicalism results from incorrect religious beliefs, ideologies, and a postcolonial disposition. Therefore, responding to Islamophobia and racism is framed from a spiritual and ethical perspective rather than a political one. For seekers looking to the shaykhs for spiritual elevation, there are consistencies and disjuncture, as well as many confusions and uncertainties sometimes mitigated by an appeal to the shaykhs' authority "for knowing more than we do."

The confusion is not, however, merely a matter of political interpretation. It is a matter of religious and even eschatological concerns. Jamillah, the 18-year-old Syrian French student in Lebanon, notes she was first introduced to neo-traditionalist shaykhs in 2014. Zaytuna College posted a popular Friday sermon that Hamza Yusuf presented on the rise of ISIS (Islamic State of Iraq and Syria).[17] She told me:

> I was introduced to Shaykh Hamza Yusuf through the internet. That was the first video I ever saw on ISIS and how they were a prophetic prediction. Many people were attacking [Islam], and I did not know how to answer. I knew this wasn't Islam. I like the fact that every time he would say something, he would back it up with sources and with ḥadīth or Qurʾān. It was very credible. It is [a] cliché, but Islam is a religion of peace. This is why you have extremists. You have a distorted idea of what religion is. Spiritually you are empty. Politically, you are full of this fire that's from an empty source.

For Yusuf, Islamic radicalism is a by-product of Islamized secular ideologies, particularly utopian Marxism, which was born of the postcolonial moment, on the one hand, and has eschatological implications on the other. In the sermon, Jamillah cites Yusuf explaining that the rise of ISIS—who are modern-day Kharijites—had been prophesied by the Prophet: "If you see the black flags ... it begins with a *fitna* ... and the midst of it is delusion, misguidance, error ... and it ends with atheism."[18] The marker of modern Islamic ideologies which have led to this predicament is that Muslims do not blame themselves and constantly project victimhood—as a form of postcolonial hangover. Yusuf explains, "You can blame America, you can blame Israel, but if you get to the metaphysical level, we have to deal with our sin."[19] He explains that the Prophet prophesied calamities on this earth for Muslims as a way of expiating their sins. When an earthquake happens in the Muslim world thousands of people die; when an earthquake happens in the West, only three people die. In times of *fitna*, the ḥadīth relate that Muslims should not go against the sulṭān.[20] In the typical neo-traditional appeal to authority, Yusuf then explains that modern arrogance has difficulty accepting the traditional wisdom of centuries of Muslim scholarship, which deals with obedience to the sultan and refusing to engage in *fitna*. As a Syrian, Jamillah agrees with all of Yusuf's points in the sermon. She explained:

> I would always look at the Syrian and Egyptian revolutions and wonder, what went wrong? And from an Islamic perspective, do we say that an individual's freedom is more important than society's well-being? I was never pro-regime, but I guess I was skeptical. Maybe I say this because I'm from a privileged background. I can't speak for people who have really been oppressed. But I have heard this in Rihla, and I agree. Any government is better than anarchy. People who were lost in Syria before have gone even lower on the economic social ladder. So I don't think it has done any good or can do any good because who will take power? I think it [the revolution] was a selfish move, and it came out of uneducated people. Politically, my Islamic studies have backed this argument because, in the end, this is *fitna*, and it comes out of a lack of proper knowledge and knowledge of religion particularly.

Unlike Salafism, to which they were averse, political Islam was something that most seekers noted they had been neutral about before coming to Rihla. On the retreat, the narratives of Muslim modernity highlighted how Islamism resulted from the tradition's rupture, which eventually produced radical groups. The confusion is exemplified by two conversations I had with Ahmed only a few weeks apart. In the first conversation with Ahmed, who had been a Salafi in the past but had since been bitterly disillusioned, he said:

> I have inclinations towards the Sufi scholars, but I cannot comprehend the messed-up political views many hold. You see the same kind of views held by Madkhalī types too. I love Shaykh Hamza Yusuf and Shaykh Abdal Hakim Murad, but I always found the political views of Sufis generally a bit unsettling. It is actually very similar to Madkhalīs.

In our second conversation a few weeks later, Ahmed told me he is entirely convinced of *taṣawuuf* rather than being slightly inclined toward it. He explained, "I am even anti-Ikhwān now." He maintained that he still appreciated the organizations and charities the Ikhwān inspired; however, they also inspired modernist intrusion and the dissipation of Islamic orthodoxy.

On the intellectual and theoretical levels, the seekers were generally receptive to the critique of Islamism and opted for some degree of political quietism. However, they often frame it as a form of political burnout rather than a theological or metaphysical principle. However, for the seekers, some confusion arises when neo-traditionalists apply this as social and political commentary to ongoing events. Degrees of disillusionment can set in when seekers discover that the quietist discourse is merely a caveat against another form of activism. For that reason, more seekers feel conflicted about Hamza Yusuf's politics than they do about Abdal Hakim Murad and (as even fewer feel) about Umar Faruq Abd-Allah. Therefore, it is no surprise that the two main contexts in which the neo-traditionalist political theology became contested globally are after the Arab Spring and domestically with the resurgence of the Right.

Of all the seekers I interviewed, Sabrina was unique. This young Malaysian-American woman had been a big activist after 9/11. She and her husband, a white convert, would during their time at university join protests and sit-ins against the wars in Iraq and Afghanistan. No longer a political activist, she maintains that the culture of activism is deeply flawed. She now, unequivocally and without qualification, affirms and accepts the neo-traditionalist political narratives and their policy implications. Unlike Jamillah, Mysa, and Nabila, all of whom unequivocally accepted the political narrative and policies of the shaykhs, for Sabrina, this political narrative represents a sharp shift from her upbringing and her early life. Her father had studied in Al Azhar in Egypt, where he became sympathetic to, albeit not involved in, the loosely defined political Islam reformist movement. She notes that unlike the shaykhs, and her husband, with their religious discourse, her father had a very simple understanding of religion. It did not have the intellectual or spiritual depth of the shaykhs.

She told me that Hamza Yusuf and Umar Faruq Abd-Allah, in the talks they presented at the Reviving Islamic Spirit (RIS) convention in Malaysia, stressed this deep spiritual understanding of faith. Yusuf arrived in Malaysia at a time of relative discord. There had been reports that then prime minister Najib Razak was involved in corruption scandals—for which he was later arrested.[21] In his speech, Yusuf affirmed that he knew little about Malaysian politics, but he knew that Malaysia was a stable country. He urged young people not to protest and to obey their government, that was doing its best even if it was not perfect—lest they end up like the Middle East.

Sabrina explained:

> Shaykh Hamza's whole speech in RIS was that you shouldn't go against your ruler, your country. He was very emotional. Our tradition is all about peace and harmony. It is not from our tradition to speak up against the leader. You know, when I went back to Malaysia, I was planning to join the protests, but then I realized it was wrong. I was surprised at how easy it was for me to accept this. Activism is not from our tradition. Shaykh Hamza says if you ask any person in Syria on the street in 2011 if they knew the destruction and all of this loss, would they have marched out on the streets? By far, no one would say yes. This is an example of how anarchy is worse by like a crazy number. I think like three hundred times worse than the oppression. That was easy for me and my husband to accept because we recognized we had no idea what we were doing.

For most other seekers, navigating the neo-traditionalist position, particularly that put forward by Hamza Yusuf and the Eastern shaykhs on the Arab Spring, is not as straightforward as it had been for Sabrina. The uncertainties, for some seekers, were often mitigated by two things. The first was an appeal to the shaykhs' authority and, on occasion, their sainthood, meaning they know things ordinary people are not privy to. The second was a kind of realpolitik; the real demands of power require Muslims to engage with it in such ways. Other seekers mitigate it with two opposing sets of justification. The shaykhs are well-meaning but could sometimes be a little out of touch. Or, the shaykhs did not want to engage in politics but were being forced to because people pressured them to. These justifications are put under more and more pressure as different neo-traditionalists gain closer proximity to the different locales of power, particularly in the wake of Yusuf and Bin Bayyah's relationship with the UAE and Saudi Arabia and after Yusuf's comments about the BLM. For some, this creates an existential sense of confusion. For others, the appeal to authority turns into a demand for accountability.

Junaid and Saffi Ullah fall into the first camp. They do not express quietist views by any measure, but when asked about neo-traditionalist quietism, they defer to the superior knowledge and wisdom of the shaykhs. They furthermore stress the realpolitik of necessary evil in an imperfect world. Saffi Ullah, in particular, takes sharply opposing views. The shaykhs' authority mitigates the discrepancy between his appeal for political engagement and the shaykhs' quietism. As we discussed modernity, he explained the traumatic effect that the fall of the Ottoman Empire had on Muslims. Muslims had, in effect, lost their sense of "*ummah*." He explained:

> The mistake Muslim leaders made after the fall of the Ottoman Empire was to put trust in people from outside the *ummah*. Look at the invasion of Afghanistan; the United States is seen as the safeguard of peace and security in Muslim countries that aligned themselves with them or the Soviets. That was a great error. The more we trust these foreign powers, the more we get used and abused and get our resources stolen. We need to establish a geopolitical power that is a representation and negotiate on our own terms.

I took the opportunity to ask him about his views on neo-traditionalists' politics. He explained:

> I can't really speak for the shaykhs. Especially Habib Ali Jifri, who gets a lot of criticism for being with the Egyptian government or being friends with Ramzan Kadyrov in Chechnya. I don't understand it myself. Then again, everyone operates in the public sphere. Whether you are a politician or a shaykh, there are some concessions you have to make with realpolitik.

He then added:

> If we were to do things our way and say to hell with everyone, this only leads to destruction. Teenagers get emotional, and their activism could potentially be misguided. Work on yourself, be educated, get business, and we can yield power. Young people end up hurting their cause instead of helping it.

The juxtaposition of "teenage" activism versus the "realpolitik" of scholars reflects a somewhat salient theme that mitigates the political confusion seekers often feel. The shaykhs' knowledge of reality and their wisdom supersedes the juvenile tendencies of activists. Junaid expressed similar inclinations. He explained that he, too, finds this topic "very troubling." Ultimately, scholars have wisdom we may not be privy to. For example, many people attacked the Syrian scholar Ramadan al-Buti for being anti-revolutionary to the extent that they called him a "sell-out," but ultimately, he was right.

Sara—who is half-Arab and half-Pakistani—found it more difficult to mitigate the position of the shaykhs' politics by appealing to their authority. She does not try to mitigate it at all. Like many seekers, she finds it best to avoid the potential for doubt in times of "*fitna*" altogether so as not to harm her faith. That said, it was apparent that she could not escape it completely, as she constantly asked me, with a degree of urgency, how I myself could make sense of such a troubling world and the shaykhs' evident silence. She pointed out that not every shaykh must be politically conscious or an activist. She then backtracked, because Hamza Yusuf, as she noted, was not entirely apolitical. She anxiously noted:

> You know I have a habit of just sticking my head in the sand. So that whole incident [that had] happened about the Black Lives Matter, I also heard that he made a comment about Muslim Brotherhood comparing them to communism or something. I don't; I don't, really … don't want to watch the video. So I just don't want to believe it was true and get upset … I kind of want to give him the benefit of the doubt, if I'm honest. Obviously, you don't put shaykhs on a pedestal, and they make mistakes.

The conversation then went on to cover political quietism, specifically in light of the Arab Spring. Sara explained:

> I know it is for a selfish reason why I try not to look at these things on the news because they genuinely affect me in a very physical and very strong way. Sometimes I feel like I have a responsibility to at least learn about things, and I'm just completely covering my eyes from atrocities that happen. Maybe part of it is I know Allah is the most just, and the justice will come whether I say "amen" to it or I don't. There is no way that someone [Bashar al-Assad] could have committed so much crime and Allah wouldn't punish them.

Sara makes another rhetorical detour reflecting the growing confusion seek-ers undergo, particularly after the Arab Spring: "I always wonder how much someone can actually say what they want to say when they are in these net-works? How much can they exert independent opinions if these governments can't accept them? But if they spoke freely, they would lose those contacts."

Issa, too, felt that at some point he, as had Sara, had cast away his concerns. If the neo-traditionalists had remained faithfully quiet about politics, he prob-ably would not have become as disillusioned as he is now. He recalls attending a debate between Hamza Yusuf and Tariq Ramadan in the Oxford Union. Ramadan made the point that the neo-traditionalists claim to be apolitical, but they are, in fact, very political in their engagement with governments. Issa said that this point made him think: "We saw Habib Ali *bigging* up Sisi, and we saw Hamza Yusuf working with the UAE." Online, he came across an interview Hamza Yusuf gave to an Emirati channel where he explained his politics in light of the Arab Spring. Issa recounted:

> He said he was pro-monarchy. When he was asked about the Arab Spring in Morocco, for example, he said my only regret was that the king has given up much of his executive powers. He starts *bigging* up the Emirates. For me, I come from an Asian background. I have family relatives from Bangladesh that live in the Emirates that get treated like rubbish and for him not to acknowledge that was troubling to me.

Like many seekers—even those who had passionately defended Hamza Yusuf—his relationship with the UAE and Saudi Arabia was the most trou-bling. Issa contends that while neo-traditionalist shaykhs, particularly Hamza Yusuf and his Eastern counterparts, claim to be apolitical, they participate in a kind of politics. Issa noted that the Saudi bombing of Yemen had caused a dramatic shock for many seekers, much more than Yusuf's previous quiet-ist stances. With the Saudi bombing of Yemen, he stated, "It reaches a point where it was unpalatable for many people."

Indeed, the breaking point for many was the annual Forum for Promoting Peace held between 5 and 7 December 2018.[22] Many seekers had either been unaware of the Forum's existence or it did not seem to them to be particu-larly political. This, however, changed in 2018. The human cost of the UAE/ Saudi war on Yemen became greater and greater. In addition, the brutality of the Saudi Crown Prince in imprisoning notable Islamic scholars such as Salman al-Oda—whom many Sufis saw as a sympathetic Salafi—and the brutal murder and dismemberment of the Saudi journalist Jamal Khashoggi in the Saudi embassy in Turkey also did not sit well with many.[23] In addition, in the domestic realm, there was the UAE/Saudi support for Donald Trump's Muslim ban. For many seekers, Yusuf made a mistake by being involved—even if he had been well-meaning. After all, he was not only working under the auspices of brutal regimes and inadvertently giving them legitimacy, but also sharing a stage with counterterrorism surveillance initiatives and Zionist and Islamophobic organizations.[24] As more details and streams of articles emerged, many seekers became increasingly confused—including many of those I had previously interviewed.

Indignant with the seemingly vitriolic reactions of people on social media, many seekers and shaykhs closer to Hamza Yusuf spoke out. Shaykh Adam Kelwick, who attended the Peace Forum, responded to the criticisms leveled by people on social media by saying, "I can't but help think how ironic it is for those raising issues with the UAE's involvement in Yemen to be in a position where they haven't done anything themselves. Our traditions teach that on the day of resurrection, you won't be held accountable for anyone's actions but your own, so the question now becomes, "What have YOU done for Yemen?"[25]

However, no response seemed to reverberate louder than that of Mohamed Ghilan. He had been a long-time student of Hamza Yusuf, Bin Bayyah, and other neo-traditionalist scholars. His online presence and virtual lectures on the Islamic tradition earned him a place on the "World's 500 Most Influential Muslims" list.[26] In the immediate aftermath of the Forum for Peace, Ghilan appeared on a popular young Muslim podcast called "The Mad Mamluks" to discuss Hamza Yusuf and the UAE.[27] Ghilan prefaces the interview by first saying that he understands the emotions; after all, this is right in the aftermath of Jamal Khashoggi's murder.

In the podcast, he highlights two main points: the righteous authority of the shaykhs and the lack of knowledge his critics have. Ghilan diverges into neo-traditionalist tropes on the authority of the shaykhs. He states that God wages war against two types of people: those who have enmity toward saints and those who are involved in usury. He then opts to speak frankly: how can people who live in mortgaged houses and have credit card debts attack the saintly scholars? Also, if the authority of the scholars is done away with, who will the Muslims depend on? He then affirms, "*man lā shaykh lah f'al shaytānu shaykhuh*"—he who has no shaykh will have Satan as his shaykh.

The second point Ghilan makes is that very few people can know about what is happening. The scholars may be political intermediaries behind the scenes, and ordinary people are not privy to it. Additionally, Muslims and activists do not recognize the metaphysical dimensions of political realities. He cites the Qur'an (6:129): "And thus will We make some of the wrongdoers allies of others for what they used to earn." He states: "Now you have taken away the inheritors of the prophet, who do you have? You're going to listen to activists who do not know how to recite the *Fatiha*. They are going to be your moral guides?"

Only a few days after his decisive interview with "The Mad Mamluks," Ghilan changed his position drastically. As a seeker who appealed to the spiritual authority of Yusuf and Bin Bayyah as saints, he found that that appeal for trust quickly turned into a demand for accountability. Ghilan retained a tone of love and respect. At the same time, he could not make sense of Bin Bayyah's praise of Saudi Arabia and Muhammad bin Salman. He starts with a short poem that he wrote capturing his disillusionment:

Peace is the whip
Scholars use to
Beat
Justice
Out of
Muslim
Consciousness.[28]

Ghilan then explained that the crux of his disappointment was that "I've gone to the end of the world in bringing up all kinds of alternative interpretations and explanations for what Shaykh Abdullah bin Bayyah and Shaykh Hamza Yusuf are doing with the Peace Forum in the UAE."[29] Ghilan has since changed his views again, giving the shaykhs the benefit of the doubt. In many ways, Ghilan's changing reactions represent the struggle of many seekers, who see the neo-traditionalist shaykhs as saints and appeal to their authority and defer to their knowledge when their proximity to the locales of power becomes undeniable. Likewise, in a post-interview conversation I had with Junaid on the Forum for Promoting Peace, he expressed confusion and disappointment with Hamza Yusuf's position. "I hope to God that these scholars, with their wisdom, have seen something the rest of us cannot." He expressed the same fears Ghilan had in his podcast: if the scholar's esteem is tarnished, then who will fill the vacuum?

Adam, a young American seeker, explains his total disillusionment with Hamza Yusuf, particularly after the Peace Forum. He asserted:

> To say that I'm confused about Shaykh Hamza Yusuf's political position-ing would be an understatement. This year's forum (2018) is nothing new. Nothing unprecedented in both the context of his political trajectory and the grand scheme of contemporary Muslim affairs. This year's conference managed to strike a nerve. Between the new murder and butchering of Jamal Khashoggi, the internment of Uyghur Muslims in China, and the very, very fresh memory of Abdullah Bin Zayed inciting against Western Muslims and the compounded and sustained abysmal state of *ummah* poli-tics in so much of the world, and the crescendo of Emirati-axis haughtiness that seems hell-bent on being complicit in so much of the aforementioned ... This and so much more had me primed to not exactly be thrilled at the site of people I admire and respect and see as leaders of our community being celebrated in a photo-op shared by the CEO of the ADL [Anti-Defamation League].

Adam notes that his increased discomfort with Yusuf's political alliances led to the question of his complete political metaphysics. He explains that while Yusuf and Bin Bayyah call for a disavowal of worldly contingencies for more immutable metaphysical principles, their actions are very *this-worldly*, very political, and do not live up to their own stated metaphysical claims. He notes that their appeal to spiritual authority to denounce criticism comes down to the level of spiritual shaming. Much like Morsi and Issa, Adam experienced confu-sion before experiencing a complete disillusionment with neo-traditionalists.

The Question of Authority

The appeal to authority becomes a salient theme in mitigating differ-ent elements of the shaykhs' traditionalism and the uneasy reality. This is sometimes a spiritual authority, a charismatic authority, or an intellec-tual authority, as in the case of Abdal Hakim Murad. As I have shown above, the authority of Hamza Yusuf has been contested and put under pressure in the wake of three incidents. The first was his meeting with George Bush. The second was the RIS Black Lives Matter scandal, and the third was the Forum for Promoting Peace. Despite the criticisms, for many of his fervent followers the nature of his authority was untarnished. This authority relates to the entire myth on which neo-traditionalism is based.

That is, the shaykhs derive their authority from being a part of an unbroken chain of transmission that connects them with traditional scholarship in the East.

By 2017, a crisis in religious authority was instigated in the wider Anglo-American Muslim community when a popular preacher (not a neo-traditionalist) was accused of spiritual abuse, abuse of power, and sexual misconduct.[30] Although this was not the first time a religious leader was accused of comparable misconduct, the public nature of the accusations on social media polarized the Muslim community. Since then, religious appeals to authority have been tested after more allegations of spiritual abuse surfaced implicating male religious leaders across the board, including some junior neo-traditionalist shaykhs. These allegations included abuses of power, such as financial abuse of students, secret marriages, verbal abuse, and lying about credentials. In the context of a shaykh–murīd relationship, however, when such abuses occur, the results are often detrimental.

As a result, in February 2021, Walead Mosaad gave a lecture on "Spiritual Authority and Spiritual Abuse."[31] Mosaad stressed that religious authoritativeness is the foremost deterrent to spiritual abuse. He contends, "We have a dearth, we don't really have that many true I would say scholars, people who have studied with people who have studied with people who ... really carry that knowledge and really embody it. And as a result, I think this is what we're seeing is happening." The *ijāza* system, he explains, used to function as a system of checks and balances preventing abuses by imposters. When the shaykhs of *taṣawwuf* are imposters, Mosaad stressed, they could be more detrimental than any other type of shaykh. He adds that a sign of a true shaykh of *taṣawwuf* would be that they are authorized by their shaykh. Most abusive shaykhs do not have that authorization or *idhn* since the *idhn* is not just from the shaykh but is guided by Allah.

Mosaad was then asked about shaykhs who enter into secret marriages with their students. He responded: "I have people I consider friends and colleagues who may have been accused of that or may have done what you're just talking about. And I'm not judging them ... I would recommend to people not to see their students as potential wives." He then noted that for him as a Mālikī, secret marriages are not considered valid; however, they may be in other *madhhabs*. Mosaad was then asked to advise a seeker who recognized being in a spiritually abusive relationship with their shaykh but was trauma-bonded. He responded:

First and foremost, if you have a recognition that it is an abusive relationship and [the] thing that is keeping you in it is this sense of comfort, that is not coming from the higher aspect of your being. It's coming from the lower aspect, which we refer to as the *nafs* … Recognize that's not the best part of you that wants that. It's the worst part of you that wants that. The only way really to get from the worst part of you to the best part of you is to seek help from Allah … Secondly would be to seek some of the true servants of God who can help you with that, find it a true teacher, a true shaykh, and they exist.

Danish Qasim, the founder of "In Shaykh's Clothing," argued in a podcast with Muslim Matters that it is, in fact, these views that allow abuse to occur. Qasim stressed that authorized scholars with *ijāza*s and *idhn* can be abusive and that credentials do not deter a corruptible person from abusing their power. He explained: "some people say they don't follow the scholars without *ijāza*s … follow the ones with the *ijaza* … they're the ones who are rightly guided, they're the ones who won't harm you. And this is what people do, who market religion, who market these religious retreats, especially the traditionalist circles." He added: "They themselves emphasize personal and deferential relationships then after abuses uncovered … they say, well, these aren't the real shaykh, or never put someone on a pedestal."

The presenter then asked him how these differential relationships facilitate abuse. Qasim explained that firstly it is by allowing them to "reshape your whole reality." Then, when you notice there may be something that is questionable,

> they'll say, well, there's a spiritual meaning behind it. This is very common in traditionalist circles. And if you ever go to these retreats, they're always emphasizing that these [shaykhs] are the inheritors of the prophets. These are people that you should not question, and it's your own *nafs* getting in the way of if you're seeing something wrong. And again, it's only when some of the abuses [come] to light [that] these same people become the voice of reason.[32]

In my interview with Wael, he relates a story of spiritual abuse among neo-traditionalists in Australia. Imam Afroz Ali, originally an architect, was a leading neo-traditionalist shaykh in the Australian community, so much so that he was featured in the "World's 500 Most Influential Muslims" list.[33] He founded the Al Ghazzali Centre for Islamic Sciences & Human Development and was strongly tied to SeekersHub, a neo-traditionalist educational initiative. Ali claimed to have studied with scholars in Saudi Arabia, Yemen, Mauritania, and Egypt.[34] He was also a regular teacher in Rihla, covering topics such as Ḥanafī *fiqh*, the ethics of food, and gender. Wael sent me a document titled "The Curious Case of Afroz Ali: Fraud, Lies, and Spiritual Abuse," seemingly written by a former student of Afroz Ali, Aboubakr Daqiq.[35] Daqiq states in the document that Ali had been spiritually abusive to all the volunteers he had worked with. It was later discovered that he had faked his traditional credentials.

His former students approached Hamza Yusuf to inform him of this mistreatment and financial blunder. They then discovered that Afroz Ali did not, in fact, receive an *ijāza* from Yusuf. Ali's entire credibility as a scholar lies in this claim. Daqiq writes: "further evidence was compiled and sent to Shaykh Hamza as well as to Dr Umar Abd-Allah separately seeking recourse ... Disappointingly, Shaykh Hamza noted that he did not wish to be involved further."[36] A council was formed and ruled that Ali would cease activities for several years. He would also need to go through "spiritual rehabilitation" by becoming a *murīd* of Umar Faruq Abd-Allah.[37] In December 2017, Abd-Allah met with Ali's victims. It seemed that he wanted to get past it by reminding them that the trauma they faced was not as bad as other people's.[38] To Daqiq, the more seekers pushed for retribution, the more adamant neo-traditionalist shaykhs were to rehabilitate Ali's image.[39] The document then raises questions about the notion of authority derived from *ijāza*, considering how freely they are often given. In the case of spirituality, Daqiq raises concerns over the process of making *bay'ah* or pledging allegiance to a Sufi shaykh.[40]

Laura had studied with Ali in the 2014 Rihla in Konya. She notes that she was not as affected as some might have been by the incident. Unlike many seekers, she had studied with different Islamic organizations, that had equipped her with tools for interrogating religious authority. She explained, "Had I not been given a clear understanding of the fixed parameters of orthodox Islam, I would not know that the teachers at Rihla were speaking from their framework for understanding the world. Most importantly, this allowed me to separate those who profess to be a leader in Islam." Ali taught Ḥanafī *fiqh* and a class on family and gender relations. She found his essentialisms on gender especially troubling because they were used to justify gender stereotypes.

Wael paints a more somber picture, especially regarding the Australian community. He explains that the neo-traditionalist shaykhs derived their authority from their *isnād* and their appeal to ethics and spirituality. *Isnād*, as a legitimator, posits that any knowledge outside the chain of transmission is suspect. The *isnād* allows the scholars to be the inheritors of the Prophet because they belong in his chain and embody his ethical and spiritual characteristics. He notes that this is what gives them authority over Salafis, Islamists, and progressives. He adds, "places like SeekersHub, Zaytuna, and other traditionalist outfits emphasize the centrality of 'qualified/authentic scholarship,' which means *ijāza* and the implied *akhlāq*/spirituality that comes along with it." Ali's case proved to fail them on two fronts, as the report suggests. Wael writes:

> He had no *ijāza* yet was still being praised and paraded around as someone with *ijāza* and an authentic scholar and all that he was being promoted by SeekersHub, this major center of traditionalism, and was doing events and teaching classes for them, all without any verification of his *ijāza* which is where the entire edifice of traditionalism comes into question: if they're not vetting people's *ijāzas* before parading them around as being a shaykh or someone worthy of studying with, then what is the basis for their authority? And if this is the case for him, what about everyone else? If I can't trust the very people who promote the centrality of the *isnād* to apply their own standards to themselves, then who can I trust to tell me who is or is not a legitimate scholar?

He concludes by saying, "The silence is deafening: if all of these major traditionalist scholars are so adamant about the centrality of *ijāza* to the religion itself, why are they being meek when it comes to calling out people who are lying about their *ijāzas*?"

Tradition changes meanings as it is re-contextualized in the face of modern power. The religious knowledge and methods seekers learn in the space of the retreat are not always easy to adopt as a means of guidance outside the space of the retreat and in their daily lives. The hyper-critique of modernity as an irreverent status quo becomes increasingly difficult to make sense of. Particularly when power structures and institutions are maintaining and reproducing the conditions of modernity, seekers navigate this unfamiliar terrain differently. For some, this creates a sense of complete disenchantment. Issa said, "I feel like they had a spell, and the spell is breaking. It has broken on me. Religiously, I feel homeless. I believed in them for a while. Now perhaps I am trying to find a new home."

For others, the hidden and the unknown allow for the possibility of deference to the authority of the shaykhs discursively while they maintain an independent position. The stark separation of the space of the enchanted retreat and a supposedly "disenchanted" world allows for a privatized form of religious adherence to occur. Their "traditionalism" can therefore be privatized inside the space of the retreat. Still, even this form of privatization takes different forms depending on the seeker. For some, it is a clear separation; for others, different traditional-modern hybrids emerge. In the modern space—outside the retreat—seekers all exist in the same political time; however, they do not and cannot all engage it in the same way. This is because politics does not affect them uniformly, nor with the same intensity.

Not all forms of privatization look the same. Similarly, not all seekers are affected by the status quo in the same way. The less existential pressure seekers feel from the status quo, the easier it is for them not to challenge it. Paradoxically, it is also easier for them to avoid being at odds with traditional claims. For example, it is easier for a man than for a woman to accept the traditional organization of gender roles and the traditional imaginary that goes with it, since it privileges him. Similarly, it is easier for a seeker who is not Black to look past Yusuf's comments on race during the RIS convention. The locus of attention, therefore, differs from one seeker to another depending on their gender, race, and political inclinations. The myth persists, however, because it still provides a deepened sense of rootedness in a world that seems constantly moving and in peril.

CONCLUSION

In 2021, several conservative legislatures in the United States proposed bans on teaching critical race theory (CRT) in schools. For these conservative critics, CRT—with its critiques of power structures and systematic inequalities— owed its analytical structures to Marxism. The Heritage Foundation—a conservative think tank—produced a lengthy report critiquing what it believed to be the core tenets of CRT: it is based on a "Marxist analysis of society made up of categories of oppressors, and oppressed," where "language does not accord to an objective reality but is the mere instrument of power dynamics." The report spoke of "The idea that the oppressed impede revolution when they adhere to the cultural beliefs of their oppressors," "The replacement of all systems of power and even the descriptions of those systems with a worldview that describes only oppressors and the oppressed," and "The concomitant need to dismantle all societal norms through relentless criticism."[1] While the campaign against CRT is not a historical anomaly—for example, in the 1950s, there were vehement campaigns against purported communist infiltration in schools—this campaign was emblematic of the emergence of a new Right in post-Trump America.[2]

Simultaneously, neo-traditionalist shaykhs were now leading the Muslim denunciation of critical race theory and critical theory. On an ideological level, they shared the purported concerns of the Right on the breakdown of society into oppressor–oppressed categories, the dissipation of objective truth, and the hyper-critique of the power structure and the order that restrains and maintains society. These critiques culminated in condemnation of Muslim political activism (particularly antiracist) as deeply embedded, albeit unknow-ingly, in Marxist and postmodern paradigms. Zaid Shakir succinctly summa-rized the neo-traditionalist ideological interjection. The ideologies associated with postmodernism—according to Shakir—such as feminism, critical race theory, and queer studies aimed to center the margins of society. Communities that were marginalized and oppressed in traditional societies—on the basis of race or gender—should be brought to the center to correct the historical wrongs. However, Shakir notes that in traditional Abrahamic societies, the devil was the most marginal. This, in reality, is what postmodernism centers.[3]

This book is a modest attempt that neither claims nor aims to assess the theological, institutional, or even complete intellectual potency of neo-tradi-tionalism in the West. The aim is far less ambitious than that. It is to answer a set of simpler questions. How do the seekers of sacred knowledge reconcile their different experiences and histories of marginalization with a religious ideology premised on privileging social structures and hierarchies? How is a "pure," "authentic," and, more importantly, "traditional" religious typology informed by assumptions and critiques of a modern condition? Furthermore, how is this particular critique of modernity informed by the post-Christian angst regarding a declining Western civilization? In my interviews, the one assessment that both seekers and former seekers seemed to be making over and over, albeit in different terms and with different value judgments, is that the tradition, and the neo-traditionalist shaykhs that embody (or claim to embody) such tradition, represent an objective, metaphysically sound, and orthodox Islamic practice. The seekers represent a subjective religious practice burdened with the heterodoxies of modernity or inferiority begotten by a his-tory of struggle, or simply cultural and postcolonial "baggage." How do they unmake these contingent subjectivities so that they may achieve the objectivity of the tradition? This led many seekers, and me, to ask one final question: are the shaykhs telling an objective story, or misplacing a set of white anxieties—born of a civilizational narrative—and presenting them as axiomatic and more rooted?

The structure of this book mimics two parallel trajectories: the trajectory of the seekers' spiritual journeys and the trajectory of the shaykhs' project. Thus, I have organized it into three distinct sections: Stories of Disenchantment, Places of Re-enchantment, and Locating Neo-traditionalism in Modernity. The first section, at its outset, followed the emergence of neo-traditionalism and the neo-traditionalist shaykhs. It then relayed how tradition is conceptualized and embodied. In turn, it explored the neo-traditionalist critiques of the disenchantment of modernity. This section followed the seekers of sacred knowledge and their unique experiences of disenchantment.

The second section, Places of Re-enchantment, signaled the beginning of the journey. In it I showed how the neo-traditionalist spiritual retreats become a physical and metaphorical place that seekers traverse outside modernity. In these places, the authority of the tradition is embodied, meanings are created, and the plausibility structures that seekers once held in modernity are transformed. I then show the paradigm shifts prompted by the three neo-traditionalist shaykhs. First, I explore how Hamza Yusuf posits a metaphysical intervention into politics—decidedly ushering seekers away from political activism. I then show how Abdal Hakim Murad and Umar Faruq Abd-Allah theorize a traditional approach to race, citizenship, and gender. In doing so, I show the impact of the post-Christian angst, and the panic about an impending civilizational crisis in the West, on their conceptualizations of this traditional approach. As such, the notion of tradition is not entirely theological or stable; rather, it represents an antidote to the felt loss of modernity. The active "unlearning" of modernity in the space of the retreat is consequently a project of refashioning the political and religious subjectivities of the seekers.

The third section, Locating Neo-traditionalism in Modernity, provided an assessment of the project of re-enchantment when it meets modern power. Throughout the book, it is evident that neo-traditionalist discourses have a certain amenability to the imperatives of power—particularly in the post-9/11 context. In this section, however, I show how this amenability to the imperatives of power played out after the Arab Spring. In particular, I examine the role Hamza Yusuf plays in the religious soft-power policies of the UAE, advocating for a quietist and acquiescent Islam that rejects any form of popular revolt. The concluding chapter in this section examines the political re-orientation of the seekers' political subjectivities—especially as seekers reflect on it outside the re-enchanted space of the retreat. This yields three different reactions: for some seekers, it is not entirely sustainable as they go through a process of disillusionment and burnout with neo-traditionalism. Others privatize their performance of tradition in these spaces while maintaining a different outlook outside it. Finally, some seekers are completely transformed by the process of unmaking and seek to find spaces in which to reconstruct the meanings of tradition and its political strategies. I show the congruence of this newly formed Islamic neo-traditionalism with a newly emerging religious Right and traditionalism.

Legacies of Neo-traditionalism

Since its emergence in the mid-1990s, neo-traditionalism has transformed Muslim communities in the West in a fundamental way. The practice of Sufism, for many, was either marginal or highly suspect. Neo-traditionalism changed this narrative. While there have been Sufi communities in the West long claiming that Sufism was at the heart of Islamic orthodoxy—particularly Barelvi communities or Sufi orders—they were not always successful at proselytizing this view among a wider audience. The neo-traditionalist shaykhs argued for a tempered form of Sufism. They often critiqued the excesses of Sufi orders, cementing the notion that Sufism was always at the heart of Islamic orthodoxy. For example, Rumi was not a synchronistic, heterodox love poet. He was an orthodox scholar. Similarly, the study of *kalam*, long considered suspect to some and irrelevant to others, bloomed. More and more young people opted to develop their faith by studying these once-neglected religious sciences more deeply. This, in turn, developed a generation of Muslim intellectuals and scholars concerned with deep study of the classical religious sciences. Furthermore, strict adherence to a *madhhab* was on the rise. More and more young Muslims became particularly interested in studying, specifically the Mālikī *madhhab*. Thus the impact of Hamza Yusuf, Abdal Hakim Murad, and Umar Faruq Abd-Allah extended beyond themselves or even their students. They helped create an intellectual class of Muslims interested in the in-depth study of Islam.

They built and inspired religious institutions of learning that have become foundational to community building. Aside from Rihla and other religious retreats, Zaytuna College in California and Cambridge Muslim College in Cambridge gained great esteem and have become renowned for producing exemplary scholarship. Virtual programs such as SeekersHub, too, boast an impressive trajectory of educating Muslims in traditional sciences. Ta'leef Collective—although not without controversy—was also an important initiative in disseminating traditional knowledge. More recently, a new experiment in communal living, called Al Maqasid, was started by the neo-traditionalist Shaykh Yahya Rhodus in Pennsylvania. While this community is new and understudied, previous neo-traditionalist experiments with communal living were riddled with controversy—most notably Nuh Keller's community in Jordan, which was accused of conducting forced divorces and child abuse.

On the other hand, a latent consequence of this movement was the development of a small nativist, white supremacist Muslim movement called Islam4Europeans. This movement is decidedly anti-immigrant and against race-mixing as a form of racial preservation, and aims to promote a Muslim white European culture.[4] Its website publishes several Abdal Hakim Murad and Hamza Yusuf lectures on its platforms by way of a deeper interrogation of what it means to be a Western Muslim. Among these lectures are Abdal Hakim Murad's lecture on fascist metaphysician Julius Evola, the crisis of masculinity, modesty, and the *hijab*, *nasheeds* in praise of the Prophet in an English style, and Islam in the West.[5] Hamza Yusuf's lectures have his article on abortion, his conversation with conservative philosopher Roger Scruton, and his articles "Atheists" and "Whether European Muslims Must Dress Like Arabs", along with his article on the Qur'an.[6] While this movement is quite marginal, its claims have undoubtedly impacted the community of seekers.

Seekers of Sacred Knowledge

The different paths leading young Muslims to seek knowledge with the neo-traditionalist shaykhs, notwithstanding their different personal trajectories, often relate to generalized questions of meaning in contentious religious and secular environments. Just like their non-Muslim counterparts, they are confronted by a fundamental question: is religious adherence and practice necessary for modern people in modern times? When I had initially set out to conduct my research, my primary question had been: what attracts seekers to the neo-traditionalist shaykhs as opposed to other religious trends? The more I posed this question, the more it became apparent that although the finer points of theology or politics and identity were central, they were not the most central. Seekers—as Charles Taylor notes—are cross-pressured by the plausibility of belief. They could both opt in or opt out of religious practice—depending on their spiritual and practical priorities. However, unlike for others in the secular West, being a "Muslim" is also being a religious and often a racial minority. This minority has its own history with the dominant culture—whether in the context of colonialism as with the South Asian community in the United Kingdom, or with that of slavery and structural racism as with the Black Muslims in the United States. Furthermore, with the rise of racism and Islamophobia in the aftermath of the "War on Terror," the question of religious adherence and conditions of belief had become a question of politics as well as of faith.

The personal histories and subjectivities of the seekers are subsumed within that larger story of Islam in the West. Their conception of identity and the political comes from that specific history. One example is the rise of political Islam as a way of institutionalizing and politically organizing Muslim communities for internal and global solidarity. That impacts how seekers engage with ideas regarding religious and political responsibility and the notion of the *ummah*. The inception and the last relative decline of the Salafi movement is another important point of transformation for developing the notion of orthodoxy. Another point of contention relates to the so-called "cultural" Islam, which emphasizes cultural practices more than religious normativity. Often, the intra-sectarian polemics between the Barelvi and the Deobandi mosques have been deemed a matter of "culture" as opposed to one of religion. In the context of the War on Terror, young Muslims find themselves needing to navigate their religious-political histories as well as the political pushback.

The neo-traditionalists engage in direct polemics with some religious trends and represent an alternative to others. According to neo-traditionalists, the story of Islamism and Salafism represents an enduring trauma and insecurity in the Muslim experience with the West. Neo-traditionalism provides a normative conception of Islamic belief and practice. This religious normativity is a continuation of the pre-colonial religion—untainted by the complexes of postcolonial Islam. It fashions new imaginations of a traditional past and traditional space while simultaneously positing itself as comfortably Western. However, this conscious erasure or rejection of the historical and intellectual forces that form immigrant Islam constructs a dichotomy of an immigrant Islam burdened by politicized heterodoxies unable to escape its subjectivity and an objective and "fuller" neo-traditionalist Islam.

For the neo-traditionalist shaykhs, the advent of modernity fundamentally challenged the traditional order of the world and the value systems it once upheld. This left believers existentially adrift. They contend that the Muslim story of modernity cannot be told in isolation from that of the West. This is because Muslims in the colonial period abandoned the metaphysically sound approach in dealing with the question of colonialism. Instead, facing the colonial military machine and prompted by their insecurity, Muslims posited reactionary solutions. They challenged the established religious authorities and the normative religious methods. The Islamic tradition had been preserved through an unbroken chain of transmission from student to teacher all the way back to the time of the Prophet. Instead, they posited the need to find new solutions by opening the gates of *ijtihād*. Although I do not engage with or disentangle this historical revisionism thoroughly in the book, it is worth noting that this narrative is simplistic at best and Eurocentric at worst. Rather than engaging with the array of postcolonial literature in the Muslim world, the neo-traditionalist narrative seems to suggest that intellectual and religious ingenuity stopped in the Muslim world at some point. Therefore, neo-traditionalists must excavate ideas virtually unknown to Muslims for decades after colonialism. The question therefore becomes, can the postcolonials think?

The neo-traditionalist shaykhs posit two meta-narratives of modernity—disenchantment, and the decline of metaphysics. They draw parallels between the unfolding of these two narratives in the post-Christian West and Muslim history. Although they accept (a simplified reading of the) Weberian teleology, the Reformation signifies a decline, not progress. Similarly, the Nahḍa movement (and the Wahhabi movement) also represent a decline in the Muslim world. By attacking the mystical traditions, they disenchanted the world. Human beings no longer felt the persistent intervention of the cosmos in their material world. Additionally, they contend that the rise of nominalism in both religious traditions paved the way for modern decline. This neo-Thomist reading of the history of modernity is extended to the Islamic context. The figure of Ibn Taymiyyah appears as an early modernist, in his conception of *fiṭra* that allows space for modern subjectivity and his supposed endorsement of nominalism. The narratives of disenchantment and the decline of metaphysics, in which a religious world order had been replaced with a secular one, show the destruction of value systems and the decline of order and meaning in modernity. Instead, there is disorientation, materialism, narcissism, and violence.

The politicized ways in which postcolonial Islam developed resulted from Muslims internalizing anti-metaphysical ideologies. The shaykhs contend that Marxism is essentially the invisible hand in the story of postcolonial Islam. Furthermore, Marxist influences persist in Muslim activists' conduct by leading them to internalize the Foucauldian and postmodern power critiques. The Marxist paradigm allows no space for the intervention of God or any form of metaphysics. They contend that the Marxist paradigm, fundamentally utopian in nature, attempts to establish heaven on earth, thereby eliminating the possibility of heaven in the afterlife. In their utopian search for justice, they divided the world into vanquishers, vanquished victims, and victimizers. The Islamists first internalized this paradigm and fashioned a utopian ideology out of Islam. By removing metaphysics, they no longer saw the metaphysical purpose of injustice or tribulations in the world; nor did they see their purpose regarding spiritual ascension and introspection. Instead, Islamists and later generations of Muslim activists shirked their responsibilities with power structures. In the beginning, seekers find this narrative empowering, for it focuses the lens not on the power structures but on their spiritual states. Their condition is not informed by power struggles but rather by the metaphysical state of their hearts. This, however, later becomes a more difficult position to reconcile.

The pedagogical spaces that the neo-traditionalist shaykhs construct represent their traditional vision. As they had once gone to the peripheral pockets in the East to attain traditional knowledge, so did the seekers. They trace that pedagogical journey in the religious retreats. The Western neo-traditionalist shaykhs act as bridges or intermediaries between the East and West by bringing tradition to modernity. The religious retreat has become the foremost space for traditional learning. It is a space of enchantment carved out of a disenchanted world. The boundaries between tradition and modernity enable shaykhs and seekers to critique modernity as though they were outside it. This allows the seekers to envision a dissipation of modern subjectivities and their supposed baggage. The space of the retreat is both outside modernity, by way of its spatial seclusion, and unmodern, by way of its internal traditional arrangements. Oftentimes, the retreat takes place in Eastern pockets or spaces that are perceived to have traditional religious significance. The simultaneous positioning in the East and the seclusion from the outside society in these countries allow for a change of imaginary. They are seen according to the very same terms of enchantment as the space of the retreat. They become traditional, metaphysically framed, and untainted by modernity, its values, politics, or subjectivities, or the traditional archetype, just as Mauritania has been for Hamza Yusuf.

The retreat opens the space for developing new meanings, imaginaries, and a radical interrogation of the precepts of modernity. As the shaykhs read it, the discursive deconstruction of modernity allows for different strategies to emerge. Alternative ideas about science, politics, and gender equality, which might otherwise be controversial outside the space of the retreat, become a plausible traditional counter-narrative. The hierarchical dissemination of knowledge, furthermore, establishes the plausibility of this counter-narrative. The authority of the shaykhs is established through their unmatched intellect and spiritual acumen. A clear hierarchy in which the knowledge moves from the teacher to student is traditional in disposition and knowledge—to a student still impacted by the remnants of modernity. Therefore, knowledge is seen as first and foremost traditional and untainted by modern subjectivities. Furthermore, the rules and discipline maintained in the retreat and the intensity of time-scheduling are reaffirmed between student and teacher. Seekers reconnect with their religious tradition by studying primarily the traditional religious method—in *fiqh*, *'aqīda*, *taṣawwuf*, and other "traditional" approaches. As a space presumably outside the contingencies of modernity, the social and political critiques and recommendations the shaykhs posit are authoritative and represent the spirit of tradition.

Politics and Metaphysics

The neo-traditionalist shaykhs contend that Muslims have been afflicted in their political and social lives because they have abandoned their metaphysical lens. By accepting the paradigms modernity has put forth, they have moved further from the traditional approach. Therefore, the shaykhs critique the modern approaches and then provide solutions in line with the tradition. The problem with Muslims' political approaches goes back to the neo-traditionalist narratives on modernity. The postcolonial insecurity led Muslims to absorb non-Islamic approaches and frameworks. Instead of introspection, their approaches have led to a sense of perpetual victimhood and a shirking of responsibility. Instead of spiritually developing communities and cultivating virtues, Muslims became subsumed in a culture of grievance. They later took on Marxist paradigms, which alienated them even further from a reference to God. Instead of seeking absolution in the afterlife, they attempted to find a utopian sense of justice on earth.

In this book, I examine the shaykhs' different political strategies and discourses. Hamza Yusuf, for example, stresses the problems of political dissent directly. He is outspoken in his critique of different forms of activism in Muslim-majority and Muslim-minority contexts. In the Muslim-majority context, he stresses the need to obey the leader and not revolt. Rather, people should look at tribulations from a metaphysical perspective whereby there are no victims or victimizers but only the will of God. In a Muslim-minority context, he stresses the need for the community to cultivate moral rather than political approaches. Instead of a discourse of grievance, people need to find their place with other dissenting voices in modernity. These are conservative believers.

Although Abdal Hakim Murad and Umar Faruq Abd-Allah are not as actively politically engaged as Hamza Yusuf, they, too, stress the need to form bridges with other traditional conservative believers. They contend that the activists' hyper-focus on politics and the left-wing approaches of postcolonial Islam have barred Muslims from seeing the moral priorities of their community and kept them from being acclimatized to the West. Instead, Muslims should learn from the critique of modernity in the West by internal dissenting voices such as Richard Weaver and Julius Evola. This right-wing critique of modernity has an internal metaphysical discourse on politics. The metaphysical imaginary, or as Weaver calls it the "metaphysical dream," of the Right intersects with and overshadows the Muslim story. This is apparent, especially, in these voices' discourse on family values and feminism.

Although these are framed as metaphysical interventions on political and social issues, they are embedded within political reality. The foremost political context is the War on Terror's cultivating a moderate Islamic discourse to counter that of the Islamists. Conservative think tanks posited that Sufi groups were the best fit. The context of the War on Terror signaled the beginning of instrumentalizing Sufism in general and segments of the neo-traditionalist trend to counter Islamism and Salafism. The apex of this was reached after the Arab Spring. Hamza Yusuf became an increasingly important figure for anti-Islamist and anti-revolutionary monarchies—namely the UAE. This also coincided with the rise of the Right in Europe and the United States. This context gave the alliance of conservative believers another dimension whereby the concerns of the Right had become concerns of Muslims.

Seekers Speak

As seekers move away from the enchanted space of the retreat to the disenchanted modern world, the conditions for plausibility change. The immutable metaphysical principles that govern their approach to politics are under pressure from their lived realities. It is not merely that the ideal is hard to strive for, but also that these metaphysical principles seem equally partisan. I posed the question: how do seekers navigate the shaykhs' traditional political discourse in their modern lives? The question of politics elicits different answers from seekers depending on their backgrounds and personal political values. However, the question of the authority of the shaykhs as both the representatives of an authoritative, normative tradition and spiritual leaders remains central. This authority sometimes affirms political positions which seekers readily adopt. In my research, this was a minority position (except regarding gender discourse). For others, the authority of the shaykhs played a more ambivalent

244 | NEO-TRADITIONALISM IN ISLAM IN THE WEST

role. Sometimes, it mitigated concerns. Seekers often appeal to the shaykhs' vast knowledge and spiritual authority versus their personal lack thereof to mitigate their concerns. The shaykhs' authority must mean they have access to knowledge or are privy to the hidden wisdom that allows them to adopt such positions. Seekers with these positions typically compartmentalize their opposing systems of beliefs, thereby holding both simultaneously. The last group of seekers are those who have undergone a form of "burnout." This is when the authority of the shaykhs can no longer mitigate the contradictions of value systems. The immutable objectivity attributed to the metaphysical principles is then seen as the prioritization of the shaykhs' personal subjectivities. The act of replacing the postcolonial narrative with a Western one becomes a form of erasure.

The call for an alliance of conservative believers coincides with the rise of right-wing politics in the United States and Europe. For many—particularly male seekers—those on the Right share similar traditional values regarding feminism and traditional family structures. They also share the same concerns about postmodernity and what they call "cultural Marxism." This has allowed a space for the development in which neo-traditionalists engaged and borrowed from the dissenting discourse of the alt-right. For example, Abdal Hakim Murad's lecture on Julius Evola inadvertently inspired an online Muslim counterculture of esoteric critique of modernity based on essentialist categories. The introduction of figures such as Roger Scruton and other right-wing thinkers by Hamza Yusuf—notwithstanding his Islamophobia—gave rise to a new traditional imaginary. This is an imaginary that conservatives from different faith traditions can relate to, but one that also reflects the loss of power and esteem in the West following the periods of decolonization. This new imaginary allows some seekers who espouse radical traditionalist tendencies to share the views of the Right on issues of race and gender. As was noted by seekers who had undergone a form of burnout, the radical interrogation of so-called modern subjectivities by young seekers who espouse traditionalism becomes a form of policing.

Contributions, Limitations, and Recommendations

As a fairly recent but increasingly salient religious trend, neo-traditionalism has not been as extensively studied as other religious trends. This book has aimed to contribute to the wider study of Islam in the West in more general terms. Muslims have raised the question of modernity, metaphysics, and the impact of colonialism in different historical periods. They have come up with varying solutions and made different references to the historical experience of Islam. This book has not only presented the different strategies posited by neo-traditionalist shaykhs but has also addressed how seekers make sense of these strategies in their material and social worlds. I have also aimed to show the impact of the reading of modernity on the neo-traditionalists' socio-political vision. Furthermore, I have shown how the wider context impacts the development of meanings and strategies, particularly after the War on Terror, and the need to promote a moderate Islam to counter politically assertive interpretations.

Due to the limited scope of my research, I have not provided a textual analysis or criticism of the main precepts of neo-traditionalism. Instead, I have focused on framing these precepts and how they are brought to the fold of discourse and meaning for selected individual seekers. The shaykhs' innovative engagement with metaphysics also highlights the need for scholars of 'ilm al-Kalām to engage more fully with the sociology of religion and theories of modernity. Furthermore, the involvement of Hamza Yusuf in global politics can be studied to a greater degree alongside other neo-traditionalist figures in the Middle East and Russia. Throughout this research, I have been careful not to essentialize a "Sufi" approach to politics. As evidenced by history, there is not a monolithic Sufi approach. It could be useful to contrast the different political strategies of different Sufi groups and what prompted the difference. Furthermore, the rise of Muslim neo-traditionalists in the West has coincided with the rise of other traditional religious revivals, most prominently in the Catholic tradition. A comparative study of the two sets of revivals and how they engage with modernity would be very useful. For the seekers, the seemingly separate spheres of modernity and tradition are cross-referenced with mutual bearings. For this reason, each informs and relates to the other.

NOTES

Foreword

1 Translated by Michael Mumisa.

Introduction

1 Richard Weaver, *Ideas Have Consequences* (University of Chicago Press, 2013), 131–2.
2 The Queen's Journal, "Protest Outside Jordan Peterson's Visit to Queen's campus," YouTube, https://www.youtube.com/watch?v=odRiqkdgDnE&ab_channel=TheQueen%27sJournal (last accessed October 2, 2022).
3 Shuja Haider, "Postmodernism Did Not Take Place: On Jordan Peterson's 12 Rules for Life," *Viewpoint Magazine*, January 23, 2018, https://viewpointmag.com/2018/01/23/postmodernism-not-take-place-jordan-petersons-12-rules-life/?fbclid=IwAR2p7rgE8LPRF39CBsrhjRWbc32x3RocOQaRtmTEve-27rYJBblmvCPUeFw (last accessed October 2, 2022).
4 Jordan B. Peterson, "Why Is the Feminine Represented as Chaos?," YouTube, June 5, 2021, https://www.youtube.com/watch?v=rY9X6a-xxFo&t=1408s&ab_channel=JordanBPeterson (last accessed October 2, 2022).
5 Nellie Bowles, "Jordan Peterson, Custodian of the Patriarchy," *New York Times*, May 18, 2018, https://www.nytimes.com/2018/05/18/style/jordan-peterson-12-rules-for-life.html (last accessed October 2, 2022).
6 Ibid.
7 Yahya Birt, "Interview: Jordan Peterson, White Supremacy, and the Perils of Engagement," Medium, July 27, 2022, https://yahyabirt.medium.com/intervi

246

ew-jordan-peterson-white-supremacy-and-the-perils-of-engagement-a80518ad
92f4 (last accessed October 2, 2022).

8 Ibid.

9 "Originally (9th/10th cent. CE) a way of classifying the rules and methods by
which a mystical approach to god might be sustained, it became a term for the
different Sūfī systems themselves, along with their rules and rituals." John Bowker,
"Ṭarīqa," in *The Concise Oxford Dictionary of World Religions* (Oxford University
Press, 2000), https://www.oxfordreference.com/view/10.1093/acref/9780192
800947.001.0001/acref-9780192800947-e-7241 (last accessed May 29, 2019).

10 Kasper Mathiesen, "Anglo-American 'Traditional Islam' and Its Discourse of
Orthodoxy," *Journal of Arabic and Islamic Studies* 13 (2013): 198.

11 Ibid.

12 Tahir Abbas, *Muslim Britain: Communities Under Pressure* (Zed Books, 2005),
9.

13 Ibid., 8.

14 R. A. Greaves, "The Reproduction of Jamaati Islami in Britain," in *Islam and
Christian–Muslim Relations* 6, no. 2 (1995): 197.

15 Ibid., 343.

16 Sadek Hamid, "The Development of British Salafism," *Isim Review* 21 (2008): 10.

17 Hamid Mahmood, *The Dars-e- Niẓāmī and the Transnational Traditionalist
Madāris in Britain* (London, 2012).

18 Yoginder S. Sikand, "The Origins and Growth of the Tablighi Jamaat in Britain,"
Islam and Christian-Muslim Relations 9, no. 2 (1998), 171.

19 Hamid, "The Development of British Salafism," 10.

20 Sylvia Chan-Malik, *Being Muslim: A Cultural History of Women of Color in
American Islam* (New York University Press, 2018), 5.

21 Ibid.

22 Ibid., 34.

23 Edward E. Curtis, *Black Muslim Religion in the Nation of Islam, 1960–1975*
(University of North Carolina Press, 2006), 17.

24 Curtis, *Muslims in America*, 37.

25 Ibid., 18.

26 Jamillah Karim, *American Muslim Women: Negotiating Race, Class, and Gender
within the Ummah* (NYU Press, 2008), 14.

27 Michele Dillo, *Handbook of the Sociology of Religion* (Cambridge University
Press, 2003), 225.

28 Zareena Grewal, *Islam Is a Foreign Country: American Muslims and the Global
Crisis of Authority* (NYU Press, 2013), 131–2.

29 Curtis, *Muslims in America*, xii.

30 Ansari, *The Infidel Within*, 160.
31 Shadee Elmasry, "The Salafis in America: The Rise, Decline and Prospects for a Sunni Muslim Movement among African-Americans," *Journal of Muslim Minority Affairs* 30, no. 2 (2010): 217.
32 Elmasry, "The Salafis in America," 221–2.
33 Hamid, "The Attraction of 'Authentic' Islam," 391.
34 Iddo Tavory and Daniel Winchester, "Experiential Careers: The Routinization and De-Routinization of Religious Life," *Theory and Society* 41, no. 4 (2012): 367.
35 Marta Bolognani, "Islam, Ethnography and Politics: Methodological Issues in Researching amongst West Yorkshire Pakistanis in 2005," *International Journal of Social Research Methodology* 10, no. 4 (2007): 281–4.
36 Maryam Kashani, "Seekers of Sacred Knowledge: Zaytuna College and the Education of American Muslims" (PhD diss., University of Texas at Austin, 2014), 24.
37 Judith Okely, "Anthropology and Autobiography: Participatory Experience and Embodied Knowledge," in *Anthropology and autobiography*, ed. Judith Okely and Helen Callaway (Routledge, 1992), 3.
38 "Spring Lodge Retreat," http://www.naqa.org.uk/spring-lodge-retreat/ (last accessed February 2, 2019).

> One of the main problems I have encountered was that—despite being renowned as public intellectuals—the shaykhs produced more public lectures than written work. Furthermore, seekers were less likely to have read the written material the shaykhs produced. The first book Hamza Yusuf published was *The Creed of Imam al-Tahawi*. His best-known books are *Purification of the Heart: Signs, Symptoms and Cures of the Spiritual Diseases of the Heart*, which is a translation and commentary of Imam Mawlūd's Mātharāt Al-Qulūb, and *The Prayer of the Oppressed*, which is a translation and commentary of al-Duʿāʾ al-Naṣīrī by Imam al-Darʿī. He also co-wrote *Agenda to Change Our Condition* with Zaid Shakir. Yusuf also contributed a chapter in Reza Shah Kazemi's book *Common Ground between Islam and Buddhism* titled "Buddha in the Qurʾān?" Yusuf explores how Buddhism was perceived by scholars in the past. He builds on the work of the Persian philosopher and scholar Muhammad al-Shahrastānī in arguing that Buddha may have been the Qurʾanic figure of al-Khiḍr, who was sent as a guide to Moses. Furthermore, he wrote *Caesarean Moon Births: Calculations, Moon Sighting, and the Prophetic Way*. Most of Yusuf's articles appear either on his personal website Sandala or in the journal of Zaytuna College, *Renovatio*.

Abdal Hakim Murad's most recent book (2020)—*Travelling Home: Essays on Islam in Europe*—is based on a series of edited lectures he presented over the years. In 2012, he wrote *Commentary on the Eleventh Contentions*, based on his aphorisms. He also wrote *Muslim Songs of the British Isles: Arranged for Schools* and *Understanding the Four Madhhabs: Facts About Ijtihad and Taqlid*. The majority of Abdal Hakim Murad's written work is found at http://masud.co.uk/ As for Umar Faruq Abd-Allah, his most accessed written contribution was his essay "Islam and the Cultural Imperative."

39 That said, Abd-Allah has written three books in English—*Mālik and Medina: Islamic Legal Reasoning in the Formative Period* (based on his PhD thesis), *The Islamic Struggle in Syria* (written in the 1980s; his perspectives have changed fundamentally since), and, most recently, *A Muslim in Victorian America: The Life of Alexander Russell Webb*. Abd-Allah also wrote a book in Arabic, *Al-Imān Fitra*, which is not in circulation. Most seekers—particularly the younger ones—note that they discovered the neo-traditionalist shaykhs through their material online before attending their retreats. I therefore gathered most of the material from lectures and articles posted online. Additionally, the lectures in Rihla are livestreamed, and most of them are saved as videos on https://www.deenstream .tv/

Chapter 1

1 "Rihla: Course Pack," Deen Intensive Foundation, 2012, https://www.scribd .com/doc/98729274/Rihla-2012-Coursepack (last accessed January 10, 2019).

2 "40 Hadith Nawawi 2," sunnah.com/nawawi40 (last accessed January 13, 2016).

3 Brendan Peter Newlon, "American Muslim Networks and Neotraditionalism," (PhD diss., University of California, Santa Barbara, 2017), 74.

4 Kasper Mathiesen, "Anglo-American 'Traditional Islam' and its Discourse of Orthodoxy," *Journal of Arabic and Islamic Studies* 13 (2013): 198.

5 Anabel Inge, *The Making of a Salafi Muslim Woman: Paths to Conversion* (Oxford University Press, 2017), 26.

6 Richard Bulliet, David Cook, Roxanne L. Euben, Khaled Fahmy, Frank Griffel, Bernard Haykel, Robert W. Hefner, Timur Kuran, Jane McAuliffe, and Ebrahim Moosa, *The Princeton Encyclopedia of Islamic Political Thought* (Princeton University Press, 2013), 483.

7 Ibid., 484.

8 Robert Gleave. "Taqlid," in *Encyclopedia of Islam and the Muslim World*, ed. Richard C. Martin (Gale, 2016).

9 Sadek Hamid, "The Attraction of 'Authentic' Islam," Salafism and British Muslim Youth," in *Global Salafism: Islam's New Religious Movement*, ed. R. Meijer (Hurst, 2009), 358.

10 Ibid., 361.

11 Inge, *The Making of a Salafi Woman*, 33.

12 Ibid., 34.

13 Shadee Elmasry, "The Salafis in America: The Rise, Decline and Prospects for a Sunni Muslim Movement among African-Americans," *Journal of Muslim Minority Affairs* 30, no. 2 (2010): 222.

14 Hamid, "The Attraction of 'Authentic' Islam," 361.

15 Terje Østebø, "Salafism, State-Politics, and the Question of 'Extremism' in Ethiopia," *Comparative Islamic Studies* 8 (2012), 177.

16 Anas El Gomati, "Libya's Islamists and the 17 February Revolution: A Battle for a Revolutionary Theology," in *Routledge Handbook of the Arab Spring*, ed. Larbi Sadiki (Routledge, 2014), 120.

17 Sadek Hamid, "The Development of British Salafism," *Isim Review* 21, no. 1 (2008): 11.

18 Abdal Hakim Murad, "Islamic Spirituality: the forgotten revolution," http://ma sud.co.uk/ISLAM/ahm/fgtnrevo.htm

19 Inge, *Making of a Salafi Woman*, 233.

20 Hamza Yusuf, "The Dajjal and New World Order" (lecture, London, 1998), https://www.youtube.com/watch?v=oky3TSlEt4A&t=4320s

21 "The Muslim 500: The World's Most Influential Muslims," https://themuslim5 00.com/

22 Zareena Grewal, *Islam Is a Foreign Country: American Muslims and the Global Crisis of Authority* (NYU Press, 2013), 160.

23 Hamza Yusuf, "Religion: A Pretext for Conflict?," Davos Open Forum at the World Economic Forum Annual Meeting (session with Tony Blair, David Rosen, Hamza Yusuf Hanson, Mina Oraibi, and Thabo Cecil Makgoba, Davos, 2015), https://www.youtube.com/watch?v=BYs6Mm9BTaM (last accessed January 10, 2019).

24 Haifaa A. Jawad, *Towards Building a British Islam: New Muslims' Perspectives* (A & C Black, 2011), 132.

25 Bob Roberts and Hamza Yusuf, "Shaykh Hamza Yusuf & Bob Roberts Jr | Muslim Scholar Talks Jesus with Evangelical Pastor," in Bold Love (podcast), October 14, 2020, https://www.youtube.com/watch?v=vcRiogk9EKM&ab_ch annel=BobRobertsJr. (last accessed January 25, 2022).

26 "David Joseph Hanson Obituary," *New York Times*, 2017, https://www.legacy .com/us/obituaries/nytimes/name/david-hanson-obituary?pid=185113929

27 Hamza Yusuf, "On the Passing of My Mother, Elizabeth George Hanson," *Sandala* https://sandala.org/blogs/uncategorized/on-the-passing-of-my-mother

28 Grewal, *Islam Is a Foreign Country*, 160.

29 Yusuf, "On the Passing of My Mother."
30 Ibid.
31 Akbar Ahmed, *Journey into America: The Challenge of Islam* (Brookings Institution Press, 2010), 315.
32 Roberts and Yusuf, "Muslim Scholar Talks Jesus with Evangelical Pastor."
33 Ahmed, *Journey into America*, 315.
34 Yusuf, "On the Passing of My Mother."
35 Sharify-Funk Meena, William Rory Dickson, and Shobhana Xavier Merin, *Contemporary Sufism Piety, Politics, and Popular Culture* (Routledge, 2017), xiv.
36 Hamza Yusuf, "A Spiritual Giant in an Age of Dwarfed Terrestrial Aspirations," *Q-News* 363 (2005): 53–8.
37 Roberts and Yusuf, "Muslim Scholar Talks Jesus with Evangelical Pastor."
38 Grewal, *Islam Is a Foreign Country*, 160.
39 Jawad, *Towards Building a British Islam*, 156.
40 Ibid.
41 Ian Abdal Latīf Whiteman, *Average Whiteman: Adventures with Quakers, Architects, Rock Stars & Sufi Sages* (Editorial Qasida, 2021), 100.
42 Sardar, *Desperately Seeking Paradise*, 69.
43 Grewal, *Islam Is a Foreign Country*, 160.
44 Ibid.
45 Nathan Spannaus and Christopher Pooya Razavian, "Zaytuna College and the Construction of an American Muslim Identity," in *Modern Islamic Authority and Social Change, Volume 2: Evolving Debates in the West*, ed. Masooda Bano (Edinburgh University Press, 2017), 42.
46 Grewal, *Islam Is a Foreign Country*, 162.
47 Deniz Baran, "A Voice to the World from Chicago: Dr Umar Faruq Abd-Allah," June 8, 2017, in worldbulletin, https://www.worldbulletin.net/interviews-in-de pth/a-voice-to-the-world-from-chicago-dr-umar-faruq-abd-allah-h190556.html (last accessed January 10, 2019).
48 "Dr. Umar Faruq Abd-Allah Wymann-Landgraf" (last accessed October 18, 2019), http://www.themodernreligion.com/profile/sh-Umar-Faruq-Abd-Allah .html
49 "Donald Eugene Weinman" (last accessed January 25, 2022), https://www.finda grave.com/memorial/47072342/donald-eugene-weinman
50 Umar Faruq Abd-Allah, "The Fitra" (lecture, Malaysia, 2017).
51 "Dr. Umar Faruq Abd-Allah," ALIM American Learning Institute for Muslims, https://www.alimprogram.org/scholars/dr-umar/ (last accessed January 10, 2019).

52 https://www.alimprogram.org/dr-umar-faruq-abd-allah.html

53 Umar Faruq Abdallah, "Keynote," Malikiyyah Conference (Norwich, 1982), https://www.youtube.com/watch?v=_e1nrkU1q0g (last accessed January 10, 2019).

54 Ahmed Peerbux dirs, *Blessed Are the Strangers* (C Media, 2017).

55 Ziauddin Sardar, *Desperately Seeking Paradise: Journeys of a Sceptical Muslim* (Granta, 2005), 69.

56 Whiteman, *Average Whiteman*, 107.

57 Ibid., 152.

58 Sardar, *Desperately Seeking Paradise*, 69.

59 Whiteman, *Average Whiteman*, 180–1.

60 Abd-Allah, "The Fitra."

61 Justine Howe, *Suburban Islam* (Oxford University Press, 2018), 49.

62 "Obituaries: John Winter," *The Daily Telegraph*, November 23, 2012, https://www.telegraph.co.uk/news/obituaries/9699534/John-Winter.html

63 Jawad, *Towards Building a British Islam*, 117.

64 Tom Peck, "Timothy Winter: Britain's Most Influential Muslim—and It Was All Down to a Peach," *The Independent*, August 20, 2010, https://www.independent.co.uk/news/people/profiles/timothy-winter-britain-s-most-influential-muslim-and-it-was-all-down-to-a-peach-2057400.html

65 Ibid.

66 Abdal Hakim Murad, "Why I Converted to Islam," interview with Joan Bakewell, BBC Radio 3 (December 2009), https://www.youtube.com/watch?v=GGfc6Ob1UAY (last accessed January 10, 2019).

67 Jawad, *Towards Building a British Islam*, 117.

68 Abdal Hakim Murad, "Abdal Hakim Murad on Tablighi Jamaat," YouTube, April 3, 2012, https://www.youtube.com/watch?v=ZLWnUjZEJN0 (last accessed January 10, 2019).

69 According to Habib Ali Jifri.

70 Yahya Birt, "Fuad Nahdi, Q-News and the Forging of British Islam: Some Personal Reflections," March 30, 2020, https://yahyabirt.medium.com/fuad-nahdi-q-news-and-the-forging-of-british-islam-some-personal-reflections-9182c15b4ca8

71 Innes Bowen, *Medina in Birmingham, Najaf in Brent: Inside British Islam* (Oxford University Press, 2014), 122–3.

72 Sadek Hamid, "The Rise of the 'Traditional Islam' Network(s): Neo-Sufism and British Muslim Youth," *Sufism in Britain*, 2013, 184.

73 Sadek Hamid, *Sufis, Salafis and Islamists: The Contested Ground of British Islamic Activism* (I. B. Tauris, 2016), 79.

74 Hamid, *Sufis, Salafis and Islamists*, 80.

75 Spannaus and Pooya Razavian, "Zaytuna College and the Construction of an American Muslim Identity," 39.

76 Hamid, *Sufis, Salafis and Islamists*, 81.

77 Ibid.

78 Marcia Hermansen, "American Sufis and American Islam: From Private Spirituality to the Public Sphere," *Islamic Movements and Islam in the Multicultural World: Islamic Movements and Formation of Islamic Ideologies in the Information Age*, ed. Denis Brilyov, 2013, 201.

79 Peter M. Haas, "Introduction: Epistemic Communities and International Policy Coordination," *International Organization* 46, no. 1 (1992), 3.

80 Masooda Bano breaks down neo-traditionalists to three generations. The first generation being Hamza Yusuf, Abdal Hakim Murad, Umar Faruq Abd-Allah, alongside the other shaykhs who started teaching in the 1990s. These shaykhs were central to the epistemic, religious, institutional formation of neo-traditionalism. The second generation are some of the younger shaykhs and *ustadh*s—such as Usama Canon, Yahya Rhodus, Mustafa Davis, Faraz Rabbani, and others. The second generation and the institution they built—such as Ta'leef Collective, Maqasid, or SeekersHub—were inspired by the first generation. The third generation are the seekers of sacred knowledge in neo-traditionalists spaces. Masooda Bano, *The Revival of Islamic Rationalism: Logic, Metaphysics and Mysticism in Modern Muslim Societies* (Cambridge University Press, 2020), 23.

81 For a more comprehensive mapping of the network see Brendan Peter Newlon, "American Muslim Networks and Neotraditionalism" (PhD diss., University of California, Santa Barbara, 2017), 154–6.

82 Sajida Jalalzai, "Muslim Chaplaincy and Female Religious Authority in North America," in *The Routledge Handbook of Islam and Gender* (Routledge, 2020), 209.

83 Kasper Mathiesen, "Anglo-American 'Traditional Islam' and its Discourse of Orthodoxy," *Journal of Arabic and Islamic Studies* 13 (2013): 198.

84 Nazim Baksh, "In the Spirit of Tradition," www.masud.co.uk/ISLAM/misc/tradition.htm (last accessed January 13, 2016).

85 Abdal Hakim Murad, *Travelling Home: Essays on Islam in Europe* (The Quilliam Press, 2020), 3.

86 Umar Faruq Abd-Allah, "Modernity and Post-Modernity: Definitions, History, Responses" (lecture, Zawiya, 2014).

87 Yusuf has used *turāthī* on occasion in interviews conducted in Arabic.

88 Muḥammad ʿādil al-Tirīkī, "Al-ʾaṣālah' w-al- muʿāṣara fī al-fikr al-ʿarabī al-muʿāṣir," January, 18, 2011, maghress.com, https://www.maghress.com/tettawen/1838 (last accessed January 10, 2019).

89 As they objected to identifying as "modernist" or ḥadāthīyūn.

90 Abdullah bin Hamid Ali, "'Neo-Traditionalism' vs 'Traditionalism,'" January 22, 2012, Lamppost Foundation Initiative, https://lamppostedu.org/neo-traditionalism-vs-traditionalism-shaykh-abdullah-bin-hamid-ali/ (last accessed December 15, 2020).

91 Ibid.

92 Ibid.

93 Newlon, "American Muslim Networks and Neotraditionalism," 33–7. Abdelwahab El-Affendi, *The People on the Edge: Religious Reform and the Burden of the Western Muslim Intellectual* (Vol. 19. International Institute of Islamic Thought (IIIT), 2010), 13.

94 I discuss this in Chapter 6.

95 Dawud Israel, "3 Miracles of Murabit al-Hajj—Yahya Rhodus at SeekersRetreat 2014," filmed 2014, YouTube video, 6:58, posted November 2015, https://www.youtube.com/watch?v=PdeooPMD5y4 (last accessed January 13, 2016).

96 Hamza Yusuf, "Faces of Islam," BBC documentary, 1999, https://www.youtube.com/watch?v=h0ZlEyx0040 (last accessed January 10, 2019).

97 Grewal, *Islam Is a Foreign Country*, 166.

98 Ibid.

99 Yusuf, "Faces of Islam."

100 Grewal, *Islam Is a Foreign Country*, 165.

101 I discuss enchantment, disenchantment, and re-enchantment in greater detail in the following chapters.

102 Grewal, *Islam Is a Foreign Country*, 167.

103 Ibid., 165.

104 Yusuf, "Faces of Islam."

105 Hamza Yusuf, "Speech," in AlMarkaz al-'ālamī l'l-Tajdīd wal Tarshīd (speech, Mauritania, April 2013), https://www.youtube.com/watch?v=Rpma1aaWwds&t=148s (last accessed January 10, 2019).

106 أما الخيام فإنها كخيامهم... وأرى نساء الحي غير نسائها

لا والذي حجت قريش حجت بيته ... مستقبلين الركن من بطحائها.

ما أبصرت عيني خيام قبيلة ... إلا ذكرت أحبتي بفنائها.

107 Yusuf, "Speech," in AlMarkaz al-'ālamī l'l-Tajdīd wal Tarshīd.

108 In fact, long before the Arab Spring, Mauritania had its own democratic experience in 2007, which ended in a military coup in 2008.

109 Yusuf, "Faces of Islam."

110 Mathiesen, "Anglo-American 'Traditional Islam' and Its Discourse of Orthodoxy," 210.

Chapter 2

1 Umar Faruq Abd-Allah, "Modernism and Post-Modernism in the Light of the Prophetic Belief: session 6" (lecture, Samsun, 2016), https://deenstream.vhx.tv/videos/drumar-faruq-modernist-session-6

2 Ibid.

3 Abdal Hakim Murad, *Travelling Home: Essays on Islam in Europe* (The Quilliam Press, 2020), 3.

4 Abd-Allah, "Modernity and Post-Modernity."

5 Umar Faruq Abd-Allah defines Islamism as "highly politicized twentieth-century revivalist movements with essentialist interpretations of Islam, generally advocating particular state and party ends as Islam's chief or virtually unique focus. Islamists tend toward literalism but selectively retrieve the texts they follow, often contravening well established interpretations within Islam's scholarly tradition." Umar Faruq Abd-Allah, "Islam and the Cultural Imperative," *Islam and Civilisational Renewal* 1, no. 1 (2009): 11.

6 Umar Faruq Abd-Allah, "Modernism and Post-Modernism in the Light of the Prophetic Belief: Session 3a" (lecture, Samsun, 2016), https://deenstream.vhx.tv/modernism-and-post-modernism-in-the-light-of-prophetic-belief/season:1/videos/drumar-faruq-modernist-session-3-part-a

7 Ibid.

8 Zaytuna College, "Hamza Yusuf: A Crisis of Metaphysics," YouTube, September 29, 2015, https://www.youtube.com/watch?v=NKrxbX3_PWc (last accessed June 26, 2018).

9 Hamza Yusuf, "Is the Matter of Metaphysics Immaterial? Yes and No," *Renovatio: The Journal of Zaytuna College* (May 10, 2017), https://renovatio.zaytuna.edu/article/the-matter-of-metaphysics

10 Umar Faruq Abd-Allah, "Modernism and Post-Modernism in the Light of the Prophetic Belief: session 5b" (lecture, Samsun, 2016), https://deenstream.vhx.tv/modernism-and-post-modernism-in-the-light-of-prophetic-belief/season:1/videos/drumar-faruq-modernist-session-5-part-b

11 Michael J. Loux and Thomas M. Crisp, *Metaphysics: A Contemporary Introduction* (Routledge, 2017), 45.

12 Hamza Yusuf, "Is the Matter of Metaphysics Immaterial? Yes and No," *Renovatio: The Journal of Zaytuna College* (May 10, 2017), https://renovatio.zaytuna.edu/article/the-matter-of-metaphysics (last accessed January 10, 2019).

13 Abdurrahman Mihirig, "The Myth of Intellectual Decline: A Response to Shaykh Hamza Yusuf," *The Maydan*, November 27, 2017, https://www.themaydan.com/2017/11/myth-intellectual-decline-response-shaykh-hamza-yusuf/ (last accessed June 26, 2018).

14 Yusuf, "Is the Matter of Metaphysics Immaterial? Yes and No."

15 Hamza Yusuf, *Prayer of the Oppressed* (Sandala Productions, 2010), 9–10.

16 Umar Faruq Abdullah, "Modernist and Post-Modernist Belief," parts 1 and 4, Rihla, 2016.

17 Walaa Quisay, "The Neo-Traditionalist Critique of Modernity and the Production of Political Quietism," in *Political Quietism in Islam: Sunni and Shi'i Practice and Thought* (I. B. Tauris, 2019): 246.

18 Umar Faruq Abdullah, "Modernist and Post-Modernist Belief," part 6, Rihla, 2016.

19 Abdal Hakim Murad, "The Destitute: A Discussion on the Spirituality of Poverty" (lecture, London: SOAS, 2014), https://www.youtube.com/watch?v=ciBmrwrLn98

20 Murad, "The Destitute."

21 Abdal Hakim Murad, "Contentions," *Rihla*, 2016.

22 Murad, "The Destitute."

23 Omar Qureshi, "Virtue Ethics," Rihla, 2017.

24 Abdal Hakim Murad, "Riding the Tiger of Modernity" (lecture, Cambridge, 2016), https://www.youtube.com/watch?v=07Ien1qo_qI&t=1082s (last accessed January 21, 2019).

25 Umar Faruq Abd-Allah, "Modernity and Post-Modernity: Definitions, History and Responses," Zawiya 2014 notes, 5.

26 Ibid., 287.

27 Dustin J. Byrd, *Islam in a Post-Secular Society: Religion, Secularity, and the Antagonism of Recalcitrant Faith* (Brill, 2016), 8.

28 Byrd, *Islam in a Post-secular Society*, 8.

29 Nicholas Gane, *Max Weber and Postmodern Theory: Rationalization versus Re-Enchantment* (Springer, 2002), 20.

30 Max Weber and Stephen Kalberg, "The Protestant Sects and the Spirit of Capitalism," *Essays in Sociology 3*, 1946, xii.

31 Gane, *Max Weber and Postmodern Theory*, 12.

32 Charles Taylor, *A Secular Age* (Harvard University Press, 2007), 29–30.

33 Ibid.

34 Bob Roberts and Hamza Yusuf, "Shaykh Hamza Yusuf & Bob Roberts Jr | Muslim Scholar Talks Jesus with Evangelical Pastor," in Bold Love (podcast), October 14, 2020, https://www.youtube.com/watch?v=vcRiogk9EKM&ab_channel=BobRobertsJr. (last accessed January 25, 2022).

35 James K. A. Smith, *How (Not) To Be Secular: Reading Charles Taylor* (Eerdmans, 2014), 70–1.

36 Ibid., 140.

37 Umar Faruq Abd-Allah (Rihla, 2017).

38 Murad, "Contentions."

39 Hamza Yusuf, "Is the Matter of Metaphysics Immaterial? Yes and No," *Renovatio: The Journal of Zaytuna College*, May 10, 2017, https://renovatio.zaytuna.edu/article/the-matter-of-metaphysics

40 Abd-Allah, "Modernism and Post-Modernism in the Light of the Prophetic Belief: Session 1."

41 Abdal Hakim Murad, "Faith in the Future: Islam after the Enlightenment" (lecture, Islamabad, December 23, 2002), http://masud.co.uk/ISLAM/ahm/postEnlight.htm

42 Cairo Review, "Cairo Review interviews Shaykh Hamza Yusuf," https://imamsonline.com/cairo-review-interviews-shaykh-hamza-yusuf/ (last accessed January 4, 2021).

43 Rasha Elass, "Muslim Liberal Arts College Aims for a Restoration," *The Arab Weekly*, November 20, 2015, https://thearabweekly.com/muslim-liberal-arts-college-aims-restoration (last accessed January 4, 2021).

44 Sherman A. Jackson, *Islam and the Blackamerican: Looking toward the Third Resurrection* (Oxford University Press, 2005), 77.

45 Ibid.

46 Yusuf, "Is the Matter of Metaphysics Immaterial? Yes and No."

47 Ibid.

48 Aftab Ahmad Malik, *The Broken Chain: Reflections upon the Neglect of the Tradition* (Amal Pres, 2001), 8, 9.

49 Islam on Demand, "The Salafi Fallacy—Abdal Hakim Murad," YouTube, https://www.youtube.com/watch?v=1MRXs5fqlXQ (last accessed January 13, 2016).

50 Abdal Hakim Murad, *Bombing without Moonlight: The Origins of Suicidal Terrorism* (Amal Press, 2008).

51 Hamza Yusuf and Tariq Ramadan, "Rethinking Reform," debate, University of Oxford Union, Oxford, May 26, 2010.

52 Ibid.

53 Islam on Demand, "The Concept of Ihsan—By Hamza Yusuf (Foundations of Islam Series: Session 4)," YouTube, https://www.youtube.com/watch?v=SLhogmk-Wug (last accessed February 15, 2017).

54 Albert Hourani, "Rashid Rida and the Sufi Orders: A Footnote to Laoust," *Bulletin d'études orientales* 29 (1977): 231–41.

55 Henri Lauzière, "The Construction of Salafiyya: Reconsidering Salafism from the Perspective of Conceptual History," *International Journal of Middle East Studies* 42, no. 3 (2010): 375.

56 Abdal Hakim Murad, "Understanding the Four Madhhabs: The Problem with Anti-Madhhabism," 1999, http://masud.co.uk/understanding-the-four-madhh abs-the-problem-with-anti-madhhabism/ (last accessed March 7, 2018)

57 Abdal Hakim Murad, *Commentary on the Eleventh Contention* (The Quilliam Press), 124.

58 Yusuf and Ramadan. "Rethinking Reform."

59 Murad, *Bombing without Moonlight.* Yusuf and Ramadan, "Rethinking Reform."

60 Abu Bakr, "Shaykh Hamza Yusuf—Framing Islam into Marxist Thought," YouTube, July 18, 2016, https://www.youtube.com/watch?v=Kjh6x_vbgcY (last accessed March 7, 2018).

61 Ibid.

62 Q News, "'Love Even Those Who Revile You,'" *Arab News*, 2005, http://www .arabnews.com/node/265421 (last accessed March 7, 2018).

63 Umar Faruq Abd-Allah, "Islam and the Cultural Imperative," *CrossCurrents* (2006): 373.

64 Hamza Yusuf and Zaid Shakir, *Agenda to Change Our Condition* (Zaytuna Institute, 2008), 5.

65 Abd-Allah, "Modernism and Post-Modernism in the Light of the Prophetic Belief: session 4."

66 Murad, "Contentions," 124.

67 See e.g. Ayaan Hirsi Ali, *Heretic: Why Islam Needs a Reformation Now* (Knopf Canada, 2015).

68 "President Bush Addresses the Nation," September 20, 2001, https://www.wash ingtonpost.com/wpsrv/nation/specials/attacked/transcripts/bushaddress_0920 01.html

69 Edward E. Curtis IV, *Muslims in America: A Short History* (Oxford University Press, 2009), 100.

70 Rosemary R. Corbett, *Making Moderate Islam: Sufism, Service, and the "Ground Zero Mosque" Controversy* (Stanford University Press, 2016), 11.

71 Sylvia Chan-Malik, *Being Muslim: A Cultural History of Women of Color in American Islam* (New York University Press, 2018), 22.

72 Ibid., 92.

73 Corbett, *Making Moderate Islam*, 12.

74 Saba Mahmood, "Secularism, Hermeneutics, and Empire: The Politics of Islamic Reformation," *Public Culture* 18, no. 2 (2006): 326–7.

75 Ibid., 328.

76 Su'ad Abdul Khabeer, *Muslim Cool: Race, Religion, and Hip Hop in the United States* (New York University Press, 2016), 9; Sylvia Chan-Malik, "'Common

Cause': On the Black-Immigrant Debate and Constructing the Muslim American," *Journal of Race, Ethnicity, and Religion* 2, no. 8 (2011): 12.

77 Abdul Khabeer, *Muslim Cool*, 13.

78 The MCB is an umbrella organization with a stated aim of representing British Muslims, and, Stephen Jones notes, "with its affiliates mostly being aligned with the Deobandi tradition and reformist Islamist (specifically Jamaat-i-Islami influenced) movements. Over the years, British Shia, Ahmadi and Barelvi groups have periodically complained of their marginalization and relative lack of influence in the organization." Stephen H. Jones, *Islam and the Liberal State: National Identity and the Future of Muslim Britain* (Bloomsbury, 2020), 121.

79 *Islam and the Liberal State: National Identity and the Future of Muslim Britain*, 120.

80 Khadijah Elshayyal, *Muslim Identity Politics: Islam, Activism and Equality in Britain* (Bloomsbury, 2018), 102–4.

81 Ibid., 119.

82 Ibid., 118.

83 Stephen H. Jones, "New Labour and the Re-making of British Islam: The Case of the Radical Middle Way and the 'Reclamation' of the Classical Islamic Tradition," *Religions* 4, no. 4 (2013): 566.

84 Ibid., 557.

85 Jonathan (Yahya) Birt, "Good Imam, Bad Imam: Civic Religion and National Integration in Britain post-9/11." *The Muslim World* 96, no. 4 (2006): 687.

86 Fait Muedini, *Sponsoring Sufism: How Governments Promote "Mystical Islam" in Their Domestic and Foreign Policies* (Springer, 2015), 158.

87 Simon Stjernholm, *Lovers of Muhammad: A Study of Naqshbandi-Haqqani Sufis in the Twenty-First Century*, Vol. 29 (Lund University, 2011), 280.

88 Corbett, *Making Moderate Islam*, 71.

89 Ibid., 88.

90 Richard H. Curtiss, "Dispute Between U.S. Muslim Groups Goes Public," *Washington Report on Middle East Affairs*, April/May 1999, 71, 101, https://www.wrmea.org/1999-april-may/dispute-between-u.s.-muslim-groups-goes-public.html

91 Sharify-Funk Meena, William Rory Dickson, and Shobhana Xavier Merin, *Contemporary Sufism: Piety, Politics, and Popular Culture* (Routledge, 2017), 82.

92 Cheryl Benard, Andrew Riddile, Peter A. Wilson, and Steven W. Popper, *Civil Democratic Islam: Partners, Resources, and Strategies* (Rand Corporation, 2004), 40.

93 Jonathan Rauch, "Islam Has Been Hijacked, and Only Muslims Can Save It," University of Chicago Press, 2001, https://www.press.uchicago.edu/sites/daysafter/911rauch.html (last accessed January 21, 2019).

94 Zareena Grewal, *Islam Is a Foreign Country: American Muslims and the Global Crisis of Authority* (NYU Press, 2013), 306.
95 Ibid.
96 Geneive Abdo, *Mecca and Main Street: Muslim Life in America after 9/11* (Oxford University Press, 2006), 13.
97 Grewal, *Islam Is a Foreign Country*, 307.
98 'Abdullah bin Al-Shaykh Al-Maḥfūẓ bin Bayyah, "Shāhid Mādhā Qāl al-ʿalāmah Ibn Bayyah l'lQadhāffī Wajān li Wajh?," YouTube, March 30, 2014. https://www.youtube.com/watch?v=LadvZVGiIE4 (last accessed January 21, 2019).
99 Abdo, *Mecca and Main Street*, 14.
100 Ibid., 22.
101 Ibid.
102 Ibid., 20.
103 Ibid.
104 "Radical Middle Way," http://impacteurope.eu/partners/radical-middle-way/ (last accessed January 21, 2019).
105 Jones, "New Labour and the Re-making of British Islam," 558.
106 "Radical Middle Way Project," https://www.idealist.org/en/nonprofit/aecf 97897e024310a217d0fddb02442c-radical-middle-way-london (last accessed January 21, 2019).
107 Jones, "New Labour and the Re-making of British Islam," 559.
108 Christopher Hope, "Ministers spend £90,000 a Day on 'Soft Schemes' To Tackle Extremism," *The Telegraph*, March 23, 2009, https://www.telegraph.co.uk/news/uknews/law-and-order/5038157/Ministers-spend-90000-a-day-on-soft-schemes-to-tackle-extremism.html (last accessed January 21, 2019).
109 Jones, "New Labour and the Re-making of British Islam," 561–2.

Chapter 3

1 They were partly compiled in his 2012 book *Commentary on the Eleventh Contentions*, and the remainder could be found on www.masud.com.
2 Abdal Hakim Murad, "Contentions," Samsun, 2016.
3 Alqueria De Rosales Campus, "Studies of Imam Al-Ghazali Program," YouTube, September 26, 2017, https://www.youtube.com/watch?v=c1d5GP7Rh5A&feature=youtube (last accessed January 13, 2019).
4 Umar Faruq Abd-Allah, "Islam and The Cultural Imperative," in Seekers Hub (lecture, December 10, 2011), https://www.youtube.com/watch?v=44ycrsABA 2s&t=1s (last accessed January 13, 2019).

5 Gregory B. Willson, Alison J. McIntosh, and Anne L. Zahra, "Tourism and Spirituality: A Phenomenological Analysis," *Annals of Tourism Research* 42 (2013): 152.

6 Brooke Schedneck, "Religious and Spiritual Retreats," in *The Routledge Handbook of Religious and Spiritual Tourism*, ed. Daniel H. Olsen, and Dallen J. Timothy (Routledge, 2021),

7 Melanie Kay Smith, "Religion, Spirituality, and Wellness Tourism," in *The Routledge Handbook of Religious and Spiritual Tourism*, ed. Daniel H., Olsen, and Dallen J. Timothy (Routledge, 2021), 69.

8 Haifaa Jawad, "De-radicalization through Conversion to Traditional Islam: Hamza Yusuf's Attempt to Revive the Sacred Knowledge with a North Atlantic Context," in *Moving In and Out of Islam*, ed. Karin van Nieuwkerk (University of Texas Press, December 5, 2018), 215.

9 Hall, *The Ways Out*, 51.

10 Ibid.

11 Darius Liutikas, "Travel Motivations of Pilgrims, Religious Tourists, and Spirituality Seekers," in *The Routledge Handbook of Religious and Spiritual Tourism*, ed. Daniel H. Olsen, and Dallen J. Timothy (Routledge, 2021), 226.

12 Melanie Kay Smith, "Religion, Spirituality, and Wellness Tourism," in *The Routledge Handbook of Religious and Spiritual Tourism*, ed. Daniel H. Olsen, and Dallen J. Timothy (Routledge, 2021), 69.

13 Ibid.

14 Ibid.

15 DeenIntensive, "Deen Intensive *Rihla* 2010/1431 Trailer," YouTube, January 31, 2010, https://www.youtube.com/watch?v=9LI6xKk3CCM&feature=you tu.be&fbclid=IwAR2eGvRd2_uykCLy9tSSH3ImwQ_H13EHfGK6Da3YRy uzny-cidMNIKKBE0s (last accessed January 13, 2019).

16 Smith, "Religion, Spirituality, and Wellness Tourism," 69.

17 Alex Norman, *Spiritual Tourism: Travel and Religious Practice in Western Society* (Bloomsbury, 2011), 25.

18 Smith, "Religion, Spirituality, and Wellness Tourism," 69.

19 Norman, *Spiritual Tourism*, 31.

20 Charles Taylor, *A Secular Age* (Harvard University Press, 2007), 28.

21 Ibid., 3.

22 Sophia Rose Arjana, *Buying Buddha, Selling Rumi: Orientalism and the Mystical Marketplace* (Simon & Schuster, 2020), 12.

23 Carole M. Cusack, "A New Spiritual Marketplace: Comparing New Age and New Religious Movements in an Age of Spiritual and Religious Tourism," in *The*

Routledge Handbook of Religious and Spiritual Tourism, ed. Daniel H. Olsen, and Dallen J. Timothy (Routledge, 2021), 81.

24 John Preston, *Grenfell Tower: Preparedness, Race and Disaster Capitalism* (Springer, 2018), 33.

25 Ibid.

26 Robert Booth and Calla Wahlquist, "Grenfell Tower Residents Say Managers 'Brushed Away' Fire Safety Concerns," *The Guardian*, June 14, 2017, https://www.theguardian.com/uk-news/2017/jun/14/fire-safety-concerns-raised-by-grenfell-tower-residents-in-2012 (last accessed December 13, 2020).

27 Lynsey Hanley, "Look at Grenfell Tower and See the Terrible Price of Britain's Inequality," *The Guardian*, June 16, 2017, https://www.theguardian.com/commentisfree/2017/jun/16/grenfell-tower-price-britain-inequality-high-rise (last accessed December 13, 2022).

28 Hawes Spencer, *Summer of Hate: Charlottesville, USA* (University of Virginia Press; 2019).

29 Ibid.

30 Ibid.

31 Joe Heim, "Charlottesville Timeline—How White Supremacist Protests Turned Deadly over 24 Hours," *Washington Post*, August 14, 2017, https://www.washingtonpost.com/graphics/2017/local/charlottesville-timeline/?utm_term=.6298c843f478

32 Anabel Inge, *The Making of a Salafi Muslim Woman: Paths to Conversion*, illustrated edition (New York: Oxford University Press, 2016), 99.

33 Zareena A. Grewal, "Marriage in Colour: Race, Religion and Spouse Selection in Four American Mosques, Ethnic and Racial Studies," 2009, 32, no. 2, 325.

34 Mahdi Tourage, "Performing Belief and Reviving Islam: Prominent (White Male) Converts in Muslim Revival Conventions," *Performing Islam* 1, no. 2 (2013): 207–26.

35 See Chapter 2.

36 Yahya Birt, "Interview: Jordan Peterson, White Supremacy, and the Perils of Engagement," *Medium*, July 27, 2022, https://yahyabirt.medium.com/interview-jordan-peterson-white-supremacy-and-the-perils-of-engagement-a80518ad92f4 (last accessed October 2, 2022).

37 Aftab Ahmad Malik, *The Broken Chain: Reflections upon the Neglect of the Tradition* (Amal Pres, 2001), 8, 9.

38 Zareena Grewal, *Islam Is a Foreign Country: American Muslims and the Global Crisis of Authority* (New York University Press, 2014), 132.

39 Ibid.

40 Hamza Yusuf, RIS, 2016.

41 Abu Bakr, "Shaykh Abdul Hakim Murad—Progressive Islam Movements," YouTube, March 15, 2018, https://www.youtube.com/watch?v=NMR1xq5 cZM4 (last accessed June 27, 2018).

42 Michael Muhammad Knight, "Islamotopia: Revival, Reform, and American Exceptionalism," in *Islam After Liberalism*, ed. Faisal Devji and Zaheer Kazmi (Oxford University Press, 2017), 238.

43 Ibid.

44 Abdal Hakim Murad, "Crisis of Modern Consciousness," Masjid Negara (lecture, Kuala Lumpur, March 28, 2010), https://www.youtube.com/watch?v=R WOKaOb33K4&t=75s (last accessed January 10, 2019).

45 Ibid.

46 Grewal, *Islam as Foreign Country*, 168.

47 Herbert Whyte, *HP Blavatsky: An Outline of Her Life* (Рипол Классик, 1920), 33.

48 Mark Sedgwick, *Against the Modern World: Traditionalism and the Secret Intellectual History of the Twentieth Century* (Oxford University Press, 2009), 79.

49 Arjana, *Buying Budhha, Selling Rumi*, 50.

50 Yusuf, "Faces of Islam."

51 "24th Annual Dowra," www.thedowra.org (last accessed January 10, 2019).

52 Michael Gunn, "Sufism in Jordan: A Prism of Spirituality," *Qantara.de* https://en.qantara.de/content/sufism-in-jordan-a-prism-of-spirituality (last accessed January 26, 2022).

53 Zara Choudhary, "A Mauritanian Retreat: In Search of Murabit Al-Hajj," *Sacred Footsteps*, 2014 https://www.sacredfootsteps.org/2014/06/02/mauritania/ (last accessed January 13, 2019).

54 Spring Lodge Retreat, 2015.

55 DeenIntensive, "Deen Intensive Foundation—*Rihla* 2015 Konya & Istanbul, Turkey," YouTube, March 13, 2015, https://www.youtube.com/watch?v=Lb0 9KN7hLTI (last accessed January 13, 2019).

56 Masooda Bano, *The Revival of Islamic Rationalism: Logic, Metaphysics and Mysticism in Modern Muslim Societies* (Cambridge University Press, 2020), 168.

57 Hall, *The Ways Out*, 20.

Chapter 4

1 Abdal-Hakim Murad, "Contentions 2," masud.co.uk/ISLAM/ahm/contention s2.htm (last accessed January 13, 2019).

2 Umar Faruq Abd-Allah, "Modernism and Post-Modernism in the Light of the Prophetic Belief: session 1" (lecture, Samsun, 2016).

3 John R. Hall, *The Ways Out: Utopian Communal Groups in an Age of Babylon* (Routledge & Kegan Paul, 1978), 85–6.

4 Ibid., 83.

5 David Chidester, "Time," in *The Oxford Handbook of the Study of Religion*, ed. Michael Stausberg, and Steven Engler (Oxford University Press, 2016), 349.

6 Dawud Israel, "Towards a Traditionally American Mosque and Culture, filmed December 2011, YouTube video, 5:57, posted December 2011, https://www.yo utube.com/watch?v=w8vZrS3epmU (last accessed January 13, 2016).

7 "Rihla 2017: A Journey of a Lifetime," *Dear Sarina*, May 20, https://www.dea rsarina.com/dearsarina/2017/9/6/rihla-2017-journey-of-a-lifetime (last accessed March 26, 2019).

8 Rihla booklet.

9 Ibid.

10 Hall, *The Ways Out*, 47.

11 Chidester, "Time," 346.

12 Ibid.

13 In Rihla 2017, Shaykh Ninowy did in fact give students an *ijāza*, but the three neo-traditionalist shaykhs to the best of my knowledge had not done so.

14 Zahra, Ayubi, "Owning Terms of Leadership and Authority: Toward a Gender-Inclusive Framework of American Muslim Religious Authority," In *A Jihad for Justice: Honoring the Work and Life of Amina Wadud*, ed. Ali Kecia, Juliane Hammer, and Laury Silvers (University Texas Press, 2012): 50.

15 Juliane Hammer, *American Muslim Women, Religious Authority, and Activism: More than a Prayer* (University of Texas Press, 2012), 116.

16 TheEmpireofFaith, "Shaykh Hamza Yusuf Witnesses Karamah of Dr Umar Farooq Abdullah," YouTube, 29 August 2014, www.youtube.com/watch?v=b _3DK1GNF-o. (last accessed January 10, 2019).

17 Rihla booklet, 2012 and 2017.

18 The same text was studied in other years as well (2013, 2014, 2015).

19 Walead Mosaad, "Foundations of the Spiritual Path — Shaykh Walead Mosaad" (lecture, Istabul, 2012), https://deenstream.vhx.tv/foundations-of-the-spiritual -path-shaykh-walead-mosaad (last accessed January 13, 2016).

20 The Ba'alawī litany.

21 TheEmpireofFaith, "Shaykh Hamza Yusuf Witnesses Karamah of Dr Umar Farooq Abdullah," YouTube, 29 August 2014, www.youtube.com/watch?v=b _3DK1GNF-o (last accessed January 10, 2019).

22 I have not encountered any stories of *karāmāt* associated with Abdal Hakim Murad.

23 "Khiḍr in the Islamic Tradition," khidr.org/khidr.htm (last accessed January 13, 2019).

24 "Where the Two Seas Meet: Al-Khidr and Moses, the Qurʾanic Story of al-Khidr and Moses in Sufi Commentaries as a Model for Spiritual Guidance."

25 In Chapter 7, I show how this was used to justify the relationship Abdullah bin Bayyah has with the government of the UAE.

26 Of the Perennialist school.

27 Wolfgang Smith, *Ancient Wisdom and Modern Misconceptions: A Critique of Contemporary Scientism* (Sophia Perennis, 2013) [older version of the same book: Wolfgang Smith, *The Wisdom of Ancient Cosmology: Contemporary Science in Light of tradition* (Foundation for Traditional Studies, 2003)].

28 Talal Asad, "The Idea of an Anthropology of Islam," *Qui Parle 17*, no. 2 (2009), 15–16.

29 Justice Muhammad Taqi Usmani has stated that he was not a signatory of the actual Amman message.

30 "Amman Message," http://ammanmessage.com/ (last accessed January 13, 2019).

31 "The Rihla is a journey with a purpose: an inner transformation rooted in sound knowledge and spiritual discipline," http://www.deenintensive.com/the-rihla-program (last accessed January 26, 2022).

32 Remona Aly," Alqueria de Rosales, Spain: A Calm Haven," *Emel*, August 2009, www.emel.com/article?id=61&a_id=1443 (last accessed January 13, 2019).

Chapter 5

1 Eissa Bougary, "Riḥla mʿa al-shaykh Ḥamza Yusūf: Episode 5," MBC television show, 2016, https://shahid.mbc.net/ar/shows/%D8%B1%D8%AD%D9%84%D8%A9%3A-%D9%85%D8%B9-%D8%A7%D9%84%D8%B4%D9%8A%D8%AE-%D8%AD%D9%85%D8%B2%D8%A9-%D9%8A%D9%88%D8%B3%D9%81-%D8%A7%D9%84%D9%85%D9%88%D8%B3%D9%85-1-%D8%A7%D9%84%D8%AD%D9%84%D9%82%D8%A9-5/episode-142320 (last accessed January 20, 2019).

2 Eissa Bougary, "Riḥla mʿa al-shaykh Ḥamza Yusūf: Episode 6," MBC television show, 2016, https://shahid.mbc.net/ar/shows/%D8%B1%D8%AD%D9%84%D8%A9%3A-%D9%85%D8%B9-%D8%A7%D9%84%D8%B4%D9%8A%D8%AE-%D8%AD%D9%85%D8%B2%D8%A9-%D9%8A%D9%88%D8%B3%D9%81-%D8%A7%D9%84%D9%85%D9%88%D8%B3%D9%85-1-%D8%A7%D9%84%D8%AD%D9%84%D9%82%D8%A9-5/episode-142320 (last accessed January 20, 2019).

3 Ibid., episode 2.

4 See Chapter 7.

5 See Chapter 2.

6 Peter L. Berger, *The Sacred Canopy: Elements of a Sociological Theory of Religion* (Doubleday, 1967), 39.

7 Ibid., 33.

8 Ibid., 36.

9 Berger, *The Sacred Canopy*, 36–7.

10 Ibid.

11 Hamza Yusuf, *Prayer of the Oppressed* (Sandala Productions, 2010), 9–10.

12 Zaytuna College, "Hamza Yusuf: A Crisis of Metaphysics," YouTube, September 29, 2015, https://www.youtube.com/watch?v=NKrxbX3_PWc (last accessed January 20, 2019).

13 Ibid.

14 Umar Faruq Abdullah, "Modernist and Post-Modernist Belief part 4," Rihla, 2016.

15 Abdal Hakim Murad, "Contentions," Rihla, 2016.

16 The Ink of Scholars channel, "Britain's Void of Meaning—Timothy Winter," YouTube, October 26, 2014, https://www.youtube.com/watch?v=D5UTDzf S0Wc (last accessed February 15, 2017).

17 Umar Faruq Abdullah, "Modernist and Post-Modernist Belief part 4," Rihla, 2016.

18 Umar Faruq Abdullah, "Modernist and Post-Modernist Belief part 1," Rihla, 2016.

19 Umar Faruq Abdullah, "Modernist and Post-Modernist Belief part 3/a," Rihla, 2016

20 Umar Faruq Abdullah, "Modernist and Post-Modernist Belief part 1," Rihla, 2016.

21 Mo987665, "Shaykh Hamza Yusuf—Miracles of the Awliya," YouTube, July 28, 2012, https://www.youtube.com/watch?v=7gwqus452ns (last accessed February 15, 2017).

22 Yusuf, *Prayer of the Oppressed*, 9–10.

23 Hamza Yusuf, "Tribulation, Patience and Prayer," in *The State We Are In: Identity, Terror and the Law of Jihad*, ed. Aftab Ahmad, Malik, and Tahir Abbas (Amal Press, 2006), 32.

24 Eissa Bougary, "Riḥla mʿa al-shaykh Ḥamza Yusūf: Episode 5," MBC television show, 2016 https://shahid.mbc.net/ar/shows/%D8%B1%D8%AD%D9%84 %D8%A9%3A-%D9%85%D8%B9-%D8%A7%D9%84%D8%B4%D9%8A%D8 %AE-%D8%AD%D9%85%D8%B2%D8%A9-%D9%8A%D9%88%D8%B3%D9 %81-%D8%A7%D9%84%D9%85%D9%88%D8%B3%D9%85-1-%D8%A7%D9

%84%D8%AD%D9%84%D9%82%D8%A9-5/episode-142320 (last accessed January 20, 2019).

25 Hamza Yusuf in RIS 2018.

26 Walaa Quisay and Thomas Parker, "On the Theology of Obedience: An Analysis of Shaykh Bin Bayyah and Shaykh Hamza Yusuf's Political Thought," *The Maydan*, January 8, 2019, https://www.themaydan.com/2019/01/theology-ob edience-analysis-shaykh-bin-bayyah-shaykh-hamza-yusufs-political-thought/?fb clid=IwAR3xQzi-SC2md2gEie8nlPjxaHBK2Ur1MtA_cceg3muWermp9rc349 0AJI4 (last accessed January 20, 2019).

27 TRT World, "Hamza Yusuf under Fire for Comments about the Syrian Revolution," 2019, https://www.youtube.com/watch?v=x96kvfDNjhs. (last accessed January 27, 2022).

28 Hamza Yusuf, "Don't Curse the People of Syria—Hamza Yusuf, 2019," https://www.youtube.com/watch?v=YcYNdmaA-Oo. (last accessed January 27, 2022).

29 Abu Bakr, "Shaykh Hamza Yusuf—Framing Islam into Marxist Thought," YouTube, July 18, 2016, https://www.youtube.com/watch?v=Kjh6x_vbgcY (last accessed March 7, 2018).

30 Hamza Yusuf, "A Grammar of Tolerance," *World Literature Today*, November 2017, https://www.worldliteraturetoday.org/2017/november/grammar-toleran ce-hamza-yusuf (last accessed January 20, 2019).

31 Ibid.

32 Murad, "Contentions 125."

33 Imran A. Khan, "Shaykh Hamza Yusuf and the Age of Feeling," *Wordpress*, March 25, 2018, https://blogofthebeardedone.wordpress.com/2018/03/25/sha ykh-hamza-yusuf-and-the-age-of-feeling/ (last accessed January 20, 2019).

34 Hamza Yusuf, RIS, 2017.

35 See Chapter 2.

36 Quisay and Parker, "On the Theology of Obedience."

37 Jibril Latif, "Muslim American Cyber Contestations between Scholars and Activists Debating Racism, Islamophobia and Black Lives Matter," *Journal of Religion, Media and Digital Culture* 7, no. 1 (2018): 75.

38 H. Yusuf, "Trip to Princeton," *Sandala*, October 8, 2010, https://sandala.org /trip-to-princeton/; "Religious Freedom: Why Now? A Conversation on Islam and Religious Freedom with Dr. Robert P. George and Shaykh Hamza Yusuf," Religious Freedom Project—Berkeley Center for Religion, Peace and World Affairs, March 1, 2012, https://berkleycenter.georgetown.edu/publications/re ligious-freedom-why-now-a-conversation-on-islam-and-religious-freedom-with -dr-robert-p-george-and-shaykh-hamza-yusuf; B. Dempsey, "Religious Liberty in the Eyes of Evangelicals, Catholics, Mormons, & Muslims," *Juicy Ecumenism*,

June 1, 2016, https://juicyecumenism.com/2016/06/01/religious-liberty-eyes
-evangelicals-catholics-mormons-muslims/; J. S. Bryson, "Princeton's Robert
George and Islam," *Muslim Matters*, April 9, 2012, http://muslimmatters.org
/2012/04/09/princetons-robert-george-and-islam/; S. G. Chachila, "Peaceful
Muslims View US LGBT Issues as 'Completely Insane,' Says Muslim leader,"
Christian Times, May 28, 2016, http://www.christiantimes.com/article/musli
ms-view-us-lgbt-issues-as-completely-insane-says-muslim-leader/56058.htm; E.
Bristow, "Russell Moore Announces Multi-Faith Statement Opposing California
Assault on Religious Liberty in Higher Education," Ethics & Religious Liberty
Commission of the Southern Baptist Convention, August 9, 2016, http://erlc
.com/resource-library/press-releases/russell-moore-announces-multi-faith-state
ment-opposing-california-assault-on-religious-liberty-in-higher-education; R. P.
George and H. Yusuf, "Religious Exemptions Are Vital for Religious Liberty,"
Wall Street Journal, March 23, 2014, https://www.wsj.com/articles/SB100014
24052702304914204579397170026645290; "Burwell v. Hobby Lobby Stores,
Inc.," Supreme Court of the United States Blog, August 1, 2014, http://www.sc
otusblog.com/case-files/cases/sebelius-v-hobby-lobby-stores-inc/
39 Tradachieve, "A Sacred Alliance of Conservative Believers—Abdal Hakim
Murad," YouTube, July 13, 2017, https://www.youtube.com/watch?v=QbIo6
5dKk0o (last accessed January 20, 2019).
40 This was not always the case, but became increasingly so after 9/11, and especially
after the period 2012–13, as Chapter 8 will show (and contextualize). Yusuf has
also lent his support to notions of dissent if they are within the bounds of the
political system of a given country and do not challenge it structurally or cause its
collapse.
41 Bougary, "Riḥla mʿa al-shaykh Ḥamza Yusūf: Episode 5."
42 Ibid.
43 Ibid.
44 Omar Bajwa, "A Rhetorical Analysis of Hamza Yusuf's Discourse on Education"
(Cornell University, August 2006), 19.
45 "الثوره نفسها مشتقه من ثوريعني هم يثورون كحيوان لا يتصرفون كعقلاء"; Bougary, "Riḥla mʿa
al-shaykh Ḥamza Yusūf: Episode 6."
46 Inkofknowledge, "Is Islam A Political Ideology?—Shaykh Hamza Yusuf |
Powerful," YouTube, November 26, 2016, https://www.youtube.com/watch
?v=872N34Jxiw8&t=1s (last accessed February 15, 2017).
47 Yusūf Zaydān, *Fiqh al-Thawra*, Google Books (Dar al-Shurūq, 2013), https://
books.google.co.uk/books?id=gi4lDAAAQBAJ&pg=PT64&lpg=PT64&dq=
%D8%A7%D9%84%D8%AB%D9%88%D8%B1%D8%A9+%D9%87%D9%8A+
%D8%A7%D9%86%D8%AB%D9%89+%D8%A7%D9%84%D8%AB%D9%88

%D8%B1&source=bl&ots=xTMUMrXirD&sig=u4eEovDdZx5VzZxjVFJfpizw
vcA&hl=en&sa=X&ved=0ahUKEwjj4e23qr_aAhXKAcAKHRDQDw84ChD
oAQhFMAU#v=onepage&q&f=false section 7

48 http://blogs.aljazeera.net/blogs/2016/8/30/%D8%A3%D9%88%D8%B1%D8
%A7%D9%82-%D8%A7%D9%84%D8%B1%D8%A8%D9%8A%D8%B9-2-%D8
%A7%D9%84%D8%AB%D9%88%D8%B1%D8%A9-%D9%84%D9%8A%D8
%B3%D8%AA-%D8%A3%D9%86%D8%AB%D9%89-%D8%A7%D9%84%D8
%AB%D9%88%D8%B1 (last accessed February 15, 2017).

49 Khaled Abou El Fadl, *Rebellion and Violence in Islamic Law*, Cambridge University Press, 2006, 76.

50 Kecia Ali, *Imam Shafi'i: Scholar and Saint* (Oneworld, 2011) (Kindle edition).

51 Joseph Van Ess, "Theology and Society in the Second and Third Centuries of the Hijra: A History of Religious Thought in Early Islam," Almanca'dan İngilizce'ye, trans. John O'Kane, ed. Maribel Fierro (Brill 2017), 510.

52 Abū al-Faraj 'Abd al-Raḥmān, *The Life of Ibn Hanbal* (NYU Press, 2016), 202.

53 Bougary, "Riḥla m'a al-shaykh Ḥamza Yusūf: Episode 5."

54 Naquib Al Attas was also taught in Rihla 2017.

55 Muhammad Naguib Al-Attas, *Islām and Secularism* (Muslim Youth Movement of Malaysia, 1978), 78.

56 Bougary, "Riḥla m'a al-shaykh Ḥamza Yusūf: Episode 6."

57 Hamza Yusuf, "Forum for Promoting Peace in Muslim Societies, Abu Dhabi 2016," https://www.youtube.com/watch?v=r7k1-iW2qb0 (last accessed January 20, 2019).

58 Yusuf, "Tribulation, Patience and Prayer," 32.

59 Yusuf, *Prayer of the Oppressed*, 8.

60 Ibid., 20.

61 Ibid., 18.

62 Ibid., 9–10.

63 Ibid., 4.

64 Ibid., 20.

65 RIS 2017.

66 See Chapter 8 for more context.

67 Turkī al-Shaykh, "'Iḍā'āt ma'a Ḥamza Yusūf," interview, *Al Arabiya*, October 5, 2011, https://www.youtube.com/watch?v=WhV791UyT0o (last accessed January 20, 2019).

68 Bougary, "Riḥla m'a al-shaykh Ḥamza Yusūf: Episode 5."

69 Ibid.

70 Ibid.

71 Ibid.

72 Abou El Fadl, *Rebellion and Violence in Islamic Law*, 283–7.

73 Quisay and Parker, "On the Theology of Obedience."

74 Office of the Mufti, "Can Muslims Participate in Modern Democracy? (Sh Hamza Yusuf)," YouTube, November 5, 2017, https://www.youtube.com/watch?v=qn5KRg0neaI (last accessed January 20, 2019).

75 Quisay and Parker, "On the Theology of Obedience."

76 Yusuf, "Forum for Promoting Peace in Muslim Societies, Abu Dhabi 2016."

77 Haneen Dajani, "Arabs and Emiratis Put Nationality First, UAE Forum Hears," *The National*, December 19, 2016, https://www.thenational.ae/uae/arabs-and -emiratis-put-nationality-first-uae-forum-hears-1.201087 (last accessed January 20, 2019).

78 Hamza Yusuf, "When Evil Fails and Goodness Prevails: Regarding the Recent Coup Attempt in Turkey," *Sandala*, July 31, 2016, https://sandala.org/when-ev il-fails/ (last accessed January 20, 2019).

79 al-Shaykh, "ʿIḍāʾāt maʿa Ḥamza Yusūf."

80 Ibid.

81 Their relationship would later sour, as I show in Chapter 7.

82 Yusuf, "When Evil Fails and Goodness Prevails."

83 Latif Jibril, "Muslim American Cyber Contestations between Scholars and Activists Debating Racism, Islamophobia and Black Lives Matter," *Journal of Religion, Media and Digital Culture* 7, no. 1 (2018), 70.

84 Ibid., 73.

85 Riz Khan, "Interview with Hamza Yusuf," *Al Jazeera*, June 13, 2007, https:// www.youtube.com/watch?v=ve0Sgm0PFyk (last accessed January 20, 2019).

86 Riz Kan, "Rising Anti-Muslim Rhetoric?: Interview with Hamza Yusuf," March 10, 2011, https://www.youtube.com/watch?v=EkzDUJHEw8Q (last accessed January 20, 2019).

87 Khan, "Interview with Hamza Yusuf."

88 H. Yusuf, "We Shall Overcome," *Sandala*, November 15, 2016, https://sandala .org/we-shall-overcome/ (last accessed January 20, 2019).

89 Yahya Birt, "Blowin' in the Wind: Trumpism and Traditional Islam in America," in *Medium*, February 14, 2017, https://medium.com/@yahyabirt/https-medi um-com-yahyabirt-blowin-in-the-wind-trumpism-and-traditional-islam-in-amer ica-40ba056486d8 (last accessed January 20, 2019).

90 RabwahTimes, "U.S. Muslim cleric Hamza Yusuf calls Trump 'A Servant of God' during Racist Rant against Black Lives Matter," *Rabwah Times*, December 25, 2016, https://www.rabwah.net/muslim-hamza-yusuf-racist-rant/ (last accessed January 20, 2019).

91 Birt, "Blowin' in the Wind."

92 #RIS2016 Shaykh Hamza Yusuf Controversy," Muslim Wellness Foundation, January 5, 2017, http://www.blackmuslimpsychology.org/ris2016controversy; "U.S. Muslim Cleric Hamza Yusuf Calls Trump 'A Servant of God' during Racist Rant against Black Lives Matter," *Rabwa Times*, December 25, 2016, https://www.rabwah.net/muslim-hamza-yusuf-racist-rant/, which includes the full recording of the interview at the bottom of the page.

93 The Black Lives Matter movement (BLM) first emerged as an online response to the shooting of the Black teenager Trayvon Martin and the subsequent acquittal of George Zimmerman. It became an important voice protesting excessive policing and racism. It especially protested the many shootings of unarmed Black people by the police. Jordan T. Camp and Christina Heatherton, eds., *Policing the Planet: Why the Policing Crisis Led to Black Lives Matter* (Verso, 2016).

94 Hamza Yusuf and John Sexton, "The Secular and the Sacred in Higher Education: A Conversation with Shaykh Hamza Yusuf and Dr. John Sexton" (Fritzi Weitzmann Owens Memorial Lecture, September 2016), https://www.yo utube.com/watch?v=oQJnjfq_aMk

95 https://www.youtube.com/watch?v=oQJnjfq_aMk

96 Latif, "Muslim American Cyber Contestations between Scholars and Activists Debating Racism, Islamophobia and Black Lives Matter," 78.

97 http://www.patheos.com/blogs/nbamuslims/2017/01/05/risgate-3-things-amo ng-many-muslims-did-right/ (last accessed January 20, 2019).

98 I'm forced to address what was said by Sh. Hamza because it was irresponsible and harmful. I'm not speaking from a personal perspective but a religious one. What the sheikh said was wrong, he should correct it, and the organizers should distance themselves from his words. Shortly after his talk, four scholars contacted me, expressing their sadness and frustration with him. This is not an attempt to take shots at the Sheikh. I love him. I respect him. I admire him. But it is that love and respect that demands I share these concerns.

I walked in towards the end of his interview, and what initially caught my attention was his dismissal of the Black Lives Matter movement, police brutality against blacks in America, the racial bias in the criminal justice system in the US, sentencing guidelines, prison terms and a few other issues that, as a white man, he should address with extreme care. Privilege aside, using religion as support is unacceptable to speak that way.

Two goals of our faith are the protection of life and the establishment of justice. From the crime bill of 1994 to the new Jim Crow of the 2000s, there is no way we can dismiss the clear, egregious treatment of people of color today in America, nor can we dismiss its historical roots in America's foundation. Supporting the victims of injustice is a fard full stop, and the role of prophetic communities is to defend the rights of the marginalized and the victims of injustice.

Suhaib Webb's Facebook page, https://www.facebook.com/suhaib.webb/posts /10154763543928080 (last accessed January 20, 2019).

99 This is not a criticism he addresses in the conferences he attends in the UAE. Many seekers of South Asian descent were equally upset by him not leveling this critique at Arab racism in the Gulf.

100 Hamza Yusuf, RIS, 2016.

101 Yusuf, *Prayer of the Oppressed*, 4.

102 Ryan R. Williams, "Black Pathology in the American Muslim Community."

Chapter 6

1 Abdal Hakim Murad, "On Migrating to Lands of Melancholy," *Renovatio*, February 19, 2021, https://renovatio.zaytuna.edu/article/on-migrating-to-lands-of-melancholy

2 Ibid.

3 Ibid.

4 Ibid.

5 Umar Faruq Abd-Allah, "Foundations of the Islamic Worldview," course, *Bayan Claremont*, Spring 2017 www.bayanclaremont.org/academics/spring-2017-courses/abdallah/ (last accessed January 21, 2019).

6 Richard M. Weaver, *Ideas Have Consequences: Expanded Edition* (University of Chicago Press, 2013), 1.

7 Yusuf quotes Richard Weaver in his joint lecture with the controversial right-wing British philosopher Roger Scruton. Renovatio: The Journal of Zaytuna College, "Sacred Truths in a Profane World | Hamza Yusuf & Roger Scruton," YouTube, June 19, 2018, https://www.youtube.com/watch?v=OQoi9xPooKo &t=25s (last accessed June 21, 2018).

8 Weaver, *Ideas Have Consequences*, 3.

9 Ibid., 2–3.

10 Aaron McLeod, *A Condensation of Richard Weaver, Ideas Have Consequences* (Alabama Policy Institute, 2012), 5—this summary was used by seekers as reading material.

11 Ibid., 6.

12 . Weaver, *Ideas Have Consequences*, 11

13 Alastair Bonnett, "From White to Western: 'Racial Decline'and the Rise of the Idea of the West in Britain, 1890–1930," in *The Idea of the West* (Palgrave, London, 2004), 14.

14 Ibid., 19.

15 Ibid., 15.

16 Corey Robin, *The Reactionary Mind: Conservatism from Edmund Burke to Sarah Palin* (Oxford University Press, 2011), 16.

17 Traditionalist with a capital "T" from the School of René Guénon: otherwise referred to as "Perennialists."

18 Weaver, *Ideas Have Consequences*, 34.

19 Ibid.

20 Weaver, *Ideas Have Consequences*, 34.

21 McLeod, *A Condensation of Richard Weaver's Ideas Have Consequences*, 34.

22 Weaver, *Ideas Have Consequences*, 4.

23 Abdal Hakim Murad, "British Muslims and the Rhetoric of Indigenisation," in *Travelling Home: Essays on Islam in Europe* (The Quilliam Press, 2020), 72.

24 Abdal Hakim Murad, *Travelling Home: Essays on Islam in Europe* (The Quilliam Press, 2020), 8–9.

25 Ibid.

26 Truth with a capital "T" refers to the ultimate immutable Truth relating to God.

27 Abdal Hakim Murad, "The Destitute: a Discussion on the Spirituality of Poverty" (lecture, London: SOAS, 2014), https://www.youtube.com/watch?v=ciBmrwr Ln98 (last accessed 21 January 2019).

28 Abdal Hakim Murad, "Crisis of Modern Consciousness," Masjid Negara (lecture, Kuala Lumpur, March 28, 2010), https://www.youtube.com/watch?v=R WOKaOb33K4&t=75s (last accessed January 10, 2019).

29 Abdal Hakim Murad, "Muslims and National Populism," in *Travelling Home: Essays on Islam in Europe* (The Quilliam Press, 2020), 51.

30 Murad, "On Migrating to Lands of Melancholy."

31 Murad, "Muslims and National Populism," 35.

32 Ibid.

33 Ibid., 36.

34 Ibid., 36–7.

35 Ibid., 37.

36 Christopher Pooya Razavian, "The Neo-Traditionalism of Tim Winter," in *Modern Islamic Authority and Social Change, Volume 2: Evolving Debates in the West*, ed. Masooda Bano (Edinburgh University Press, 2017), 85.

37 Abdal Hakim Murad, "British and Muslim?," http://masud.co.uk/ISLAM/ahm /british.htm. (last accessed January 21, 2019).

38 Ibid.

39 Murad, "Muslims and National Populism," 63.

40 Ibid.

41 Abdal Hakim Murad, "The Venomous bid'a of tanfîr," in *Travelling Home: Essays on Islam in Europe* (The Quilliam Press, 2020), 125.

42 Ibid., 119–20.

43 Abdal Hakim Murad, "Muslim Loyalty and Belonging: Some Reflections on the Psychosocial Background," January 2003, http://masud.co.uk/ISLAM/ahm/loy alty.htm (last accessed January 21, 2019).

44 https://www.youtube.com/watch?v=1RbkhXfBphw (last accessed January 21, 2019).

45 Ibid.

46 See the discussion of Charles Taylor in Chapter 2.

47 Tradarchive, "Identity Politics ~ Abdal Hakim Murad," YouTube, March 11, 2018, https://www.youtube.com/watch?v=1RbkhXfBphw (last accessed January 21, 2019).

48 Ibid.

49 Ibid.

50 Murad, *Travelling Home*, 4.

51 Murad, "The Venomous bid'a of tanfîr," 125.

52 Abdal Hakim Murad, "Good Anger, Bad Anger and Shirk Al-Asbāb," in *Travelling Home: Essays on Islam in Europe* (The Quilliam Press, 2020), 161.

53 Murad, "Muslims and National Populism," 61–2.

54 Ibid., 62.

55 Evola also influenced Steve Bannon: Joshua Green, "Inside the Secret, Strange Origins of Steve Bannon's Nationalist Fantasia," *Vanity Fair*, July 17, 2017, https://www.vanityfair.com/news/2017/07/the-strange-origins-of-steve-banno ns-nationalist-fantasia (last accessed January 21, 2019).

56 In reference to the French Traditionalist/Perennialist metaphysician René Guénon.

57 Abdal Hakim Murad, "Riding the Tiger of Modernity" (lecture, Cambridge, 2016), https://www.youtube.com/watch?v=07Ien1qo_qI&t=1082s

58 Ibid.

59 Mark Sedgwick, *Against the Modern World: Traditionalism and the Secret Intellectual History of the Twentieth Century* (Oxford University Press, 2009), 98–104.

60 Ibid.

61 Sedgwick, *Against the Modern World*, 98–104.

62 Murad uses this term to indicate the end of times. This is a term used by the Guénonians, borrowed from Hindu cosmic cycles. He used it in two instances, in Rihla 2017 and in "Riding the Tiger of Modernity."

63 Itzchak Weismann, *The Naqshbandiyya: Orthodoxy and Activism in a Worldwide Sufi Tradition* (Routledge, 2007), 27–8.

64 Kate Zebiri, *British Muslim Converts: Choosing Alternative Lives* (Oneworld, 2014), 174.

65 Murad, "Muslim Loyalty and Belonging."

66 Zebiri, *British Muslim Converts*, 189.

67 Ibid.

68 Dawud Israel, "What Can We Do for Palestine?—Shaykh Abdal Hakim Murad," YouTube, December 11, 2011, https://www.youtube.com/watch?v=qxAo5ki-2RU (last accessed January 21, 2019).

69 Gulnaz Sibgatullina and Tahir Abbas, "Political Conversion to Islam Among the European Right," *The Journal of Illiberalism Studies* Vol. 1 No. 2 (2021): 4.

70 Joram van Klaveren, *Apostate: From Christianity to Islam in Times of Secularisation* (Kennishuys & Sunni Publications, 2019).

71 Ibid., 19–20.

72 Ibid., 177–8.

73 Umar Faruq Abd-Allah, "Islam and the Cultural Imperative," *Islam and Civilisational Renewal 1*, no. 1 (2009): 1.

74 Ibid., 3.

75 Ibid., 9.

76 Justine Howe, *Suburban Islam* (Oxford University Press, 2018), 64.

77 Ibid., 84.

78 Abd-Allah, "Islam and the Cultural Imperative," 2.

79 Ibid.

80 Ibid.

81 Ibid., 12.

82 Umar Faruq Abd-Allah, "Balancing Reason and Tradition in the Contemporary Context," in *IKEM* (lecture, Malaysia, May 2018), https://soundcloud.com/iamalik/sets/dr-umar-faruq-abd-allah-the-malaysia-lectures (last accessed January 21, 2019).

83 Abd-Allah, "Islam and the Cultural Imperative," 5.

84 Ibid., 2.

85 Ibid.

86 Umar Faruq Abd-Allah, "Islam and The Cultural Imperative," in SeekersHub (lecture, 2011), https://www.youtube.com/watch?time_continue=1428&v=44ycrsABA2s (last accessed January 21, 2019).

87 Abd-Allah, "Islam and the Cultural Imperative," 9.

88 Ibid.

89 Abd-Allah, "Islam and The Cultural Imperative" (lecture).

90 Ibid., 10.

91 Ibid., 12.

92 I discuss this in Chapter 7.

93 Weaver, *Ideas Have Consequences*, 161.

94 Ibid., 160.

95 Abdal Hakim Murad, "Fall of the Family," June 2015, www.masud.co.uk/fall-of -the-family-part-1/ (last accessed January 21, 2019).

96 MishkatMedia, "Star Wars and the Crisis of Modern Masculinity," YouTube, March 9, 2016, https://www.youtube.com/watch?v=3kDbqABvEN0 (last accessed January 21, 2019).

97 "Joseph Campbell," www.moongadget.com/origins/myth.html (last accessed January 21, 2019).

98 Ibid.

99 Andrew Pulver, "Star Wars Director JJ Abrams: We Always Wanted Women at the Centre of The Force Awakens," *The Guardian*, December 17, 2015, https://www.theguardian.com/film/2015/dec/17/star-wars-director-jj-abrams -women-the-force-awakens-daisy-ridley-lupita-nyongo-carrie-fisher (last accessed February 2, 2019).

100 Bishop Robert Barron, "The Jordan Peterson Phenomenon," *Strange Notions: The Digital Areopagus—Reason, Faith, Dialogue*, https://strangenotions.com /the-jordan-peterson-phenomenon/ (last accessed February 2, 2019).

101 Ibid.

102 David G. Brown, "Why Star Wars: The Force Awakens Is a Social Justice Propaganda Film," Return of Kings, December 20, 2015, www.returnofkings .com/75991/why-star-wars-the-force-awakens-is-a-social-justice-propaganda -film (last accessed February 2, 2019).

103 P. Claire Dodson, "J.J. Abrams Thinks Trolls Lashed Out About 'The Last Jedi' Because They're 'Threatened' by Female Characters," February 18, 2018, https://hellogiggles.com/news/jj-abrams-last-jedi-trolls/ (last accessed February 2, 2019).

104 MishkatMedia, "Star Wars and the Crisis of Modern Masculinity," YouTube, March 9, 2016 https://www.youtube.com/watch?v=3kDbqABvEN0 (last accessed January 21, 2019).

105 Although the genealogy could be traced to Carl Jung, the same claim is made by Perennialists. It is on this understanding of the Transcendental unity of religion that Sachiko Murata wrote the *Tao of Islam*, which the shuykh reference in their discourse on gender essentialisms.

106 Murad, *Travelling Home*, 8.

107 Kelefa Sanneh, "Jordan Peterson's Gospel of Masculinity," *The New Yorker*,

March 5, 2018, https://www.newyorker.com/magazine/2018/03/05/jordan
-petersons-gospel-of-masculinity (last accessed January 21, 2019).

108 Umar Faruq Abd-Allah, "The Fitra," *Rihla* (lecture, Malacca, 2017)—this reference relates to this whole section.

109 Renovatio: The Journal of Zaytuna College, "Learning To Be Human: Umar
Faruq Abd-Allah & Hamza Yusuf (Part II)," YouTube, April 21, 2018, https://
www.youtube.com/watch?v=TulCWOZnd5o (last accessed January 21, 2019).

110 Friedrich Engels, *The Origin of the Family, Private Property and the State*
(Penguin, 2010).

111 With the exception of Syed Muhammad Naquib al-Attas.

112 Whitehall Perry, *The Unanimous Tradition: Essays on the Essential Unity of All
Religions*, ed. Ranjit Fernando (Sri Lanka Institute of Traditional Studies Press,
1999).

113 Renovatio, "Learning to Be Human."

114 Ibid.

Chapter 7

1 Forum For Promoting Peace, "Hamza Yusuf: Al-Miḥwar
al-Rabiʿ: Ishām al-Islām fī al-Silm al-ʿālmī -Dawr al-ʿulamāʾ
w-al Iʿlām fī taʿzīz al-silm" (lecture: Abu Dhabi, 2014), https://
www.youtube.com/watch?v=g7_isEsApX8&t=2079s&ab_channel=Fo
rumforPromotingPeace%D9%85%D9%86%D8%AA%D8%AF%D9%89
%D8%AA%D8%B9%D8%B2%D9%8A%D8%B2%D8%A7%D9%84%D8%B3
%D9%84%D9%85

2 Letter from Jawdat Said to Bin Bayyah, April 22, 2015:

In the Name of Allah, the Most Beneficent, the Most Merciful
The honorable blessed brother, Shaykh ʿAbdullah bin al-Shaykh al-Maḥfūdh
bin Bayyah
Peace and blessings of Allah be upon you,
{"Praise belongs to Allah, and peace be on those of His servants whom He has
chosen and who bid for justice}

When I first met my brother Wahiduddin Khan over twenty years ago, he told
me something I had not heard before. As far as I remember, he said: intellectuals and scholars are responsible for the crises that young Muslims now face. I
thanked him wholeheartedly for this profound observation. Seven years ago, I
was invited to a conference in Belgium that discussed the role of religious scholars in peacebuilding and democracy; there, I noted that crises arise in thinking
before in reality. The crisis emerges in the scholar's mind before in the politician's actions. The world is in crisis because scholars are in crisis. This includes

all of the world's major crises: the climate crisis, the food crisis, the economy, conflict, and wars. All these crises begin by intellectual crises. The Bible says: If therefore the light that is in you is darkness, how great is the darkness!

Intellectuals and scholars are responsible for our current crises: whether it is things they have written, a sermon they presented, ideas they have disseminated, or even issues they chose to be silent about. For that reason, I would like to speak earnestly to the degree that might be inappropriate: it is a great scam and fraudulence for Muslim scholars to be gathered like this and pretend to be saviors. It is more appropriate that they come as criminals seeking repentance, radical self-criticism, and transformation.

Herbert George Wells stated that the history of mankind was nothing but books in closed boxes for those personalities who met to found the United Nations around 100 years ago. They were not aware of human history, and it was not possible to serve humanity if you were ignorant of its history. A short look into the realities ... the Muslim world is experiencing is enough to reveal the truth that we are absent from the world and we have not yet learned the alphabet of human knowledge. I admit guilt, negligence, and responsibility, and I have often stated that I have failed as a teacher. And I say that if we want something useful to come out of any meeting with scholars, we must first acknowledge our responsibility and shortcomings, and that we are almost an obstacle on the way to a solution. It is rare to hear an admirable sentence from any of the scholars living today. They cannot influence their students positively, let alone influence governments.

Scholars and jurists have long deemed it impermissible to go to ḥajj in a car or use a cell phone. Still, may today deem it impermissible for a woman to drive or deny even the basics of ḥadīth scholarship. This only goes to show how far they are from reality. It also shows the extent to which such scholars are co-opted to the point that they are silent in the face of corruption and oppression. They accept the privileges given to them, and whenever politicians summon them, they just tell them what they want to hear, not what should be said. The jurists legitimize coups against democracy, legitimate rule, and the consensus of the masses in one place while claiming they support legitimate rule in other places. This form of co-option is, as French scholar Pierre Bourdieu would say, the primary reason for the situation we are in.

Today we draw from the same sources of knowledge. All of the texts of Islamic jurisprudence were written after the Muslims had lost their senses and adapted to the rule of tyranny and oppression to this very day. I do not distinguish here Sunni from Shia from Kharijite. I contend that those who study jurisprudence and confine themselves to books of fiqh cannot get out of the darkness nor get others out of it. The sources that have caused this crisis cannot save us from it.

Here we are, as Arabs, witnessing Europeans unite and abolish the death sentence. They are twenty-eight nations with twenty-four languages and multiple ethnicities. Whereas we speak the same language, and the book is the Qur'an. No one has the right to speak of unity. Whoever speaks of unity is either a traitor or insane. Those leaders demand that each is alone the leader with no one else sharing his power. Peace and non-violence is the greatest form of jihād. But it is not the path of cowards of deference, silence, and submission to tyranny. Instead, it is the path to bear witness to truth and disobedience in the face of sinfulness (No! Do not obey him. But prostrate and draw near [to Allāh]). The path is that of democracy and mutual consultation we have lost a long way. It is the path of the Prophets who said (And we will surely be patient against whatever harm you should cause) until they convinced humanity of the doctrines of justice and goodness.

Although I am pleased with your kind gesture, the reality confirms that I do not deserve it. I apologize; I cannot accept it, and I will not be attending. I thank you for your trust, and I hope that God will produce from our loins a generation that will serve this religion and elevate the message of his Prophet.

Peace and blessing and mercy of Allah be upon you.
Jawdat Saʿīd Muḥammad
Istanbul, 22 April 2015

3 Hamza Yusuf, "Role of Muslims in the West," Islam—The Only for Humanity Conference in London Arena (lecture, London, August 1995), https://www.yo utube.com/watch?v=-DjcJniCMt0 (last accessed January 21, 2019).

4 MuslimCanuck, "Interview of Sh. Hamza Yusuf w/ Tim Winter (1/3)," YouTube, May 6, 2013, https://www.youtube.com/watch?v=Oj-MkZ2wagY& t=1s (last accessed January 21, 2019).

5 Umar F. Abd-Allah, *The Islamic Struggle in Syria* (Mizan Press, 1983).

6 El-Sayed el-Aswad, "Images of Muslims in Western Scholarship and Media after 9/11," *Digest of Middle East Studies* 22, no. 1 (2013): 39–56.

7 Charles Kimball, "The War on Terror and Its Effects on American Muslims," In *The Oxford Handbook of American Islam* (Oxford University Press, 2015), 493.

8 Mahmood Mamdani, *Good Muslim, Bad Muslim: America, the Cold War, and the Roots of Terror* (Harmony, 2005), 15.

9 Ibid.

10 Peter Mandaville and Shadi Hamid, "Islam as Statecraft: How Governments Use Religion in Foreign Policy," Brookings Institute, November 2018, 3.

11 Cheryl Benard, Andrew Riddile, Peter A. Wilson, and Steven W. Popper, *Civil Democratic Islam: Partners, Resources, and Strategies* (Rand Corporation, 2004); Zeyno Bara, ed., *Understanding Sufism and its Potential Role in US Policy* (Nixon Center Conference Report, March 2004).

12 "Bernard Lewis, an eminent historian of Islam who traced the terrorist attacks of Sept. 11, 2001, to a declining Islamic civilization, a controversial view that influenced world opinion and helped shape American foreign policy under President George W. Bush," Douglas Martin, "Bernard Lewis, Influential Scholar of Islam, Is Dead at 101," *New York Times*, May 21, 2018, https://www.nytimes.com /2018/05/21/obituaries/bernard-lewis-islam-scholar-dies.html (last accessed January 21, 2019).

13 Bara, ed., *Understanding Sufism and its Potential Role in US Policy.*

14 Ibid.

15 Ibid., 20.

16 Ibid., 18.

17 Ibid.

18 Hamza Yusuf was involved in organizing some of these conferences. He had no connection to some, for example the conference in Chechnya and Document on Human Fraternity for World Peace and Living Together, and was only a signatory to others, such as the Amman Message.

19 Peter M. Haas, "Introduction: Epistemic Communities and International Policy Coordination," *International Organization* 46, no. 1 (1992), 3.

20 Karin D. Knorr-Cetina, "Scientific Communities or Transepistemic Arenas of Research? A Critique of Quasi-economic Models of Science," *Social studies of science* 12, no. 1 (1982), 103.

21 Emanuel Adler, "The Emergence of Cooperation: National Epistemic Communities and the International Evolution of the Idea of Nuclear Arms Control," *International Organization* 46, no. 1 (1992): 101.

22 Nukhet Ahu Sandal, "Religious Actors as Epistemic Communities in Conflict Transformation: The Cases of South Africa and Northern Ireland," *Review of International Studies* 37, no. 3 (2011): 930.

23 Haas, "Introduction: Epistemic Communities and International Policy Coordination," 3.

24 Ibid., 21.

25 Emanuel Adler and Peter M. Haas, "Conclusion: Epistemic Communities, World Order, and the Creation of a Reflective Research Program," *International Organization* 46, no. 1 (1992): 381.

26 Emanuel Adler, "The Emergence of Cooperation: National Epistemic

Communities and the International Evolution of the Idea of Nuclear Arms Control," *International Organization* 46, no. 1 (1992): 124.

27 Adler and Haas, "Conclusion: Epistemic Communities, World Order, and the Creation of a Reflective Research Program," 381.

28 Imran Khan's official Facebook account, March 14, 2019, https://www.facebook.com/143462899029472/posts/3321630521212678/ (last accessed March 22, 2019).

29 "Mission and Vision," https://alqadir.edu.pk/mission-vision/

30 "The Centre of Islamic Spirituality at Al-Qadir," http://alqadir.edu.pk/academic-centers-at-al-qadir/

31 "Global Advisors," http://alqadir.edu.pk/team/#advisors

32 "Prime Minister Imran Khan and Global Muslim Scholar Dialogue," https://www.youtube.com/watch?v=zQ8RMDjhtBc

33 Prime Minister Imran Khan, Twitter post, January 2022, 6:19 a.m., https://twitter.com/PakPMO/status/1477600512002437122; Al Qadir University Project Trust, "An excerpt from a meeting between #PMImranKhan, Shaykh Abdal Hakim Murad, Dr. Zeeshan & Dr. Arif Butt," YouTube, October 11, 2021, https://www.youtube.com/watch?v=Czp99rIoUcM&ab_channel=AlQadirUniversityProjectTrust; Abdullah bin Bayyah, "Shaykh Bin Bayyah Responds to Prime Minister's Question: What Advice Would You Give to the Youth?," YouTube, January 2, 2022, https://youtu.be/AGwHlYtLrSo

34 Human Rights Watch, "Egypt: Rab'a Killings Likely Crimes against Humanity No Justice a Year Later for Series of Deadly Mass Attacks on Protesters," *HRW*, August 2014, https://www.hrw.org/news/2014/08/12/egypt-raba-killings-likely-crimes-against-humanity (last accessed January 21, 2019).

35 CNN Library, "2011 Libya Civil War Fast Facts," *CNN*, August 30, 2018, https://edition.cnn.com/2013/09/20/world/libya-civil-war-fast-facts/index.html (last accessed January 21, 2019); BBC News, "Syria: The Story of the Conflict," *BBC News*, March 11, 2016, https://www.bbc.com/news/world-middle-east-26116868 (last accessed January 21, 2019).

36 Declan Walsh, "In Saudi Arabia's War in Yemen, No Refuge on Land or Sea," *New York Times*, December 17, 2018, https://www.nytimes.com/2018/12/17/world/middleeast/yemen-fishing-boats-saudi.html (last accessed January 21, 2019).

37 https://allahcentric.wordpress.com/2011/01/31/shaykh-hamza-yusuf-on-the-revolution-in-tunisia/

38 Ibid.

39 Walaa Quisay and Thomas Parker, "On the Theology of Obedience: An Analysis of Shaykh Bin Bayyah and Shaykh Hamza Yusuf's Political Thought," *The*

Maydan, January 8, 2019, https://www.themaydan.com/2019/01/theology-ob
edience-analysis-shaykh-bin-bayyah-shaykh-hamza-yusufs-political-thought/?fb
clid=IwAR3xQzi-SC2md2gEie8nlPjxaHBK2Ur1MtA_cceg3muWermp9rc349
0AJI4 (last accessed January 21, 2019).

40 Hamza Yusuf, "When the Social Contract Is Breached in Egypt," in *Last Prophet*
[originally published in *Sandala*], February 2011, www.lastprophet.info/when
-the-social-contract-is-breached-in-egypt (last accessed January 21, 2019).

41 Ibid.

42 Ibid.

43 David D. Kirkpatrick, "Named Egypt's Winner, Islamist Makes History," *New
York Times*, June 24, 2012, https://www.nytimes.com/2012/06/25/world/mi
ddleeast/mohamed-morsi-of-muslim-brotherhood-declared-as-egypts-president
.html (last accessed January 21, 2019).

44 Usaama al-Azami, *Islam and the Arab Revolution* (Hurst, 2022), 100.

45 Al-Azami, *Islam and the Arab Revolution*, 96.

46 Sharify-Funk Meena, William Rory Dickson, and Shobhana Xavier Merin,
Contemporary Sufism Piety, Politics, and Popular Culture (Routledge, 2017), 84.

47 Zekeria ould Ahmed Salem, "Zekeria ould Ahmed Salem," Middle East Research
and Information Project, April 13, 2021, https://merip.org/2021/04/the-impor
tance-of-mauritanian-scholars-in-global-islam/ (last accessed January 31, 2022).

48 "Biography of Shaykh Abdallah bin Bayyah," www.binbayyah.net/english/bio/
(last accessed January 21, 2019).

49 Ibid.

50 David H. Warren, *Rivals in the Gulf: Yusuf al-Qaradawi, Abdullah Bin Bayyah,
and the Qatar-UAE Contest Over the Arab Spring and the Gulf Crisis* (Routledge,
2021), 166.

51 Ibid., 79.

52 Al-Azami, *Islam and the Arab Revolutions*, 106.

53 Ibid., 106–7.

54 Ibid., 107.

55 Warren, *Rivals in the Gulf*, 87–8.

56 Abdullah bin Bayyah, "Khiṭāb Istiqālat ʿAbdullāh b. Bayyah min al-Ittiḥād
al-ʿĀlamī li-ʿUlamāʾ al-Muslimīn," Binbayyah.net, September 13, 2013, http://bi
nbayyah.net/arabic/archives/1454 (trans. David Warren).

57 http://binbayyah.net/arabic/archives/1412 (also *Islam and the Arab Revolutions*,
119).

58 http://binbayyah.net/english/world-leaders-unite-to-grant-all-children-a-healt
hy-start-to-their-lives-during-the-first-world-summit-for-vaccines/

59 Quisay and Parker, "On the Theology of Obedience."

60 Bin Bayyah official website, "Al-ʿalāmah ʿAbdullāh Bin Bayyah mutaḥadithān fī Iḥtifālliyāt "yawm Zāyid l' lʿamal alʿinsāni" http://binbayyah.net/arabic/archives /1448 (last accessed January 21, 2019).

61 Jeremy Ravinsky, "Friends Again? Saudi Arabia, UAE Jump In to Aid Egypt," *Christian Science Monitor*, 2013, https://www.csmonitor.com/World/Global -Issues/2013/0710/Friends-again-Saudi-Arabia-UAE-jump-in-to-aid-Egypt (last accessed January 21, 2019), https://carnegieendowment.org/files/egyptian_arm ed_forces.pdf p16

62 The Tabah Foundation is a UAE-based non-profit organization that offers suggestions and recommendations to opinion makers in order that they assume a wise approach that is beneficial to society. It also sets up practical projects that serve the exalted values of Islam and bring out its splendor as a civilization, http:// www.nakhwah.org/en/organizations/783-Tabah-Foundation (last accessed January 21, 2019).

63 Muḥammad ʿAmāsha, "Al-ʾEmirāt w-al Ṣūfiyyah fī Miṣr: Kharāʾit al-Fikr wa-l-Ḥaraka," *Eipss*, October 18, 2018.

64 Farah El Sharif, "The Problem of 'Political Sufism,'" *The Maydan*, December 15, 2018, https://www.themaydan.com/2018/12/problem-political-sufism/ (last accessed January 21, 2019).

65 Warren, *Rivals in the Gulf*, 94.

66 Christopher Davidson, *From Sheikhs to Sultanism Statecraft and Authority in Saudi Arabia and the UAE* (Hurst, 2021), 102.

67 Ibid., 213.

68 Muḥammad ʿAmāsha, "Al-ʾEmirāt w-al Ṣūfiyyah fī Miṣr: Kharāʾit al-Fikr wa-l-Ḥaraka," *Eipss*, October 18, 2018.

69 *Rivals in the Gulf*, 82–3.

70 "Saḥb al-Jinsiyyah al-ʾEimārātiyyah min 6 ʿAshkhāṣ litwaruṭhum bil-masās bi-ʾāmn al-dawla," *Emarat al-Youm*, December 22, 2011, https://www.emarata lyoum.com/local-section/other/2011-12-22-1.447078 (last accessed January 21, 2019).

71 Matthew Hedges and Giorgio Cafiero, "The GCC and the Muslim Brotherhood: What Does the Future Hold?," *Middle East Policy* 24, no. 1 (2017) [incidentally, the author of this article was also arrested by the UAE and held on charges of spying] and *From Sheikhs to Sultanism*, 215.

72 Warren, *Rivals in the Gulf*, 83.

73 Davidson, *From Sheikhs to Sultanism*, 202.

74 Dominic Waghorn, "Mohammed bin Salman: Reformer or Tyrant?," *Sky News*, https://news.sky.com/story/mohammed-bin-salman-reformer-or-tyrant-1152 9990 (last accessed January 21, 2019).

75 Dilip Hiro, "Mohammed bin Salman Never Was a Reformer. This Has Proved It," *The Guardian*, October 18, 2018, https://www.theguardian.com/comme ntisfree/2018/oct/18/mohammed-bin-salman-brutality-saudi-jamal-khashoggi (last accessed January 21, 2019).

76 Morris Loveday, "The High Price of Feminism in the 'New' Saudi Arabia," *Washington Post*, May 20, 2018, https://www.washingtonpost.com/world/mi ddle_east/the-high-price-of-feminism-in-thenew-saudi-arabia/2018/05/20/99 d6dfde-5c3f-11e8-b656-236c6214ef01_story.html?utm_term=.d706db01427f (last accessed January 21, 2019).

77 Chiara Pellegrino, "Mohammad Bin Salman and the Invention of Tradition," *OASIS*, June 19, 2018, https://www.oasiscenter.eu/en/mbs-saudi-arabia-moder ate-islam (last accessed January 21, 2019).

78 https://www.bbc.com/news/world-europe-45812399

79 El Sharif, "The Problem of "Political Sufism."

80 Davidson, *From Sheikhs to Sultanism*, 105.

81 Ibid., 105.

82 Ibid.

83 El Sharif, "The Problem of Political Sufism."

84 Shu'ūn Islāmiyya', "Abu Dhabi's Network of Political Sufism," 4.

85 Ibid.

86 Ibid.

87 Quisay and Parker, "On the Theology of Obedience."

88 BBC, "Turkey's President Erdogan opens Cambridge 'Eco-mosque,'" *BBC News*, December 5, 2019, https://www.bbc.co.uk/news/uk-england-cambridgeshire -50666385 (last accessed October 2, 2020).

89 Ibid.

90 Warren, *Rivals in the Gulf*, 107–8.

91 Stacey Gutkowski, "We Are the Very Model of a Moderate Muslim State: The Amman Messages and Jordan's Foreign Policy," *International Relations* 30, no. 2 (2016).

92 Mandaville, Hamid, "Islam as Statecraft," 19–20.

93 Yahya Michot, "Ibn Taymiyya's 'New Mardin Fatwa.' Is Genetically Modified Islam (GMI) Carcinogenic?," *The Muslim World* 101, no. 2 (2011), 137.

94 Ibid., 149–50.

95 Ibid.

96 Ibid., 156.

97 Quisay and Parker, "On the Theology of Obedience."

98 Morgan Lee, "Morocco Declaration: Muslim Nations Should Protect Christians

from Persecution," *Christianity Today*, January 27, 2016, https://www.christian itytoday.com/news/2016/january/marrakesh-declaration-muslim-nations-christian-persecution.html (last accessed January 21, 2019).

99 "The Marrakesh Declaration," http://www.marrakeshdeclaration.org/ (last accessed January 21, 2019).

100 Mandaville, Hamid, "Islam as Statecraft," 21.

101 "The Marrakesh Declaration."

102 Zaytuna College, "Special Address by Hamza Yusuf," YouTube, February 23, 2016, https://www.youtube.com/watch?v=yMzuRe8LPA4 (last accessed January 21, 2019).

103 Quisay and Parker, "On the Theology of Obedience."

104 Haneen Dajani, "Arabs and Emiratis Put Nationality First, UAE Forum Hears," *The National*, December 19, 2016, https://www.thenational.ae/uae/arabs-and -emiratis-put-nationality-first-uae-forum-hears-1.201087 (last accessed January 20, 2019).

105 Warren, *Rivals in the Gulf*, 95.

106 Davidson, *From Sheikhs to Sultanism*, 233.

107 Ibid., 234–5; The United Arab Emirates' Government Portal, "Minister of Tolerance and Coexistence," https://u.ae/en/about-the-uae/culture/tolerance /tolerance-initiatives/minister-of-tolerance

108 Abdullah bin Bayyah, "In Pursuit of Peace: Framework Speech for the Forum for Promoting Peace in Muslim Societies," trans. Tarek El Gawhary, ed. Krista Bremer in *The Forum for Promoting Peace in Muslim Societies* (lecture, Abu Dhabi, March 9–10, 2014), 22.

109 Ibid.

110 Davidson, *From Sheikhs to Sultanism*, 234–5.

111 Shireena Al Nowais, "Some Fatwas Are Dangerous … And Some Are Ridiculous, Says Renowned Muslim Scholar Hamza Yusuf," *The UAE National News*, June 28, 2018, https://www.thenationalnews.com/uae/uae-fatwa-council-to-deliv er-moderate-voice-to-islamic-discourse-says-sheikh-hamza-yusuf-1.744932 (last accessed January 26, 2022).

112 Warren, *Rivals in the Gulf*, 103.

113 Al Arabiya News, "UAE Blacklists 82 Groups as 'Terrorist,'" *Al Arabiya News*, November 15, 2014, https://english.alarabiya.net/News/middle-east/2014/11/15/ UAE-formally-blacklists-82-groups-as-terrorist-(last accessed January 26, 2022).

114 Yahya Birt, "Blowin' in the Wind: Trumpism and Traditional Islam in America," *Medium*, February 14, 2017, https://medium.com/@yahyabirt/https-medium -com-yahyabirt-blowin-in-the-wind-trumpism-and-traditional-islam-in-ameri ca-40ba056486dt8 (last accessed January 26, 2022).

115 Al-Ghad, "Majlis al-Iftā' al-Imārātī yuṣnif al-Ikhwān munadhama irhābiyyah," *Al-Ghad*, November 23, 2020, https://www.alghad.tv/%D8%A5%D9%81%D8%AA%D8%A7%D8%A1-%D8%A7%D9%84%D8%A5%D9%85%D8%A7%D8%B1%D8%A7%D8%AA-%D9%8A%D8%A4%D9%83%D8%AF-%D8%AA%D8%AC%D8%B1%D9%8A%D9%85-%D8%AA%D9%86%D8%B8%D9%8A%D9%85-%D8%A7%D9%84%D8%A5/ (last accessed January 26, 2022).
116 Warren, *Rivals in the Gulf*, 89.
117 Davidson, *From Sheikhs to Sultanism*, 234–5.
118 Robin Gomes, "Abrahamic Family House in Abu Dhabi to Open in 2022," *Vatican News*, https://www.vaticannews.va/en/vatican-city/news/2021-06/abu-dhabi-abrahamic-family-house-2022-human-fraternity.html (last accessed January 26, 2022).
119 Hae Won Jeong, "The Abraham Accords and Religious Tolerance: Three Tales of Faith-Based Foreign-Policy Agenda Setting," *Middle East Policy* (2021), 38.
120 Al Bayān, "Muntadā Ta'zīz al-Silm Yushid b-ḥikmat Muḥammad Bin Zāyed," *al-Bayān*, August 17, 2020, https://www.albayan.ae/across-the-uae/news-and-reports/2020-08-17-1.3938162 (last accessed January 26, 2022).
121 Benjamin Harbaugh, "Abraham Accords and Religious Freedom," *International Christian Concern*, https://www.persecution.org/2020/09/16/abraham-accords-religious-freedom/ (last accessed January 26, 2022).
122 5Pillars, "Shaykh Hamza Yusuf Denies Supporting Israel Peace Deal, Blames Media for 'Lying,'" *5Pillars*, August 24, 2020, https://5pillarsuk.com/2020/08/24/hamza-yusuf-denies-supporting-israel-peace-deal-blames-media-for-lying/; Hamza Yusuf, Facebook post, August 2020, https://www.facebook.com/permalink.php?story_fbid=327523151940240&id=114544283238129
123 https://www.trtworld.com/magazine/uae-attempt-to-get-muslim-scholars-to-endorse-israel-deal-falls-flat-39189 (last accessed January 26, 2022).
124 Birt, "Blowin' in the Wind."
125 Ibid.
126 Quisay and Parker, "On the Theology of Obedience."
127 Birt, "Blowin' in the Wind."
128 Ibid.
129 "History of the Alliance Virtue," https://www.allianceofvirtues.com/english/history.asp
130 Martino Diez, "The Alliance of Virtue: Towards an Islamic Natural Law?," *Oasis*, March 30, 2020, https://www.oasiscenter.eu/en/emirates-chart-new-alliance-of-virtue (last accessed January 26, 2022).
131 Kent R. Hill, "The Charter of the New of Virtue," *The Catholic Thing*, March

5, 2020, https://www.thecatholicthing.org/2020/03/05/the-charter-of-the -new-alliance-of-virtue/ (last accessed January 26, 2022).

132 Dignitatis Humanae, "Declaration on Religious Freedom," Second Vatican Council (1965), https://www.vatican.va/archive/hist_councils/ii_vatican _council/documents/vat-ii_decl_19651207_dignitatis-humanae_en.html (last accessed January 26, 2022).

133 Samuel Smith, "Trump's New Religious Freedom Amb. Praises Islamic Scholars in First Public Speech," *Christian Post*, February 6, 2018, https://www.christi anpost.com/news/trump-new-religious-freedom-ambassador-sam-brownback -islamic-scholars-first-public-speech-216586/ (last accessed January 26, 2022).

134 Ibid.

135 Princeton MLP, "Mawlid! A Conversation with Sh. Hamza Yusuf + Songs & Poetry Celebrating the Prophet's Birth," Facebook lecture, October 29, 2020, https://www.facebook.com/princetonmlp/videos/418041562918666 (last accessed January 26, 2022).

136 Birt, "Blowin' in the Wind."

137 Ibid.

138 Umar Farooq, "US Muslim Scholar Joins Trump's Human Rights Panel," *Anadolu Agency*, July 9, 2019, https://www.aa.com.tr/en/americas/us-muslim -scholar-joins-trumps-human-rights-panel/1527283 (last accessed January 26, 2022).

139 Kenneth Roth, "Pompeo's Commission on Unalienable Rights Will Endanger Everyone's Human Rights," *Human Rights Watch*, August 27, 2020, https:// www.hrw.org/news/2020/08/27/pompeos-commission-unalienable-rights-wi ll-endanger-everyones-human-rights (last accessed January 26, 2022).

140 "UAE Fatwa Council Member among Experts of US 'Commission on Unalienable Rights,'" *Emirates News Agency*, July 9, 2019, http://wam.ae/en /details/1395302773134 (last accessed January 26, 2022).

141 Renovatio: The Journal of Zaytuna College, "What Conservatism Really Means—Roger Scruton in Conversation with Hamza Yusuf," YouTube, June 5, 2018, https://www.youtube.com/watch?v=iawSzFZg-vw&t=1s (last accessed June 21, 2018); Renovatio: The Journal of Zaytuna College, "Sacred Truths in a Profane World | Hamza Yusuf & Roger Scruton," YouTube, June 19, 2018, https://www.youtube.com/watch?v=OQoi9xPooKo&t=25s (last accessed June 21, 2018).

142 Patrick Maguire, "Theresa May Urged to Sack Roger Scruton over Comments on Eugenics," *NewStatesman America*, November 8, 2018, https://www.newst atesman.com/politics/uk/2018/11/theresa-may-urged-sack-roger-scruton-over -comments-eugenics (last accessed June 21, 2018).

143 Roger Scruton, "The Future of European Civilization: Lessons for America," The Heritage Foundation (Russell Kirk Lecture, October 2015), https://www.youtube.com/watch?v=WMz3clGp_MY (last accessed June 21, 2018).

144 "Vita et Veritas: Guide to Politics, Policy Making, and Social Trends in the Pro-Life Movement," https://www.vitaetveritas.com/ (last accessed January 26, 2022).

145 Hamza Yusuf, "When Does a Human Fetus Become Human?," *Renovatio*, June 22, 2018, https://renovatio.zaytuna.edu/article/when-does-a-human-fetus-become-human (last accessed January 26, 2022).

146 See Chapter 2.

147 Warren, *Rivals in the Gulf*, 109.

148 Davidson, *From Sheikhs to Sultanism*, 233; Mona El-Naggar, "Sundays Off: U.A.E. Changes Its Weekend to Align with West," *New York Times*, December 10, 2021, https://www.nytimes.com/2021/12/07/world/middleeast/uae-weekend-shift.html (last accessed January 26, 2022) and Emma Graham-Harrison, "UAE Decriminalises Alcohol and Lifts Ban on Unmarried Couples Living Together," *The Guardian*, November 9, 2020, https://www.theguardian.com/world/2020/nov/07/united-arab-emirates-to-relax-islamic-laws-on-personal-freedoms (last accessed January 26, 2022).

Chapter 8

1 John R. Hall, *The Ways Out: Utopian Communal Groups in an Age of Babylon* (Routledge and Kegan Paul, 1978), 36.

2 José Casanova, *Public Religions in the Modern World* (University of Chicago Press, 2011), 52.

3 Hall, *The Ways Out*, 33–4.

4 Abdal Hakim Murad voiced his discomfort with the degree of the Gulf States' relationship and utilization of neo-traditionalism as an expedient form of theology. Murad insisted on separation of the power of the state and scholars, citing that it was the role of the madrasa to cultivate a moral self and be a voice of society rather than that of power. Murad then cited the RAND Corporation's attempt at so-called "religion building" by sponsoring moderate Muslim networks. Alluding to Hamza Yusuf's relationship with the UAE/Saudi block, he insisted on the example of independent traditional scholars who spoke truth to power. Modern Muslim states, he contends, use the "fig leaf of counter radicalisation" as a caveat against *fatwā* production, often excommunicating any dissenting or independent voices. Murad notes that the arrest of Salman al-Oda is a primary example of this, or the fact that scholars aligned with the Saudi state now deem the blockade of Qatar as almost divinely mandated. Abdal Hakim Murad, "How

Islamic is 'Islamic Studies'?," Cambridge Muslim College (lecture, Cambridge, 2018), https://www.youtube.com/watch?v=cGNyFVXrBqs&t=2004s (last accessed January 20, 2019): 32:08.

5 Hall, *The Ways Out*, 34.

6 Yassir Morsi, *Radical Skin, Moderate Masks: De-Radicalising the Muslim and Racism in Post-Racial Societies* (Rowman & Littlefield, 2017), 75.

7 Ibid., 76.

8 Hamza Yusuf Hanson, "A Time for Introspection," *Q-News*, http://www.masud.co.uk/ISLAM/misc/shhamza_sep11.htm (last accessed January 26, 2022).

9 Morsi, *Radical Skin, Moderate Masks*, 82–3.

10 Donna Auston and Sylvia Chan-Malik, "Drawing Near to God's Pleasure: A Dialogue on the Black Muslim Political Tradition and the Moral–Ethical Imperative of American Islam," in *Muslims and US politics Today: A Defining Moment*, ed. Mohammad Hassan Khalil (Harvard University Press), 196.

11 "Black Muslim Psychology | RIS2016 Controversy," https://www.blackmuslim psychology.org/ris2016controversy. (last accessed April 24, 2020).

12 Abdullah Ali, "From Frames of the Familiar: Concerning Shaykh Hamza Yusuf," Lamppost Education Initiative [blog], December 29, 2016, https://lamppostedu .org/frames-shaykh-hamza-yusuf; Zaid Shakir, "Shaykh Hamza Yusuf Is Not a Racist," *New Islamic Directions—Imam Zaid Shakir* (blog), https://newislamic directions.com/nid/articles/shaykh_hamza_yusuf_is_not_a_racist (last accessed April 24, 2020).

13 "Hamza Yusuf and the Dangers of Black Pathology," *Struggles of a Covered Girl* [blog], https://strugglinghijabi.tumblr.com/post/154946891650/hamza-yusuf -and-the-dangers-of-black-pathology. (last accessed April 24, 2020).

14 Ubaydullah Evans, "Discussing Controversy: Hamza Yusuf at RIS Convention-Ustadh Ubaydullah Evans," Lamppost Education Initiative [blog], December 28, 2016, https://lamppostedu.org/discussing-controversy-hamza-yusuf-at-ris-conv ention-ustadh-ubaydullah-evans

15 "Hamza Yusuf and the Dangers of Black Pathology."

16 Much as in his lecture on the crisis of masculinity, Murad presented the arche-types of gender in traditional societies as the ideal. This traditional setting affirmed tropes about purity and chivalry as intrinsic to womanhood and manhood respec-tively.

17 Hamza Yusuf, "The Crisis of ISIS: A Prophetic Prediction," Zaytuna College (sermon, Berkeley, 2014), https://www.youtube.com/watch?v=hJo4B-yaxfk (last accessed January 20, 2019).

18 Ibid.

19 Ibid.

20 Ibid.

21 Associated Press Reporter, "Former Malaysian Prime Minister Najib Razak Arrested by Anti-corruption Agency," *The Independent*, September 19, 2018, https://www.independent.co.uk/news/world/asia/malaysia-former-prime -minister-najib-razak-anti-graft-agency-corruption-1mdb-a8544886.html (last accessed January 20, 2019).

22 Hassan Bashir, "5th Annual Conference of Forum for Promoting Peace in Muslim Societies Continues for Second Day," Emirates New Agency, December 12, 2018, http://wam.ae/en/details/1395302725704 (last accessed January 20, 2019).

23 In my interview in 2015 with Habib Ali Jifri, he said that Salman al-Oda wanted to build bridges and dialogue between Sufis and Salafis.

24 Areeb Ullah, "Sara Khan to Speak in UAE Alongside Trump Envoy Who 'Lobbied for Tommy Robinson,'" *Middle East Eye*, December 4, 2018, https:// www.middleeasteye.net/news/sara-khan-speak-uae-alongside-trump-envoy-who -lobbied-tommy-robinson-1923785718 (last accessed January 20, 2019).

25 Adam Kelwick Facebook page, December 9, 2018, https://www.facebook.com /adam.kelwick/posts/10155566451901330 (last accessed January 20, 2019).

26 "Mohamed Ghilan, "The Muslim 500," https://www.themuslim500.com/profil es/mohamed-ghilan/ (last accessed December 10, 2018).

27 Mohammad Ghilan, "EP 130: Hamza Yusuf and UAE—Mohamed Ghilan," interview, The Mad Mamluks, December 8, 2018, https://www.youtube.com /watch?v=wxPOSa_awdg (December 10, 2018).

28 Mohammad Ghilan's Facebook page, December 13, 2018, https://www.face book.com/drmohamedghilan/posts/2431167480246862?__tn__=K-R (last accessed December 13, 2018).

29 Ibid.

30 Hannah Allam, "Payoffs, Threats, and Secret Marriages: How an Accused Preacher Is Fighting To Save His Empire," *Buzzfeed News*, December 21, 2017, https://www.buzzfeednews.com/article/hannahallam/payoffs-threats-and-sh am-marriages-women-say-a-celebrity (last accessed December 26, 2022).

31 Walead Mosaad, "Spiritual Authority and Spiritual Abuse," Facebook lecture, *Sabeel Community*, https://www.facebook.com/sabeelcommunity/videos/2950 979931842859

32 Zeba Khan, "Uncovering the Wolf in Shaykh's Clothing | Danish Qasim," pod- cast with Danish Qasim, *Muslim Matters*, March 22, 2021. https://muslimma tters.org/2021/03/22/podcast-uncovering-the-wolf-in-shaykhs-clothing-danish -qasim/

33 "Afroz Ali," *The Muslim 500: The World's Most Influential Muslims*, https://

www.themuslim500.com/profiles/imam-afroz-ali/ (last accessed January 20, 2019).

34 "Afroz Ali," Berkeley Centre for Religion, Peace & World Affairs, https://berkle ycenter.georgetown.edu/people/afroz-ali (last accessed January 20, 2019).

35 Aboubakr Daqiq, "The Curious Case of Afroz Ali: Fraud, Lies, and Spiritual Abuse," https://static1.squarespace.com/static/59df0672e9bfdf961234faa8 /t/5b452dc2575d1f3762c3b93b/1531260438971/AfrozAli.pdf (last accessed January 20, 2019).

36 Ibid., 4.

37 Ibid., 5.

38 Ibid., 7.

39 Ibid., 9.

40 Ibid., 13–14.

Conclusion

1 Jonathan Butcher and Mike Gonzalez, "Critical Race Theory, the New Intolerance, and Its Grip on America," *Heritage Foundation Backgrounder* 3567, December 2020.

2 Stephen Sawchuk, "What Is Critical Race Theory, and Why Is It Under Attack," *Education Week*, https://www.edweek. org/leadership/what-is-critical-race-the ory-and-why-is-it-under-attack/2021/05 (last accessed February 13, 2022).

3 Zaid Shakir and Yasir Qadhi, "Imam Zaid Shakir's Story | Interview by Shaykh Dr Yasir Qadhi," February 11, 2022, https://www.youtube.com/watch?v=oZt3Py DFy3w (last accessed February 13, 2022).

4 *Islam4Europeans*, http://islam4europeans.com/

5 "Abdal Hakim Murad," *Islam4Europeans*, http://islam4europeans.com/tag/ab dal-hakim-murad/

6 "Hamza Yusuf," *Islam4Europeans*, http://islam4europeans.com/tag/hamza-yu suf/

BIBLIOGRAPHY

"24th Annual Dowra." www.thedowra.org (last accessed January 10, 2019).

"40 Hadith Nawawi 2." www.sunna.com/nawawi40 (last accessed January 13, 2016).

Adam Kelwick Facebook page. December 9, 2018. https://www.facebook.com/adam .kelwick/posts/10155566451901330 (last accessed January 20, 2019).

"Afroz Ali." *Berkeley Centre for Religion, Peace & World Affairs*. https://berkleycent er.georgetown.edu/people/afroz-ali (last accessed January 20, 2019).

"Afroz Ali." *The Muslim 500: The World's Most Influential Muslims*. https://www .themuslim500.com/profiles/imam-afroz-ali/ (last accessed January 20, 2019).

"Biography of Shaykh Abdallah Bin Bayyah." www.binbayyah.net/english/bio/ (last accessed January 21, 2019).

"Donald Eugene Weinman." https://www.findagrave.com/memorial/47072342/do nald-eugene-weinman (last accessed January 25, 2022).

"Dr. Umar Faruq Abd-Allah." *ALIM American Learning Institute for Muslims* (last accessed January 10, 2019). https://www.alimprogram.org/scholars/dr-umar/

"Joseph Campbell." www.moongadget.com/origins/myth.html (last accessed January 21, 2019).

"Khiḍr in the Islamic Tradition." khidr.org/khidr.htm (last accessed January 13, 2019).

"Mohamed Ghilan." *The Muslim 500*. https://www.themuslim500.com/profiles /mohamed-ghilan/ (last accessed December 10, 2018).

"Obituaries: John Winter." *Daily Telegraph*, November 23, 2012. https://www.teleg raph.co.uk/news/obituaries/9699534/John-Winter.html

"President Bush Addresses the Nation." September 20, 2001. https://www.washing

tonpost.com/wp-srv/nation/specials/attacked/transcripts/bushaddress_092001
.html

"Rihla 2017: A Journey of a Lifetime." *DearSarina*, May 20. https://www.dearsarina
.com/dearsarina/2017/9/6/rihla-2017-journey-of-a-lifetime (last accessed March
26, 2019).

"The Muslim 500: The World's Most Influential Muslims." https://themuslim500
.com/

"#RIS2016 Shaykh Hamza Yusuf Controversy." *Muslim Wellness Foundation*,
January 5, 2017. http://www.blackmuslimpsychology.org/ris2016controversy
(last accessed March 26, 2019).

"Abdal Hakim Murad." *Islam4Europeans*. http://islam4europeans.com/tag/abdal
-hakim-murad/ (last accessed January 13, 2019).

"Amman Message." http://ammanmessage.com/ (last accessed January 13, 2019).

"Black Muslim Psychology | RIS2016 Controversy." https://www.blackmuslimpsyc
hology.org/ris2016controversy. (last accessed April 24, 2020).

"Burwell v. Hobby Lobby Stores, Inc." Supreme Court of the United States Blog,
August 1, 2014. http://www.scotusblog.com/case-files/cases/sebelius-v-hobby
-lobby-stores-inc/ (February 15, 2017).

"David Joseph Hanson Obituary." *New York Times*, 2017, https://www.legacy.
com/us/obituaries/nytimes/name/david-hanson-obituary?pid=185113929.
(last accessed April 24, 2020).

"Dr. Umar Faruq Abd-Allah Wymann-Landgraf." http://www.themodernreligion
.com/profile/sh-Umar-Faruq-Abd-Allah.html (last accessed October 18, 2019).

"Global Advisors." http://alqadir.edu.pk/team/#advisors (last accessed October 18,
2019).

"Hamza Yusuf and the Dangers of Black Pathology." *Struggles of a Covered Girl*
[blog]. https://strugglinghijabi.tumblr.com/post/154946891650/hamza-yusuf
-and-the-dangers-of-black-pathology (last accessed April 24, 2020).

"Hamza Yusuf." *Islam4Europeans*. http://islam4europeans.com/tag/hamza-yusuf/
(last accessed April 24, 2020).

"History of the Alliance Virtue." https://www.allianceofvirtues.com/english/history
.asp (last accessed April 24, 2020).

"Islam4Europeans." http://islam4europeans.com/ (last accessed April 24, 2020).

"Mission and Vision." https://alqadir.edu.pk/mission-vision/

"Mohammad Ghilan's Facebook page." December 13, 2018. https://www.facebook
.com/drmohamedghilan/posts/2431167480246862?__tn__=K-R (last accessed
December 13, 2018).

"Prime Minister Imran Khan and Global Muslim Scholar Dialogue." https://www.yo
utube.com/watch?v=zQ8RMDjhtBc (last accessed April 24, 2020).

"Radical Middle Way Project." https://www.idealist.org/en/nonprofit/aecf97897e0
24310a217d0fddb02442c-radical-middle-way-london (last accessed January 21,
2019).

"Radical Middle Way." http://impacteurope.eu/partners/radical-middle-way/ (last
accessed January 21, 2019).

"Rihla: Course Pack." Deen Intensive Foundation, 2012. https://www.scribd.com
/doc/98729274/Rihla-2012-Coursepack (last accessed January 10, 2019).

"Saḥb al-Jinsiyyah al-'Eimārātiyyah min 6 'Ashkhāṣ litwaruṭhum bil-masās bi-'āmn al-
dawla." Emarat al-Youm, December 22, 2011. https://www.emaratalyoum.com
/local-section/other/2011-12-22-1.447078 (last accessed January 21, 2019).

"Spring Lodge Retreat." http://www.naqa.org.uk/spring-lodge-retreat/ (last accessed
February 2, 2019).

"The Centre of Islamic Spirituality at Al-Qadir." http://alqadir.edu.pk/academic-ce
nters-at-al-qadir/

"The Marrakesh Declaration." http://www.marrakeshdeclaration.org/ (last accessed
January 21, 2019).

"The Rihla Is a Journey with a Purpose: An Inner Transformation Rooted in Sound
Knowledge and Spiritual Discipline." http://www.deenintensive.com/the-rihla
-program (last accessed January 26, 2022).

"U.S. Muslim Cleric Hamza Yusuf calls Trump 'A Servant of God' During Racist
Rant against Black Lives Matter." *Rabwa Times*, December 25, 2016. https://
www.rabwah.net/muslim-hamza-yusuf-racist-rant/ (last accessed March 26,
2019).

"Vita et Veritas: Guide to Politics, Policy Making, and Social Trends in the Pro-
Life Movement." https://www.vitaetveritas.com/ (last accessed January 26,
2022).

Bougary, "Riḥla mᶜa al-shaykh Ḥamza Yusūf: Episode 6." "الثوره نفسها مشتقه من ثوريعني هم يثورون كحيوان لا يتصرفون كعقلاء"

5Pillars. "Shaykh Hamza Yusuf Denies Supporting Israel Peace Deal, Blames Media
for Lying." *5Pillars*, August 24, 2020. https://5pillarsuk.com/2020/08/24
/hamza-yusuf-denies-supporting-israel-peace-deal-blames-media-for-lying/ (last
accessed January 26, 2022).

Abbas, Tahir. *Muslim Britain: Communities Under Pressure.* Zed Books, 2005.

'Abd al-Raḥmān, Abū al-Faraj. *The Life of Ibn Hanbal.* NYU Press, 2016.

Abd-Allah, Umar Faruq. *The Islamic Struggle in Syria.* Mizan Press, 1983.

Abd-Allah, Umar Faruq. "Balancing Reason and Tradition in the Contemporary
Context." *IKEM* (lecture, Malaysia, May 2018). https://soundcloud.com/iam
alik/sets/dr-umar-faruq-abd-allah-the-malaysia-lectures (last accessed January 21,
2019).

Abd-Allah, Umar Faruq. "Foundations of the Islamic Worldview." Course, in *Bayan Claremont*, Spring 2017. www.bayanclaremont.org/academics/spring-2017-cou rses/abdallah/ (last accessed January 21, 2019).

Abd-Allah, Umar Faruq. "Islam and the Cultural Imperative." *Islam and Civilisational Renewal* 1, no. 1 (2009).

Abdallah, Umar Faruq. "Keynote." Malikiyyah Conference, Norwich, 1982. https:// www.youtube.com/watch?v=_e1nrkU1q0g (last accessed January 10, 2019).

Abd-Allah, Umar Faruq. "Modernism and Post-Modernism in the Light of the Prophetic Belief: session 6." Lecture, Samsun, 2016. https://deenstream.vhx.tv /videos/drumar-faruq-modernist-session-6 (last accessed January 21, 2019).

Abd-Allah, Umar Faruq. "Modernism and Post-Modernism in the Light of the Prophetic Belief: session 3a." Lecture, Samsun, 2016. https:// deenstream.vhx.tv/modernism-and-post-modernism-in-the-light-of-prophetic-belief/season:1/videos/drumar-faruq-modernist-session-3-part-a (last accessed January 21, 2019).

Abd-Allah, Umar Faruq. "Modernism and Post-Modernism in the Light of the Prophetic Belief: session 1." Lecture, Samsun, 2016.

Abd-Allah, Umar Faruq. "Modernity and Post-Modernity: Definitions, History, Responses." Lecture, Zawiya, 2014.

Abd-Allah, Umar Faruq. "Modernity and Post-Modernity: Definitions, History and Responses." Zawiya 2014 notes.

Abd-Allah, Umar Faruq. "The Fitra." Lecture, Malaysia, 2017.

Abd-Allah, Umar Faruq. Modernism and Post-Modernism in the Light of the Prophetic Belief: session 5b." Lecture, Samsun, 2016. https://deenstream.vhx.tv /modernism-and-post-modernism-in-the-light-of-prophetic-belief/season:1/vid eos/drumar-faruq-modernist-session-5-part-b

Abdo, Geneive. *Mecca and Main Street: Muslim Life in America after 9/11*. Oxford University Press, 2006.

Abdul Khabeer, Su'ad. *Muslim Cool: Race, Religion, and Hip Hop in the United States*. New York University Press, 2016.

Abdullah bin Bayyah. "Shaykh Bin Bayyah Responds to Prime Minister's Question: What Advice Would You Give to the Youth?" YouTube, January 2, 2022. https://youtube/AGwHlYtLrSo (last accessed January 26, 2022).

Abou El Fadl, Khaled. *Rebellion and Violence in Islamic Law*. Cambridge University Press, 2001.

Adler, Emanuel, and Peter M. Haas. "Conclusion: Epistemic Communities, World Order, and the Creation of a Reflective Research Program." *International Organization* 46, no. 1 (1992): 381.

Adler, Emanuel. "The Emergence of Cooperation: National Epistemic Communities

and the International Evolution of the Idea of Nuclear Arms Control."
International Organization 46, no. 1 (1992): 101–45.

Ahmed, Akbar. *Journey into America: The Challenge of Islam*. Brookings Institution
Press, 2010.

Al Arabiya News. "UAE Blacklists 82 Groups as 'Terrorist.'" *Al Arabiya News*,
November 15, 2014. https://english.alarabiya.net/News/middle-east/2014/11
/15/UAE-formally-blacklists-82-groups-as-terrorist- (last accessed January 26,
2022).

Al Bayān. "Muntadā Taʿzīz al-Silm Yushid b-ḥikmat Muḥammad Bin Zāyed."
al-Bayān, August 17, 2020. https://www.albayan.ae/across-the-uae/news-and
-reports/2020-08-17-1.3938162 (last accessed January 26, 2022).

Al Nowais, Shireena. "Some Fatwas Are Dangerous … And Some Are Ridiculous,
Says Renowned Muslim Scholar Hamza Yusuf." *The UAE National News*, June
28, 2018. https://www.thenationalnews.com/uae/uae-fatwa-council-to-deliv
er-moderate-voice-to-islamic-discourse-says-sheikh-hamza-yusuf-1.744932 (last
accessed January 26, 2022).

Al Qadir University Project Trust. " An Excerpt from a Meeting between
#PMImranKhan, Shaykh Abdal Hakim Murad, Dr. Zeeshan & Dr. Arif Butt."
YouTube, October 11, 2021. https://www.youtube.com/watch?v=Czp99rIo
UcM&ab_channel=AlQadirUniversityProjectTrust (last accessed January 26,
2022).

Al-Attas, Muhammad Naguib. *Islām and Secularism*. Muslim Youth Movement of
Malaysia, 1978.

al-Azami, Usaama. *Islam and the Arab Revolution*. Hurst, 2022.

Al-Ghad, "Majlis al-Iftā' al-Imārātī yuṣnif al-Ikhwān munadhama irhābiyyah."
Al-Ghad, November 23, 2020. https://www.alghad.tv/%D8%A5%D9%81%D8
%AA%D8%A7%D8%A1-%D8%A7%D9%84%D8%A5%D9%85%D8%A7%D8
%B1%D8%A7%D8%AA-%D9%8A%D8%A4%D9%83%D8%AF-%D8%AA%D8
%AC%D8%B1%D9%8A%D9%85-%D8%AA%D9%86%D8%B8%D9%8A%D9
%85-%D8%A7%D9%84%D8%A5/ (last accessed January 26, 2022).

Ali, Abdullah bin Hamid. "'Neo-Traditionalism' vs 'Traditionalism.'" January 22,
2012, Lamppost Foundation Initiative. https://lamppostedu.org/neo-tradition
alism-vs-traditionalism-shaykh-abdullah-bin-hamid-ali/ (last accessed December
15, 2020).

Ali, Abdullah. "From Frames of the Familiar: Concerning Shaykh Hamza Yusuf."
Lamppost Education Initiative [blog], December 29, 2016. https://lamppostedu
.org/frames-shaykh-hamza-yusuf (last accessed January 21, 2019).

Ali, Ayaan Hirsi. *Heretic: Why Islam Needs a Reformation Now*. Knopf Canada,
2015.

Ali, Kecia. *Imam Shafi'i: Scholar and Saint*. Oneworld, 2011.

Allam, Hannah. "Payoffs, Threats, and Secret Marriages: How an Accused Preacher Is Fighting to Save His Empire." *Buzzfeed News*, December 21, 2017. https:// www.buzzfeednews.com/article/hannahallam/payoffs-threats-and-sham-marria ges-women-say-a-celebrity (last accessed December 26, 2022).

Alqueria De Rosales Campus. "Studies of Imam Al-Ghazali Program." Youtube, September 26, 2017. https://www.youtube.com/watch?v=c1d5GP7Rh5A&fea ture=youtu.be (last accessed January 13, 2019).

Al-Shaykh, Turkī. "'Iḍā'āt ma'a Ḥamza Yusūf." Interview, *Al Arabiya*, October 5, 2011. https://www.youtube.com/watch?v=WhV791UyT0o (last accessed January 20, 2019).

Al-Tirīkī, Muḥammad 'ādil "Al- 'aṣālah' w-al- mu'āṣara fī al-fikr al-'arabī al-mu'āṣir." January 18, 2011. maghress.com. https://www.maghress.com/tettawen/1838 (last accessed January 10, 2019).

Aly, Remona. "Alqueria de Rosales, Spain: A Calm Haven." *Emel*, August 2009, www.emel.com/article?id=61&a_id=1443 (last accessed January 13, 2019).

'Amāsha, Muḥammad. "Al-'Emirāt w-al Ṣūfiyyah fī Miṣr: Kharā'it al-Fikr wa-l-Ḥaraka." *Eipss*, October 18, 2018.

Arjana, Sophia Rose. *Buying Buddha, Selling Rumi: Orientalism and the Mystical Marketplace*. Simon & Schuster, 2020.

Asad, Talal. "The Idea of an Anthropology of Islam." *Qui Parle* 17, no. 2 (2009): 1–30.

Associated Press Reporter. "Former Malaysian Prime Minister Najib Razak Arrested by Anti-corruption Agency." *The Independent*, September 19, 2018. https:// www.independent.co.uk/news/world/asia/malaysia-former-prime-minister -najib-razak-anti-graft-agency-corruption-1mdb-a8544886.html (last accessed January 20, 2019).

Auston, Donna and Sylvia Chan-Malik. "Drawing Near to God's Pleasure: A Dialogue on the Black Muslim Political Tradition and the Moral–Ethical Imperative of American Islam." In *Muslims and US Politics Today: A Defining Moment*, edited by Mohammad Hassan Khalil. Harvard University Press.

Ayubi, Zahra. "Owning Terms of Leadership and Authority: Toward a Gender-Inclusive Framework of American Muslim Religious Authority." In *A Jihad for Justice: Honoring the Work and Life of Amina Wadud*, edited by Ali Kecia, Hammer Juliane, and Laury Silvers, 47–55. University of Texas Press, 2012.

Bajwa, Omar. *A Rhetorical Analysis of Hamza Yusuf's Discourse on Education*. Cornell University Press, 2006.

Bakr, Abu. "Shaykh Abdul Hakim Murad—Progressive Islam Movements."

YouTube, March 15, 2018. https://www.youtube.com/watch?v=NMR1xq5
cZM4 (last accessed June 27, 2018).

Bakr, Abu. "Shaykh Hamza Yusuf—Framing Islam into Marxist Thought." YouTube,
July 18, 2016. https://www.youtube.com/watch?v=Kjh6x_vbgcY (last accessed
March 7, 2018).

Baksh, Nazim. "In the Spirit of Tradition." www.masud.co.uk/ISLAM/misc/traditi
on.htm (last accessed January 13, 2016).

Bano, Masooda. *The Revival of Islamic Rationalism: Logic, Metaphysics and Mysticism
in Modern Muslim Societies*. Cambridge University Press, 2020.

Baran, Deniz. "A Voice to the World from Chicago: Dr Umar Faruq Abd-Allah."
June 8, 2017, *worldbulletin*. https://www.worldbulletin.net/interviews-in-depth
/a-voice-to-the-world-from-chicago-dr-umar-faruq-abd-allah-h190556.html (last
accessed January 10, 2019).

Barron, Bishop Robert. "The Jordan Peterson Phenomenon." *Strange Notions: The
Digital Areopagus—Reason, Faith, Dialogue*. https://strangenotions.com/the-jo
rdan-peterson-phenomenon/ (last accessed February 2, 2019).

Bashir, Hassan. "5th Annual Conference of Forum for Promoting Peace in Muslim
Societies Continues for Second Day." *Emirates New Agency*, December 12, 2018.
http://wam.ae/en/details/1395302725704 (last accessed January 20, 2019).

BBC News, "Syria: The Story of the Conflict." *BBC News*, March 11, 2016. https://
www.bbc.com/news/world-middle-east-26116868 (last accessed January 21,
2019).

BBC. "Turkey's President Erdogan opens Cambridge 'eco-mosque.'" *BBC*, December
5, 2019. https://www.bbc.co.uk/news/uk-england-cambridgeshire-50666385
(last accessed October 2, 2020).

Benard, Cheryl, Andrew Riddile, Peter A. Wilson, and Steven W. Popper. *Civil
Democratic Islam: Partners, Resources, and Strategies*. Rand Corporation, 2004.

Bara, Zeyno. *Understanding Sufism and Its Potential Role in US Policy*. Nixon Center
Conference Report, March 2004.

Berger, Peter L. *The Sacred Canopy; Elements of a Sociological Theory of Religion*.
Garden City, NY: Doubleday, 1967.

Bin Bayyah Official Website. "Al-'alāmah 'Abdullāh Bin Bayyah mutaḥadithān fī
Iḥtifālliyāt 'yawm Zāyid l' l'amal al'insāni.'" http://binbayyah.net/arabic/archiv
es/1448 (last accessed January 21, 2019).

Bin Bayyah, 'Abdullah Bin Al-Shaykh Al-Maḥfūẓ. "Shāhid Mādhā Qāl al-'alāmah Ibn
Bayyah l'lQadhāffī Wajān li Wajh?" YouTube, March 30, 2014. https://www.yo
utube.com/watch?v=LadvZVGiIE4 (last accessed January 21, 2019).

Bin Bayyah, Abdullah. "In Pursuit of Peace: Framework Speech for the Forum for
Promoting Peace in Muslim Societies." Translated by Tarek El Gawhary, edited

by Krista Bremer in *The Forum for Promoting Peace in Muslim Societies*. Lecture, Abu Dhabi, March 9–10, 2014.

Bin Bayyah, Abdullah. "Khiṭāb Istiqālat ʿAbdullāh b. Bayyah min al-Ittiḥād al-ʿĀlamī li-ʿUlamāʾ al-Muslimīn." Translated by David Warren. Binbayyah.net, September 13, 2013. http://binbayyah.net/arabic/archives/1454

Birt, Jonathan (Yahya). "Good Imam, Bad Imam: Civic Religion and National Integration in Britain post-9/11." *The Muslim World* 96, no. 4 (2006) 687–705.

Birt, Yahya. "Blowin' in the Wind: Trumpism and Traditional Islam in America." *Medium*, February 14, 2017. https://medium.com/@yahyabirt/https-medium -com-yahyabirt-blowin-in-the-wind-trumpism-and-traditional-islam-in-america -40ba056486d8 (last accessed January 20, 2019).

Birt, Yahya. "Fuad Nahdi, Q-News and the Forging of British Islam: Some Personal Reflections." March 30, 2020. https://yahyabirt.medium.com/fuad-nahdi-q-ne ws-and-the-forging-of-british-islam-some-personal-reflections-9182c15b4ca8

Birt, Yahya. "Interview: Jordan Peterson, White Supremacy, and the Perils of Engagement." *Medium*, July 27, 2022. https://yahyabirt.medium.com/intervi ew-jordan-peterson-white-supremacy-and-the-perils-of-engagement-a80518ad 92f4 (last accessed October 2, 2022).

Bolognani, Marta. "Islam, Ethnography and Politics: Methodological Issues in Researching amongst West Yorkshire Pakistanis in 2005." *International Journal of Social Research Methodology* 10, no. 4 (2007): 279–93.

Bonnett, Alastair. "From White to Western: 'Racial Decline' and the Rise of the Idea of the West in Britain, 1890–1930." In *The Idea of the West*, 14–39. Palgrave, 2004.

Booth, Robert and Calla Wahlquist, "Grenfell Tower Residents Say Managers 'Brushed Away' Fire Safety Concerns." *The Guardian*, June 14, 2017. https:// www.theguardian.com/uk-news/2017/jun/14/fire-safety-concerns-raised-by-gr enfell-tower-residents-in-2012 (last accessed December 13, 2020).

Bougary, Eissa. "Riḥla mʿa al-shaykh Ḥamza Yusūf: Episode 5." MBC television show, 2016. https://shahid.mbc.net/ar/shows/%D8%B1%D8%AD%D9%84%D8%A9 %3A-%D9%85%D8%B9-%D8%A7%D9%84%D8%B4%D9%8A%D8%AE-%D8 %AD%D9%85%D8%B2%D8%A9-%D9%8A%D9%88%D8%B3%D9%81-%D8 %A7%D9%84%D9%85%D9%88%D8%B3%D9%85-1-%D8%A7%D9%84%D8 %AD%D9%84%D9%82%D8%A9-5/episode-142320 (last accessed January 20, 2019).

Bougary, Eissa. "Riḥla mʿa al-shaykh Ḥamza Yusūf: Episode 6." MBC television show, 2016. https://shahid.mbc.net/ar/shows/%D8%B1%D8%AD%D9%84%D8%A9 %3A-%D9%85%D8%B9-%D8%A7%D9%84%D8%B4%D9%8A%D8%AE-%D8 %AD%D9%85%D8%B2%D8%A9-%D9%8A%D9%88%D8%B3%D9%81-%D8

%A7%D9%84%D9%85%D9%88%D8%B3%D9%85-1-%D8%A7%D9%84%D8
%AD%D9%84%D9%82%D8%A9-5/episode-142320 (last accessed January 20,
2019).

Bougary, Eissa. "Riḥla mʿa al-shaykh Ḥamza Yusūf: Episode 5." MBC television show,
2016. https://shahid.mbc.net/ar/shows/%D8%B1%D8%AD%D9%84%D8%A9
%3A-%D9%85%D8%B9-%D8%A7%D9%84%D8%B4%D9%8A%D8%AE-%D8
%AD%D9%85%D8%B2%D8%A9-%D9%8A%D9%88%D8%B3%D9%81-%D8
%A7%D9%84%D9%85%D9%88%D8%B3%D9%85-1-%D8%A7%D9%84%D8
%AD%D9%84%D9%82%D8%A9-5/episode-142320 (last accessed January 20,
2019).

Bowen, Innes. *Medina in Birmingham, Najaf in Brent: Inside British Islam.* Oxford
University Press, 2014.

Bowker, John. "Ṭarīqa." In *The Concise Oxford Dictionary of World Religions.*
Oxford University Press, 2000. https://www.oxfordreference.com/view/10.10
93/acref/9780192800947.001.0001/acref-9780192800947-e-7241 (last accessed
May 29, 2019).

Bowles, Nellie. "Jordan Peterson, Custodian of the Patriarchy." *New York Times,* May
18, 2018. https://www.nytimes.com/2018/05/18/style/jordan-peterson-12-rul
es-for-life.html (last accessed October 2, 2022).

Bristow, E. "Russell Moore Announces Multi-Faith Statement Opposing California
Assault on Religious Liberty in Higher Education." Ethics & Religious Liberty
Commission of the Southern Baptist Convention, August 9, 2016. http://erlc
.com/resource-library/press-releases/russell-moore-announces-multi-faith-st
atement-opposing-california-assault-on-religious-liberty-in-higher-education
(February 15, 2017).

Brown, David G. "Why Star Wars: The Force Awakens Is a Social Justice Propaganda
Film." *Return of Kings,* December 20, 2015. www.returnofkings.com/759
91/why-star-wars-the-force-awakens-is-a-social-justice-propaganda-film   (last
accessed February 2, 2019).

Bryson, J. S. "Princeton's Robert George and Islam." *Muslim Matters,* April 9, 2012.
http://muslimmatters.org/2012/04/09/princetons-robert-george-and-islam/
(last accessed February 15, 2017).

Bulliet, Richard, David Cook, Roxanne L. Euben, Khaled Fahmy, Frank Griffel,
Bernard Haykel, Robert W. Hefner, Timur Kuran, Jane McAuliffe, and Ebrahim
Moosa. *The Princeton Encyclopedia of Islamic Political Thought.* Princeton
University Press, 2013.

Butcher, Jonathan and Mike Gonzalez. "Critical Race Theory, the New Intolerance,
and Its Grip on America." *Heritage Foundation Backgrounder* 3567, December
2020.

Byrd, Dustin J. *Islam in a Post-Secular Society: Religion, Secularity, and the Antagonism of Recalcitrant Faith*. Brill, 2016.

Cairo Review. "Cairo Review Interviews Shaykh Hamza Yusuf." https://imamsonl ine.com/cairo-review-interviews-shaykh-hamza-yusuf/ (last accessed January 4, 2021).

Calvin, John. *The Epistles of Paul to the Galatians, Ephesians, Philippians and Colossians*. Eerdmans, 1965.

Camp, Jordan T. and Christina Heatherton. *Policing the Planet: Why the Policing Crisis Led to Black Lives Matter*. Verso, 2016.

Casanova, José. *Public Religions in the Modern World*. University of Chicago Press, 2011.

Chachila, S. G. "Peaceful Muslims View US LGBT Issues as 'Completely Insane,' Says Muslim Leader." *Christian Times*, May 28, 2016. http://www.christiantim es.com/article/muslims-view-us-lgbt-issues-as-completely-insane-says-muslim-le ader/56058.htm last accessed (February 15, 2017).

Chan-Malik, Sylvia. "'Common Cause': On the Black-Immigrant Debate and Constructing the Muslim American." *Journal of Race, Ethnicity, and Religion* 2, no. 8 (2011): 1–39.

Chan-Malik, Sylvia. *Being Muslim: A Cultural History of Women of Color in American Islam*. New York University Press, 2018.

Chidester, David. "Time." In *The Oxford Handbook of the Study of Religion*, edited by Michael Stausberg, and Steven Engler. Oxford University Press, 2016.

Choudhary, Zara. "A Mauritanian Retreat: In Search of Murabit Al-Hajj." *Sacred Footsteps*, 2014. https://www.sacredfootsteps.org/2014/06/02/mauritania/ (last accessed January 13, 2019).

CNN Library. "2011 Libya Civil War Fast Facts." *CNN*, August 30, 2018. https:// edition.cnn.com/2013/09/20/world/libya-civil-war-fast-facts/index.html (last accessed January 21, 2019).

Corbett, Rosemary R. *Making Moderate Islam: Sufism, Service, and the "Ground Zero Mosque" Controversy*. Stanford University Press, 2016.

Curtis IV, Edward E. *Muslims in America: A Short History*. Oxford University Press, 2009.

Curtis, Edward E. *Black Muslim Religion in the Nation of Islam, 1960–1975*. University of North Carolina Press, 2006.

Curtiss, Richard H. "Dispute Between U.S. Muslim Groups Goes Public." *Washington Report on Middle East Affairs*, April/May 1999, 71, 101. https:// www.wrmea.org/1999-april-may/dispute-between-u.s.-muslim-groups-goes-pu blic.html

Cusack, Carole M. "A New Spiritual Marketplace: Comparing New Age and New

Religious Movements in an Age of Spiritual and Religious Tourism." In *The Routledge Handbook of Religious and Spiritual Tourism*, edited by Daniel H., Olsen, and Dallen J. Timothy, 79–89. Routledge, 2021.

Dajani, Haneen. "Arabs and Emiratis Put Nationality First, UAE Forum Hears." *The National*, December 19, 2016. https://www.thenational.ae/uae/arabs-and-emiratis-put-nationality-first-uae-forum-hears-1.201087 (last accessed January 20, 2019).

Daqiq, Aboubakr. "The Curious Case of Afroz Ali: Fraud, Lies, and Spiritual Abuse." https://static1.squarespace.com/static/59df0672e9bfdf961234faa8/t/5b452dc2575d1f3762c3b93b/1531260438971/AfrozAli.pdf (last accessed January 20, 2019).

Davidson, Christopher. *From Sheikhs to Sultanism Statecraft and Authority in Saudi Arabia and the UAE*. Hurst, 2021.

DeenIntensive, "Deen Intensive Foundation—*Rihla* 2015 Konya & Istanbul, Turkey." YouTube, March 13, 2015. https://www.youtube.com/watch?v=Lb09KN7hLTI (last accessed January 13, 2019).

DeenIntensive, "Deen Intensive *Rihla* 2010/1431 Trailer." YouTube, January 31, 2010. https://www.youtube.com/watch?v=9LI6xKk3CCM&feature=youtu.be&fbclid=IwAR2eGvRd2_uykCLy9tSSH3ImwQ_H13EHfGK6Da3YRyuzny-cidMNIKKBE0s (last accessed January 13, 2019).

Dempsey, B. "Religious Liberty in the Eyes of Evangelicals, Catholics, Mormons, & Muslims," *Juicy Ecumenism*, June 1, 2016. https://juicyecumenism.com/2016/06/01/religious-liberty-eyes-evangelicals-catholics-mormons-muslims/ (last accessed January 21, 2019).

Diez, Martino "The Alliance of Virtue: Towards an Islamic Natural Law?" *Oasis*, March 30, 2020. https://www.oasiscenter.eu/en/emirates-chart-new-alliance-of-virtue (last accessed January 26, 2022).

Dillo, Michele. *Handbook of the Sociology of Religion*. Cambridge University Press, 2003.

Dirs, Ahmed Peerbux. *Blessed Are the Strangers*. C Media, 2017.

Dodson, P. Claire. "J.J. Abrams Thinks Trolls Lashed Out About 'The Last Jedi' Because They're 'Threatened' by Female Characters." February 18, 2018, https://hellogiggles.com/news/jj-abrams-last-jedi-trolls/ (last accessed February 2, 2019).

E Fatwa Council Member among Experts of US 'Commission on Unalienable Rights.'" *Emirates News Agency*, 9 July 2019. http://wam.ae/en/details/139530 2773134. (last accessed January 26, 2022).

El Fadl, Khaled Abou. *Rebellion and Violence in Islamic Law*. Cambridge University Press, 2006.

El Gomati, Anas. "Libya's Islamists and the 17 February Revolution: A Battle for a

Revolutionary Theology." *In Routledge Handbook of the Arab Spring*, edited by Larbi Sadiki, 118–32. Routledge, 2014.

El Sharif, Farah. "The Problem of "Political Sufism." *Maydan*, December 15, 2018. https://www.themaydan.com/2018/12/problem-political-sufism/ (last accessed January 21, 2019).

El-Affendi, Abdelwahab. *The People on the Edge: Religious Reform and the Burden of the Western Muslim Intellectual*, Vol. 19. International Institute of Islamic Thought, 2010.

Elass, Rasha. "Muslim Liberal Arts College Aims for a Restoration." *The Arab Weekly*, November 20, 2015. https://thearabweekly.com/muslim-liberal-arts-co llege-aims-restoration (last accessed January 4, 2021).

El-Aswad, El-Sayed. "Images of Muslims in Western Scholarship and Media after 9/11." *Digest of Middle East Studies* 22, no. 1 (2013): 39–56.

Elmasry, Shadee. "The Salafis in America: The Rise, Decline and Prospects for a Sunni Muslim Movement among African-Americans." *Journal of Muslim Minority Affairs* 30, no. 2 (2010): 217–36.

El-Naggar, Mona. "Sundays Off: U.A.E. Changes Its Weekend to Align with West." *New York Times*, December 10, 2021. https://www.nytimes.com/2021/12/07 /world/middleeast/uae-weekend-shift.html (last accessed January 26, 2022).

Elshayyal, Khadijah. *Muslim Identity Politics: Islam, Activism and Equality in Britain*. Bloomsbury, 2018.

Engels, Friedrich. *The Origin of the Family, Private Property and the State*. Penguin, 2010.

Ess, Joseph Van. "Theology and Society in the Second and Third Centuries of the Hijra: A History of Religious Thought in Early Islam." *Almanca'dan İngilizce'ye*. Translated by John O'Kane, edited by Maribel Fierro. Brill 2017.

Evans, Ubaydullah. "Discussing Controversy: Hamza Yusuf at RIS Convention— Ustadh Ubaydullah Evans." Lamppost Education Initiative [blog], December 28, 2016. https://lamppostedu.org/discussing-controversy-hamza-yusuf-at-ris-conv ention-ustadh-ubaydullah-evans

Farooq, Umar. "US Muslim Scholar Joins Trump's Human Rights Panel." *Anadolu Agency*, July 9, 2019. https://www.aa.com.tr/en/americas/us-muslim-scholar-joi ns-trumps-human-rights-panel/1527283 (last accessed January 26, 2022).

Forum For Promoting Peace. "Hamza Yusuf: Al-Miḥwar al-Rabiʿ: Ishām al-Islām fī al-Silm al-ʿālmī -Dawr al-ʿulamāʾ w-al Iʿlām fī taʿzīz al-silm." Lecture: Abu Dhabi, 2014. https://www.youtube.com/watch?v=g7_isEsApX8&t=2079s&ab_chan nel=ForumforPromotingPeace%D9%85%D9%86%D8%AA%D8%AF%D9%89 %D8%AA%D8%B9%D8%B2%D9%8A%D8%B2%D8%A7%D9%84%D8%B3 %D9%84%D9%85

Gane, Nicholas. *Max Weber and Postmodern Theory: Rationalization Versus Re-enchantment*. Springer, 2002.

George, R. P. and H. Yusuf, "Religious Exemptions Are Vital for Religious Liberty." *Wall Street Journal*, 23 March 2014. https://www.wsj.com/articles/SB1000142 4052702304914204579397170026645290 (last accessed February 15, 2017).

Ghilan, Mohammad. "EP 130: Hamza Yusuf and UAE—Mohamed Ghilan." Interview, *The Mad Mamluks*, December 8, 2018. https://www.youtube.com /watch?v=wxPOSa_awdg (December 10, 2018).

Gleave, Robert. "Taqlid." In *Encyclopedia of Islam and the Muslim World*, edited by Richard C. Martin. Gale, 2016.

Gomes, Robin. "Abrahamic Family House in Abu Dhabi to Open in 2022." *Vatican News* https://www.vaticannews.va/en/vatican-city/news/2021-06/abu-dhabi-abrahamic -family-house-2022-human-fraternity.html (last accessed January 26, 2022).

Graham-Harrison, Emma. "UAE Decriminalises Alcohol and Lifts Ban on Unmarried Couples Living Together." *The Guardian*, November 9, 2020. https://www.th eguardian.com/world/2020/nov/07/united-arab-emirates-to-relax-islamic-laws -on-personal-freedoms (last accessed January 26, 2022).

Greaves, R. A. "The Reproduction of Jamaati Islami in Britain." *Islam and Christian–Muslim Relations* 6, no. 2 (1995): 187–210.

Green, Joshua. "Inside the Secret, Strange Origins of Steve Bannon's Nationalist Fantasia." *Vanity Fair*, July 17, 2017. https://www.vanityfair.com/news/20 17/07/the-strange-origins-of-steve-bannons-nationalist-fantasia (last accessed January 21, 2019).

Grewal, Zareena A. "Marriage in Colour: Race, Religion and Spouse Selection in Four American Mosques." *Ethnic and Racial Studies*, 2009.

Grewal, Zareena. *Islam Is a Foreign Country: American Muslims and the Global Crisis of Authority*. New York University Press, 2014.

Gunn, Michael. "Sufism in Jordan: A Prism of Spirituality." *Qantara.de* https://en.qa ntara.de/content/sufism-in-jordan-a-prism-of-spirituality (last accessed January 26, 2022).

Gutkowski, Stacey. "We Are the Very Model of a Moderate Muslim State: The Amman Messages and Jordan's Foreign Policy." *International Relations* 30, no. 2 (2016): 206–26.

Haas, Peter M. "Introduction: Epistemic Communities and International Policy Coordination." *International Organization* 46, no. 1 (1992): 1–35.

Haider, Shuja. "Postmodernism Did Not Take Place: On Jordan Peterson's 12 Rules for Life." *Viewpoint Magazine*, January 23, 2018. https://viewpointmag.com /2018/01/23/postmodernism-not-take-place-jordan-petersons-12-rules-life/?fb

clid=IwAR2p7rgE8LPRF39CBsrhjRWbc32x3RocOQaRtmTEve-27rYJBblmv
CPUeFw (last accessed October 2, 2022).

Hall, John R. *The Ways Out: Utopian Communal Groups in an Age of Babylon.*
Routledge & Kegan Paul, 1978.

Hamid, Sadek. "The Development of British Salafism," *Isim Review* 21 (2008): 10–11.

Hamid, Sadek. "The Attraction of 'Authentic' Islam." Salafism and British Muslim
Youth." In *Global Salafism: Islam's New Religious Movement,* edited by
R. Meijer, 358. Hurst, 2009.

Hamid, Sadek. "The Rise of the 'Traditional Islam' Network(s): Neo-Sufism and
British Muslim Youth." *Sufism in Britain,* 2013.

Hamid, Sadek. *Sufis, Salafis and Islamists: The Contested Ground of British Islamic
Activism.* I. B. Tauris, 2016.

Hammer, Juliane. *American Muslim Women, Religious Authority, and Activism:
More Than a Prayer.* University of Texas Press, 2012.

Hanley, Lynsey. "Look at Grenfell Tower and See the Terrible Price of Britain's
Inequality." *The Guardian,* June 16, 2017. https://www.theguardian.com/co
mmentisfree/2017/jun/16/grenfell-tower-price-britain-inequality-high-rise (last
accessed December 13, 2022).

Hanson, Hamza Yusuf. "A Time for Introspection," *Q-News.* http://www.masud.co
.uk/ISLAM/misc/shhamza_sep11.htm (last accessed January 26, 2022).

Harbaugh, Benjamin. "Abraham Accords and Religious Freedom." *International
Christian Concern.* https://www.persecution.org/2020/09/16/abraham-accords
-religious-freedom/ (last accessed January 26, 2022).

Hedges, Matthew, and Giorgio Cafiero. "The GCC and the Muslim Brotherhood:
What Does the Future Hold?" *Middle East Policy* 24, no. 1 (2017): 129–53.

Heim, Joe. "Charlottesville Timeline—How White Supremacist Protests Turned
Deadly over 24 Hours." *Washington Post,* August 14, 2017. https://www.washi
ngtonpost.com/graphics/2017/local/charlottesville-timeline/?utm_term=.6298
c843f478 (February 15, 2019).

Hermansen, Marcia. "American Sufis and American Islam: From Private Spirituality to
the Public Sphere." In *Islamic Movements and Islam in the Multicultural World:
Islamic Movements and Formation of Islamic Ideologies in the Information Age,*
edited by Denis Brilyov, 189–208. Kazan Federal University Publishing House,
2013.

Hill, Kent R. "The Charter of the New of Virtue." *The Catholic Thing,* March 5,
2020. https://www.thecatholicthing.org/2020/03/05/the-charter-of-the-new-al
liance-of-virtue/ (last accessed January 26, 2022).

Hiro, Dilip. "Mohammed bin Salman Never Was a Reformer. This Has Proved It."
The Guardian, October 18, 2018. https://www.theguardian.com/commentisf

ree/2018/oct/18/mohammed-bin-salman-brutality-saudi-jamal-khashoggi (last accessed January 21, 2019).

Hope, Christopher. "Ministers Spend £90,000 a Day on 'Soft Schemes' to Tackle Extremism." *The Telegraph*, March 23, 2009. https://www.telegraph.co.uk/ne ws/uknews/law-and-order/5038157/Ministers-spend-90000-a-day-on-soft-sche mes-to-tackle-extremism.html (last accessed January 21, 2019).

Hourani, Albert. "Rashid Rida and the Sufi Orders: A Footnote to Laoust." *Bulletin d'études orientales* 29, 1977: 231–41.

Howe, Justine. *Suburban Islam*. Oxford University Press, 2018.

Human Rights Watch. "Egypt: Rab'a Killings Likely Crimes against Humanity No Justice a Year Later for Series of Deadly Mass Attacks on Protesters." *HRW*, August 2014. https://www.hrw.org/news/2014/08/12/egypt-raba-killings-like ly-crimes-against-humanity (last accessed January 21, 2019).

Humanae Dignitatis. "Declaration on Religious Freedom." In *Second Vatican Council* (1965). https://www.vatican.va/archive/hist_councils/ii_vatican_council/docu ments/vat-ii_decl_19651207_dignitatis-humanae_en.html (last accessed January 26, 2022).

Imran Khan's official Facebook account, March 14, 2019. https://www.facebook .com/143462899029472/posts/3321630521212678/ (last accessed March 22, 2019).

Inge, Anabel. *The Making of a Salafi Muslim Woman: Paths to Conversion*. Oxford University Press, 2017.

Inkofknowledge." Is Islam a Political Ideology?—Shaykh Hamza Yusuf | Powerful." YouTube, November 26, 2016. https://www.youtube.com/watch?v=872N34Jx iw8&t=1s (last accessed February 15, 2017).

Islam On Demand. "The Concept of Ihsan—by Hamza Yusuf (Foundations of Islam Series: Session 4)." YouTube. https://www.youtube.com/watch?v=SLhogmk -Wug (last accessed February 15, 2017).

Islam On Demand. "The Salafi Fallacy—Abdal Hakim Murad." YouTube. https:// www.youtube.com/watch?v=1MRXs5fqlXQ (last accessed January 13, 2016).

Israel, Dawud. "3 Miracles of Murabit al-Hajj—Yahya Rhodus at SeekersRetreat 2014." Filmed 2014. YouTube video, 6:58, posted November 2015. https:// www.youtube.com/watch?v=PdeooPMD5y4 (last accessed January 13, 2016).

Israel, Dawud. "Towards a Traditionally American Mosque and Culture". Filmed December 2011. YouTube video, 5:57, posted December 2011, https://www.yo utube.com/watch?v=w8vZrS3epmU (last accessed January 13, 2016).

Israel, Dawud. "What Can We Do for Palestine?—Shaykh Abdal Hakim Murad." YouTube, December 11, 2011. https://www.youtube.com/watch?v=qxAo5ki -2RU (last accessed January 21, 2019).

Jackson, Sherman A. *Islam and the Blackamerican: Looking Toward the Third Resurrection*. Oxford University Press, 2005.

Jalalzai, Sajida. "Muslim Chaplaincy and Female Religious Authority in North America." In *The Routledge Handbook of Islam and Gender*, 209–21. Routledge, 2020.

Jawad, Haifaa A. *Towards Building a British Islam: New Muslims' Perspectives*. A & C Black, 2011.

Jawad, Haifaa. "De-radicalization through Conversion to Traditional Islam: Hamza Yusuf's Attempt to Revive the Sacred Knowledge with a North Atlantic Context." In *Moving In and Out of Islam*, edited by Karin van Nieuwkerk. University of Texas Press, 2018.

Jeong, Hae Won. "The Abraham Accords and Religious Tolerance: Three Tales of Faith-Based Foreign-Policy Agenda Setting." *Middle East Policy* (2021): 36–50.

Jibril, Latif. "Muslim American Cyber Contestations between Scholars and Activists Debating Racism, Islamophobia and Black Lives Matter." *Journal of Religion, Media and Digital Culture* 7, no. 1 (2018): 67–89.

Jones, Stephen H. "New Labour and the Re-making of British Islam: The Case of the Radical Middle Way and the "Reclamation" of the Classical Islamic Tradition." *Religions* 4, no. 4 (2013): 550–66.

Jones, Stephen H. *Islam and the Liberal State: National Identity and the Future of Muslim Britain*. Bloomsbury, 2020.

Karim, Jamillah. *American Muslim women: Negotiating Race, Class, and Gender within the Ummah*. NYU Press, 2008.

Kashani, Maryam. "Seekers of Sacred Knowledge: Zaytuna College and the Education of American Muslims." PhD diss., University of Texas at Austin, 2014.

Khan, Imran A. "Shaykh Hamza Yusuf and the Age of Feeling." *Wordpress*, March 25, 2018. https://blogofthebeardedone.wordpress.com/2018/03/25/shaykh-hamza -yusuf-and-the-age-of-feeling/ (last accessed January 20, 2019).

Khan, Riz "Interview with Hamza Yusuf." *Al Jazeera*, June 13, 2007. https://www.yo utube.com/watch?v=ve0Sgm0PFyk (last accessed January 20, 2019).

Khan, Riz "Rising anti-Muslim Rhetoric?: Interview with Hamza Yusuf." March 10, 2011. https://www.youtube.com/watch?v=EkzDUJHEw8Q (last accessed January 20, 2019).

Khan, Zeba. "Uncovering the Wolf in Shaykh's Clothing | Danish Qasim." Podcast with Danish Qasim, in *Muslim Matters*, March 22, 2021. https://muslimmatte rs.org/2021/03/22/podcast-uncovering-the-wolf-in-shaykhs-clothing-danish-qa sim/ (last accessed January 31, 2022).

Kimball, Charles. "The War on Terror and Its Effects on American Muslims." In *The Oxford Handbook of American Islam*. Oxford University Press, 2015.

Kirkpatrick, David D. "Named Egypt's Winner, Islamist Makes History." *NYT*, June 24, 2012. https://www.nytimes.com/2012/06/25/world/middleeast/mohamed-morsi-of-muslim-brotherhood-declared-as-egypts-president.html (last accessed January 21, 2019).

Klaveren, Joram van. *Apostate: From Christianity to Islam in Times of Secularisation.* Kennishuys & Sunni Publications, 2019.

Knight, Michael Muhammad. "Islamotopia: Revival, Reform, and American Exceptionalism." In *Islam After Liberalism*, edited by Faisal Devji and Zaheer Kazmi, 219–40. Oxford University Press, 2017.

Knorr-Cetina, Karin D. "Scientific Communities or Transepistemic Arenas of Research? A Critique of Quasi-economic Models of Science." *Social Studies of Science* 12, no. 1 (1982): 101–30.

Latif, Jibril. "Muslim American Cyber Contestations between Scholars and Activists Debating Racism, Islamophobia and Black Lives Matter." *Journal of Religion, Media and Digital Culture* 7, no. 1 (2018): 67–89.

Lauzière, Henri. "The Construction of Salafiyya: Reconsidering Salafism from the Perspective of Conceptual History." *International Journal of Middle East Studies* 42, no. 3 (2010): 375.

Lee, Morgan. "Morocco Declaration: Muslim Nations Should Protect Christians from Persecution." *Christianity Today*, January 27, 2016. https://www.christianitytoday.com/news/2016/january/marrakesh-declaration-muslim-nations-christian-persecution.html (last accessed January 21, 2019).

Lee, Umar. "The Rise and Fall of the Salafi Dawah in America: A Memoir by Umar Lee." Kindle edition, 2014.

Liutikas, Darius. "Travel Motivations of Pilgrims, Religious Tourists, and Spirituality Seekers." In *The Routledge Handbook of Religious and Spiritual Tourism*, edited by Daniel H. Olsen, and Dallen J. Timothy. Routledge, 2021.

Loux, Michael J. and Thomas M. Crisp. *Metaphysics: A Contemporary Introduction.* Routledge, 2017.

Loveday, Morris. "The High Price of Feminism in the 'New' Saudi Arabia." *Washington Post*, May 20, 2018. https://www.washingtonpost.com/world/middle_east/the-high-price-of-feminism-in-thenew-saudi-arabia/2018/05/20/99d6dfde-5c3f-11e8-b656-236c6214ef01_story.html?utm_term=.d706db01427f (last accessed January 21, 2019).

Maguire, Patrick. "Theresa May Urged to Sack Roger Scruton over Comments on Eugenics." *NewStatesman America*, November 8, 2018. https://www.newstatesman.com/politics/uk/2018/11/theresa-may-urged-sack-roger-scruton-over-comments-eugenics (last accessed June 21, 2018).

Mahmood, Hamid. *The Dars-e- Niẓāmī and the Transnational Traditionalist Madāris in Britain*. London, 2012.

Mahmood, Saba. "Secularism, Hermeneutics, and Empire: The Politics of Islamic Reformation." *Public Culture* 18, no. 2 (2006): 323–47.

Malik, Aftab Ahmad. *The Broken Chain: Reflections upon the Neglect of the Tradition*. Amal Pres, 2001.

Mamdani, Mahmood. *Good Muslim, Bad Muslim: America, the Cold War, and the Roots of Terror*. Harmony, 2005.

Mandeville, Peter and Shadi Hamid. "Islam as Statecraft: How Governments Use Religion in Foreign Policy." Brookings Institute, November 2018.

Martin, Douglas. "Bernard Lewis, Influential Scholar of Islam, Is Dead at 101." *NYT*, May 21, 2018. https://www.nytimes.com/2018/05/21/obituaries/bernard-lewis -islam-scholar-dies.html (last accessed January 21, 2019).

Mathiesen, Kasper. "Anglo-American 'Traditional Islam' and Its Discourse of Orthodoxy." *Journal of Arabic and Islamic Studies* 13 (2013).

McLeod, Aaron. *A Condensation of Richard Weaver's Ideas Have Consequences*. Alabama Policy Institute, 2012.

Meena, Sharify-Funk, William Rory Dickson, and Shobhana Xavier Merin. *Contemporary Sufism Piety, Politics, and Popular Culture*. Routledge, 2017.

Michot, Yahya. "Ibn Taymiyya's 'New Mardin Fatwa.' Is Genetically Modified Islam (GMI) Carcinogenic?" *The Muslim World* 101, no. 2 (2011): 130–81.

Mihirig, Abdurrahman. "The Myth of Intellectual Decline: A Response to Shaykh Hamza Yusuf." *The Maydan*, November 27, 2017. https://www.themaydan .com/2017/11/myth-intellectual-decline-response-shaykh-hamza-yusuf/ (last accessed June 26, 2018).

MishkatMedia. "Star Wars and the Crisis of Modern Masculinity." YouTube, March 9, 2016. https://www.youtube.com/watch?v=3kDbqABvEN0 (last accessed January 21, 2019).

Mo987665. "Shaykh Hamza Yusuf—Miracles of the Awliya." YouTube, July 28, 2012. https://www.youtube.com/watch?v=7gwqus452ns (last accessed February 15, 2017).

Morsi, Yassir. *Radical Skin, Moderate Masks: De-Radicalising the Muslim and Racism in Post-Racial Societies*. Rowman & Littlefield, 2017.

Mosaad, Walead. "Foundations of the Spiritual Path—Shaykh Walead Mosaad." Lecture, Istabul, 2012. https://deenstream.vhx.tv/foundations-of-the-spiritual -path-shaykh-walead-mosaad (last accessed January 13, 2016).

Mosaad, Walead. "Spiritual Authority and Spiritual Abuse." Facebook lecture. *Sabeel Community*. https://www.facebook.com/sabeelcommunity/videos/295097993 1842859 (last accessed January 13, 2016).

Muedini, Fait. *Sponsoring Sufism: How Governments Promote "Mystical Islam" in their Domestic and Foreign Policies.* Springer, 2015.

Murad, Abdal Hakim. "Contentions." Rihla, 2016.

Murad, Abdal Hakim. "Islamic Spirituality: The Forgotten Revolution." http://mas ud.co.uk/ISLAM/ahm/fgtnrevo.htm

Murad, Abdal Hakim. "Abdal Hakim Murad on Tablighi Jamaat." YouTube, April 3, 2012. https://www.youtube.com/watch?v=ZLWnUjZEJN0 (last accessed January 10, 2019).

Murad, Abdal Hakim. "Crisis of Modern Consciousness." Masjid Negara, lecture, Kuala Lumpur, 28 March 2010. https://www.youtube.com/watch?v=RWOKa Ob33K4&t=75s (last accessed January 10, 2019).

Murad, Abdal Hakim. "Crisis of Modern Consciousness." Masjid Negara, lecture, Kuala Lumpur, 28 March 2010, https://www.youtube.com/watch?v=RWOKa Ob33K4&t=75s (last accessed January 10, 2019).

Murad, Abdal Hakim. "Fall of the Family." June 2015. www.masud.co.uk/fall-of-the -family-part-1/ (last accessed January 21, 2019).

Murad, Abdal Hakim. "How Islamic Is 'Islamic Studies'?" Cambridge Muslim College, lecture, 2018. https://www.youtube.com/watch?v=cGNyFVXrBqs&t =2004s: 32:08 (last accessed January 26, 2022).

Murad, Abdal Hakim. "Understanding The Four Madhhabs: The Problem with Anti-Madhhabism." 1999. http://masud.co.uk/understanding-the-four-madhh abs-the-problem-with-anti-madhhabism/ (last accessed March 7, 2018)

Murad, Abdal Hakim. "Why I Converted to Islam." Interview with Joan Bakewell, BBC Radio 3 (December 2009). https://www.youtube.com/watch?v=GGfc6O b1UAY (last accessed January 10, 2019).

Murad, Abdal Hakim. "British and Muslim?" http://masud.co.uk/ISLAM/ahm/brit ish.htm (last accessed January 21, 2019).

Murad, Abdal Hakim. "British Muslims and the Rhetoric of Indigenisation." In *Travelling Home: Essays on Islam in Europe.* The Quilliam Press, 2020.

Murad, Abdal Hakim. "Contentions." *Samsun,* 2016.

Murad, Abdal Hakim. "Faith in the Future: Islam after the Enlightenment." Lecture, Islamabad, December 23, 2002. http://masud.co.uk/ISLAM/ahm/postEnlight .htm (last accessed January 21, 2019).

Murad, Abdal Hakim. "Good Anger, Bad Anger and Shirk Al-Asbāb." In *Travelling Home: Essays on Islam in Europe,* Chapter 6. The Quilliam Press, 2020.

Murad, Abdal Hakim. "Muslim Loyalty and Belonging: Some Reflections on the Psychosocial Background." January 2003. http://masud.co.uk/ISLAM/ahm/lo yalty.htm (last accessed January 21, 2019).

Murad, Abdal Hakim. "Muslims and National Populism." In *Travelling Home: Essays on Islam in Europe*, Chapter 2. The Quilliam Press, 2020.

Murad, Abdal Hakim. "Riding the Tiger of Modernity." Lecture, Cambridge, 2016. https://www.youtube.com/watch?v=07Ien1qo_qI&t=1082s (last accessed January 21, 2019).

Murad, Abdal Hakim. "The Destitute: A Discussion on the Spirituality of Poverty." Lecture, London: SOAS, 2014. https://www.youtube.com/watch?v=ciBmrwrLn98 (last accessed 21 January 2019).

Murad, Abdal Hakim. "The Destitute: A Discussion on the Spirituality of Poverty." Lecture, London: SOAS, 2014. https://www.youtube.com/watch?v=ciBmrwrLn98 (last accessed January 21, 2019).

Murad, Abdal Hakim. "The Venomous bidʿa of tanfīr." In *Travelling Home: Essays on Islam in Europe*, Chapter 5. The Quilliam Press, 2020.

Murad, Abdal Hakim. *Bombing without Moonlight: The Origins of Suicidal Terrorism*. Amal Press, 2008.

Murad, Abdal Hakim. *Commentary on the Eleventh Contention*. The Quilliam Press.

Murad, Abdal Hakim. "On Migrating to Lands of Melancholy." *Renovatio*, February 19, 2021. https://renovatio.zaytuna.edu/article/on-migrating-to-lands-of-melancholy (last accessed January 31, 2022).

Murad, Abdal Hakim. *Travelling Home: Essays on Islam in Europe*. The Quilliam Press, 2020.

Murad, Abdal-Hakim. "Contentions 2." www.masud.co.uk/ISLAM/ahm/contentions2.htm (last accessed January 13, 2019).

MuslimCanuck. "Interview of Sh. Hamza Yusuf w/ Tim Winter (1/3)." YouTube, May 6, 2013. https://www.youtube.com/watch?v=Oj-MkZ2wagY&t=1s (last accessed January 21, 2019).

Newlon, Brendan Peter. "American Muslim Networks and Neotraditionalism." PhD diss., University of California, Santa Barbara, 2017.

Norman, Alex. *Spiritual Tourism: Travel and Religious Practice in Western Society*. Bloomsbury, 2011.

Office of the Mufti. "Can Muslims Participate in Modern Democracy? (Sh Hamza Yusuf)." YouTube, November 5, 2017. https://www.youtube.com/watch?v=qn5KRg0neaI (last accessed January 20, 2019).

Okely, Judith. "Anthropology and Autobiography: Participatory Experience and Embodied Knowledge." In *Anthropology and Autobiography*, edited by Judith Okely and Helen Callaway, 1–28. Routledge, 1992.

Østebø, Terje. "Salafism, State-Politics, and the Question of 'Extremism' in Ethiopia." *Comparative Islamic Studies* 8 (2012): 165–84.

Peck, Tom. "Timothy Winter: Britain's Most Influential Muslim—and It Was All Down to a Peach." *The Independent*, August 20, 2010. https://www.independ ent.co.uk/news/people/profiles/timothy-winter-britain-s-most-influential-musl im-and-it-was-all-down-to-a-peach-2057400.html

Pellegrino, Chiara. "Mohammad Bin Salman and the Invention of Tradition." *OASIS*, June 19, 2018. https://www.oasiscenter.eu/en/mbs-saudi-arabia-moderate-islam (last accessed January 21, 2019).

Perry, Whitehall. *The Unanimous Tradition: Essays on the Essential Unity of All Religions*, edited by Ranjit Fernando. Sri Lanka Institute of Traditional Studies Press, 1999.

Peterson, Jordan B. "Why Is the Feminine Represented as Chaos?" YouTube, June 5, 2021. https://www.youtube.com/watch?v=rY9X6a-xxFo&t=1408s&ab_chann el=JordanBPeterson (last accessed October 2, 2022).

Preston, John. *Grenfell Tower: Preparedness, Race and Disaster Capitalism*. Springer, 2018.

Prime Minister Imran Khan. Twitter post, January 2022, 6:19 a.m.. https://twitter .com/PakPMO/status/1477600512002437122

Princeton MLP. "Mawlid! A Conversation with Sh. Hamza Yusuf + Songs & Poetry Celebrating the Prophet's Birth." Facebook lecture, October 29, 2020. https:// www.facebook.com/princetonmlp/videos/418041562918666 (last accessed January 26, 2022).

Pulver, Andrew. "Star Wars Director JJ Abrams: We Always Wanted Women at the Centre of The Force Awakens." *The Guardian*, December 17, 2015. https:// www.theguardian.com/film/2015/dec/17/star-wars-director-jj-abrams-wo men-the-force-awakens-daisy-ridley-lupita-nyongo-carrie-fisher (last accessed February 2, 2019).

Q News. "'Love Even Those Who Revile You.'" *Arab News*, 2005. http://www.arabn ews.com/node/265421 (last accessed March 7, 2018).

Quisay, Walaa and Thomas Parker. "On the Theology of Obedience: An Analysis of Shaykh Bin Bayyah and Shaykh Hamza Yusuf's Political Thought." *Maydan*, January 8, 2019. https://www.themaydan.com/2019/01/theology-obedience -analysis-shaykh-bin-bayyah-shaykh-hamza-yusufs-political-thought/?fbclid=Iw AR3xQzi-SC2md2gEie8nlPjxaHBK2Ur1MtA_cceg3muWermp9rc3490AJI4 (last accessed January 20, 2019).

Quisay, Walaa. "The Neo-Traditionalist Critique of Modernity and the Production of Political Quietism." In *Political Quietism in Islam: Sunni and Shi'I Practice and Thought*, 241–58. I. B. Tauris, 2019.

Qureshi, Omar. "Virtue Ethics." Rihla, 2017.

Rabwah Times. "U.S. Muslim Cleric Hamza Yusuf calls Trump 'A Servant of God' during Racist Rant against Black Lives Matter." *Rabwah Times*, December 25, 2016. https://www.rabwah.net/muslim-hamza-yusuf-racist-rant/ (last accessed January 20, 2019).

Rauch, Jonathan. "Islam Has Been Hijacked, And Only Muslims Can Save It." University of Chicago Press, 2001. https://www.press.uchicago.edu/sites/daysaf ter/911rauch.html (last accessed January 21, 2019).

Ravinsky, Jeremy. "Friends Again? Saudi Arabia, UAE Jump In to Aid Egypt." *Christian Science Monitor*, 2013. https://www.csmonitor.com/World/Global -Issues/2013/0710/Friends-again-Saudi-Arabia-UAE-jump-in-to-aid-Egypt (last accessed January 21, 2019).

Razavian, Christopher Pooya. "The Neo-Traditionalism of Tim Winter." In *Modern Islamic Authority and Social Change, Volume 2: Evolving Debates in the West*, edited by Masooda Bano, 72–94. Edinburgh University Press, 2017.

Renovatio: The Journal of Zaytuna College. "Sacred Truths in a Profane World | Hamza Yusuf & Roger Scruton." YouTube, June 19, 2018. https://www.youtu be.com/watch?v=OQoi9xPooKo&t=25s (last accessed June 21, 2018).

Renovatio: The Journal of Zaytuna College. "Learning To Be Human: Umar Faruq Abd-Allah & Hamza Yusuf (Part II)." YouTube, April 21, 2018. https://www.yo utube.com/watch?v=TulCWOZnd5o (last accessed January 21, 2019).

Renovatio: The Journal of Zaytuna College. "What Conservatism Really Means— Roger Scruton in Conversation with Hamza Yusuf." YouTube, June 5, 2018. https://www.youtube.com/watch?v=iawSzFZg-vw&t=1s (last accessed June 21, 2018).

Renovatio: The Journal of Zaytuna College. "Sacred Truths in a Profane World | Hamza Yusuf & Roger Scruton." YouTube, June 19, 2018. https://www.youtu be.com/watch?v=OQoi9xPooKo&t=25s (last accessed June 21, 2018).

Rihla Booklet 2012 and 2017.

RIS 2017.

Roberts, Bob, and Hamza Yusuf. "Shaykh Hamza Yusuf & Bob Roberts Jr | Muslim Scholar Talks Jesus with Evangelical Pastor." In *Bold Love* (podcast), October 14, 2020 (last accessed January 25, 2022). https://www.youtube.com/watch?v=vcR iogk9EKM&ab_channel=BobRobertsJr.

Robin, Corey. *The Reactionary Mind: Conservatism from Edmund Burke to Sarah Palin*. Oxford University Press, 2011.

Roth, Kenneth. "Pompeo's Commission on Unalienable Rights Will Endanger Everyone's Human Rights." *Human Rights Watch*, August 27, 2020. https:// www.hrw.org/news/2020/08/27/pompeos-commission-unalienable-rights-will -endanger-everyones-human-rights (last accessed January 26, 2022).

Salem, Zekeria ould Ahmed. "Zekeria ould Ahmed Salem." Middle East Research and

Information Project, April 13, 2021. https://merip.org/2021/04/the-importan ce-of-mauritanian-scholars-in-global-islam/ (last accessed January 31, 2022).

Sandal, Nukhet Ahu. "Religious Actors as Epistemic Communities in Conflict Transformation: The Cases of South Africa and Northern Ireland." *Review of International Studies* 37, no. 3 (2011): 930.

Sanneh, Kelefa. "Jordan Peterson's Gospel of Masculinity." *The New Yorker*, March 5, 2018. https://www.newyorker.com/magazine/2018/03/05/jordan-petersons-go spel-of-masculinity (last accessed January 21, 2019).

Sardar, Ziauddin. *Desperately Seeking Paradise: Journeys of a Sceptical Muslim.* Granta, 2005.

Sawchuk, Stephen. "What Is Critical Race Theory, and Why Is It Under Attack." *Education Week.* https://www.edweek. org/leadership/what-is-critical-race-the ory-and-why-is-it-under-attack/2021/05 (last accessed February 13, 2022).

Schedneck, Brooke. "Religious and Spiritual Retreats." In *The Routledge Handbook of Religious and Spiritual Tourism*, edited by Daniel H., Olsen, and Dallen J. Timothy, 191–203. Routledge, 2021.

Scruton, Roger. "The Future of European Civilization: Lessons for America." The Heritage Foundation (Russell Kirk Lecture, October 2015). https://www.youtu be.com/watch?v=WMz3clGp_MY (last accessed June 21, 2018).

Sedgwick, Mark. *Against the Modern World: Traditionalism and the Secret Intellectual History of the Twentieth Century.* Oxford University Press, 2009.

Shakir, Zaid and Yasir Qadhi, "Imam Zaid Shakir's Story | Interview by Shaykh Dr Yasir Qadhi." February 11, 2022. https://www.youtube.com/watch?v=oZt3Py DFy3w (last accessed February 13, 2022).

Shakir, Zaid. "Shaykh Hamza Yusuf Is Not a Racist." New Islamic Directions—Imam Zaid Shakir [blog]. https://newislamicdirections.com/nid/articles/shaykh_ham za_yusuf_is_not_a_racist. (last accessed April 24, 2020).

Shu'ūn Islāmiyya'. "Abu Dhabi's Network of Political Sufism."

Sibgatullina, Gulnaz and Tahir Abbas. "Political Conversion to Islam Among the European Right." *The Journal of Illiberalism Studies* 1, no. 2 (2021): 1–17.

Sikand, Yoginder S. "The Origins and Growth of the Tablighi Jamaat in Britain." *Islam and Christian–Muslim Relations* 9, no. 2 (1998): 171–92.

Smith, James K. A. *How (Not) To Be Secular: Reading Charles Taylor.* Eerdmans, 2014.

Smith, Melanie Kay. "Religion, Spirituality, and Wellness Tourism." In *The Routledge Handbook of Religious and Spiritual Tourism*, edited by Daniel H. Olsen, and Dallen J. Timothy, 69. Routledge, 2021.

Smith, Samuel. "Trump's New Religious Freedom Amb. Praises Islamic Scholars in First Public Speech." *Christian Post*, February 6, 2018. https://www.christianp

ost.com/news/trump-new-religious-freedom-ambassador-sam-brownback-islam ic-scholars-first-public-speech-216586/ (last accessed January 26, 2022).

Smith, Wolfgang *Ancient Wisdom and Modern Misconceptions: A Critique of Contemporary Scientism*. Sophia Perennis, 2013.

Spannaus, Nathan and Pooya Razavian. "Zaytuna College and the Construction of an American Muslim Identity." In *Modern Islamic Authority and Social Change, Volume 2: Evolving Debates in the West*, edited by Masooda Bano, 39–71. Edinburgh University Press, 2017.

Spencer, Hawes. *Summer of Hate: Charlottesville, USA*. University of Virginia Press, 2019.

Stjernholm, Simon. *Lovers of Muhammad: A Study of Naqshbandi-Haqqani Sufis in the Twenty-First Century*, Vol. 29. Lund University, 2011.

Suhaib Webb's Facebook page. https://www.facebook.com/suhaib.webb/posts/101 54763543928080 (last accessed January 20, 2019).

Tavory, Iddo, and Daniel Winchester. "Experiential Careers: The Routinization and De-Routinization of Religious Life." *Theory and Society* 41, no. 4 (2012): 351–73.

Taylor, Charles. *A Secular Age*. Harvard University Press, 2007.

The Ink of Scholars channel. "Britain's Void of Meaning—Timothy Winter." YouTube, October 26, 2014. https://www.youtube.com/watch?v=D5UTDzf S0Wc (last accessed February 15, 2017).

The Queen's Journal. "Protest Outside Jordan Peterson's visit to Queen's Campus." YouTube. https://www.youtube.com/watch?v=odRiqkdgDnE&ab_channel= TheQueen%27sJournal (last accessed October 2, 2022).

The United Arab Emirates' Government Portal. "Minister of Tolerance and Coexistence," https://u.ae/en/about-the-uae/culture/tolerance/tolerance-initia tives/minister-of-tolerance

TheEmpireofFaith. "Shaykh Hamza Yusuf Witnesses Karamah of Dr Umar Farooq Abdullah." YouTube, 29 August 2014. www.youtube.com/watch?v=b_3DK1 GNF-o (last accessed January 10, 2019).

Tourage, Mahdi. "Performing Belief and Reviving Islam: Prominent (White Male) Converts in Muslim Revival Conventions." *Performing Islam* 1, no. 2 (2013): 207–26.

Tradachieve. "A Sacred Alliance of Conservative Believers ~ Abdal Hakim Murad." YouTube, July 13, 2017. https://www.youtube.com/watch?v=QbIo65dKk0o (last accessed January 20, 2019).

Tradarchive. "Identity Politics ~ Abdal Hakim Murad." YouTube, March 11, 2018. https://www.youtube.com/watch?v=1RbkhXfBphw (last accessed January 21, 2019).

TRT World. "Hamza Yusuf Under Fire for Comments about the Syrian Revolution."

2019. https://www.youtube.com/watch?v=x96kvfDNjhs (last accessed January 27, 2022).

Ullah, Areeb. "Sara Khan to Speak in UAE alongside Trump Envoy Who 'Lobbied for Tommy Robinson.'" *Middle East Eye*, December 4, 2018. https://www.middle easteye.net/news/sara-khan-speak-uae-alongside-trump-envoy-who-lobbied-tom my-robinson-1923785718 (last accessed January 20, 2019).

Waghorn, Dominic. "Mohammed bin Salman: Reformer or Tyrant?" *Sky News*. https://news.sky.com/story/mohammed-bin-salman-reformer-or-tyrant-1152 9990 (last accessed January 21, 2019).

Walsh, Declan. "In Saudi Arabia's War in Yemen, No Refuge on Land or Sea." *NYT*, December 17, 2018. https://www.nytimes.com/2018/12/17/world/middleeast /yemen-fishing-boats-saudi.html (last accessed January 21, 2019).

Warren, David H. *Rivals in the Gulf: Yusuf al-Qaradawi, Abdullah Bin Bayyah, and the Qatar-UAE Contest Over the Arab Spring and the Gulf Crisis*. Routledge, 2021.

Weaver, Richard M. *Ideas Have Consequences: Expanded Edition*. University of Chicago Press, 2013.

Weber, Max, and Stephen Kalberg. "The Protestant Sects and the Spirit of Capitalism." *Essays in Sociology 3*, 302–22 (1946).

Weismann, Itzchak. *The Naqshbandiyya: Orthodoxy and Activism in a Worldwide Sufi Tradition*. Routledge, 2007.

Whiteman, Ian Abdal Latīf. *Average Whiteman: Adventures with Quakers, Architects, Rock Stars & Sufi Sages*. Editorial Qasida, 2021.

Whyte, Herbert. *HP Blavatsky: An Outline of Her Life*. Рипол Классик, 1920.

Williams, Ryan R. "Black Pathology in the American Muslim Community." https:// www.researchgate.net/profile/Ryan-Williams-31/publication/313673723_Bla ck_Pathology_in_the_American_Muslim_Community/links/58a2915492851 c7fb4c1cab1/Black-Pathology-in-the-American-Muslim-Community.pdf (last accessed January 22, 2023).

Willson, Gregory B., Alison J. McIntosh, and Anne L. Zahra, "Tourism and Spirituality: A Phenomenological Analysis." *Annals of Tourism Research* 42 (2013): 150–68.

Yusuf, Hamza. "Trip to Princeton," *Sandala*, October 8, 2010. https://sandala.org /trip-to-princeton/

Yusuf, Hamza. "We Shall Overcome," *Sandala*, November 15, 2016. https://sandala .org/we-shall-overcome/ (last accessed January 20, 2019).

Yusuf, Hamza, and John Sexton. "The Secular and the Sacred in Higher Education: A Conversation with Shaykh Hamza Yusuf and Dr. John Sexton." Fritzi Weitzmann

Owens Memorial Lecture, September 2016. https://www.youtube.com/watch
?v=oQJnjfq_aMk

Yusuf, Hamza and Tariq Ramadan. "Rethinking Reform." Debate, University of
Oxford Union, Oxford, May 26, 2010.

Yusuf, Hamza, and Zaid Shakir. *Agenda to Change Our Condition*. Zaytuna Institute,
2008.

Yusuf, Hamza. "A Grammar of Tolerance." *World Literature Today*, November
2017. https://www.worldliteraturetoday.org/2017/november/grammar-toleran
ce-hamza-yusuf (last accessed January 20, 2019).

Yusuf, Hamza. "A Spiritual Giant in an Age of Dwarfed Terrestrial Aspirations."
Q-News 363 (2005): 53–8.

Yusuf, Hamza. *Faces of Islam*. BBC documentary, 1999. https://www.youtube.com
/watch?v=h0ZlEyx0040 (last accessed January 10, 2019).

Yusuf, Hamza. "On the Passing of My Mother, Elizabeth George Hanson." *Sandala*.
https://sandala.org/blogs/uncategorized/on-the-passing-of-my-mother

Yusuf, Hamza. "Religion: A Pretext for Conflict?" Davos Open Forum at the World
Economic Forum Annual Meeting (session with Tony Blair, David Rosen,
Hamza Yusuf Hanson, Mina Oraibi, and Thabo Cecil Makgoba, Davos, 2015).
https://www.youtube.com/watch?v=BYs6Mm9BTaM (last accessed January
10, 2019).

Yusuf, Hamza. "Role of Muslims in the West." in Islam—The Only for Humanity
Conference in London Arena. Lecture, London, August 1995.

Yusuf, Hamza. "The Crisis of ISIS: A Prophetic Prediction." Zaytuna College
(sermon, Berkeley, 2014). https://www.youtube.com/watch?v=hJo4B-yaxfk
(last accessed January 20, 2019).

Yusuf, Hamza. "The Dajjal and New World Order." Lecture: London, 1998. https://
www.youtube.com/watch?v=oky3TSlEt4A&t=4320s (last accessed January 20,
2019).

Yusuf, Hamza. "When Evil Fails and Goodness Prevails: Regarding the Recent Coup
Attempt in Turkey." *Sandala*, July 31, 2016. https://sandala.org/when-evil-fa
ils/ (last accessed January 20, 2019).

Yusuf, Hamza. "When the Social Contract is Breached in Egypt." *Last Prophet* [origi-
nally published in *Sandala*], February 2011. www.lastprophet.info/when-the-so
cial-contract-is-breached-in-egypt (last accessed January 21, 2019).

Yusuf, Hamza. "Speech." *AlMarkaz al-ʿālamī l'l-Tajdīd wal Tarshīd*. Speech,
Mauritania, April 2013. https://www.youtube.com/watch?v=Rpma1aaWwds
&t=148s (last accessed January 10, 2019).

Yusuf, Hamza. "Don't Curse the People of Syria—Hamza Yusuf, 2019." https://
www.youtube.com/watch?v=YcYNdmaA-Oo (last accessed January 27, 2022).

Yusuf, Hamza. Facebook post. August 2020. https://www.facebook.com/permali nk.php?story_fbid=327523151940240&id=114544283238129 (last accessed January 26, 2022).

Yusuf, Hamza. "Forum for Promoting Peace in Muslim Societies, Abu Dhabi 2016."

Yusuf, Hamza. "Is the Matter of Metaphysics Immaterial? Yes and No." *Renovatio: The Journal of Zaytuna College*, May 10, 2017. https://renovatio.zaytuna.edu/ar ticle/the-matter-of-metaphysics (last accessed January 20, 2019).

Yusuf, Hamza. "Tribulation, Patience and Prayer." In *The State We Are In: Identity, Terror and the Law of Jihad*, edited by Aftab Ahmad, Malik, and Tahir Abbas. Amal Press, 2006.

Yusuf, Hamza. "When Does a Human Fetus Become Human?" *Renovatio*, June 22, 2018, https://renovatio.zaytuna.edu/article/when-does-a-human-fetus-become -human (last accessed January 26, 2022).

Yusuf, Hamza. *Prayer of the Oppressed*. Sandala Productions, 2010.

Yusuf, Hamza. RIS, 2016.

Yusuf, Hamza, "Religious Freedom: Why Now? A Conversation on Islam and Religious Freedom with Dr. Robert P. George and Shaykh Hamza Yusuf." Religious Freedom Project—Berkeley Center for Religion, Peace and World Affairs, March 1, 2012. https://berkleycenter.georgetown.edu/publications/re ligious-freedom-why-now-a-conversation-on-islam-and-religious-freedom-with -dr-robert-p-george-and-shaykh-hamza-yusuf (last accessed January 21, 2019).

Zaydān, Yusūf *Fiqh al-Thawra*. Dar al-Shurūq, 2013.

Zaytuna College. "Special Address by Hamza Yusuf." YouTube, February 23, 2016. https://www.youtube.com/watch?v=yMzuRe8LPA4 (last accessed January 21, 2019).

Zaytuna College. "Hamza Yusuf: A Crisis of Metaphysics." YouTube, September 29, 2015. https://www.youtube.com/watch?v=NKrxbX3_PWc (last accessed June 26, 2018).

Zebiri, Kate. *British Muslim Converts: Choosing Alternative Lives*. Oneworld, 2014.

INDEX

Printed in the USA
CPSIA information can be obtained
at www.ICGtesting.com
LVHW081931071123
763286LV00009B/136